STANDING UP SPACE FORCE

Titles in the Series

The Other Space Race: Eisenhower and the Quest for Aerospace Security

An Untaken Road: Strategy, Technology, and the Mobile Intercontinental Ballistic Missile

Strategy: Context and Adaptation from Archidamus to Airpower

Cassandra in Oz: Counterinsurgency and Future War

Cyberspace in Peace and War

Limiting Risk in America's Wars: Airpower, Asymmetrics, and a New Strategic Paradigm

Always at War: Organizational Culture in Strategic Air Command, 1946–62

How the Few Became the Proud: Crafting the Marine Corps Mystique, 1874–1918

Assured Destruction: Building the Ballistic Missile Culture of the U.S. Air Force

Mars Adapting: Military Change during War

Cyberspace in Peace and War, Second Edition

Rise of the Mavericks: The U.S. Air Force Security Service and the Cold War

Transforming War
Paul J. Springer, editor

To ensure success, the conduct of war requires rapid and effective adaptation to changing circumstances. While every conflict involves a degree of flexibility and innovation, there are certain changes that have occurred throughout history that stand out because they fundamentally altered the conduct of warfare. The most prominent of these changes have been labeled "Revolutions in Military Affairs" (RMAs). These so-called revolutions include technological innovations as well as entirely new approaches to strategy. Revolutionary ideas in military theory, doctrine, and operations have also permanently changed the methods, means, and objectives of warfare.

This series examines fundamental transformations that have occurred in warfare. It places particular emphasis upon RMAs to examine how the development of a new idea or device can alter not only the conduct of wars but their effect upon participants, supporters, and uninvolved parties. The unifying concept of the series is not geographical or temporal; rather, it is the notion of change in conflict and its subsequent impact. This has allowed the incorporation of a wide variety of scholars, approaches, disciplines, and conclusions to be brought under the umbrella of the series. The works include biographies, examinations of transformative events, and analyses of key technological innovations that provide a greater understanding of how and why modern conflict is carried out, and how it may change the battlefields of the future.

STANDING UP SPACE FORCE

THE ROAD TO THE NATION'S SIXTH ARMED SERVICE

FORREST L. MARION

Naval Institute Press
Annapolis, MD

Naval Institute Press
291 Wood Road
Annapolis, MD 21402

© 2023 by the U.S. Naval Institute
All rights reserved. No part of this book may be reproduced or utilized in any form or by any means, electronic or mechanical, including photocopying and recording, or by any information storage and retrieval system, without permission in writing from the publisher.

Library of Congress Cataloging-in-Publication Data

Names: Marion, Forrest L., author.
Title: Standing up space force : the road to the nation's sixth armed service / Forrest L. Marion.
Description: Annapolis, MD : Naval Institute Press, [2023] | Series: Transforming war | Includes bibliographical references and index.
Identifiers: LCCN 2023024971 (print) | LCCN 2023024972 (ebook) | ISBN 9781682472392 (hardcover) | ISBN 9781682472439 (ebook)
Subjects: LCSH: United States. Space Force--History. | National security--United States. | Outer space--Strategic aspects. | BISAC: HISTORY / Military / Aviation & Space | HISTORY / United States / 21st Century
Classification: LCC UG1523 .M34 2023 (print) | LCC UG1523 (ebook) | DDC 358/.8070973--dc23/eng/20231006
LC record available at https://lccn.loc.gov/2023024971
LC ebook record available at https://lccn.loc.gov/2023024972

♾ Print editions meet the requirements of ANSI/NISO z39.48-1992 (Permanence of Paper).
Printed in the United States of America.

31 30 29 28 27 26 25 24 23   9 8 7 6 5 4 3 2 1
First printing

To Professor Dino A. Lorenzini and his
fellow early space force proponents:

Thus says the LORD,
Who gives the sun for light by day,
And the fixed order of the moon and the stars for light by night,
Who stirs up the sea so that its waves roar;
The LORD of hosts is His name.

And in memory of my parents,
Professor and Mrs. Jerry B. Marion;
and my beloved and beautiful sister-in-law,
April Geist McCready (1976–2022):

Those who hope in the Lord will renew their strength.
They will soar on wings like eagles.

CONTENTS

FOREWORD   xi

PREFACE   xxiii

PROLOGUE   xxix

1. Survey of U.S. National Security Space, 1996–2000   1
2. U.S. National Security Space: The Bush Years, 2001–2008   26
3. U.S. National Security Space: The Obama Years, 2009–2016   53
4. Mixed Momentum for a Space Service, 2017–2018   80
5. Standing Up, 2019–2020   112

Epilogue. Service Fundamentals, 2021   146

APPENDIX 1: SPACE POLICY DIRECTIVE-4, 19 FEBRUARY 2019   163

NOTES   169

SELECTED BIBLIOGRAPHY   227

INDEX   247

FOREWORD

As of December 2022, the United States Space Force (USSF) remains a work-in-progress.

To those within the space community prophesying a coming new age of dominant space power, the USSF is a necessary first step, yet one that doesn't go far enough, its name grandly hinting more of what it might become at some future point rather than the reality of what it actually is in the present.

To its critics it constitutes an impulsive, reflexive, unnecessary, and potentially wasteful response by the Trump administration to the rapid globalization of space technology and capabilities, particularly as pursued by four disturbingly aggressive international actors: China, Russia, North Korea, and Iran.

While there is some truth in both of these positions, it is worth noting that these responses are themselves largely reflexive and characteristic: when a new military branch or command is established (often reflecting the emergence of some new technology and its actual or potential exploitation and implementation by a likely foe), advocates and critics typically regard it in such dualistic Manichaean terms. The nascent branch or command never goes far enough to satisfy its staunchest advocates, while going too far in the minds of critics who, typically, are military traditionalists committed to one form or another of power projection.

The circumstances of the Space Force's birth, coming as they did in the tumultuous years of President Donald Trump's administration, exacerbated the debate. As a consequence, its creation has been cast in partisan terms, particularly because its most prominent adherents included the charismatic, fiery, and mercurial Donald Trump and former Georgia congressman Newt Gingrich, architect of the "Contract with America," credited with securing

Republican control of the House of Representatives in 1994 for the first time in forty years. Not appreciated was that, irrespective of their politics, both men were long-standing space advocates. As far back as the early 1990s, Gingrich had advocated for a greater American effort in space. For his part, just months after assuming office, Donald Trump had revived the National Space Council (moribund for almost a quarter-century).

If the idea of a Space Force stirred political emotions, there were nevertheless both urgencies and substantial reasons undergirding its establishment. On 23 August 2018, during the summer of intense debate over Space Force, skeptics, advocates, and the simply curious gathered at a symposium held at the Washington headquarters of the Institute for Defense Analyses' Science and Technology Policy Institute (IDA-STPI), an influential federally funded research and development center (FFRDC). This FFRDC, located across from the White House, was established in 1990 to furnish objective analytical inputs and insights on science and technology policy issues primarily to support the White House Office of Science and Technology Policy (OSTP). Organized by then–STPI director Dr. Mark J. Lewis, and Dr. Teasel Muir-Harmony, a curator in the Department of Space History at the Smithsonian Institution's National Air and Space Museum (SI-NASM), it served as a forum to address arguments and views on both sides.[1] There was a general recognition that the United States had reached a point in its national journey where Americans were facing a fork in the road—persist on the road taken, heedless of increasing complacency and risk, or, as at the beginning of the air age and the beginning of the jet age, boldly opt for a new path that was opening up, one already sought by others who do not share American values or the American outlook. At an informal gathering afterward, attendees generally conceded that on the whole, the pro-Space Force side carried the day.

At the symposium that day, I suggested that creation of the Space Force would mirror Great Britain's earlier establishment of the Royal Air Force (RAF, the world's first independent air force) on 1 April 1918, seven months before an armistice brought the First World War to a close, noting as well the irony of now, exactly a century later discussing forming the world's first independent Space Force. I also suggested that for Americans, it mirrored the transformation of the United States Air Force (USAF)

FOREWORD xiii

from the Army-subordinate (at least on paper) United States Army Air Forces (USAAF) into an independent service on 18 September 1947.[2]

The circumstances of both warrant brief review. The RAF was a response to a military-political crisis reflecting deeper longer-standing discontents within the British military aviation enterprise. The crisis was disturbingly frequent mass bombing attacks on metropolitan London and other British urban, industrial, and harbor areas by zeppelin airships and bomber airplanes, and resulting public and political uproar with understandable demands for Lloyd George's government to do something. The public, politicians, and military leaders alike recognized that the British Army's Royal Flying Corps (RFC) and the Royal Naval Air Service (RNAS) weren't effectively countering the threat, for a variety of reasons.

Understandably, both were focused on how their air branches could support their own service's combat operations at sea and on land. As well, their traditionalist surface-oriented leadership held blinkered views of air power aside from land and maritime reconnaissance and land and ship-based artillery observation and control. Despite prewar zeppelin hysteria and popular speculation by novelists as disparate as H. G. Wells and Erskine Childers, and aviation journalists such as *The Aeroplane*'s Charles G. "C. G." Grey—they little appreciated the profound political dimensions of air power until bombs began falling over Britain itself. They had only a limited appreciation for air superiority operations (and then only directly over the fleet or the forward edge of battle—think "battlespace" in the current vernacular). There was little to no emphasis on coordinated air operations across all mission areas, as advocated by airmen, most notably Britain's Major General Hugh Trenchard and America's Brig. Gen. William "Billy" Mitchell (a Trenchard acolyte). British Army and Royal Navy airmen realized all this and were thus generally dissatisfied with their service's excessively surface-focused leadership at the strategic and operational level of war. Thus, it was the airmen of both branches—particularly the RNAS, which incidentally furnished a large number of transferred airmen who subsequently rose to high RAF rank—that drove for independence and the creation of the RAF.

Establishing the RAF had one major strategic consequence: by 1939 Britain possessed a specialist military force focused on defense of the homeland as well as prosecution of long-range strategic air warfare, typified by RAF Fighter Command and the Chain Home (CH) radar net, and RAF Bomber Command. The former greatly influenced the outcome of the Battle of Britain, the latter was of more consequence for operations from 1942 onward. If the UK had had instead an Army-controlled RFC in 1940, it would in all likelihood have lacked the Chain Home integrated air defense system, at least to the degree that CH was in place in the late summer of 1940 (think Pearl Harbor, where radars sent—on British advice—to Pearl Harbor were promptly stored by the U.S. Army while its civil engineers prioritized routine construction projects, leaving only one in place and functioning when Japan attacked on December 7).

Worse, in the debacle that followed Germany's invasion of France, an RFC would have been unable to resist the calls to send more of its precious Spitfire and Hurricane fighters—if indeed it would have even possessed these aircraft—to be fed into the Moloch maw of Northern France, leaving southern and eastern England unable to resist the Luftwaffe from June onward except with legacy Gloster Gladiator biplanes (and others less advanced than this). While the Royal Navy arguably could have frustrated any German invasion attempt in the short term, the longer-term question is far less certain, particularly given the subsequent demonstrated vulnerability of its ships to Axis air and submarine attacks elsewhere, particularly off Crete and Malaya. Absent control of the air, and given the large number of influential defeatists within the United Kingdom—and there were sadly many—it is likely the British establishment would have cast Churchill aside and opted for a settlement with Hitler, shattering any hope of an independent Britain serving as a springboard for the liberation of western Europe. In short, forming—or not forming—military services with important new capabilities and strengths has consequences. The U.S. Air Force was also created in response to a threat and a recognition, and its creation had a strategic consequence and a significant outcome. The threat was the uncertainties of a dramatically changed post–World War II world: an emergent foe—the USSR—with formidable air capabilities and the intent to control Europe; the inability of Britain's RAF (for multiple reasons, primarily size and economic) to assume the mantle of responsibility for western Europe's air needs after World War II; the new global strategic

FOREWORD   XV

responsibilities of the United States; a new nation-destroying weapon (the atomic bomb) and revolutionary new supporting technologies: jet aircraft, supersonic flight, guided missiles, advanced electronics; and, finally, the beginning of the synergistic confluence of traditional aeronautical research, development, test, and evaluation (RDT&E) with the emergent and rapidly accelerating (if still largely nascent) computer revolution.

Air Force independence was also stimulated by the recognition that America's prewar airpower had long suffered by being organizationally, even artificially, constrained within the structure of both the Army and the Navy, which were still largely dominated by a surface warfare perspective. While nowhere as serious as in Britain at the time of the "Great War," it nevertheless had worked to limit expenditures and investment in military aviation technology—indeed, in the interwar years it was America's investment in civil aircraft development from 1919 to 1934 that was more significant in promoting a dual-use civilian-military (notice I do not say military-civilian) industrial base than investment in military aeronautics.

Given the extraordinary traditionalism of the leadership of both the Army and the Navy, full credit must be given to the leaders of the aviation programs in these services. In the Navy, Adm. William Moffett, and in the Army, two generals—Billy Mitchell and Henry "Hap" Arnold—deserve particular acknowledgement for succeeding as well as they did. Additionally, much credit within the Army goes to the Air Corps Tactical School, predecessor of today's Air University. Nevertheless, as the Second Sino-Japanese War, the Spanish Civil War, and outbreak of World War II revealed, we were militarily inferior to foreign powers, particularly in the structuring of combat forces at the operational and tactical levels of war, and in air-land, and air-sea command and control. Our early battle experiences—Kasserine in North Africa, and the South Pacific and Solomons—revealed this.

As interim steps, in 1941 the U.S. Army Air Corps was expanded and rechristened the U.S. Army Air Forces (AAF). Then, after the debacle of Kasserine in 1943, Chief of Staff Gen. George C. Marshall (a strong airpower proponent) issued Army Field Manual FM 100–20, which recognized airpower and land power as coequal and interdependent, noting "neither is an auxiliary of the other." The document was subsequently hailed as the "Declaration of Independence of the U.S. Air Force." By 1944 the AAF was operating effectively as a de facto independent air arm. After the war, no less a luminary than General Dwight Eisenhower championed the creation of the USAF as an independent service given its wartime performance. Critics of independence were less concerned by alleged loss of military competencies than they were by fears of being superseded (the cultural divide between the older era of 2-D-focused surface warfare and the twentieth century's advent of 3-D war above and below the surface) or having to give up their own aviation forces.

The strategic consequence of Air Force independence was that by 1951 America possessed a specialist military force focused on defense of the homeland as well as prosecution of strategic air warfare—in this case, up to and including global atomic warfare, and including as well global strategic mobility (and the beginning of the "tanker bridge"). Admittedly, after Korea it overly focused on nuclear operations, but this was driven by the Soviet nuclear threat and American national defense strategy rather than by the service itself. (And, somewhat ironically, it was that Soviet threat that drove the first investment of the USAF into strategic rocketry, leading to the Thor, Atlas, Titan, and Minuteman that introduced America into both the world of intercontinental ballistic missiles (ICBMs) and routine space access for military, civil, and exploratory satellites and probes.)

The most significant outcome of Air Force independence was that all through the Cold War, Europe—the potential area of greatest risk and conflict—was effectively shielded by the USAF, the RAF, and the NATO air forces, particularly Strategic Air Command (SAC), United States Air Forces in Europe (USAFE), and RAF Strike Command, coupled, where applicable, with naval carrier-based striking forces and long-range maritime patrol aircraft. NATO doctrine and plans from the outset in 1949 recognized this: it emphasized overwhelming use of air power to confront Soviet aggression, not prioritizing getting into an attritional war between opposing surface armies.

In short, the challenges of the post-1945 world were, as a group, something that required a full-service 24–7–365 independent Air Force, and which could not be met by services having aviation as just one of multiple combat arms branches within them. This does not mean that services such as armies and navies (and, in the American context, the Marine

FOREWORD

xvii

Corps) should not have aviation branches—quite the opposite! Indeed, every service should—and must—exploit the third dimension to whatever degree is appropriate to it, just as with cyber and artificial intelligence (AI) more recently. But there needs to be a recognition that an independent full-service air force frees other services to focus their aviation capabilities on the primary mission areas and combat needs of their forces. Today, there needs to be an equal recognition that a full-service Space Force does much the same.

Now, to Space Force and some final reflections: First, the Air Force, the Navy, and the Army have been in space for more than sixty years. They got there via the ballistic missile and/or space launch vehicles like the Redstone (Army), Jupiter (Army), Atlas (USAF), Thor (USAF), Viking (Navy), Vanguard (Navy), etc. Another path was what we term "transatmospheric vehicles"—most notably the NASA-AF-USN X-15, but others as well, including the Space Shuttle.

As a consequence of the emergent "space race" we began to speak of "aerospace"—first popularized by the Air Force, and now a generic term across the global aerospace community.

Today, the space community faces—as the creators of the RAF did in 1918, as the creators of the USAF did in 1947—a threat and a recognition.

The threat is the prospect of losing space superiority (defined as control of our space assets, and freedom to employ our space capabilities) to an aggressor, thanks to a radically transformed military environment reflecting the linkage of rapidly expanding and diverse international space launch nations and actors; ever-smaller and more capable satellites; the still-astonishing pace of Moore's Law–driven computational architectures and their now-pervasive and near-ubiquitous information netting and sharing; the emergence of relatively cheap (and increasingly so in future) commercial space launch; and the readily discerned evidence of adversaries—some potential, and some already actively hostile—playing against us in the cyber field. All we depend upon in our national life—our fielded combat forces; our national defense; our daily reliance upon complex and vulnerable networks of transportation, law enforcement, financial services, health services, power/water/sewage, and access to food and goods—would be endangered by the loss of space superiority.

The growing recognition leading to Space Force was that the existing management and control of space within a five-service Department of Defense was simply not adequate for the future looming before us. What was required was a new organizational construct, namely a purpose-focused Space Force composed in large measure of an extraction across the services of those capabilities—in some cases wastefully duplicative—that can be incorporated within a single unified service, together with the standing up of new organizational elements including a space secretariat and an office of a space chief of staff akin to the secretarial and chief of staff/Chief of Naval Operations structure that currently characterizes the national defense establishment.

Was the idea of creating a Space Force a good one? Yes. Frankly, the Air Force has too many missions and responsibilities on its plate, and inadequate numbers of systems, personnel, resources, and budget to fulfill them.[3] It has been in a constant warfighting mode since August 1990, with heavy air (and AF space) involvement by limited numbers of systems that are simply worn out. It operates across the spectrum of conflict from low to high, but most recently, particularly in counterinsurgency and air mobility. Yet now it is tasked with responsibility both for atmospheric operations and operations in space—effectively global air, and near-Earth space. It is being overtasked and not given its share of budget and technical investment to match the need. Space is so crucial and so vital to all the American military enterprise does that there was an evident need to let the USAF concentrate on what it does better than anyone else—atmospheric operations—and establish space as a distinct service.

With Air Force Space Command (created in 1982), the service already effectively had a "Space Corps" within the Air Force, and elements of naval and Army space are very close to being a space corps themselves. At the end of the 1990s, the Air Force already bore the dominant share of America's military space presence, with 90 percent of the Department of Defense's (DoD) space personnel, 85 percent of the space budget, 86 percent of the space assets, and 90 percent of the space infrastructure.[4]

But just as the RFC-RNAS and USAAF model of airpower was inadequate in the air age, the notion of space subordinate to atmospheric and

FOREWORD

xix

surface forces makes no sense. The twenty-first century world is a world linking sensors, platforms, and weapons within a sphere of cyber/artificial intelligence, and space takes that beyond a regional/theater construct to a global construct that, indeed, extends to lunar orbit.

Was now the right time to do it? Yes, certainly, though it might have been done sooner. As early as 8 January 1997, then–Air Force chief of staff Gen. Ronald H. Fogleman presciently stated, "Not too far into the 21st Century, the USAF will be an Air and Space Force, and by the end of the First Quarter of the 21st Century, we will be a Space and Air Force."[5]

Here, too, history, if not repeating itself, certainly rhymed. It took America from 1908 to 1947 to get an Air Force, even after the formation of the RAF in 1918. The Department of Defense had its first "full service" experience with space war in 1991, when we used a broad range of space capabilities—intelligence, surveillance, and reconnaissance (ISR); threat detection and warning; weapon cuing; weather; navigation; and communications—during Operation Desert Storm in January–March 1991, though it should be noted that space ISR played a significant role in Vietnam a quarter-century earlier.[6] Space partisans immediately after Desert Storm were already championing a separation, and relatively shortly thereafter issued a notable compilation of papers on space doctrine and space thought.[7] The subsequent history of space—particularly the linkage of space comm, weather, navigation, and weapons cuing—and "conventional" warfare has largely rendered irrelevant questions over the weaponization of space because, frankly, space is already weaponized. The terrorist killed by a joint direct attack munition or another GPS-cued munition dropped or fired from a multiservice aircraft or ship or submarine or mobile launcher that themselves are reliant on space-based navigation, weather, and communications, has, in effect, been killed from space.

Now, given establishment of the Space Force, what are the challenges? I believe them to be more cultural and political than technical and organizational. These include

1. Institutional resistance across the other services, that is likely to lead to a "with all deliberate speed" slow-rolling, including the fear of shedding and losing control over parochial institutional capabilities.

2. The extraordinarily confrontational, indeed poisonous, political environment, in which an idea is immediately placed into a party politics framework, with one side predictably for and one side predictably against. We didn't have that in the great aviation and aerospace initiatives of the distant past (think Air Commerce Act of 1926, or the National Defense Act creating the USAF in 1947), and certainly not with the Kennedy-launched space program of the 1960s. It began after 1969, has accelerated to an astonishing degree after 2000, and by now has grown so that it is frighteningly destructive of good governance and stewardship.

3. Ensuring the strong and understandable RDT&E mindset that has traditionally characterized military space does not constrain the quest for time-sensitive operational flexibility and military utility. General Chuck Horner famously encountered this when he took over AF Space Command after Desert Storm, once joking he would paint an overly delayed Titan IV booster brown and give it a building number if delays continued. He found his biggest challenge was convincing space personnel that they were war fighters; encouragingly, once he did so, they took to it like ducks to water. It is particularly important in future that Space Force acquisition be modeled on successful rapid-turn exemplars of past and present, such as Lockheed Martin's famed "Skunk Works," or the Air Force's own Rapid Capabilities Office (RCO).

Finally, what is the most pressing need? I would argue the most pressing need is finding accomplished, charismatic, and decisive leaders to run Space Force. In my ideal world, there would be a space "czar" with powers and oversight and long-term—at least a decade—continuity such as America had with Leslie Groves (Pentagon and A-bomb), Bernard Schriever (ICBM force), Hymen Rickover (naval nuclear power), William Raborn (submarine-launched ballistic missile (SLBM) force), James Webb (national space program), and Jim Abrahamson (Ballistic Missile Defense).[8]

Above all, the creation of Space Force reflects urgency. As others have noted, the United States cannot afford to lose the first space war, for the consequences of such a defeat are unthinkable. Such a loss would have grand strategic implications at least as calamitous for America and its place in the world today as was Spain's loss of mastery of the sea to England in 1588, or the Byzantine Empire's collapse before the Ottomans in 1453, or Russia's loss to Japan in the Tsushima Straits in 1905.

For that reason, it is well and good that we have this fine institutional study by Dr. Forrest Marion, a distinguished warrior-scholar of a critical slice in time in the formative years of the Space Force. Through his digging, we now have not only a solid historical record, but an intriguing glimpse into the workings and thinking of those who labored to make Space Force a reality.

—DR. RICHARD P. HALLION
Former senior advisor for air and space issues to the Air Force Directorate of Security, Counterintelligence, and Special Programs Oversight

PREFACE

Fifty years ago, my devoted father, Dr. Jerry B. Marion of the University of Maryland's Department of Physics and Astronomy, wrote these words in one of his many college-level physics textbooks:

> One of the significant steps forward in Man's understanding of the behavior of Nature was the realization that it is the Earth that moves around the Sun, and not the Sun that moves around the Earth. The simple statement that "the Earth moves around the Sun" represents a new dimension in physical thinking. As important as this idea is, nevertheless, it is incomplete. We cannot say that we really understand a physical phenomenon until we have reduced the description to a statement involving *numbers*. Physics is a precise science and its natural language is mathematics. Only when Johannes Kepler gave a mathematical description of planetary motion and Isaac Newton derived the same results on the basis of his theory of universal gravitation could it be said that a proper analysis of the motion of the Earth and the planets had finally been made.[1]

That analysis and many others eventually enabled Man to extend his reach into the heavens—outer space—facilitating his usage of the new domain "for better or for worse." The decades-long road to the establishment of the United States Space Force was opened—an example, arguably, *for better*.[2]

This book's initiation coincided with the COVID-19 pandemic, making for especially difficult early going. On 2 January 2020—two weeks after the "stand-up" of the U.S. Space Force with President Donald Trump's signing of the national defense authorization act on 20 December

xxiv PREFACE

2019—I was advised by my agency's director to begin planning for a new book project. I was not thrilled. I had already received an official tasking, with orders in hand, to serve later that year as the deployed Air Force historian at the combined air operations center in Qatar, for which duty I had volunteered.

During January, I prepared a prospectus for the project, then in early February attended a week-long operations security conference at March Air Reserve Base, California. The attendees were aware that some two hundred Americans had recently been housed at the base upon their evacuation by air from Wuhan, China, fearing possible infection with the new virus that was about to change the way of life for billions worldwide over the next several years.[3] On the conference's final day, the instructors received a Defense Department message detailing the operational concerns in connection with the virus known as Coronavirus Disease 2019, or COVID-19 for short. For practice, we discussed the message's implications and possible responses as operations security managers. Then everyone left for home. We had no idea what was coming.

On my way to the conference, at Montgomery's Dannelly Airport I had providentially bumped into then–Brig. Gen. Ed Thomas, the Air Force's director of public affairs. From his time in Montgomery when he served a command tour at Maxwell Air Force Base's (AFB) Gunter Annex as well as attending Eastwood Presbyterian Church, we had been acquainted. He apparently had the lead on getting the book project assigned to an author, and I had just been selected by the air staff but was yet to be notified— until he told me once we both passed through airport security and talked briefly inside the gate area.

By then I was getting excited about the book, which was to address the up-and-down journey to establishing the Space Force. It was intended basically as an administrative-legislative, anecdote-filled history—not a dry, technical, classified work—a layman's narrative of how we had gained the first new armed service since the U.S. Air Force in 1947. Because other works had covered the early decades, my assignment was to begin around the year 2000. My history program director's guidance to me was simply, "Make it a bestseller."

PREFACE

I wrapped up other duties by early March, then began reading books on space. By that time, the whole country—the Defense Department included—was preparing to shut down as the mysterious COVID-19 continued to spread. On 25 March, Maxwell AFB closed down and almost all personnel were sent home. I took a stack of Air University Library books with me.

That stack put me in good stead. By the time my agency returned to work in July, I had a fairly good knowledge base including my own notes made from various readings. In the months that followed, however, it became clear that the book's priority at the air staff and senior history offices in Washington, DC, had dropped from what it had been pre-COVID. In early 2021, I was given the choice whether to continue working on the book, which was no longer an air-staff sponsored project. The funding for official travel to capture the dozens of initially anticipated oral history interviews, and the related transcription support, dropped from $80,000 to zero. As events developed, I was able to conduct a small number of in-person interviews at Maxwell, as well as a few telephone interviews with key space leaders—which were considerably helpful, albeit by no means the equal of in-person interviews. Having conducted well over five hundred interviews in the last twenty-five years, I am convinced that the element of personal rapport cannot be replicated over any remote system. That said, I am grateful for each person who participated in an interview in support of this book, whether conducted in-person or remotely.

I am greatly indebted to several individuals whose assistance was indispensable in bringing this book to life. Noted airpower historian Dr. Richard P. "Dick" Hallion, who retired two decades ago as *the* Air Force historian—and has remained heavily engaged in air and space power research and writing—provided counsel and feedback, books to include in my research, and steady encouragement at every step. A true mentor and friend, he and his engaging wife—"Miss Chris" in the Deep South's traditional vernacular—kindly hosted me on several occasions both at their home and fine dining establishments in the Destin, Florida, area. Unfortunately for the Air Force history program, Dr. Hallion was the last "Air Force historian." When he left, the position was redesignated as "director" of Air Force history, and later downgraded. In the years since 11 September 2001, successive administrations and Department of Defense leaders have tasked the Air Force with many new responsibilities and missions, while at the same time failing to provide it with the resources necessary to adequately undertake those taskings. This has forced the service to scavenge from within to find the necessary funding and resources needed, and sadly, one of the organizations that has suffered is Air Force history, which today operates at greatly reduced size, with minimal funding and little ability to undertake the kind of extensive outreach and publishing it did in the past.

At the Air Force Historical Research Agency, where a small number of historians, archivists, information technology specialists, and technical support staff continue to punch well above their weight class—truly a customer-oriented organization—Maranda Gilmore and Kara Newcomer offered their critical support. Maranda, possessing strong editorial experience from a previous job and now the deputy director at the agency, supported the book's completion long after some had lost interest. She also permitted Kara, a former U.S. Marine Corps photo archivist who transferred into the Air Force history program during the difficult days of COVID, to apply her expertise in finding, verifying the suitability of, and preparing the photographs for this work. I am deeply grateful to both of them.

Also at Maxwell AFB, three space advocates affiliated with the Air Command and Staff College (ACSC)—Peter Garretson, Michael "Coyote" Smith, and Brent Ziarnick—not only sat for interviews but provided valuable follow-up assistance including contacts, photographs, and feedback. Two other ACSC faculty members were of considerable help: John Terino provided inputs regarding ACSC's space curriculum over the years, and Paul J. Springer—also the editor of the series to which this book belongs—provided his usual stern—but incredibly helpful—feedback on an early draft of the manuscript.

In yet another—and much earlier—ACSC connection, from 1996 to 1997 I had the opportunity to get to know two of my seminar mates, Ed Lorenzini and Matt Donovan. Unknown to me at the time, Ed's father, Dr. Dino Lorenzini, had co-authored the 1981 essay in the *Naval War College Review* that proposed a United States Space Force within twenty years. A quarter-century after Ed, Matt, and I graduated from ACSC, I came across

PREFACE

the essay and realized that it formed the logical starting point for the present work. Following his military career, Matt Donovan eventually served as the undersecretary of the Air Force (2017–19) and for an important four-month period in 2019, as the acting secretary of the Air Force. When I contacted him in 2021 about the book project, he responded kindly to the blast-from-the-past, answering my questions, reviewing several draft paragraphs, and offering valuable insights.

John Coyle of Air University's public affairs office provided a timely and comprehensive review of the manuscript that facilitated its submission to the Naval Institute Press in mid-2022. Additionally, Dr. Greg Ball, the U.S. Space Force historian, and several other individuals provided copies of space interviews conducted pre–COVID-19 as well as other space-related documents, offered expertise on several issues, and answered my questions during the research and writing.

Finally, I wish also to acknowledge my dear wife, April—whose maiden name, April McCready, is the same as our beloved sister-in-law, April Geist McCready, who died unexpectedly during the book's preparation. Especially on those days when this book seemed a bridge too far due to COVID restrictions, canceled interviews, and reimaged computers, my wife's steady encouragement, support, and prayers kept me going.

During nearly the entirety of the twenty-plus-year road to establishing the Space Force, the focus of U.S. national security concerns was on non-state terrorist threats, not on great power or near-peer competition. That trend has reversed. In that context, the U.S. Space Force has a critical role to play. If this book helps its readers appreciate how this new player on the national security space scene got into the game—and why it needs to be there—it will have served its purpose.

—FORREST L. MARION, PHD
Crossville, Tennessee
Columbus Day, October 10, 2022

PROLOGUE

Space historian David N. Spires referred to the early 1970s as a period of "disarray" and "disinterest" for the American space community. The final two Apollo lunar missions were scrapped, and the uncertainty of what the post-Apollo era might look like for civil and military space programs carried over into uncertainty regarding roles and missions and organizational structures. Further, "the President eliminated important advisory bodies for space issues." Coupled with the demands of the war in Southeast Asia, an ongoing social agenda stemming from the Great Society of the 1960s, and oil shortages resulting from the Arab-Israeli conflict in 1973, an "ambitious military space agenda" was out of the question. But a decade later, the prospects for military space had improved, in part by Air Force leadership building consensus for a centralized space organization, the operational maturing of space systems themselves, and the impetus the Space Shuttle provided for change within the Air Force. The most significant upgrading of military space crystalized in the USAF's establishment of Space Command in 1982. It was redesignated Air Force Space Command in 1985 in conjunction with the establishment of the unified combatant command known as United States Space Command.[1]

Shortly before the 1982 establishment, however, in the earliest known initiative in U.S. military circles to vigorously promote the creation of a separate service for space, two U.S. Air Force officers took their advocacy to the readership of the *Naval War College Review*. At least one other similar initiative followed soon after.[2] In their 1981 article, the duo sought a U.S. Space Force by the year 2001. Presciently, Lt. Col. Dino Lorenzini, an astronautical engineer with a doctorate of science from the Massachusetts Institute of Technology (MIT), and Maj. Charles Fox, previously a political science professor at the Air Force Academy, posited that within twenty

xxix

years, "space activity for both peaceful and military purposes will increase significantly, with signal importance for continued international stability." For his doctorate, Lorenzini conducted "original research on improving the guidance and control of vehicles through space using gyroscopes," which contributed to the navigational system of the developing Global Positioning System (GPS). He went on to serve as a deputy director for the original GPS program. During the 1980s Lorenzini played significant roles in the Strategic Defense Initiative as head of the Pilot Architecture Study and at the Defense Advanced Research Projects Agency leading "the first space-based laser program."[3]

Twenty years after the 1981 article by Lorenzini and Fox, in January 2001 the report of a congressionally mandated commission on national security space (NSS) appeared. It was a watershed moment on the often-turbulent course of establishing the U.S. Space Force two decades later.[4]

In the early 1980s the Soviet Union continued in the midst of a vigorous national effort "to surpass the United States in every area of military capability." At least numerically, they appeared to be succeeding in nearly every one. In space, the United States had won the race to the moon a decade earlier and still enjoyed the technological edge over its Cold War competitor. During this period retired Lt. Gen. Daniel O. Graham's High Frontier—a private, nonprofit organization—emphasized the U.S. technological advantage in space. The former Defense Intelligence Agency's director, Graham advocated a "technological end-run" around the Soviets as a means of ditching the "mutual assured destruction" doctrine and replacing it with what he called "assured survival," founded upon a space-based, non-nuclear, strategic defense using existing technologies. Writing not long after Lorenzini and Fox, Graham also urged "serious consideration" of the idea of a U.S. Space Force.[5]

The Soviets had been far more active in space during the 1970s than the Americans, launching many times more payloads into space than their competitors. While Soviet cosmonauts were spending prolonged periods of time in space in preparation for establishing a permanently manned space station, no U.S. astronaut had been to space since 1975. Lorenzini and Fox warned, "Although the U.S. Space Shuttle will provide easier and less expensive access to space, nothing approaching the scale of Soviet

Official U.S. government information about the Global Positioning System and related topics
Graphic by the United States government

space activity is planned for the United States."[6] Soviet expenditures to develop high-energy lasers capable of employment as space weapons were several times greater than America's, and the USSR already possessed an anti-satellite (ASAT) capability, something that remained on the drawing board in the United States. In later years, U.S. space officials' concern regarding ASATs increased, particularly after January 2007 when the People's Republic of China (PRC) destroyed one of their own defunct satellites on orbit.[7]

Since the 1950s, U.S. presidential administrations had maintained an official policy of space for peaceful purposes. There were voices that questioned such a policy. In 1959, Air Force Col. Lee V. Gossick—a P-40 pilot credited with two aerial victories over German Me-109s in the Mediterranean theater in mid-1943—argued in his Air War College thesis against a space program divided between military and civil—or so-called peaceful—projects. Earlier that year, Adm. John E. Clark, deputy director of the Advanced Research Projects Agency, wrote, "The Russians do not concern themselves with the academic problem of peaceful or military uses of space. They marshal their capability under a central authority, accomplish their projects, and get on with the job." Gossick, a future major general, went further and opined, "The separation of our space program into 'civilian' and 'military' projects has added to the difficulties of reaching decisions, has given rise to further competition for funds available for our space effort, and has made more complex and time-consuming the task of coordination and overall management of our total program." At about the same time, in a statement before the U.S. House of Representatives Space Committee, Rear Adm. John T. Hayward, assistant chief of naval operations, called for "a single U.S. Space Agency to handle the national programs, both military and civil." It was an early expression that leaned toward a separate space service.[8]

Since the early 1960s, the secretive work of satellites under the National Reconnaissance Office (NRO)—deemed critical to keeping an eye on Soviet strategic capabilities—was unknown to the public. When Americans thought of space, most of them thought only of the National Aeronautics and Space Administration (NASA). After the lunar landing in 1969, most Americans' interest in space waned; they were ready to move

PROLOGUE   xxxiii

on to the next big thing. In contrast to one school of thought that viewed space as a sanctuary, Air Force leaders were disinclined to adopt the view of those whom *Air Force Magazine* called "fuzzy thinkers." In 1974 retired USAF general Jacob E. Smart wrote that the United States "must be prepared to defend itself against aggression *in* space and *from* space. We cannot surrender the 'high ground' without a contest" [emphasis in original]. Air Force doctrine at the time called for space to be preserved for peaceful purposes, but it balanced that affirmation with the warning that no nation should be allowed to gain a "strategic military advantage" through the exploitation of the space domain. In 1980, *Air Force* magazine opined that the Soviets, "unencumbered by moralistic views about the peaceful and humanitarian character of the cosmos, [treat] space as a predominantly military high ground that needs to be seized and exploited" by their armed forces. Note that the high ground metaphor for military space—already well established in Air Force thinking at the time—was destined to remain the preferred descriptor of NSS thinkers up to the present. Lorenzini and Fox sought to stir U.S. policy makers to take the initiative to choose the nation's military role in the new, advantageous domain before it was consigned—perhaps permanently, they feared—to second place.[9]

The Air Force officers—faculty members of the Naval War College's management department—were well qualified to admonish the Pentagon for "studying . . . to death" the concept of high-energy laser weapons that official Washington anticipated becoming a reality. Lorenzini and Fox acknowledged that the size and complexity of present-day strategic systems required "increasingly more time and effort" to move "a new concept from the laboratory to the field." Under such circumstances, they had little confidence that, if the Soviets surprised the West with a demonstrated laser weapon capability from space, the United States could catch up even with a "'crash effort' program." The tendency to study space problems excessively continued to be a cause for concern among space professionals, for example, on the part of Gen. John E. Hyten four decades later.[10]

There were three international agreements that impinged particularly on national security space initiatives: the Limited Test Ban Treaty, the Anti-Ballistic Missile (ABM) Treaty, and the Outer Space Treaty (OST). The first, whose major provision prohibited conducting nuclear explosions in the atmosphere, under water, or in outer space, the authors judged unlikely to influence considerably the signatories' military activities in space. The ABM Treaty allowed each of the two superpowers to establish one ABM system to protect either the nation's capital or to defend an intercontinental ballistic missile (ICBM) launch area. The United States elected to defend an ICBM site in North Dakota, while the Soviet Union defended its capital, Moscow. The ABM Treaty was intended "to promote strategic stability" since both countries remained susceptible to an ICBM attack by the other.[11]

Of the three treaties, the 1967 OST was of greatest consequence for the space initiatives of the more than a hundred signatories. The first of two significant provisions forbade one to place in orbit around the earth, on the moon or another celestial body, "or otherwise stationing in outer space *nuclear* or any other *weapons of mass destruction*" [emphasis in original]. The second provision limited the use of the moon and other celestial bodies "to peaceful purposes" and disallowed the establishing of military installations or weapons testing on celestial bodies. The authors predicted that difficulties were certain to arise over defining weapons of mass destruction. They concluded there was little doubt that the Soviets were unlikely to be "constrained by the provisions of military arms arrangements when they can see distinct advantages accruing from their violation." One more complicating factor the USAF authors brought to the fore in their discussion of high-energy laser weaponry was that such a laser's inherent beaming capability rendered it arguably beyond the bounds of a weapon of mass destruction. One analyst considered it "a clean, discriminating weapon," not a mass destruction weapon. The difficulty of defining weapons in space was to continue for decades.[12]

Lorenzini and Fox discussed four options, from doing nothing in space, to negotiating agreements designed to slow Soviet progress in space, to hedging against a Soviet technological breakthrough, to a national commitment "to exploit the medium of space to our own advantage, thus seizing the high ground before the Soviets do." They recommended "*Option 4: Compete*" [emphasis in original].[13]

Anticipating the charge from certain quarters that their proposal was bound to lead to an arms race, the two airmen argued that the Soviets already seemed committed to an arms race, one that thus far was unilateral in nature. That a considerable and increasing imbalance in two competing nations' military capabilities could lead to hostilities had been suggested 2,500 years ago by the Greek city-states of Athens and Sparta. The Greek historian Thucydides posited that what made the Peloponnesian War "inevitable was the ... growth of Athenian power and the fear which this caused in Sparta." In contrast with the Greek city-states of old, Lorenzini and Fox feared the Athens-like United States becoming the descendant power and the Sparta-like Soviet Union the ascendant power. In 2021, noted aerospace historian Richard P. Hallion observed that the writers four decades earlier could not have foreseen that the actual ascendant power was not to be the USSR; rather, it was the PRC.[14]

Calling for a new vision, organizational structure, and funding for military space, the authors sought a renewed national commitment along the lines of President John F. Kennedy's goal, two decades earlier, "of landing a man on the Moon and returning him safely to the Earth." To turn vision into reality, however, the two proponents argued strenuously for creating, out of existing military and civilian agencies that presently were involved in space, "a separate and distinct military organization to focus our efforts and to make operational the military applications of space." Lorenzini and Fox left no doubt that by the year 2001 "the eventual goal of our proposal is the creation of the U.S. Space Force, independent of the other military services." Presaging some of the familiar arguments voiced in later years, the writers were convinced that a separate military space service was the best means to "provide the much needed organizational cohesiveness that is now lacking in the military space program." Moreover, a separate space organization was also best equipped to secure the increased funding necessary for pursuing its mission in space. The Soviets already had demonstrated the viability of a new military service for space with the establishment of the Soviet Strategic Rocket Forces, which was "the preeminent and elite arm of the Soviet Armed Forces." In the two decades of its existence, the rocket forces had surpassed the Americans' "nuclear delivery potential" and carved out a major role in the Soviet space program.[15]

At almost the same time as the Lorenzini/Fox article appeared, Lt. Col. David E. Lupton, USAF, worked on similar questions during a period that evinced greater Air Force activity with respect to space than in the previous decade. In April 1981, the Air Force Academy hosted a three-day military space doctrine symposium. For the 1981–82 academic year the Air War College (AWC), the service's professional military education program for lieutenant colonels (O-5) and colonels (O-6), incorporated its "first extensive block of instruction on space." Also in 1982, the USAF established Space Command, with space operations as its primary mission, headquartered at Peterson Air Force Base (AFB), Colorado.[16]

One of the initial research fellows at Air University's Airpower Research Institute at Maxwell AFB, Alabama, in the early 1980s, Lupton asked the basic question, "Should there be a military component to U.S. space power?" Lupton wrote insightfully on the historical precedents, doctrines, and schools of thought that dealt with space activities and the potential of space warfare. He argued that Billy Mitchell's advocacy for airpower's separation from the U.S. Army in the 1920s dealt with "the same types of organizational questions" as those that were to occupy space power proponents, if not presently, then in the decades to come. As airpower came to be valued more highly for its military capabilities, its position in the "bureaucratic advocacy structure" rose accordingly, eventually leading to an independent Air Force in 1947, shortly after the world war in which airpower had made immense contributions to victory.[17]

Agreeing with Lorenzini and Fox on the organizational inadequacies of existing military space entities, Lieutenant Colonel Lupton asked: might not the relationship between the perceived value of space power and its organizational structure within the defense bureaucracy lead to a space force in the not-too-distant future? Lupton argued against a space force being "formed today" because of the many years of work that are "required to overcome the organizational neglect" of twenty-five years of "the sanctuary doctrine's antimilitary organizational tenets." In addition, the Air Force must learn to incorporate into its personnel management systems a means to develop experienced space personnel, an assessment destined for a long and valid track record. Ultimately, David Lupton made clear his belief "that a space force will be required in the future." He was convinced that "one day the term *spaceman* will mean a military member of the United States Space Force, not a creature from some other planet."[18]

1

SURVEY OF U.S. NATIONAL SECURITY SPACE, 1996–2000

The starting point for this study was debatable. Why begin in the middle of a two-term administration in which space occupied a low-to-middling priority? Because the president of the United States bears the responsibility to set national space policy, the issuance of President William J. Clinton's space policy directive in 1996 argued in favor of that year as a reasonable starting point for the present study of the path to establishing the U.S. Space Force. That fourteen years later the space policy directive of President Barack H. Obama looked back to the 1996 document strengthened the case for beginning with Clinton's policy.

The White House billed Clinton's directive of 19 September 1996 as "the first post–Cold War assessment of American space goals and activities." The president's assistant for science and technology, John H. Gibbons, announced the policy following a year-long study by the National Science and Technology Council and the National Security Council (NSC). The fact that neither of those entities had the word "space" in their title indicated their scope was broader than the new domain in the heavens; space

1

was not their top priority. In the 1980s the National Space Council, "under the direction of the Vice President, developed U.S. space policy within the government." But in 1993 the space council, which focused squarely on that domain, was allowed to languish although the law governing that body was never repealed. In 2022 Robert S. Walker, former Republican representative from Pennsylvania and chairman of the U.S. House Committee on Science who possessed extensive experience in commercial aerospace, observed that the Clinton administration was "not very favorable" toward space programs. In 1997 the Pentagon's dismantling of the two-year-old office of deputy undersecretary of defense for space buttressed Walker's assessment. He argued the country needed the kind of "coordination function" the National Space Council provided, in part because getting space-related resources matched between the military and NASA was critical.[1]

One former Arms Control and Disarmament Agency acting director considered the National Space Council's demise as having "killed the only mechanism the government had for coordinating government space policy."[2] In 2000 John E. Hyten, later a four-star general in the Air Force, wrote in a published paper,

> The military, as a minority player in space and in the absence of a coherent national strategy, is finding it increasingly difficult to develop the means to deal with conflict in space in the next century. Therefore, it is impossible for the military alone to effectively plan for and deal with all the elements of space as it relates to national security. It is a national problem and must be dealt with in a coherent manner by the executive branch—integrating all the elements of national power into a coherent policy.[3]

Hyten's critique was similar to that of Bob Smith, the former Republican senator from New Hampshire, and more, than a decade later, Mike Rogers, the Republican representative from Alabama. A quarter-century passed before the presidential-level advisory body was revived in 2017, the year that Congress expressed its seriousness on the possibility of a separate space service in the fiscal 2018 national defense authorization act.[4]

SURVEY OF U.S. NATIONAL SECURITY SPACE, 1996–2000   3

In any case, on a Saturday night early in Walker's last term in Congress (1995–97), he took a call from the White House asking if he could accompany the president to Houston the next morning. The Clinton staff had learned that Bob Walker was highly qualified to lead the president on a tour of the Johnson Space Center. He was glad to do so, and during the three-hour flight on board Air Force One Walker joined the president for a cigar in his cabin while the two men talked uninterrupted about space policy and programs. While their discussion had highlighted the need for the administration to focus on space matters, it was months later when the Clinton space policy directive was issued. Any specific policy impact from Walker's time with the president was unclear.[5]

In the 1996 directive, the White House highlighted the civil space program—of which NASA was the best-known organization—and reaffirmed America's commitment to the International Space Station, new launch vehicles, and "an aggressive space science program including the sustained robotic exploration of Mars." The best-publicized NASA flight in the late 1990s was seventy-seven-year-old senator John Glenn's return to space as a payload specialist on board the space shuttle *Discovery* on mission STS-95. Thirty-six years earlier Glenn—one of the original seven Mercury astronauts—became the first American to fly an orbital mission. In 1961 Soviet cosmonaut Yuri Gagarin had orbited the Earth once, but in 1962 Glenn completed three orbits in the *Friendship 7* space capsule.[6]

In 1994 an Air Force chief of staff–directed study called Spacecast 2020 concluded there "is an area of fusion or overlap between the range of civilian and military responses to the new world, specifically in the medium of space. . . . States with affordable and as-required access to space will have commercial and military advantages over those who do not." Eight decades earlier, shortly after the armistice of 11 November 1918, the American Expeditionary Force's Third Aviation Instruction Center in France published a piece on aviation's future. Looking ahead, the center's newspaper, *Plane News*, predicted: "In a commercial way the airplane promises great things, and many of the older trade routes are likely to be again changed." By the 1990s, space was changing many of the older trade patterns. Reflecting the overlap of civil, commercial, and national security space (NSS) sectors, the 1996 Clinton space policy directed U.S.

4 CHAPTER 1

government agencies to purchase "commercially available space goods and services to the fullest extent feasible"—such as satellite time for military communications—without compromising national security or public safety. The best-known program in civil-commercial-NSS space was the U.S. Global Positioning System (GPS), and the administration encouraged the intersection of the three space sectors regarding GPS as a cost-effective measure. The Air Force was slow to adapt to GPS; in the early 1990s only 5 percent of its aircraft had GPS receivers installed.[7]

In early 1996, President Clinton approved new guidelines for the GPS, "opening the door for rapid growth in a burgeoning civil and commercial GPS market" that was expected to add 100,000 jobs to the U.S. economy by the year 2000. Widely recognized for its role in the success of U.S./coalition military forces against Iraq in Operation Desert Storm in 1991, the constellation of GPS satellites and associated ground stations and facilities made it possible, the White House said five years later, to determine one's "position and navigate anywhere in the world." The U.S. Air Force announced its support for the new policy on GPS and affirmed its intent to maintain the twenty-four-satellite constellation as long as required.[8]

National Security Space

The NSS section of Clinton's policy was expressed in traditional terms: "The United States will conduct those space activities necessary for national security," it began. The 1990s was a period of adjustment following the end of the Cold War during which the mission of the U.S. military was murky at times, including increased attention to humanitarian operations, peacekeeping, and the unwieldy term of "military operations other than war" (MOOTW). "Improving our ability to support military operations worldwide" in addition to fulfilling various monitoring and intelligence functions from space were "key priorities" for NSS. In short, while the Clinton policy appeared, as space scholar Everett C. Dolman wrote, "to conform to a notion of grand strategy," in reality the policy was "no more than a somewhat organized collection of existing *ad hoc* national space policy declarations of the previous decade" [emphasis in original]. Michael O'Hanlon summarized the Clinton administration's attention to military space, stating Clinton shifted "missile defense efforts from strategic to theater systems, for which weapons based in space did not figure prominently. ... Even when Clinton reemphasized national missile defense in mid-decade, his plan called for land-based interceptors." Encouraged by the Cold War's end, a season of détente with Russia, and a greater affinity for U.S. domestic concerns, the Clinton administration viewed military space as a low priority.[9]

In the late 1990s, the state of America's NSS organizations and programs was something of a mixed bag. In June 1998 the USAF renamed Falcon Air Force Base (AFB), near Colorado Springs, Colorado, as Schriever AFB—the first time the USAF had bestowed that honor on a living person. It was fitting for the base that controlled the service's satellites to bear the name of Gen. Bernard A. Schriever, who was widely recognized as the "father of Air Force missiles and space," and whose work had been indispensable to U.S. national security during the Cold War.[10]

One month later, a commission that assessed the ballistic missile threat to the United States, led by former secretary of defense Donald H. Rumsfeld, reported that a Third World country could threaten America within five years and with little warning.[11] Almost on cue, a month later the North Koreans surprised U.S. analysts when they launched a three-stage rocket—called Taepo Dong 1—later determined to have been an attempted satellite launch. While the rocket might have reached Alaska, it failed over the Pacific Ocean east of Japan. Nonetheless, North Korea's launch was a wake-up call in two ways: first, U.S. analysts determined the launch was intended as a threat, and second, the technology required to attain the thrust needed to place a satellite in orbit was similar to that required for launching a ballistic missile.[12]

At the same time that analysts concerned themselves with rogue actors in space, the Air Force experienced a rash of booster rocket failures that led *Spaceflight* magazine to refer to a launcher crisis. Between August 1998 and May 1999, the USAF sustained six losses, including three Titan IV launches in a row. In April 1999, in the second Titan IV failure, a USAF Defense Support Program (DSP) 19 early warning satellite was stranded in a useless orbit when its Titan IVB inertial upper stage (IUS) booster failed. The three Titan failures alone cost the Air Force a hefty $3.4 billion.[13]

6   CHAPTER 1

In addition to the second and third Titan IV failures, the spring 1999 failure of one Delta III and an Athena 2 booster—all four mishaps were within twenty-five days—led President Clinton to order a full investigation. The Air Force conducted its own review into the military launch failures, which, disturbingly, resembled the pattern of failures witnessed in 1985–86. Space historian David Spires called the launch failures a "wake-up call for the Air Force," one that dealt with "the most fundamental element of the space program," and its "Achilles heel." L. Parker Temple III, senior policy analyst in national security and space programs, wrote, "When trends involve critical national assets, they become obvious only after some serious damage has been done to national security and national defense. . . . The dollar value of these launch vehicle and satellite losses ranged into billions. The monetary loss, though, did not compare with the impacts to national security and national defense. Satellites are not built quickly, so the nation suffered years of diminished or lost capabilities as replacements were built."[14]

Concerns in Washington led the Air Force to delay its planned launch of a NRO satellite at Vandenberg AFB, California, for which the payload remained unknown to outside experts.[15]

China and Russia

A troublesome aspect of space technology was the difficulty of distinguishing between systems intended for civil or military purposes. Space systems capable of being employed for either or both purposes were identified as dual-use technology. Particularly, the fluid relations enjoyed by the People's Republic of China (PRC) with more-or-less private Chinese space entities probably guaranteed that Western technology shared with Chinese companies also ended up in the hands of the PRC or the People's Liberation Army (PLA), statutes and agreements intended to protect the shared technology notwithstanding. Miniaturization satellite technology constituted one example of dual-use technology, which might in the near term be modified from scientific or communications usage into parasitic microsatellites capable of attaching themselves—in the proper position, unseen—to larger, target satellites, to be employed as anti-satellite weapons at the time of the operator's choosing. In 2000, the Air Force's Scientific Advisory

Board (SAB) posited the near impossibility of predicting the "most significant applications of highly miniaturized space satellites, which are still in their infancy." The SAB noted that previous "disrupting technologies" had not foreseen major applications that followed, such as the Internet and World Wide Web that came twenty-five years after the computer. As of 2000, some miniature satellites already envisioned included those for purposes of inspection, protection of one's own satellites, space debris detection and elimination, and suicide missions.[16]

At the start of 1999 the White House rejected, for the first time, a license intended to allow Hughes Space and Communications to execute a nearly one-half billion dollar satellite deal with China, citing national security reasons. Reports stated the Commerce Department had favored approving the license, but the State Department and Department of Defense opposed it. The Satellite Industry Association, the industry's lobbying group, charged the rejection was for "purely political motives," and, to no one's surprise, the Chinese expressed "strong resentment" and issued a protest. The case highlighted John Hyten's point that if "U.S. companies were prohibited from competing because of fear of transferring critical technologies to potential enemies, these customers would just go elsewhere. This is the dilemma; a need to allow U.S. companies to compete fairly without allowing a loss of critical technologies."[17]

Subsequent events led the U.S. Senate Intelligence Committee to conclude that China pressured American satellite companies seeking business in Asia to lobby for the loosening of U.S. export laws, and for a time enhanced U.S. restrictions brought certain PRC Long March ballistic missile launches to a halt. The Senate committee concluded the previous arrangements had enabled the PLA to improve its ballistic missile technology. Soon after, President Clinton "cleared the export of satellite propellant and other equipment to China," enabling the latter to resume its Long March 2C/SD launches of Motorola Iridium satellites. Transfer of technology concerns were to continue in the years ahead.[18]

While the PRC pushed ahead with its space programs and related technologies, conditions in the Russian Federation deteriorated. The economic, social, and other dislocations in the aftermath of the breakup of the Soviet Union reached crisis level by 1996. That fall, with most of the army not having been paid for several months and top-priority defense needs going unfunded, the Russian minister of defense spoke words of warning. General of the Army Igor Rodionov—a decade earlier the distinguished commander of the USSR's 40th Army in Afghanistan—stated that due to chronic underfunding, "the Army is now at a point beyond which extremely dangerous and uncontrollable processes could arise." Not long after, Rodionov wrote, "One of Russia's most important institutions and mainstays—the Armed Forces—is not being strengthened but is being destroyed." The deputy chairman of the state Duma's Committee on Defense, Aleksei Arbatov, acknowledged, "Not since June 1941 has the Russian military stood as perilously close to ruin as it does now." In that grave context, the head of the country's Military Space Forces (VKS), Vladimir Ivanov, was relieved of command just after having appeared on a Moscow television program that recognized the space forces and coincided with the anniversary of the Sputnik mission of 4 October 1957. The Military Space Forces had been a separate branch of the Soviet (later, Russian) armed forces since 1982, but in attempting to save rubles they were reunited with the Strategic Rocket Forces of which the VKS had been a part prior to its independence. More than two decades later, the issue of military space separatism was to echo in the halls of the U.S. Congress regarding the United States Space Force.[19]

An Air and Space Force to a Space and Air Force?

Especially in the budget-constrained, post–Cold War 1990s, neither Pentagon nor USAF leaders envisioned an independent space service in the near or intermediate future. Near the end of 1997, the Air Force chief of staff, Gen. Michael E. Ryan, referred to the Persian Gulf conflict six years earlier, Operation Desert Storm, as the first "space-aided war," a more accurate phrasing for what some liked to call the first space war. Gen. Tom Moorman, then the commander of Air Force Space Command (AFSPC), said that satellites, ground systems, and their controllers played a crucial role in the conflict's outcome: "Space owned the battlefield." Space systems provided significant operational support to the warfighters especially in terms of communication and navigation capabilities during the desert campaign against Saddam Hussein's Iraq.[20] Drawing upon the Air Force's

SURVEY OF U.S. NATIONAL SECURITY SPACE, 1996–2000   9

1996 vision statement, *Global Engagement*, Ryan told the Air Force Association's (AFA) national gathering that his goal was to see the USAF "evolve from an Air and Space Force, which we call ourselves now, into a Space and Air Force." But it was decades away. The chief's immediate focus was to transition the Air Force into "an air and space EXPEDITIONARY force" [emphasis in original].[21]

In his reference to nomenclature, General Ryan hinted that the Air Force had yet to attain the reality of an air and space force. *Air Force* magazine stated the USAF was "now transitioning from an 'air' force into an 'air and space' force." That also was the wording used by *Global Engagement*. At the moment, the USAF remained mostly "an *air* force." Perhaps Ryan's willingness to adopt a somewhat premature designation was grounded in his conviction that "Air and Space are a continuum—forever." Ryan called for "seamless Air and Space power," and he proposed "there is no delineation, break, or boundary in the third dimension." Such language regarding air and space pointed to a foundational concept, one strongly disputed by a number of space professionals. Ryan may or may not have helped his cause when he stated to the AFA, "The air and space realm touches 100 percent of the world's surface." At best, the words "and space" were unnecessary.[22]

The commander-in-chief of U.S. Space Command, Gen. Howell M. Estes III, addressed the same AFA gathering as did his Air Force Academy classmate, Mike Ryan. Like him, Estes also seemed to question the propriety, in the late 1990s, of informally calling the USAF an air and space force. But unlike the Air Force chief, General Estes gave more attention to fiscal concerns: "We will never become an Air and Space Force if we do not begin to invest greater sums in space. . . . Space must expand and become a larger part of the Air Force budget every year. It has to be this way because it is unlikely anyone is going to give the Air Force a bigger slice of the pie to cover our expansion into space."[23]

At that time, the Air Force was responsible for about 85 to 90 percent of the military space budget and provided 93 percent of military space personnel. In 1993, the AFSPC budget was $2.7 billion, its largest of the decade. For the next half-decade, however, while commercial space was booming and the threats to U.S. satellites from potential adversaries remained somewhat unknown, Air Force funding for space never exceeded $1.77 billion.[24]

Estes acknowledged that should Washington be unwilling to provide the necessary funding for military space, the USAF "can choose to relinquish its leadership of space in favor of another organization, perhaps a new organization [that] will lead our nation into space." While he affirmed the requirement for increased funding, the commander of U.S. Space Command had raised the possibility of a separate space organization, doing so before the same air and space proponents to which the Air Force chief of staff had just expressed his vision for an eventual space and air force.[25]

Having peered over the edge, in a sense, General Estes stepped back and affirmed, "We claim space as an Air Force domain," and he proposed the Air Force's "biggest mistake" at that moment would be to "impede our development as a Space and Air Force." Perhaps it was noteworthy that Estes did not proclaim a seamless space and air domain.[26]

Wrapping up his address, Estes turned to culture. He stated the potential of military space could not be realized without the Air Force changing its culture to embrace the responsibility "for the role of space and its importance to the future national security interests of our country." The Air Force's need for cultural change with respect to space was Estes' main theme and the basis for his speech's title: "The Air Force at a Crossroad." Over the next two decades, a number of space professionals and writers agreed with him. In 2014, Air Force colonel Jeffrey J. Smith wrote of the transition that began in the late 1990s from the USAF's "*fighter-operations* perspective" to a "*synergistic-operations* perspective" [emphasis in original]. A decade after the start of the global war on terror, Smith concluded, "The dominant and most important capabilities required of the USAF do not come from the fighter-operations community; rather, those responsible for intelligence, surveillance, and reconnaissance, together with space-based capabilities, cyberspace operations, logistics, tactical airlift, and special operations are dominating current conflicts."[27]

Accordingly, Smith anticipated the synergistic-operations perspective to become the USAF's new norm, of which an evolving culture was one element. Because space-based capabilities comprised no small part of the new perspective, the logic of Smith's argument could reasonably be expected to lead to a new dominant culture, "an amalgamation of numerous operational capabilities," one that could hardly leave military space unaffected in the process.[28]

Space as a Supporting Force

While Ryan and Estes spoke of an air and space force in somewhat different terms, in 1998 Secretary of Defense William Cohen viewed the nation's space forces as providing "unique benefits" to the United States and its allies not only in terms of military activities but also in civil and commercial enterprises. Cohen stated that space forces "are fundamental to sustaining U.S. global commitments," providing support to enable the air, land, and sea forces during deployments around the globe. One year later, the defense secretary issued a memorandum and accompanying directive updating the department's space policy and aligning it with the current presidential policy. In Pentagon parlance, space was to be a "strategic enabler," especially in the realm of information superiority—which included for deterrence purposes—and was to be integrated into all U.S. military strategies, doctrines, concepts of operations, education, training, and activities. The DoD was to seek increased international cooperation and partnerships in space and to provide support to commercial space.[29]

Clearly, the Clinton administration, including the Cohen-led Pentagon, expected military space to remain primarily a supporting force to terrestrial warfighters for some time to come. As yet, there was no hint of an independent military space corps or force on the horizon, but within two years the landscape was to change at the outset of the next administration.

Senator Bob Smith's Challenge of Space Power

In the meantime, one United States senator took the lead to advocate an independent space corps or service. In November 1998, Sen. Bob Smith of New Hampshire gave an address at Tufts University that quickly led to him writing an article entitled "The Challenge of Space Power." Smith had become well versed on space from his time in the House of Representatives. Upon his election to the Senate in 1990, his support for space programs deepened, marked by his chairmanship of the Strategic Forces Subcommittee on Armed Services.[30]

Already convinced of America's need to maintain "our constant supremacy in space," Senator Smith received multiple communications from at least one constituent who argued for a separate space service. A mid-grade Air Force space weapons officer during the 1990s, Michael V. Smith (no relation) had embraced the idea of an independent space entity, in part, after learning of the Air Force's practice of redirecting funds that Congress intended for space programs to some of its needy air programs instead. At least one USAF space leader, Lt. Gen. Roger DeKok, later the AFSPC vice commander, opined that the reason the service called itself an aerospace organization was "so the Air Force can help itself to the space budget and space personnel, and forget space." It was a well-known phenomenon within space circles. In 1997 retired Gen. Charles Horner, who had commanded AFSPC and then the U.S. Strategic Command, pointed to the same basic issue when he told *Space News*, "If the Air Force clings to its ownership of space, then tradeoffs will be made between air and space, when in fact the tradeoff should be made elsewhere." Both senior leaders expressed a basic viewpoint held in military space circles—where Air Force satellites might go unfunded in favor of USAF aircraft programs, including the fifth-generation fighter, the F-22 Raptor.[31]

In any case, Senator Smith argued that despite the lead in space the United States enjoyed at the moment, future dominance was not assured. The country's leaders must take advantage of the lack of a peer competitor—perhaps lasting only briefly—to combine "expansive thinking with a sustained and substantial commitment of resources" to establish a "dedicated, politically powerful, independent advocate for space power." Smith stated the use of space could enable U.S. forces, when necessary, to inflict violence on an adversary "with great precision and nearly instantaneously and often more cheaply" than by terrestrial-based means. Additionally, space capabilities were going to be required to protect the increasing commerce in space for ourselves and our allies. Smith's point regarding commerce brought to mind the thinking of Sir Julian Corbett. In his highly regarded 1911 work, *Principles of Maritime Strategy*, Corbett argued, "By no conceivable means is it possible to give trade absolute protection. We cannot make an omelette without breaking eggs. We cannot make war without losing ships. To aim at a standard of naval strength or a strategical distribution which would make our trade absolutely invulnerable is to march to economic ruin."[32]

Many space scholars have commented on the parallels of Corbett's maritime strategies with strategic thinking regarding space. Corbett's concerns for the protection of ocean-going trade at reasonable economic cost appeared well worth consideration in a space context. John Hyten employed the maritime analogy to point out the greater difficulty faced by nations in the twenty-first century attempting to protect space-going trade:

> With regard to the commons of the sea, strategic military advantages and economic advantages are easily discernable. Ships of war and ships of commerce are, for the most part, completely different. In space, particularly in the future, satellites of war and satellites of commerce may be one and the same. The national response to a threat from a ship of war is clear. The national response to a satellite that has a military and commercial "dual-use" is not so clear.[33]

Not all agreed with the broad comparison between space and the sea, however. A decade later, one team of three scholars viewed as "deeply flawed" the comparing of the commons of space to that of the high seas. Michael Krepon, Theresa Hitchens, and Michael Katz-Hyman observed that whereas ships damaged at sea during hostilities might find shelter and repairs at a friendly port, "No nation can expect there to be safe havens in space," at least not for years to come. Moreover, the debris resulting from kinetic operations in space did not sink so as no longer to pose a hazard to other craft, as did debris resulting from combat at sea. Instead, space debris lingered for decades, or longer, constituting a hazard to any spacecraft regardless of nationality in the vicinity of the orbit where the strike occurred. Unlike Hyten, for Krepon, Hitchens, and Katz-Hyman the dual-use nature of satellites—which made defensive measures in space more difficult than at sea—appeared to be a significant factor in their rejection of the sea-space analogy.[34]

The senator echoed other leaders such as Secretary Cohen to make the point that as of 1998, U.S. space assets were "basically dedicated to supporting nonspace forms of power projection." That was not space warfare. Rather, it was using space to support air warfare, mainly in the form of information superiority—with which several congressmen and space advocates at Air University were to agree some years later. While he embraced the integration of space-based information capabilities into current systems and organizations as "an important near-term goal," Smith viewed true space warfare going well beyond those capabilities related strictly to information. Writing not long after Smith, RAND's Benjamin Lambeth encouraged the Air Force to go beyond air-space integration, and to pursue land-space and maritime-space integration as well.[35]

Bob Smith charged the Air Force with failure to make critical investments in two areas: space and technology programs, and career space personnel development. Most important, the USAF had not devoted significant resources to "space-based missile-defense development" programs such as kinetic-energy satellites and the space-plane. During the previous two decades, the service had not made the personnel investments in those officers who sought careers in the space field. As a result, of eleven general officers then in AFSPC, none were career space officers, and six of the Air Force Space Command generals were serving in their first space assignment. Moreover, the senator noted the Air Force's tendency "to combine space and missile personnel"—to which some space proponents objected—and to place non-space officers in charge of space organizations. The latter went well beyond the accepted practice of broadening the experience of up-and-coming officers by assigning them outside their area of expertise for an assignment or two.[36]

Of Senator Smith's top two priorities, first was the need for a space-power culture. There must be a leadership cadre or clearinghouse that facilitated an environment that rewarded—rather than punished or viewed indifferently—creative thinking about space power, in a manner akin to Gen. Henry "Hap" Arnold and the Scientific Advisory Board regarding airpower near the end of World War II The speaker of the House from 1995 to 1998, Rep. Newt L. Gingrich (R-Ga.), agreed, later recalling he had been convinced, probably since the 1980s when he worked with High Frontier, "It was obvious that the culture of the Air Force made it virtually impossible to really have people who were willing to explore the full potential of space."[37] During that period, as retired Lt. Gen. William T. Lord (who commanded Air Force Cyberspace Command [Provisional] from 2007 to 2009) recalled, Air Force space and cyber professionals needed to begin communicating their requirements and capabilities in language that resonated with the rest of the USAF, to "speak in a language, and act in a language, and train in a language that is very similar to . . . the rated force." Lord credited then–brigadier general Dale W. Meyerrose, director of communications and information and chief information officer, Headquarters, Air Combat Command, with that initiative.

Smith's second priority was to promote aggressively, and cost-effectively, greater "cooperation between military, civil, and commercial space practitioners," but without compromising national security interests. Twenty years later, both of his concerns had become part of the ongoing conversation on the new U.S. Space Force, from debates over the service's rank structure and other cultural elements to its reliance on large numbers of satellites being launched by commercial entities such as Elon Musk's SpaceX.[38]

Smith presented three options if the nation expected to dominate what he called "the permanent frontier." The USAF could change by shedding "big chunks of today's Air Force to pay for tomorrow's"—a very painful choice, he acknowledged. The senator added his voice to General Horner's and others who made clear that the Air Force had no inherent primary role in space. Smith asked, "Just because space hardware and signals move about over our heads, must space be the exclusive domain of the Air Force?" In a second option that also fell short of creating a new armed force or corps, Smith suggested that U.S. Space Command might establish—in the pattern of U.S. Special Operations Command's funding—a separate major force program (MFP) structure for space power in order to provide adequate control over the development, acquisitions, promotions, and assignments of a unique community. In 2001, the Rumsfeld Space Commission unanimously recommended that very measure. Smith mused that Congress might also consider creating a new assistant secretary of defense for space, an idea the commission modified.[39]

The third option was to create a new service. Smith viewed that, perhaps dramatic, step as an increasingly viable option, one that he and others

16   CHAPTER 1

saw as something of a parallel with U.S. Army aviation in the 1910s when
the Signal Corps held responsibility for "aeronautical equipment." Under
the Signal Corps, army aviation remained in its infancy, without planning
for its funding, development, employment, or the career progression of
personnel. There was only a vague notion that aviation might support the
Signal Corps' communications mission.[40]

The Granite State's senior senator argued that if the Air Force failed to
demonstrate its commitment to becoming a true space and air force and
the special operations MFP model appeared to be unworkable, then the
only other way to enable military space to compete successfully for funding
was as a new service, perhaps as a space corps similar to the U.S. Marine
Corps within the Department of the Navy. Bob Smith's commitment was
clear: "Space dominance is simply too important to allow any bureaucracy,
military department, service mafia, or parochial concern to stand in the
way. I intend to muster all of the political support I can to take any step
necessary to make true space power and space dominance a reality for the
United States of America."[41]

Two years later the Rumsfeld Commission viewed a new service as a
distinct option, one to be "dictated by circumstances over the next five to
ten years."[42]

Air Force Tradeoffs

At the AFA's national symposia in February 1999, Gen. Richard B. Myers
spoke of what he called the next step regarding space. The forum brought
together space leaders, experts, and advocates from industry, academia, government, and the armed forces. Following remarks intended to calm the
anxieties of many caused by the approach of Y2K (the year 2000), the U.S.
Space Command's boss informed the audience of the exponential growth
of commercial space activities. He affirmed that "space is driving a new
American way of making wealth," observing that the gap between worldwide commercial space revenues and military space expenditures continued to widen. Space industries were growing annually at an astounding 20
percent. Space proponents predicted that in the next several years spacefaring nations around the world "will pump another $500 billion into space,"
launching 1,000 to 1,500 satellites.[43]

But while there was cause for encouragement especially with respect to commercial space, including various shared arrangements with the DoD, General Myers acknowledged the unfortunate reality that "the Air Force has so many bills to pay." As a result, he was forced to slip the command's top space acquisition priority—the Space-Based Infrared System (SBIRS)—by two years. It was one of the very painful choices Senator Smith had warned about, and an inauspicious realization for a program that David Spires labeled as experiencing "a history of developmental problems." Lt. Col. John Hyten likened the Air Force's decision to delay SBIRS—albeit by no means a unique case within military circles—to a hypothetical Army decision to delay the M-1 tank because the M-60 could last a few more years; or a Navy delay of its newest carrier because an older carrier could hang on for longer. The future commander of U.S. Space Command, U.S. Strategic Command, and Joint Chiefs of Staff (JCS) vice chairman wrote, "It is not just about how long a system lasts, but the need to update out-of-date technology and take advantage of new capabilities. Failure to treat space systems with equal importance to other military programs sends the wrong message." This was General Horner's tradeoff fear with a vengeance.[44]

Unfortunately, under the organization and funding structures of the day, the Air Force's "so many bills to pay" lacked a solution. In 2000, an *Aerospace Power Journal* article pointed out, "The Air Force is expected to equally prioritize funding opportunities for its own direct war-fighting capabilities as well as its own and its customers' support needs. These space services represent non-core, non-war-fighting services that carry some of our nation's largest must-pay bills," among them launch range services, navigation, and surveillance. The writer, Lt. Col. Cynthia McKinley, USAF, noted that many of the organizations using those services were outside the USAF, the one "paying the bills." The GPS was a prime example, for which McKinley observed, "Regardless of the number of GPS receivers—one or one million—the satellite constellation must be a certain size in order to provide navigation services." McKinley's logic led her to conclude that a United States Space Guard, "a fusion of civil, commercial, and military space personnel and missions"—in many ways similar to the Coast Guard in the maritime domain—was a viable solution. During wartime,

18   CHAPTER 1

the Space Guard could become an arm of the Air Force, as is the case with the Coast Guard vis-a-vis the Navy.[45]

Before the AFA, General Myers went on to express additional funding concerns, especially for the GPS operational and control system's prospects as part of the ongoing Minuteman intercontinental ballistic missile (ICBM) modernization. He noted that Space Command's retention issues required attention, including dollars, particularly because sharp, experienced enlisted space personnel were easily hired into the booming commercial space sector. Confirming the likelihood that some space leaders had expressed—among them General Horner and Senator Smith—Myers told the gathering, "We must energize space funding at a national level. It is more than we can do in the Air Force." At almost the same time, the retired Horner stated, "Right now, space is sick, and the only way it's going to get well is at the expense of needed air programs." While some if not much of the problem was beyond its control, nonetheless, the Air Force needed help.[46]

Thinking Colored by Culture?

At the same AFA meeting in 1999, General Ryan was asked where the service stood in its efforts to integrate air and space. The chief of staff responded with clarity, stating, "We are there, and we declare victory. . . . We are an aerospace force so interlocked that you cannot pull it apart. . . . It just does not make any operational sense. And it certainly does not make any tactical sense. And I do not think that it makes any strategic sense."[47]

But the extent to which Ryan's thinking was influenced by the Air Force's air culture was unclear, keeping in mind that not all players—especially space proponents—bought into the notion that the service had become an air and space force, a question that was inseparable from whether air and space constituted a single domain or two. After all, the service was called the U.S. Air Force, a designation that by law carried with it the obligation of delivering airpower to meet national security objectives. More than a year later, Ryan pointed out that he lacked Title 10 authority for the space mission.[48]

Another AFA speaker at the Orlando, Florida, event, former Air Force Chief of Staff Gen. Michael J. Dugan, addressed what he considered the service's apparent decline over the previous decade in the institution's ability to think about the future of air and space power. Perhaps the decline resulted in part from the perception of no longer having a near-peer competitor after the Cold War, but Air Force culture appeared also to be a factor. General Dugan observed that in contrast with the sister services, USAF members—particularly the operators of aircraft—tended to self-identify with the community of their particular aircraft type, a point long-recognized by the Air Force faculty at Squadron Officer School. From Dugan's perspective, they considered themselves "heavy equipment operators"—his term, and one that some objected to—rather than as members of the U.S. Air Force or those who served or defended their country. On the other side of the cultural aisle, in 1994 retired Air Force general Michael P. C. Carns had addressed the need to change "a testing mindset in space undertakings—every launch unique, long pad-prep times, heavy contractor reliance, extremely long recycle times, and extremely costly charges." Rather, the Air Force should assume space launch and control responsibilities from contractors, and Air Force space specialists needed to begin viewing themselves as players in the "operationalization of space."[49]

To the extent that Dugan was correct—others including Carl Builder have agreed with his perspective—the existence of space personnel and their mission within the institutional Air Force appeared likely to stoke the cultural stovepiping the former chief described, perhaps exacerbated by a degree of self-identification by space personnel as developers and testers. Moreover, space personnel from that period recalled no shortage of cultural prejudice, mainly from the operators, or as Jeffrey Smith termed it, the fighter-operations community that ran the Air Force.[50]

Emerging Space Threats

In November 1999, General Myers returned to the AFA forum to talk about space. He made the point that space superiority was "fleeting," and that although up to that time the nation assumed space superiority over all potential competitors, it ought not to be assumed any longer. "Make no mistake, we are vulnerable, because many of our space systems lack the basic self-defense measures like those [that are] integral to our air missions," he said. Already, Myers counted several countries that possessed

20   CHAPTER 1

lasers capable of blinding the optical sensors on U.S. satellites. O'Hanlon noted that a laser may undergo testing "for beam strength and pointing accuracy as a ballistic missile defense device, without being identified as an ASAT." Myers said others were developing ballistic missile technologies "to disperse tiny shrapnel into low earth orbit [LEO]" which could "create a space version of an interstate pileup since even small objects can produce disastrous collisions at orbital speeds of 17,000 miles per hour." Bluntly, if simplistically, one study opined that "a $1 bag of marbles, properly inserted into [low-earth orbit], could destroy a $1 billion satellite." Several of General Myers' concerns were to bear repeating over the next two decades.[51]

The Space Command's boss was particularly concerned for vulnerable commercial satellites on which the Pentagon depended—or might depend in future—for various missions. Myers warned that the DoD's reliance on commercial space had "created a new center of gravity that can easily be exploited by our adversaries." He cited exercises in which young lieutenants, playing the role of an adversary, went to Radio Shack and with a few cheap purchases, brought down expensive military space systems. Begrudgingly, Myers affirmed how easy it was: "This is not rocket science, it turns out. The previous was." In one U.S. Army test in 1997, "a low-powered laser with little more wattage than a refrigerator lightbulb" temporarily blinded a U.S. satellite. In another case, Air Force engineers built "a working jammer" from "a Honda electrical generator, copper tubing and PVC pipe from a local home supply store and electronic components at a swap meet," for $7,500.[52]

Myers also addressed the need to replace older GPS satellites that were outliving their intended life span. From a warfighter's perspective, it was bad news that GPS satellites were lasting longer than expected, he argued, because "we have capability on orbit designed for a previous era and not responsive to our current needs." Those in Washington holding the purse strings were reluctant to spend money to replace still-functioning satellites when there were so many other unmet requirements, such as the F-22 program. While Myers may not have been aware of Hyten's work, both the current general and the future four-star were on the same page. Myers clarified that the eighteen satellites then available to be launched as

SURVEY OF U.S. NATIONAL SECURITY SPACE, 1996–2000   21

GPS replacements, which could comprise a constellation of twenty-seven satellites, "don't provide the totality of the new capability that we need." Moreover, their life expectancy had just been extended by eight years, which meant an even longer period during which the United States lacked required capabilities such as M-code (signal) jam-resistance and increased power output. Moreover, the faint signal made GPS satellites "highly susceptible to jamming."[53]

Deliberate or not, the GPS was susceptible to human inputs. In a 2000 work addressing space power in the twenty-first century, Simon P. Worden—promoted that year to brigadier general in the Air Force—addressed the critical importance of GPS for a host of applications including air traffic management. Its "potentially most far-reaching application is in timing," Worden surmised. To make his point, the new vice director of operations at Headquarters U.S. Space Command summarized an incident on 17 March 1997:

> A small manual input error was made in a routine update to one of the constellation's 24 satellites that resulted in a small time error being broadcast on a single satellite for only six seconds. While this would have little impact on the use of GPS as a navigation tool since most GPS receivers will ignore a single out-of-range error, the same is not the case for users of the system interested only in timing. Those users will get a time "hack" from the nearest satellite. These time readings have many uses, but one of the most important is to time the use of "time-shared circuits." . . . Cellular telephone systems are just one such time-shared circuit. Thus, the single errant time-hack satellite was duly picked up by the cellular networks in the eastern United States; 110 of 800 cellular sites in that part of the country failed . . . circuits were no longer correctly time-shared and the entire system responded by "crashing" for a good many hours.[54]

Astrophysicist Worden concluded, wryly, "It doesn't take a rocket scientist to figure out that someone interfering with the GPS timing signal can have devastating impacts on national or even international operations." Although Worden had long since retired when the U.S. Space

22 CHAPTER 1

Force came into being in 2019, several younger space proponents who were around to see that long-anticipated event considered him to have been not only a forward-thinking space pioneer, but also a valued mentor and friend.[55]

A Seamless Domain (Or, No Need for Space Separatism?)

At the November AFA gathering in 1999, the Air Force chief of staff, General Ryan, again affirmed his conviction of a seamless aerospace domain that encompassed air and space, stating, "The first half of the next century will mature the aerospace realm. The domain that it will encompass will be from the surface of the earth to the most distant satellite or spacecraft." Refuting the viewpoint held by a number of space proponents, he continued, "There are those who would want to separate the aerospace domain. . . . But for me, that would be like separating the mountains from the valleys or the oceans from the seas. It makes no military sense, and for the foreseeable future, the aerospace realm will remain earth-centric. Though we may explore, as we have in the past, planets or other objects in our solar system, commercialization or colonization of those bodies will have to wait for some time."[56]

Spires observed, "While the so-called indivisibility of 'aerospace' provided a conceptual approach to space that supported the service's quest for military space missions, it did not contribute effectively to a planning process that required consideration of space as a separate medium."[57]

Borrowing the idea from an unnamed space weapons officer later self-identified as Michael V. Smith, by then at the Air Force's Air Command and Staff College, Benjamin Lambeth wrote, "Although the aerospace formula has long insisted that there is no clear line of demarcation between air and space, that formula ignores the 60-mile-high band separating the highest altitude at which air-breathing aircraft can sustain flight and the lowest at which satellites can remain on orbit." The region between about twenty-eight and ninety-three miles above the Earth's surface was "an aerospace no-man's land." No other service besides the Air Force ever bought into the seamless aerospace argument, which Lambeth called "a flawed but handy device for enabling that service to justify a roles and missions claim to space as well as to air."[58]

While Mike Ryan was not the first chief of staff to make the seamless domain argument—Gen. Thomas D. White did so in 1957—perhaps the greater issue was something Gen. John D. Ryan had said in 1970. The elder General Ryan, Mike Ryan's father and the chief of staff between 1969 and 1973, said the aerospace domain was "the operational medium in which the Air Force must be preeminent." Preeminence required dollars, lots of them. If a domain existed that included anything other than air, how reasonable was it to expect an air force to devote a significant portion of its limited funding to non-air interests, the term "aero-space" itself notwithstanding? In any case, an Air Force white paper released in 2000 affirmed the previously stated position of USAF senior leaders: "Our Service views the flight domains of air and space as a seamless operational medium. The environmental differences between air and space do not separate the employment of aerospace power within them." It was intriguing that at almost the same time, Lieutenant Colonel McKinley wrote that although USAF senior leaders' original intent with air and space integration was "as a method by which to guarantee continued Air Force stewardship of space, within months [of late 1996] . . . integration was being interpreted as the necessary and sufficient condition by which the Air Force could seize the opportunity to call itself an aerospace force." The lieutenant colonel's views earned her no favor with Air Force leadership.[59]

The younger General Ryan also highlighted the Air Force's partnering with the space industry. One example led to emblazoning a thirty-foot version of the Pizza Hut logo on a Russian Proton rocket, which in July 2000 launched the living quarters of the fledgling International Space Station. Teasing the Air Force Association crowd, Ryan quipped that it "kind of makes me wonder whether you can get a free pizza if they don't show up in 30 minutes."[60]

Once again with the AFA in November of 2000, Ryan stayed with the vision of an "aerospace domain of seamless vertical dimension." During the U.S./NATO combat operations over Kosovo and Serbia in the spring of 1999, the Air Force demonstrated "significant improvements since Desert Storm" in air and space integration in support of the joint fight, as Spires wrote. While Ryan affirmed the same, the general seemed most concerned for the Air Force's recapitalization needs for both air-breathing and space systems. He posited that space assets were the service's "most re-capitalized [*sic*] force . . . because it must be," in light of its obligations to support multiple services and the national command authority.[61]

Ryan spoke in the shadow of another commission led by Donald Rumsfeld, with a different focus from the one he had chaired two years earlier. In late 2000, Rumsfeld chaired the congressionally mandated commission to assess NSS management and organization. Gen. Ralph Eberhart of Space Command likened the space commission to a trip to the dentist—not fun, but necessary. General Ryan considered the Air Force had been "great stewards" of space, and he saw no need for a space corps or force. Rather, he sought a national commitment to increased funding to make his aerospace vision a reality. At the same time, Ryan acknowledged he had no legal obligation regarding the space realm of the vertical dimension. He anticipated some clarification stemming from the upcoming quadrennial defense review.[62]

The secretary of the Air Force, F. Whitten Peters, added his voice to those of the uniformed leaders. Perhaps more willing to share his thoughts than the generals, the secretary opined, "I really do not understand what the big problem is that justifies a national [space] commission." Like the chief of staff, Peters thought the Air Force was doing well as the steward of space and saw no reason for a separate space corps or force. Nevertheless, Peters suggested the Rumsfeld Commission, which was meeting at that very time, might work on reducing "the multitude of players in the space business." The secretary likened the decision-making process for space, especially budgeting, to "the street map of Rome"—chaotic, and with lots of dead ends. Most of all, space needed "a national integrating organization" for a seamless aerospace force, but something short of a space entity outside the Air Force. Probably more than a few space separatists in the audience noticed that when Peters acknowledged that the service had often been accused of "siphoning off money to go to the air side," he did not deny the charge. Rather, he pointed to the need for replacing an aging tanker force and the RC-135 fleet in particular. He also argued that developing aerospace leaders who were capable of the kinds of integration required by an air and space force was best accomplished by keeping space with the USAF.[63]

Conclusion

In other words, Secretary Peters agreed with Senator Bob Smith and other space separatists' arguments that many of the problems could best be resolved by creating a new space organization, but he held a different conviction on what to do about them. Air Force space was sick, and drastic changes were called for. The secretary of the Air Force and the USAF chief of staff were far from the only senior leaders who, in the words of a retired Air Force two-star, had "simply not come to grips with whether to treat space as a continuum of air power or a separate domain." Until that question was resolved once and for all, there could be no long-term restoration of space's health. Within two months of Peters' address, however, in January 2001, the Rumsfeld Commission's report was to argue the case for space separatism in Washington—although not right away. Perhaps unforeseen beforehand, the report was to enjoy the considerable advantage of its release at the same time as a new administration was arriving in town. Once all the hanging chads had been counted in Florida and George W. Bush was declared the winner of the 2000 presidential election, the president-elect began planning his administration. His team included a new secretary of defense—in fact, a former secretary of defense—the man who happened to have chaired the space commission, Donald Rumsfeld.[64]

2

U.S. NATIONAL SECURITY SPACE

THE BUSH YEARS, 2001–2008

In the National Defense Authorization Act (NDAA) of 2000, Congress mandated that the secretary of defense establish a commission "to assess the organization and management" of national security space (NSS). Given that the U.S. Air Force controlled more than 80 percent of the defense dollars spent on space, the commission's charge was, in effect, to evaluate the Air Force's stewardship of military space. Although that service's leadership considered itself "great stewards" of space, some in Congress disagreed. Some Air Force leaders, then and later, remained skeptical. In 2007, Gen. Lance W. Lord—from 2002 to 2006 the commander of Air Force Space Command (AFSPC)—considered the Rumsfeld Space Commission to have taken place in the context of various competing agendas. Military space at the time, Lord said, "was kind of an orphan."[1]

Commonly known as the Rumsfeld Space Commission or the 2001 Space Commission, Donald H. Rumsfeld chaired the thirteen-member body from early July until late December of 2000 when he was nominated by president-elect George W. Bush for the cabinet position of secretary of defense. So it was that the commission's report, issued in January 2001, arrived shortly at the desk of the new defense secretary—Rumsfeld—who, obviously, was already familiar with its content and favorably inclined toward most, if not all, of its major recommendations.[2]

This was Rumsfeld's second tour running the Pentagon. Under President Gerald Ford (1974–77), Rumsfeld was forty-three years of age when he began to serve in 1975—the youngest defense secretary in U.S. history. One of his early initiatives was to redo the Pentagon's bare, green walls, adding what a former aide called "a sense of mission on the walls," which was accomplished mainly by displaying hundreds of paintings, photographs, and exhibits highlighting the nation's military history. Rumsfeld's work helped turn the Pentagon into the tourist attraction it is today, allowing visitors to see items from George Marshall's desk to Douglas MacArthur's corncob pipe on display inside glass cases.[3]

On the day the report was issued (11 January 2001), the defense-related *Early Bird Brief* included an article on the launch of an unmanned Chinese spacecraft the day before. A Long March 2-F rocket had blasted off from the country's Gobi Desert satellite launch facility, the latest step in China's quest to become the third nation to send an astronaut—or "taikonaut" from the Chinese word for space—into orbit. In October 2003, former fighter pilot Yang Liwei joined Soviet cosmonaut Yuri Gagarin and American astronaut John Glenn in space history as his country's first man in space. His promotion several years later to major general suggested the importance the Chinese government placed on catching up to the two leading nations in military space.[4]

The commission's charter was to assess military space with an eye toward changes that, if implemented, should bolster U.S. national security. The members, totaling twelve following Rumsfeld's resignation, included four Air Force four-star generals. Three other military members included one Army three-star, one Army four-star, and one Navy four-star who had served as vice chairman of the Joint Chiefs of Staff (JCS). Each of the remaining five commissioners possessed a wealth of corporate or government civilian service in space, intelligence, or other armed services issues—some had both. Their report sailed through the commission unanimously and was submitted to each chairman and ranking member of the House and Senate armed services committees. Those four individuals and

28   CHAPTER 2

Secretary of Defense William S. Cohen had appointed the commission's members, in consultation with the director of central intelligence.[5]

Some Concerns of the 2001 Space Commission: Capability, Culture, and Cadre Building

The tasking from the Congress was no small hint that many were concerned with the Air Force's stewardship of space. It should have come as no surprise when the majority of space experts interviewed by the commission expressed their doubts regarding the USAF's ability, or willingness, to handle the changes deemed necessary. Overall, commissioners reported a "lack of confidence" on the part of those they spoke with as to whether the Air Force was fully prepared to address the military space needs of the other services. Despite the USAF doctrine of air and space integration en route to a space-and-air force at some future date, many testified to the commission that the "Air Force does not treat the two equally." Space experts told the commissioners they believed the USAF viewed space "solely as a supporting capability" to enhance the Air Force's primary mission of offensive and defensive air operations.[6]

The point was well taken. Gen. Michael E. Ryan had spoken of the 1999 Serbia air campaign as a fine example of air and space integration—also called "network- (or net-) centric warfare." It also was a case of employing space assets to enhance traditional air operations. "In less than one minute, Predator video data could be combined with three-dimensional terrain data derived from national satellites, then linked via satellite and data link to the cockpits of combat aircraft flying into Kosovo and Serbia." Integration or net-centric warfare it certainly was, but whether it was of the sort to promote a space-and-air force in the future perhaps was debatable.[7]

There were other far-reaching concerns integral to air-space integration, among them culture and cadre-building. The commission acknowledged the absence for the most part of a space culture within the Air Force, stating the service "must take steps to create a culture . . . dedicated to developing new space system concepts, doctrine, and operational capabilities"—as Army aviators had done in the decades prior to an independent air force. One cultural tangent was that Air Force space officers were accustomed to slights from their fellow airmen, from comments by macho fighter pilots on how their space peers looked in their flight suits to space memorabilia being given away rather than preserved and showcased by the owning organizations. In Gen. Chuck Horner's *Every Man a Tiger*, Horner longed "for the day when a space geek walks into a fighter pilot bar and announces, 'You boys better get out of here. I've had a bad day flying my satellite, I intend to get drunk, and if that happens I may get mean and hurt one of you.' At that point, the space pilots will have earned their spurs. 'Every man a tiger' applies to all the skies, those above the air included." While humorous and a bit overstated, Horner cleverly touched upon the need for developing a space culture within the Air Force.[8]

Perhaps worse than perceived or actual slights at the fighter pilot bar was the replacing of space memorabilia in unit display cases with the treasured relics of flying units, to which the space professionals serving in those units had no link whatsoever. The message was clear: space was not valued by the Air Force. Space culture and a space cadre were largely inseparable, however: long-serving space professionals were the very ones best equipped to promote culture change within AFSPC, if not beyond it as well.[9]

One of the biggest problems the commissioners noted was that the Air Force had not yet demonstrated a commitment to developing a space cadre within its ranks. Of more than 150 personnel in "key operational space leadership positions," fewer than one in five flag officers had career space backgrounds. That was in sharp contrast with the vast majority of senior leaders in other career fields, including the Navy's nuclear submarine force, who typically spent up to 90 percent of their years of service in their specialty or a related field. The 2001 report noted that due to limited years of duty in space-related jobs, short tour lengths, and a dearth of technical education at the appropriate points in one's career, most Air Force senior leaders in space jobs "spend most of their assignments learning about space rather than leading." Overall, the commission concluded that the defense department—especially the Air Force—"must create a stronger military space culture, through focused career development, education and training, within which the space leaders for the future can be developed."[10]

The 2001 Space Commission's Recommendations

The Rumsfeld Space Commission offered three presidential recommendations, the first of which called on the president to "consider establishing space as a national security priority." This was based upon America's "vital national interest in space," commercially and militarily. The commissioners warned that the United States was more vulnerable to attack or disruption of its space assets—by deliberate act or accident—than were other nations that were less dependent upon space. For example, in 1998 80 percent of U.S. pagers as well as credit card authorization networks and other communication systems were shut down when the Galaxy IV satellite malfunctioned. It took weeks to restore satellite service for some of the affected systems. In early 2000 "the U.S. lost all information from a number of its satellites" for several hours when ground station computers malfunctioned.[11]

Perhaps the country's single greatest space vulnerability—at least the one best known to Americans—rested with its GPS satellites. From the 1960s the U.S. Navy and U.S. Air Force had worked on developing satellite navigation systems, which efforts merged in the early 1970s. Gen. John D. Ryan, the Air Force chief of staff, established a joint program office under the Air Force Systems Command's Space Division to manage the program. By 1974 the Pentagon had authorized a validation effort using a four-satellite configuration and renamed the system the Navstar Global Positioning System. Four years later, the defense department launched the first eleven GPS test satellites, of which the navigational system owed much to the work of early space force advocate Dino Lorenzini.[12] The GPS constellation became fully operational by the mid-1990s with twenty-four satellites then in use. In 2001 the commission cautioned the U.S. leadership, "If the GPS system were to experience widespread failure or disruption, the impact could be serious. Loss of GPS timing could disable police, fire and ambulance communications around the world; disrupt the global banking and financial system, which depends on GPS timing to keep worldwide financial centers connected; and interrupt the operation of electric power distribution systems."[13]

Arguing from strategist Alfred Thayer Mahan, who more than a century ago viewed naval strength as essential for a great power, Everett C. Dolman wrote, "The United States must be ready and prepared, in Mahanian scrutiny, to commit to the defense and maintenance of these [GPS, other satellite] assets, or relinquish its power to a state willing and able to do so."[14]

It was the possibility of devastation to U.S. satellites, beginning with GPS, that led to the report's most striking warning: "The U.S. is an attractive candidate for a 'Space Pearl Harbor.'" The stirring phrase to Americans, "Pearl Harbor," could not be missed—it appeared no less than seven times in the hundred-page report. It was not the first time that theme had been employed in the context of space: in 1958 Lt. Gen. James M. Gavin's *War and Peace in the Space Age* warned of the possibility of "a technological Pearl Harbor" in connection with the launching of a Soviet satellite that might serve military purposes as part of an ICBM system. In 2001 the commissioners added, "We are on notice, but we have not noticed." Over the following two decades, some space experts found fault with the ominous warning, perhaps in cases based on what former House Speaker Newt Gingrich termed "a fantasy vision of a demilitarized space." Others, embracing astropolitik as Dolman rendered it, considered it prudent in view of China's increasing aggressiveness ranging from claiming broader sovereignty based on man-made islands in the western Pacific to conducting anti-satellite tests in space.[15]

Following the commission's advocating "space as a national security priority" and two additional presidential recommendations, the next two centered on the Pentagon chief himself, a fact perhaps noted by the former defense secretary who chaired the commission—perhaps unaware at the time they were penned that the report was to soon land on his desk. The commission viewed the relationship between the secretary of defense and director of central intelligence (DCI) to be particularly critical for addressing effectively NSS policy and objectives, so it recommended that the two "should meet regularly." Further, the defense secretary should provide for a senior space advocate in the department by establishing an undersecretary for space, intelligence, and information, at least until military space organizations had matured—one of the three major recommendations that Secretary Rumsfeld did not adopt.[16]

The next word of counsel was the first to deal specifically with the Department of the Air Force. It called for the secretary of the Air Force to assign "a four-star officer other than" the commander of U.S. Space Command (CINCSPACE) and the commander of North American Aerospace Defense Command (CINCNORAD) as commander of the Air Force Space Command. In those days, a triple-hatted arrangement existed: CINCSPACE/CINCNORAD also commanded the AFSPC. The second part of the recommendation asked the defense secretary to "end the practice of assigning only Air Force flight-rated officers to the position of CINCSPACE and CINCNORAD" to allow "an officer from any Service with an understanding of combat and space" to be eligible for the position.[17]

The report's "Military Services" section called for realignments within mainly Air Force headquarters and field commands to organize, train, and equip for prompt and sustained space operations. In what was to be the largest USAF realignment by far, the Space and Missile Systems Center (SMC)—then under the Air Force Materiel Command (AFMC), led by General Lester L. Lyles—should be reassigned to AFSPC. While the Army and Navy were expected to continue to develop and deploy their own space systems, AFSPC should be assigned the job of providing the resources to conduct "space research, development, acquisition and operations." Also, under the Military Services section, commissioners called for amending Title 10 U.S. Code to assign the Air Force statutory responsibility for "sustained offensive and defensive air *and* space operations" [emphasis in original]—Rumsfeld chose not to adopt the second recommendation, as it was already largely addressed elsewhere in terms of space. The last item under the section was to task the defense secretary to designate the Air Force as the executive agent for space within the defense department, to which Rumsfeld assented.[18]

From its founding in the early 1960s, the NRO was responsible for development and employment of U.S. national security reconnaissance satellites during the Cold War. Since the first reconnaissance satellite launch in 1962, no U.S. government office had announced a launch ahead of time, and payloads and missions never were described. Post-launch press releases were restricted to the type of rocket employed. The NRO's existence remained classified for three-and-a-half decades until President Clinton's space policy directive of September 1996, which also permitted "the identification and official titles of its senior officials." On 20 December 1996 a Titan IV booster was launched from Vandenberg AFB, California, carrying the first announced NRO satellite. The NRO's press release stated, "This event is the first time the US Government has acknowledged, in advance, the launching of a reconnaissance satellite. . . . The NRO will operate the satellite once in orbit." The payload and mission went undescribed, however.[19]

In 2001, recognizing "growing similarities between Air Force and NRO satellite acquisition and operations," the Rumsfeld Commission requested two changes to draw the USAF and NRO closer together: first, the undersecretary of the Air Force should double as the NRO director, a return to the 1960s arrangement; and, second, the undersecretary ought also to be designated the Air Force acquisition executive for space.[20]

The recommendation was despite differences in the approach to acquisition and operations in each organization. Traditionally, the NRO maintained a much closer relationship between those handling the acquisition of a satellite type and its operation—often the same people were involved—but the same was not true in the Air Force. The commissioners noted "different organizational cultures within NRO and Air Force space activities," perhaps stemming in part from the fact that military satellites often were acquired with a fleet inventory of only one or two; whereas the USAF's traditional obligations required greater numbers of airframes, which argued against the personal relationship between acquisitions and operations even in those few cases where the numbers were small.[21]

One Air University space officer viewed the NRO's culture to be marked by "Hyper-classification," mostly civilian personnel, and "A Space-Minded Culture"—all of which contrasted sharply with traditional Air Force culture. He was not alone. At a 1995 historical symposium devoted to "The USAF in Space, 1945 to the Twenty-First Century," General Schriever noted that excessive secrecy had hindered the NRO program. Historian David N. Spires added that over-classification tended to segregate space from the rest of the military. Summarizing the symposium, Dwayne A. Day of the Space Policy Institute, George Washington University, wrote, "This separation created many ancillary effects—such

34 CHAPTER 2

as poor communications between users and designers of space systems—that still exist today."[22]

The final three recommendations dealt with space research and budgeting. The commission had pushed for regular meetings between the defense secretary and the DCI. Part of the rationale for their closeness was in order to facilitate "the creation of a research, development and demonstration organization" with its focus on finding new methods for intelligence collection, including but not limited to space systems. The commissioners saw competition as a good thing and wanted the defense secretary to direct the Defense Advanced Research Projects Agency (DARPA) "and the Services' laboratories to undertake development and demonstration of innovative space technologies and systems for dedicated military missions."[23]

Lastly, the commission thought that space capabilities "are not funded at a level commensurate with their relative importance." To facilitate providing military space programs with better visibility regarding fiscal and personnel resources, the commission requested the secretary of defense to establish a major force program (MFP) for space. While commissioners initially considered the creation of an MFP-12 for space after the pattern of the U.S. Special Operations Command, in the end they opted for a more decentralized approach to funding due to the existence of U.S. Space Command, a unified command. The point was to gain clarity in terms of spending on U.S. military space, something previously unknown.[24]

The Question of a Space Corps within USAF or an Independent Military Department

Not surprisingly, the single most far-reaching issue facing the commission was the question of creating a space corps within the Air Force, or a space force presumably within its own military department. Given the interest in such possibilities on the part of Sen. Bob Smith and a growing number of space professionals, it was noteworthy that the commission was not overly focused there. Instead, the commission's broad overview was that a new, comprehensive approach was needed to further NSS; its most important conclusion was that "the critical need is national leadership to elevate space on the national security agenda." While keeping its focus on near- and mid-term changes to U.S. national security space, the commission also addressed what it considered the longer-term prospect of a new military department: "The use of space in defense of U.S. interests may require the creation of a military department for space at some future date." But in the near term, the disadvantages clearly outweighed the advantages, beginning with an insufficient number of space-qualified personnel—the space cadre.[25]

Perhaps the most important caveat to the commission's major recommendations was the clear intent that its near-term intentions were not to prejudice or preclude the likelihood of establishing a space corps under the Air Force in the intermediate term or an independent space force in the long term: the commission concluded that once the USAF's initial realignments were completed, *"a logical step toward a Space Department could be to transition from the new Air Force Space Command to a Space Corps within the Air Force"* [emphasis in original]. The timetable for such a transition was unpredictable but depended upon circumstances within the next five to ten years.[26]

The Mixed Initial Response by USAF and Bush Administration, 2001–2002

On 11 January 2001 the commission delivered its report to key members of Congress. In early 2001, many airmen assumed the recommendations were to be accepted and implemented in the main, if not entirely, especially because the commission's chairman was the new administration's secretary of defense, who, in the words of one well-connected space professional, "feels ownership" of the report. The same individual told the AFSPC vice commander, Lt. Gen. Roger G. DeKok, he had heard directly from certain commissioners that when the report was briefed to the chief of staff of the Air Force (CSAF) and the secretary of the Air Force, it was questioned, if not resisted. One commissioner reportedly was appalled at the Air Force reception of the report. The unidentified space insider—who addressed DeKok as Roger and signed his email to the general "from Bill"—was convinced it was "a total non-starter" to fight the report because Rumsfeld "believes he had an excellent Commission behind him and heard from all the right witnesses." Prudently, Bill was convinced "the smart play for the AF is to embrace the vision, lean forward and be willing to change." Rightly, he also noted, "Rumsfeld hates status quo. He wants to transform the military—it's at the top of his agenda."[27]

36   CHAPTER 2

The next morning, which was two weeks since the report's issuance and a mere five days into the George W. Bush administration, Lieutenant General DeKok wrote to Bill, saying the Air Force leadership's reaction to the report, in his view, "is generally positive . . . but not positive enough." The general was concerned with those who exercised service acquisition authority and the realigning of the SMC as well as the Air Force research laboratories under the AFSPC. Encouragingly, DeKok reported that Gen. Ralph E. Eberhart—then triple-hatted as commander of AFSPC, NORAD, and U.S. Space Command—had contacted CSAF Ryan to ask him to move up the date of the Air Force's official response to the space commission report, which was set for mid-February. General Ryan agreed to provide it by the end of January. Otherwise, DeKok feared that too much time might allow "antibodies to begin developing" against it at the air staff in the Pentagon, mostly from the acquisition community. Overall, DeKok remained upbeat and commented, "We can debate implementation details, but . . . the 'AF enthusiastically welcomes the conclusions and recommendations of the report.'"[28]

In order to coordinate USAF's response amidst a myriad of implementation details, General Ryan established a Space Commission Implementation Task Force, led by Brig. Gen. Michael A. Hamel. At the time, Hamel served as director of space operations under Headquarters, USAF; he went on to wear three stars as the SMC commander from 2005 to 2008. Meanwhile, in the spring of 2001 the Congress, air staff, JCS, and Secretary Rumsfeld expressed approval of nearly all the commission's recommendations. Senator Wayne Allard (R-Colo.)—who in 2008 chaired a follow-on commission addressing military space—stated, "I believe the commission has done an excellent job at describing why space is so important to U.S. national security, and how we can improve our ability to exploit space to enhance our security."[29]

The commission likened the transition of military space within the Air Force to the evolution of aviation within the U.S. Army, which led eventually to the Department of the Air Force—four decades after the Wright Brothers delivered the first airplane to the U.S. Army Signal Corps. It was debatable whether military space in 2001 more closely paralleled Army aviation in the pre-1918 or the pre-1947 era, but the point seemed to favor the former. Unlike the air arm in the 1942–45 period when the Army Air Forces' bombers struck countless targets and contributed materially to military victory, at the twenty-first century's outset U.S. military space forces had never fired a shot in anger and there were no weapons deployed in space. Perhaps the Army's aviation experience entered into the CSAF's thinking, but in any case, not long after the release of the space commission's report, General Ryan, addressing an aerospace conference in Washington, stated he did not see the need for a space corps or space force "for 50 years."[30]

The AFSPC commander, General Eberhart, viewed the SMC realignment from AFMC to AFSPC as "our number one priority," which he saw as "key to the success of military space in the coming decades." Moreover, SMC boasted some 2,700 personnel and a $6 billion budget. The commissioners noted, "Design, development and acquisition of space launch, command and control, and satellite systems" were conducted by AFMC, not space, personnel; they were convinced that a realignment, or consolidation of space functions, under AFSPC "would create a strong center of advocacy for space" as well as fostering the development of a cadre of space professionals. While it was a bureaucratically difficult matter for the Air Force, by May 2001 Eberhart reported the main issue of managing the career needs of those SMC personnel to be transferred to AFSPC had been worked out. In October 2001 the realignment of SMC—located at Los Angeles AFB, California—to AFSPC became a reality. DeKok enthusiastically viewed the realignment as creating "a cradle-to-grave powerhouse that's exactly the right organization for the 21st century."[31]

As the SMC realignment was being hammered out, Secretary Rumsfeld wrote to Sen. John Warner (R-Va.), the Armed Services Committee chairman, providing him an overview of his decisions. The defense secretary directed the department to implement ten of the report's thirteen key recommendations. Of the ten, seven were under the Air Force's purview. Of the thirteen recommendations, #3 (using the Government Accountability Office (GAO) report's enumeration for simplicity) required the assigning of a four-star officer as commander, AFSPC, and the general must be other than the (soon to be dual-hatted) commander in chief of U.S. Space Command and NORAD; #4 on the list of recommendations discontinued the practice of assigning only flight-rated officers as CINCSPACE/CINCNORAD to ensure the eligibility of an officer from any service who was up to the job; #5 directed the realigning of head-quarters and field commands to "organize, train, and equip for prompt and sustained [offensive, defensive] space operations"; #6 required AFSPC to conduct "space research, development, acquisition, and operations"; #8 began the work of assigning the Air Force the role of designated executive agent for military space. In addition, in directive #9 Rumsfeld assigned the Air Force undersecretary, Peter B. Teets, as NRO director; and in #10 the Pentagon chief designated the Air Force undersecretary as the Air Force acquisition executive for space.[32]

The year 2001 provided mixed developments regarding civil space. In March, NASA launched *Discovery* on a space shuttle mission to deliver supplies and equipment to the International Space Station (ISS) and to deploy the Expedition-Two crew to the ISS. The Expedition-One crew had spent four-and-a-half months "at the orbiting outpost." Also that spring, the world's "first space tourist," American millionaire Dennis A. Tito (formerly an engineer at NASA's Jet Propulsion Laboratory), traveled to the ISS with two Russian cosmonauts. His trip, which was against the wishes of NASA who cited safety concerns, "has reignited Russia's obses-sion with space and it was overjoyed to have defied the world's most pow-erful nation by being the first country to put a tourist into space," reported *Spaceflight*. Although he was considered a tourist, Tito spent considerable time at the Gagarin Cosmonaut Training Centre near Moscow in prepa-ration for the flight, and he assisted with food preparation for the cosmo-nauts while at the ISS. Upon his return, Tito testified before a U.S. House of Representatives subcommittee as it gathered information and views on the future of space tourism. At about the same time, the president and CEO of Lockheed Martin, coming off a disappointing several months in terms of satellite manufacturing, noted, "Lockheed's growth opportunities are not going to be in space."[33]

Between mid-2001 and early 2002, the Air Force continued to imple-ment recommended changes. The SMC commander became the program executive officer (PEO) for space, an important move that the AFSPC historian viewed as increasing the command's "control of the acquisition arm of space." Although Rumsfeld's decision to alter the command structure of AFSPC had been made in 2001, it was April 2002 when Lance Lord became the first four-star commander solely of the Air Force Space Command, which granted AFSPC equivalent status with the Air Force's other major commands. Lord succeeded General Eberhart, who continued as the dual-hatted commander of U.S. Space Command and NORAD.[34]

After General Lord retired in 2006, he was going through the mail at home one day and discovered a personal letter from Secretary Rumsfeld. The Pentagon chief wrote Lord that he had done "a wonderful job" at AFSPC. For Lance Lord, it was "one of life's golden moments," as well as confirmation of the wisdom of General Schriever who had mentored the younger generation of space leaders "to stick with the mission" regardless of the other important issues of the day. In a poignant moment for both men, Lord had the opportunity, not long before Schriever's death in 2005 at age ninety-four, to present him with the Air Force's newly approved space badge, soon to be worn by AFSPC personnel. Getting the badge represented an important cultural step for Air Force space professionals. Noted author Neil Sheehan wrote of Lord's presentation to Schriever,

> The badge was mounted nicely behind glass in a small brown lacquered wooden frame. It was silvered, with a rocket superimposed on a globe representing the earth and satellites circling behind it. "This is the first one and we want you to have it," Lord said as he handed the framed badge to Schriever. A citation on a little plaque within the frame read: "Gen. Lance Lord to Bernard A. Schriever, General, USAF (Retired), the First Badge to America's First Space Operator." Lord then bent down and draped a blue-and-white checkered scarf the command had also just adopted as a new accoutrement to its uniform around Schriever's neck. Bennie smiled. He seemed to understand what was happening and to be immensely pleased.[35]

The June 2002 GAO report listed six of Rumsfeld's ten directed changes as completed, with the remaining four in-progress. Cautiously, the GAO noted that because the implementation of several recommendations had been so recent, it was too early to assess their impact. Even more important, the long-range plans for "developing a cadre of space professionals and integrating military and intelligence space activities" remained incomplete. As a step in the right direction, in late 2004 AFSPC established the National Security Space Institute (NSSI), which was initially contracted off base in Colorado Springs to provide personnel with increased space education and training.[36]

By the end of 2002, only one of the approved recommendations remained to be completed. Following a departmental directive in 2003 designating the secretary of the Air Force as the DoD executive agent for space as well as the Air Force acquisition executive for space, in July the secretary of the Air Force delegated to the undersecretary all responsibilities as the DoD executive agent for space.[37]

11 September 2001 and Aftermath

While not the only reason, one explanation for the two-year delay in designating the DoD executive agent for space was that the 9/11 attacks happened only months after Secretary Rumsfeld completed his official response to the space commission's report. In one specific, unsettling, connection with subsequent events, the 2001 commission had addressed the role of military space in the U.S. intelligence community's increased collection requirements since the end of the Cold War. The example it mentioned was "the pursuit of the terrorist Osama bin Laden." On 11 September 2001, bin Laden's actions became known to the world in a horrific manner as Al Qaeda terrorists carried out his design to attack the United States for its presence and perceived corrupting influence in Islamic lands, particularly Saudi Arabia. Al Qaeda operatives hijacked four fuel-laden commercial airliners that took off from U.S. airports, flying two of them into the World Trade Center in New York, where more than 2,700 died. The third hijacked airliner crashed into the Pentagon—on the sixtieth anniversary of the building's groundbreaking, 11 September 1941. Aboard the fourth airliner, courageous passengers battled the terrorists for control of the plane, which impacted the ground in rural Somerset County, Pennsylvania. Nearly 3,000 died in the attacks.[38]

The attack on the nation's homeland not only thrust the United States immediately into wartime mode. The 9/11 attacks also served to highlight

U.S. NATIONAL SECURITY SPACE

various space support capabilities that proved critical during the response. Communication satellites kept the lines of communication open between New York and Washington when cell phone service providers could not handle the unprecedented volume of calls. David Spires wrote, "Homeland security officials relied on GPS' precise data for search and rescue work and for vehicle surveillance and tracking." Weather, national signals intelligence collection, and remote sensing satellites provided critical information to decision-makers responsible for protection and recovery activities, the monitoring and intercepting of terrorist communications and networks, and the providing of high-resolution imagery of attack-damaged areas. In the immediate aftermath, Spires counted no fewer than thirteen federal agencies responsible for homeland security functions that relied on space support, many of them already accustomed to some space support.[39]

Space Support for Operation Enduring Freedom–Afghanistan (OEF–Afghanistan)

Four weeks after the 9/11 attacks, U.S. military forces initiated combat operations in Afghanistan on the night of 7–8 October 2001. In concert with friendly Northern Alliance elements, U.S./coalition forces began the takedown of the Taliban regime, which not only provided a number of training facilities for al Qaeda operatives, it had refused to extradite bin Laden to the United States once U.S. authorities identified him as being behind the attacks. President Bush was determined to prevent another attack on U.S. soil, and he took the fight to the enemy. Space assets belonging to the U.S./coalition included nearly one hundred satellites committed especially to supporting the U.S. Central Command's combined air operations center (CAOC) at Prince Sultan Air Base, Saudi Arabia. Inside the huge CAOC facility, personnel integrated air and space elements "with a minimum of the 'stovepipes' that in the past had impeded effective cooperation across service and functional lines."[40]

Space support for OEF featured a daily space tasking order (STO), aligned with the CAOC's air tasking order (ATO) to ensure maximum integration of air and space operations. At the CAOC, a six-member space team led by Brig. Gen. Richard E. Webber—who deployed from Schriever AFB, Colorado—handled the daily planning and conducted space operations in support of the war. Bandwidth requirements were unprecedented,

42 CHAPTER 2

estimated to be between five and seven times the satellite communications bandwidth of the 1991 Iraqi conflict—while supporting only one-tenth of the force size in-theater from the decade prior.[41]

Predator and Global Hawk unmanned aerial vehicles (UAVs) accounted for much of the bandwidth demand. One author noted that a single Global Hawk "used five times the bandwidth consumed by the entire U.S. contingent in Desert Storm," mostly in providing streaming video imagery to attacking aircraft and control centers. Military planners secured much of the increased bandwidth from civil and commercial satellites. Managing bandwidth was a challenge, too, when at times UAVs did not fly as scheduled and their bandwidth went unused.[42]

The Afghanistan campaign was the first in which high-resolution commercial satellite imagery was available to military planners. Most important, the U.S. National Imagery and Mapping Agency (NIMA) contracted with Space Imaging for one-meter multispectral products coming from *Ikonos* satellites on a daily basis. Planners and aircrews used the imagery for flight simulations to familiarize themselves with Afghanistan's extremely rugged terrain and for bomb damage assessments.[43]

Overall, OEF earned high marks especially for its net-centric operations, in which space was a key player. A Marine Corps general officer commented on the space-enabled connectivity seen in OEF: "We used to measure our [space] support with a calendar, and now we're using a stopwatch."[44]

CSAF Jumper, from "Aerospace" to "Air and Space," and the Dearth of Space Leaders

In October 2001, shortly after the start of OEF–Afghanistan, the new Air Force chief of staff announced what Benjamin Lambeth called "a substantially changed direction in the Air Force's approach" to the relationship between air and space. Gen. John P. Jumper—whose first official staff meeting as CSAF had been on the morning of 11 September—said, "When I talk about space ... I don't talk about aerospace, I talk about air *and* space." Jumper's view was not a new perspective for him, but it matched that of the space commission nicely. The chief added, "To me, space ... is a separate culture. The physics that apply to orbital dynamics are different than what airmen experience in the air. And, there's a culture that has to grow up that shows the same expertise in space as airmen showed after World War II in aerial combat. We have to respect that, and we have to grow and nurture that culture until it matures."[45]

In 1957, Air Force Chief of Staff Gen. Thomas White had stated, "I want to stress that there is no division, per se, between air and space. Air and space are an indivisible field of operations." From that time until 2001, that was the Air Force's basic position. But coming so soon after the start of hostilities in Afghanistan, Jumper's game-changing approach to space probably was missed by many who were focused on the fight overseas. The Air Force's space community, however, took heart.[46]

Jumper also observed that the military had been operating in space long enough to have produced "senior, career space professionals," yet in the main the Air Force had failed to do so, as the Rumsfeld Commission had noted as well. Maj. Gen. Robert S. Dickman was one of the few exceptions, who finished his career in 2000 as the senior military officer at the NRO. His successful career notwithstanding, Dickman addressed a 1995 symposium on Air Force space, stating the Air Force had done "a poor job of training its space people and assigning and promoting them to rise to the top ranks in the Air Force in general and the space field in particular." Alluding to the practice of placing non-space officers in career-enhancing positions, he added, "I wonder how often a Naval aviator has been put in command of a submarine."[47]

Space Support for Operation Iraqi Freedom (OIF)

The planning for potential combat operations in Afghanistan and Iraq had begun almost simultaneously. When OIF finally kicked off in March 2003, satellites played a critical role in support of U.S./allied activities. The AFSPC noted, "GPS satellites provided navigational information that not only guided aircraft to the battle, but also directed precision guided munitions to their targets." Unlike a decade earlier against Iraq, in 2003 the GPS-guided weaponry—including joint direct attack munitions (JDAMs) carried by U.S. aircraft—did not require good weather and clear visibility as prerequisite for guidance to the target. Michael O'Hanlon observed that GPS enabled U.S. forces to drop "more than 6,000 satellite-guided

JDAMs" against Iraq. Moreover, just prior to the opening of hostilities in Iraq, USAF space operators "sweetened" the GPS signal to improve its accuracy.[48]

For perhaps the first time in combat, U.S. operators dealt with an adversary's attempt to jam friendly GPS signals. The Iraqis employed at least six jammers to try and throw off course U.S./coalition GPS-guided munitions. Thankfully, enemy efforts failed in that regard, and in March 2004 Air Force B-1 Lancers destroyed the Iraqi jammers, "ironically using GPS-guided munitions," as the AFSPC historian wryly observed.[49]

There were other space assets that made a difference in the Iraqi desert in 2003. The Defense Support Program (DSP) constellation of early warning satellites alerted operators to 70 percent of attacks by Iraqi heat-producing systems, allowing friendly ground forces to respond in a timely manner. Space imaging satellites provided the U.S./coalition forces with "high resolution, 3-D images of the battlefield" that were unaffected by cloud cover. The imaging satellites also allowed target areas to be assessed without granting visible indicators to the enemy. Communications satellites provided secure channels for time-critical targeting by Air Force bombers and facilitated last-minute target shifts. In some cases, the secure communications satellites enabled UAVs on reconnaissance missions to relay real-time information to commanders, improving upon imaging satellite capabilities.[50]

Just as important as satellite capabilities, however, was bandwidth. Space systems offered vastly increased bandwidth to U.S. forces than what had been available in 1991. For the first time, a four-star combatant commander designated the air component commander as directly responsible for space operations, clear acknowledgment of space's importance to the air campaign. Many observers of the Persian Gulf conflict had considered it "the first 'Space War,'" but Brig. Gen. Larry D. James—who in 2003 commanded the 50th Space Wing—concluded that "OIF was the first time we saw the true power of space capabilities to shape the battlefield, execute combat ops, provide precision and agility, and ensure success." In a similar vein, Gen. Donald J. Kutyna, who led the U.S. Space Command in 1991, called the Persian Gulf fight the "first space applications war." Space was not vital to the victory, but it might be in the future, he said.[51]

The George W. Bush Administration's National Space Policy, 2006

During most of the Bush administration, it was the previous president—Bill Clinton—whose national space policy remained in effect. Clinton's policy dated from 1996. Space did not rank high on the agenda for either Clinton or Bush. Only in the late summer of 2006, well into Bush's second term, did he issue his own space policy. The presidential lethargy was despite the nation's rapidly-increasing dependence on space, vigorously affirmed by the 2001 commission. Moreover, heavy U.S. dependence on space served as the benchmark for the commission's foremost recommendation: "*The President should consider establishing space as a national security priority*" [emphasis in original]. The commission continued, "Only the President has the authority, first, to set forth the national space policy, and then to provide the guidance and direction to senior officials, that together are needed to ensure that the United States remains the world's leading space-faring nation."[52]

The president signed the new space policy on August 31, 2006, but it was not released until early October, "on a Friday afternoon during a sleepy news cycle before the three-day Columbus Day weekend." The delayed release may have been intended to maintain the administration's low profile regarding matters of space policy.[53]

Regardless of the reason, the policy reflected a more-or-less U.S. unilateralist approach to space, certainly more so than the Clinton policy. Bush's policy stated the United States "will . . . preserve its rights, capabilities, and freedom of action in space," adding elsewhere that freedom of action in space "is as important to the United States as air power and sea power." In a third reference, the president directed the secretary of defense to ensure freedom of action in space and, "if directed, deny such freedom of action to adversaries." One space writer entitled his article, "New Bush Space Policy Unveiled, Stresses U.S. Freedom of Action." A specific guideline on orbital debris that the president directed was soon to be challenged: "The United States shall take a leadership role in international fora to encourage foreign nations . . . to adopt policies and practices aimed at debris minimization."[54]

Some space scholars remarked on the differences both in tone and substance between the 1996 and 2006 space policies. Concerned with U.S. unilateralism and what she termed "chest-thumping rhetoric about American space prowess," space scholar Joan Johnson-Freese wrote, "Whereas the 1996 NSP stated that the United States 'rejects any limitations on the fundamental right of sovereign nations to acquire data from space,' the 2006 document states that it 'rejects any limitations of the fundamental right of the *United States* to operate in and acquire data from space.' Whereas in the past the right to acquire data from space extended to all nations, now it appears only to be granted to the United States, with the right to operate in space additionally granted *to the United States*."[55]

Also, whereas Clinton's policy addressed civil space guidelines prior to those of national security space, the Bush document reversed the order and so emphasized NSS. In both policies, commercial space guidelines came last.[56]

In discussing Bush's more assertive space policy, Spires observed that while the language in 2006 "might very well lay the groundwork for the development of space weapons systems, policy and funding indications suggest that the focus of DoD and the Air Force continued to be directed to the Space Control rather than the Force Application mission." He went on to note that in the aftermath of the Chinese ASAT test, both AFSPC and Air Force leadership "responded by stressing the need for enhanced space situational awareness and the variety of non-military measures available to national decision-makers to address threats to U.S. space assets."[57]

The Chinese Anti-Satellite Test, 2007

Only months after President Bush's national space policy was released, a dramatic incident shook many space advocates worldwide, even if U.S. space professionals and other officials were not surprised by the launch itself. In early January 2007, China became the third nation to conduct a successful ASAT test when a ground-based ASAT missile achieved a direct hit, exploding a defunct Chinese weather satellite in low-Earth orbit (LEO). The Chinese intent in doing so remained a mystery, at least to American officials. The new secretary of defense, Robert M. Gates, got nowhere when he attempted to engage his counterpart on the matter during his first official visit to Beijing. In his memoir, Gates wrote that the PRC's civilian leadership may have been surprised by the test, as seemed also to have been the case in the 2011 Chinese rollout of its J-20 stealth fighter.[58] In a CSAF white paper at the end of the year, Gen. T. Michael Moseley warned, "China demonstrated the ability to hold satellites at risk and the willingness to contest the space domain." In a similar vein, Lt. Col. Anthony J. Mastalir observed that the successful test had "completely changed the functional paradigm" for space: instead of space as an uncontested environment, now it was contested.[59]

While Mastalir saw the new paradigm as an argument for an integrated, coalition-based approach to a contested environment, for others the greater consequence seemed to be the test's creation of more space debris than from any single human-initiated event in space history, and with increased risk to satellites near that altitude. No less than seven nations issued formal protests or inquiries, seeing the test as irresponsible or at least inconsistent with China's declared space-for-peaceful-purposes policy. Aside from the apparent realization that the Chinese were pursuing weapons in space, a RAND study concluded the explosion had created a debris cloud that added "2,606 trackable objects to the U.S. space catalog as of June 2010." Some estimates included an additional 35,000 or more individual particles of space debris of at least one centimeter in size.[60]

As Hollywood depicted in the popular movie *Gravity*, space debris is one of the greatest threats to the conduct of safe operations in space because very small pieces—even paint chips—may disable or destroy a spacecraft when the contact occurs at roughly 17,000 mph. Years earlier, the European Space Agency warned, "With closing speeds of thousands of [kilometers] per hour, a 1.2 [centimeter] piece of debris could destroy a satellite, while a piece 10 [centimeters] in diameter could destroy the Space Shuttle. The Shuttle orbiter Discovery had to make six evasive manoeuvres in the past year to avoid colliding with larger pieces of debris, most of which are spent rocket stages."[61]

Debris in orbit required decades, or much longer in some cases, to disintegrate or de-orbit so as to no longer pose a threat. Prior to the Chinese test, the U.S. domination of space had been assumed, especially given the breakup of the Soviet Union and the accompanying severe economic and other dislocations that affected the Russian space program in the 1990s.[62]

When news outlets announced the successful Chinese test, Beijing delayed for twelve days before providing an official statement, prompting

48   CHAPTER 2

some to surmise that following at least two failed attempts, perhaps their success had surprised certain Chinese officials.[63] In any case, not three weeks later Sen. Jon Kyl (R-Ariz.) delivered an address in the U.S. Senate in which he laid out his views of the threat to American national security posed by China. Affirming that "satellites underpin our military superiority," Kyl warned fellow senators that "the threat to our space security is real and growing." Not all of his colleagues agreed, however, and Kyl singled out Sen. Joseph Biden (D-Del.) for his questionable statement, "I don't think we should be overly worried about this at this point. We have ways to deal with that ability." As a long-serving member of the Senate Intelligence Committee, Kyl was certain that was not the case.[64]

The Arizona senator argued against an arms control approach to space, noting, "Space has long been militarized" and that attempts to replace the genie in the bottle through treaties have a dismal record. Kyl was unconvinced of the value of what he referred to as "illusory arms control agreements," and he viewed the recent Bush space policy as a step in the right direction. His reading of Bush's policy was one that allowed for developing offensive and defensive ASAT capabilities, "as well as robust missile defenses."[65]

But while Kyl considered the ASAT test a wake-up call, he cited numerous examples of the U.S. government's ambivalence, even confusion, regarding NSS both prior to, and after, the Chinese test. Senator Kyl offered ideas of his own, but his first priority was to complete the implementation of the 2001 Space Commission's recommendations. Among those that remained undone, Kyl wanted the president to designate space "a top national security priority" and to establish a presidential space advisory group and a senior interagency group for space. His second priority was to push Congress to hold hearings aimed at ensuring the Chinese ASAT program was not using shared or stolen U.S. technology—a serious, long-running concern that was destined to continue.[66]

By about the time of the ASAT incident, the People's Liberation Army Air Force (PLAAF) had begun to upgrade its technology and doctrine to include a high priority on space. In late 2009, official news outlets in China published an interview with the PLAAF commander, Gen. Xu Qiliang, that a leading U.S. defense study suggested was "an official Chinese statement endorsing the development of space weapons." Qiliang spoke of "the inevitability of military competition in air and space," and he viewed space as a "new commanding height for international strategic competition." American space strategists were quite familiar with the latter concept, which China space specialist Kevin Pollpeter viewed as a lesson the Chinese had learned from the U.S. experience in information-based, net-centric warfare between 1991 and 2003.[67]

Meanwhile, the Chinese continued to improve their successfully tested direct ascent ASAT vehicle from 2007, which was not at odds with their stated policy of opposition to the "deployment of weapons in outer space . . . so as to ensure that outer space is used purely for peaceful purposes." Pollpeter noted, "Chinese statements do not oppose the development of terrestrially-based ASAT weapons"—such as the direct ascent version. He continued, "the Chinese appear to perceive their country as more peace-loving than others," and perhaps historically with good reason. But do not most nations share that inclination? In the twentieth century, British military historian J. F. C. Fuller wrote of the practice known as "verbal inversion":

> When the accepted meaning of a word or an idea is turned upside down, not only are Communist intentions obscured, but the mind of the non-Communist is misled, and mental confusion leads to a semantic nightmare in which things appear to be firmly planted on their feet, but actually are standing on their heads.
>
> Disarmament to one means one thing, to the other another thing; so also does peace. While to the non-Communist peace is a state of international harmony, to the Communist it is a state of international discord. . . . Communists hold that peace and war are reciprocal terms for a conflict which can only end when the Marxian Beatitude is established; since their final aim is pacific, they are peace lovers.[68]

The Allard Commission, 2008

Jon Kyl was not the only leader in Washington concerned with China's increasing capabilities in space as well as the U.S. government's incomplete implementation of the 2001 commission's recommendations. His and

50 CHAPTER 2

other voices were heard, and in 2008 the congressionally directed Independent Assessment Panel (IAP) on the Organization and Management of National Security Space reported on the increased threats to America's space dominance, despite some NSS progress since 2001. The panel considered the current NSS inadequacies to be "unacceptable today and ... likely to grow, but leadership can reverse this trend." The phrase "Organization and Management of National Security Space" clearly linked the 2008 assessment to Rumsfeld's earlier commission.[69]

The independent panel—commonly associated with its chairman, Sen. Wayne Allard of Colorado—assessed that since 2001 U.S. dependence on NSS assets had increased, yet they hardly were "more secure," especially given China's rapid emergence as a space power. Allard's commission foresaw "a family of challenges" that required firm, prompt leadership for the country to keep its technological lead in the interest of national security. A major concern was that although current on-orbit assets continued to provide critical space-based capabilities, many of them were beyond their design lifespan, while the next generation of satellites had experienced various unacceptable problems including increased costs, delays, or cancellation.[70]

The Allard panel pointed to the failure to implement many of the recommendations from 2001 as well as those from a 2003 study on space acquisition. Senator Allard viewed the establishment and execution of a national space strategy and reestablishing the National Space Council as top presidential priorities.[71] That President Bush had focused his attention overseas on the wars in Iraq and Afghanistan as well as ensuring that no repeat of the 9/11 attacks took place at home was at once acknowledged and justified. But some argued, then and later, that those concerns seemed to be more an excuse for failing to act on NSS matters than a legitimate explanation for not having done so.[72]

"No one's in charge," the panel warned as it addressed the need for a clear and coordinated effort to handle NSS strategy, budgets, requirements, and acquisition. The point had been made in 1959, when *Air Force* magazine observed, "In our research on the space effort organization ... the usual sort of chart was not honestly possible." That was because "so far as we were able to determine, lines of authority are extremely difficult to locate or, even more typically, are notably absent." Moreover, the 2008 panel concluded the "limited technical talent pool" was insufficient, echoing Sen. Bob Smith's admonition a decade earlier, as well as Lt. Col. David Lupton's in the 1980s. Years later, Rep. Mike Rogers (R-Ala.) voiced the same concerns.[73]

The Schriever wargame series sought to upgrade the technical as well as the strategic talent pool. Held at Peterson AFB, Colorado—home to the AFSPC—the biennial exercise was one of the Air Force's most timely initiatives aligned with the 2001 recommendations. First held in January 2001, the 2006–7 Schriever IV wargame was led by a team from AFSPC's Space Innovation and Development Center. The capstone event took place at Nellis AFB, Nevada, in March 2007, with some four hundred participants who represented the AFSPC, U.S. Army Space and Missile Defense Command, U.S. Northern Command, U.S. Strategic Command, U.S. Joint Forces Command, and U.S. Special Operations Command. Other government agencies were represented as well, as were participants from the United Kingdom, Canada, and Australia. The global scenario was set in the year 2025 and was conducted in a classified environment. From the Army perspective, the Schriever wargame "was valuable for identifying and assessing Space operations' command-and-control seams" and pointing out the challenges for joint, coalition, industry, intelligence and interagency interoperability. The Schriever exercises seemed a bright spot in contrast with at least one Headquarters USAF assessment that in 2006 expressed its concerns over the command's "lack of training and training exercises" as well as "the length of time required for approval of the ones they had."[74]

Conclusion

The 2001 Space Commission's report, coming at the outset of the two-term George W. Bush administration—and whose defense secretary for six years, Donald Rumsfeld, had chaired the commission—encouraged the NSS community to anticipate a significant upgrading of space as a top national security priority. For various reasons, including but not limited to the 11 September attacks and the subsequent Long War, as Rumsfeld termed it, the highly anticipated upgrading did not happen. Although the Pentagon implemented certain recommendations and CSAF General Jumper (2001–5) facilitated the Air Force's formal recognition of "air and space" as opposed to "aerospace," the development of a professional space cadre and space culture lagged far behind what some wanted, including the two senators, Bob Smith (1998) and Wayne Allard (2008). Meanwhile, the late-in-coming Bush national space policy (2006) advanced a more unilateralist approach to space that met either agreement or disapprobation depending on one's niche within the space community and one's assessment of the threats. In any case, the Chinese ASAT test (2007) appeared to strengthen the unilateralist camp, but the consequences remained to be seen. By the start of 2009, a new administration was poised to take control in Washington and to adjust U.S. national security space to its own perspective and agenda.

3

U.S. NATIONAL SECURITY SPACE

THE OBAMA YEARS, 2009–2016

On 15 April 2010, President Barack Obama addressed a gathering of mostly NASA types that included former astronaut Edwin E. "Buzz" Aldrin Jr. of Gemini 12 and Apollo 11 fame. In July 1969 Aldrin had become the second man to walk on the moon, following Neil Armstrong. Four decades later, President Obama enjoyed the support of one of America's early space heroes as he gave the only speech of his presidency devoted to space.

With the space shuttle program scheduled for retirement in 2010, the previous administration of George W. Bush had pinned the country's hopes for returning American astronauts to the moon by 2020 on the Constellation program contracted with Lockheed and Boeing. But that program encountered skyrocketing costs and a slipping schedule, perhaps due in part to what some perceived as a reluctance to embrace new space technologies and inordinate risk aversion on the part of NASA. Any suspicions of risk aversion, however, had to be balanced by the grievous loss of life on two space shuttle missions: in 1986, seven astronauts died on *Challenger*; and, in 2003, the same number perished on board *Columbia*.[1]

54 CHAPTER 3

Even before his inauguration in January 2009, Obama had requested a review of the Constellation program. Led by his NASA transition team lead, Lori Garver, Constellation's problems were apparent. The most serious short-term consequence was the impending loss of the capability to launch manned space flights from American soil. After having won the race to the moon decades ago, it seemed incredible that the U.S. space program had fallen so low as to soon be dependent on the Russians for rides to space. Toward the end of 2009, an assessment by two Obama White House officials judged the program as being not only hugely over budget and two years behind schedule; worse than that, it was "unexecutable."[2]

That jarring, one-word assessment gave the president the leeway he needed to shift an innovative alternative into high gear. Relying on what author Christian Davenport in his book *The Space Barons* called "big, legacy contractors" that brought jobs to congressional districts, but not always the intended results, had become an old way of doing space. Others, like Obama's secretary of the Air Force, Deborah Lee James, observed that the hundreds of pages of technical specifications that the Air Force acquisitions process levied on prospective smaller contractors meant that "even startups with effective, inexpensive approaches to problems have a hard time entering the defense sector," and she sought ways to make the space sector more accessible to "nontraditional firms." For his part, Obama was willing to embrace the new approach that relied more on nontraditional space companies—including some dismissed as start-ups only a few years earlier—like Elon Musk's SpaceX and Jeff Bezos' Blue Origin. In early 2010 the president's cancellation of the Constellation program was a foretaste of the new paradigm.[3]

The cancellation precipitated a political battle in Washington, one that involved not only members of Congress whose districts were affected by the loss of contractor jobs. Some former NASA officials and astronauts were outspoken, including Neil Armstrong, "who wrote a scathing letter to Obama decrying the decision to cancel Constellation along with the shuttle program." With that background, on a balmy 15th of April 2010, as the president spoke at the John F. Kennedy Space Center in Florida, the prominently seated Buzz Aldrin helped to counter the criticisms of several other astronauts regarding the Constellation decision.[4]

President Obama's Speech at the Kennedy Space Center, 15 April 2010

Acknowledging to the crowd in his opening remarks that afternoon, "I actually really like Tang. I thought that was very cool," the president spoke of what he viewed as the next chapter in America's space story. Despite space occupying a low to middling priority in the Obama administration, the president tried to calm the anxieties of some, if not many, in the audience by committing himself "100 percent . . . to the mission of NASA and its future." He announced an increase in NASA's budget by $6 billion over the next five years, intended to facilitate increased "robotic exploration of the solar system, including a probe of the Sun's atmosphere, new scouting missions to Mars . . . and an advanced telescope to follow Hubble, allowing us to peer deeper into the universe than ever before."[5]

Obama announced the extension of the International Space Station (ISS) probably by at least five years. He intended to use the ISS for its original intended purpose, that of advanced research to improve life on Earth, as well as for testing and improving capabilities in space. Several months after the president spoke about the ability of space-related research to "help improve the daily lives of people here on Earth," a copper mine crisis in Chile provided NASA the opportunity to apply its experience to assist the Chilean government to sustain and, finally, after two months, to rescue thirty-three trapped miners. Initially, NASA provided "recommendations on medical care, nutrition, and psychological support," developed from its work with astronauts who—like the miners—operated in an extremely harsh environment, remained isolated for a long period of time (as at the ISS), and whose chances of a safe return home were far from certain. Later, NASA also provided recommendations for the design of a Chilean rescue capsule used to extract the miners. The American assistance was perhaps the more poignant as it contrasted with the loss of twenty-nine coal miners in Beckley, West Virginia, in early April, the worst mining accident in the United States in forty years. At least in the Chilean accident, exactly four months after the one in West Virginia, and as the president had alluded to in his speech—Tang, in addition to its orange, tasty flavor—was far from the only benefit that space brought to life on Earth.[6]

The president then moved to one of the far-reaching statements of his speech, although its significance may have been underappreciated at

56 CHAPTER 3

the time. In terms of improving space capabilities, Obama said, "This includes technologies like more efficient life support systems that will help reduce the cost of future missions. And in order to reach the space station, we will work with a growing array of private companies competing to make getting to space easier and more affordable." He spoke of those entities known as the "NewSpace actors," led by SpaceX and Blue Origin—both companies had been in existence for less than a decade. Those were companies described as "thinly self-funded or funded by venture capitalists," not dependent on the government for their survival although desiring some government business. Only two years before, SpaceX had not yet achieved orbit with one of its Falcon rockets, finally doing so in September 2008.[7]

Anticipating the objections of some in the audience, Obama argued that "NASA has always relied on private industry" for helping design and build the spacecraft to carry American astronauts, since John Glenn's first orbital flight nearly fifty years ago. By purchasing "the service of space transportation—rather than the vehicles themselves," the president argued, "we can continue to ensure rigorous safety standards ... [but] also accelerate the pace of innovation as companies—from young start-ups to established leaders—compete to design, build, and launch new means of carrying people and materials" to space. Indeed, the entrance into the space market of new companies that were doing those very things produced a stunning transfer of space industry leadership from the Lockheeds and Boeings of earlier decades to the catchy-sounding names of millennial enterprises: SpaceX, Blue Origin, Sir Richard Branson's Virgin Galactic, and others.[8]

A decade later, in March 2021, in another example of the risk-takers' rise to prominence, a SpaceX Falcon 9 rocket launched 60 Starlink internet satellites into orbit—bringing its total to some 1,300 to date in a growing constellation to provide global coverage—then, nine minutes later, successfully landed the reusable first stage booster, nailing the landing at sea on the company's drone ship. A Space.com writer termed the 2021 launch "the first rocket that the U.S. military allowed SpaceX to recover, a switch from its previous military launches in which the company discarded the booster after payload delivery. NASA recently followed suit, permitting SpaceX to reuse its rockets on crew missions." Previously, SpaceX had been landing first stage boosters—for the purpose of reusing them—only on commercial launches.[9]

New Ways of Doing Space, and New Companies

The president's overall message was one of shifting gears from an older way of conducting the business of space—epitomized by the Constellation program—and relying instead upon cutting-edge strategies and technologies developed largely by newer entrepreneurs. Those were the private companies competing to achieve easier and cheaper space transportation, especially young, innovative companies. The CEO of one of those entrepreneurial outfits, Elon Musk, in June 2016 visited with Secretary of Defense Ashton B. Carter at the Pentagon to discuss the topic of innovation. Some space experts considered the older way as tantamount to an "incestuous link between the Pentagon, Congress, and defense companies," sold to American voters because it met their number one issue: jobs. Former speaker Gingrich added, "You have huge bureaucracies, which with their combined friendships in the private sector, have such enormous investments in the past." Such challenges did not disappear, but within a few years it became clearer that the business of national security space (NSS)—not only civil or commercial space—was going to depend heavily upon the space companies of the new millennium.[10]

In view of his overall message, it was unfortunate that the most memorable part of Obama's speech was his comment about returning to the moon: "But I just have to say pretty bluntly here, we've been there before. Buzz has been there." Instead, Obama sought the strategies and technologies needed to promote the long-term space flight sustainability that allowed for exploring beyond the moon into deep space, including Mars. He envisioned astronauts orbiting Mars by the mid-2030s and returning safely to Earth. At an undetermined time after that, "a landing on Mars will follow," the president predicted. "And I expect to be around to see it."[11]

Although Mars stirred greater excitement for many than did the moon by 2010, one Space Policy Institute scholar—who served as the National Space Council's executive secretary between 2017 and 2020—wrote of the unintended consequences of the Obama administration's shift, or in his view, drift. In 2014, Dr. Scott Pace viewed Obama's decision through the eyes of U.S. allies who were potential partners in missions to the moon. "The international space community . . . which had been shifting attention to the Moon as the completion of the [ISS] drew near, felt blindsided." Pace pointed out that the moon was "the next target for all of our potential international partners," some of whom might be drawn to join a People's Republic of China (PRC)- or Russian Federation-led moon mission rather than remain associated with American-led Mars projects to which most of them lacked the capability to contribute.[12]

Regardless of how many viewers were to recall the president's twenty-six-minute address at the Kennedy Space Center, millions watched and remembered the photo-op that followed his talk. The White House wanted something that depicted Obama's new leadership in space and the staff had hoped for a photograph of him at the launch site of a joint Lockheed Martin and Boeing rocket. But the classified payload to be carried on the rocket meant that taking photos and drawing attention to the mission was undesirable. The president's staff turned to SpaceX's Falcon 9 rocket sitting nearby on pad 40. The Falcon 9 had not yet flown. As Elon Musk said later, by "a sheer accident" he was given the photo-op of a lifetime, as he and several SpaceX employees met the president at their launch site and showed him around. As Christian Davenport wrote, the photos taken that day "did everything SpaceX had hoped. . . . The images of the young president walking alongside the young entrepreneur was the greatest endorsement SpaceX could have ever received."[13]

A Momentary Faux Pas?

While Obama's Kennedy Space Center speech constituted the high point of his presidency's attention to space, a remark made by his NASA chief perhaps became the best known, and the most regrettable, space soundbite to come from his administration. In 2009, President Obama had named retired U.S. Marine Corps major general Charles F. Bolden—a fourteen-year astronaut who had experienced four space shuttle missions during his career—to lead NASA. According to Bolden, when he became the NASA administrator, the president told him to work on three things: "One, he wanted me to help re-inspire children to want to get into science and math; he wanted me to expand our international relationships; and third, and perhaps foremost, he wanted me to find a way to reach out to the Muslim world and engage much more with dominantly Muslim nations to help them feel good about their historic contribution to science, math, and engineering."[14]

Conservative political columnist Charles Krauthammer was one of several who complained about that approach, saying, "This idea of 'to feel good about your past scientific achievements' is the worst kind of group therapy, psycho-babble, imperial condescension and adolescent diplomacy. If I didn't know that Obama had told him this, I'd demand the firing of Charles Bolden." Perhaps even more to the point, noted historian Victor Davis Hanson later wrote, "'Feel good' does not ensure that rockets reach outer space." Whatever the reason for the president's counsel to Bolden, it seemed a momentary faux pas that belied an otherwise generally productive administration space policy. In any case, both the White House and NASA later offered a correction, stating Bolden had misspoken.[15]

Cyberspace Realignment and Cyber Culture

In December 2007 the previous Air Force chief of staff, Gen. T. Michael Moseley, had stated in a CSAF white paper, "No future war will be won without air, space and cyberspace superiority." A year and a half later, early in the Obama administration, the president designated cybersecurity "as a national security priority." Moreover, Obama announced his plan for a cybersecurity coordinator within the White House and released a seventy-plus page cyberspace action plan. In August 2009, the Air Force moved the cyber mission to the Air Force Space Command (AFSPC), which assigned cyber to the newly activated Twenty-Fourth Air Force at Lackland AFB, Texas. Cyber, however, was young and immature as a warfighting domain. Furthermore, the AFSPC's assumption of the mission increased significantly the number of installations worldwide—there were more than seventy where the command held responsibilities for its personnel.[16]

Seven years later, during congressional budget testimony regarding NSS for fiscal year 2017, Gen. John E. Hyten, the AFSPC commander, addressed the Cyber Mission Force, which included thirty-nine teams he was then beginning to form. "The Cyber Mission Force is a key element," Hyten stated. "It consists of national mission teams to protect the Nation, combat mission teams to support the combatant commanders, and cyber protection teams to defend our own capabilities." The GPS constellation's integrity was probably the most obvious example of the nation's requirement for cyber protection. Although behind schedule, as he acknowledged, the AFSPC commander was doing all he could to get personnel trained and out to the field. Cyberspace remained under AFSPC until 2018 when it transferred to the Air Combat Command.[17]

In early 2009 Gen. Kevin P. Chilton had been midway through his final military assignment as commander of the U.S. Strategic Command, headquartered at Offutt AFB, Nebraska. A former Air Force test pilot and for eleven years an astronaut, Chilton commanded the space shuttle orbiter *Atlantis* on STS-76—NASA's 76th shuttle mission—in 1996, his third and last space flight. The U.S. Strategic Command (USSTRATCOM) was responsible for the plans and operations of all U.S. forces that conducted strategic deterrence and all space and cyberspace operations controlled by the DoD. Various leaders and thinkers concerned with the space domain had emphasized the importance of nurturing a space culture that was distinct from the culture of air power, and cyberspace (or cyber) was closely aligned with space. Drawing upon some of the stories passed down involving aviators during the early days of World War I, General Chilton argued that cyberspace operations had reached the point of requiring cultural change: "Like the World War I aviators, we need a change in our *culture, conduct,* and *capabilities* if we are going to advance the state of the art and provide the protection and freedom of action we need in this domain" [emphasis in original].[18]

Chilton sought to develop a culture that respected "the importance of cyberspace and integrates it into our operational activities at all levels." No longer could the U.S. military continue to treat cyber capabilities—beginning with the computer on each member's desk but extending far beyond, encompassing command and control, intelligence, and more—as a mere convenience. He wrote, "We have not necessarily thought of computers as part of the war-fighting domain. Think about it! . . . This is the foundation of the cultural shift that we must make. We must now think about this domain, its tools, and its readiness as commanders should—as essential to successful military operations. . . . Our 'flights' through cyberspace are not simply a convenience anymore."[19]

The four-star general emphasized, "Changing this culture is absolutely essential, and it is going to take time, focus, and, above all, leadership." While Chilton's purpose in writing about the need for cyberspace culture was not necessarily intended as an argument for a space corps or an independent space force, his point on culture aligned well with the space separatists as well as the 2001 Space Commission.[20]

The concerns for cyberspace expressed by two four-stars, first Chilton and several years later, Hyten, were highlighted by a funding comparison related to cyber systems. In his prepared remarks to Rep. Mike Rogers' subcommittee in March 2016, General Hyten noted that while U.S. commercial entities devoted roughly $46 billion to cybersecurity annually, the DoD managed a paltry $3 billion. Despite the disparity, commercial space entities enjoyed a larger combined budget than did the DoD for space, so the difference probably was not too unreasonable.[21]

Especially since 2001, the U.S. military's reserve component had transitioned generally from a strategic to an operational reserve. In 2016 General Hyten viewed cyber requirements as ideal for reserve service: "The Guard is a perfect partner in cyber, more than maybe any other mission, because it can be done from anywhere, it requires unique training, it doesn't require 24/7, because you can come in and come out [of duty status]. It is a perfect total force mission, and we are looking at new ways to leverage the Guard and the Reserve to do that."[22]

When the U.S. Space Force was established several years later, Colorado—which hosted myriad military and commercial space entities—was one of the most obvious states to pursue a Space National Guard presence. In 1997 the 137th Space Warning Squadron of the Colorado Air National Guard (COANG) had become the first Air National Guard (ANG) unit to support the AFSPC. The state maintained space units that, in the event the Congress authorized a Space National Guard, were expected to transfer into the new component. Colorado was especially well positioned for establishing any potential units: in 2020, Lt. Gen. Michael A. Loh

62 CHAPTER 3

(COANG) became the ANG's director, while Army Maj. Gen. Gregory White of the Colorado National Guard served as the Guard's first director of space operations.[23]

AFSPC Still Maturing as a Major Command

While General Hyten worked on cyber issues, he also dealt with a maturing command. A predecessor, Gen. C. Robert Kehler, who led AFSPC from late 2007 to early 2011, perceived the command had what he called a "lanes in the road" issue. The command "wasn't clear about what it was supposed to do." It was not their fault, General Kehler made clear, but the situation stemmed from the pre-2002 triple-hatted command arrangement that changed after the Rumsfeld Space Commission's report.[24] Kehler—who had commanded a missile squadron and operations group, two space wings, and served as the command's deputy director of operations—saw the issue as his top internal priority at AFSPC:

> Many [of those Air Force senior leaders] that I chatted with, especially around Washington [DC] . . . said Air Force Space Command is not effective in Washington, doesn't know how to be a [major command], and has adopted this sort of insulated view. In fact some describe it as the "Rodney Dangerfield" command: "We don't get no respect!" The assertion that most of these people had was, "You're not a Rodney Dangerfield command because of the reasons that people in your command think. It isn't that no one likes space. It isn't that you're the step children. It isn't that the Air Force doesn't want you or like you. It's mostly that the command has never grown the attachment points that it needs to be [effective]."[25]

With that rationale in mind, General Kehler and several other key AFSPC leaders spent a lot of time in Washington attempting to establish the relationships, or attachment points, that the command needed. At one point, CSAF Gen. T. Michael Moseley told Kehler, "You can't swing a dead cat around anywhere in the building back here without [hitting] somebody [who thinks] they're in charge of space." Moseley continued, "I want one thing out of you. If somebody has a question on space, I want the phone to ring in Colorado Springs." Kehler replied, "You got it."[26]

2010: The Obama National Space Policy

When President Obama issued his administration's space policy in June 2010, a number of differences stood out from the previous policy of George W. Bush. For starters, Bush did not issue an overarching policy until late 2006—well into the sixth year of his eight-year presidency.[27] The editor and publisher of *The Space Review*, Jeff Foust, viewed Bush's policy statement, coming as late as it did, as "more of a reflection of what the administration did, or had wanted to do, rather than what it would do going forward." In any case, space had not ranked high on George W. Bush's priority list, especially after 11 September 2001. Preventing another large-scale terrorist attack on the U.S. homeland was priority number one, and rightly so. Neither did Bush deal with space issues in his 2010 memoir, *Decision Points*. Interestingly, among recent administrations, only the space policy of his father—President George H. W. Bush (1989–93)—was issued earlier in his administration than was Obama's. The elder Bush's policy appeared in November 1989, only ten months after taking office.[28]

There were more significant differences than the timing, however, particularly the tone. Marcia Smith (the founder and editor of SpacePolicy Online.com) noted the changes, first, from the Clinton policy (1996) to the Bush policy (2006), and, second, from Bush to Obama (2010): "I think the biggest difference between the Bush policy and the Clinton policy was the tone of it, and I think the biggest difference between the Obama policy and the Bush policy is the tone, the tenor." Ben Baseley-Walker, a policy advisor for the Secure World Foundation, a Colorado-based space sustainability foundation, felt the Obama policy's choice of words in key sections "really show a much less bellicose tone than the Bush policy." While some, if not many, Americans might be somewhat tone-deaf on such matters or not overly concerned with tone or tenor in any case, much of the rest of the world picked up on such differences. Marcia Smith observed that "it's perception that is so important, especially when you're dealing with our allies and other potential partners around the world."[29]

64   CHAPTER 3

Indeed, more than any other, it was the theme of international cooperation that characterized the Obama space policy, which one NSC senior official viewed as "woven throughout the new policy." The introduction offered, "All nations have the right to use and explore space [standard wording that the Bush policy also employed], but with this right also comes responsibility. The United States, therefore, calls on all nations to work together to adopt approaches for responsible activity in space." On the next page, the policy's principles emphasized—in the opening phrase—the "spirit of cooperation," in which the United States was committed to assist "all nations to act responsibly in space," including the preventing of mishaps in space, developing the commercial space sector, exploring space, and using space for peaceful purposes.[30]

The previous Bush policy, however, had used far less language of cooperation among nations. In a nutshell, in key statements where the Bush policy mentioned the United States and asserted its rights, Obama's policy spoke of "all nations" and "a nation's rights." The 2006 Bush policy had stated, "The United States considers space systems to have the rights of passage through and operations in space without interference. Consistent with this principle, the United States will view purposeful interference with its space systems as an infringement on its rights."[31]

It was unclear, however, whether the first sentence was intended to convey that the space systems of all nations have "the rights of passage"—or only those of the United States. The Obama policy, however, clarified its intent when it stated, "The United States considers the space systems of all nations to have the rights of passage ... without interference." In the Bush policy's second sentence, "the United States" was to view deliberate interference with its space systems as "an infringement on its rights." Such rights did not necessarily extend to other nations, some argued. But the Obama policy stated, "Purposeful interference with space systems ... will be considered an infringement of a nation's rights." Clearly, the latter's policy conveyed a more cooperative, internationalist approach in space. One *Florida Journal of International Law* article compared the 2006 and 2010 policies within the context of the 1967 Outer Space Treaty concluded, "While NSP10 is not a complete reversal from NSP06, it is a very important step in the right direction." The Bush policy had "largely ignored the

U.S. NATIONAL SECURITY SPACE

fundamental importance of cooperation and trust embedded in the OST," wrote Todd Barnet, associate professor of legal studies at Pace University. "Recall that the OST was signed with the purpose of avoiding a Cold War–era mentality in space." In Barnet's view, NPS06 pushed U.S. space policy back toward the Cold War's mistrust.[32]

A leading space scholar, Joan Johnson-Freese, argued from the above section in the 2006 policy that the Bush administration had adopted "unilateral primacy" as its approach to space, or more bluntly, the intent to "dominate space." Further, the 2006 policy had devoted more attention to NSS than to civil space, commercial space, or international space, and the NSS guidelines preceded the others, indicating its top priority. In 2010, Obama's intent to push back from his predecessor's policy was seen in the reordering of the guidelines: "International Cooperation" preceded a 1.5-page commercial space section, which was followed by civil space—and last of all in the document—national security space.[33]

The *New York Times* and the *Space Review* observed that the first of Obama's space goals was to "energize competitive domestic industries," to include satellite manufacturing, satellite-based services, and space launch. From the *Space Review* editor's desk, some of that energizing came from the administration's definition of commercial space, which referred to "space goods, services, or activities provided by private sector enterprises that bear a reasonable portion of the investment risk and responsibility for the activity." Jeff Foust commented that the above reasonable-investment-risk clause allowed for the U.S. government to bear some portion of the financial risk with the space companies, thereby encouraging a degree of risk-taking in what were often expensive, cutting-edge ventures.[34]

While the Obama space policy amounted mostly to a reversal of Bush's, it was also, to some degree, a return to the 1996 Clinton policy. Foust wrote, "Instead of placing a US-first emphasis in some sections of the policy, as the Bush Administration's 2006 policy had done, the Obama Administration policy returns to language used in the Clinton-era and earlier policies." In 1996, the introduction to Clinton's policy read, "The United States considers the space systems of any nation to be national property with the right of passage through and operations in space without interference." The Obama policy restored the explicit inclusion of other

66 CHAPTER 3

nations' space systems in its statement that all nations enjoyed the rights of passage through and in space.[35]

The following sentence in both 1996 and 2010 policy statements revealed similar thinking as well. Clinton's policy stated, "Purposeful interference with space systems shall be viewed as an infringement on sovereign rights." Because the preceding sentence referred to any nation, it was clear the potential infringement pertained to any nation's space systems. Whether or not it was intentional, a correct reading of the 2006 Bush policy, however, granted the infringement of rights only to the United States in cases of purposeful interference. In 2010, Obama returned to the essence of the Clinton policy in the phrasing, "will be considered an infringement of a nation's rights." Under Obama, infringement of rights belonged not only to the United States.[36]

2013–2016: Adversaries' Counterspace Trends, and Other Space Developments

In contrast with the Bush space policy that emphasized U.S. dominance, Obama's first term was characterized by a modest reining in of the Bush approach to the protection of U.S. space assets as well as a willingness to explore bilateral and multilateral diplomacy regarding space. Much of that self-imposed restraint changed, however, in response to a development in May 2013 that the PRC insisted was a high-altitude scientific mission. American space experts, both within and outside the government, disagreed. They considered it an anti-satellite test, perhaps of China's new Dong Ning-2 missile. The U.S. Air Force determined the rocket's trajectory to be inconsistent with the Chinese explanation. Brian Weeden, a former Air Force missile officer and space analyst who became a technical adviser to the Secure World Foundation, surmised the launch had tested "the rocket component of a new direct ascent [anti-satellite, or ASAT] weapons system derived from a road-mobile ballistic missile." The matter reached the president's desk, precipitating focused attention by senior officials on the growing threats in space and, in the process, more or less the demise of Obama's first-term multilateralist approach to space.[37]

The period from 2014 to 2016 witnessed growing concern in Washington regarding space security not only with respect to the PRC, but the Russian Federation as well. The deputy assistant defense secretary for space policy, Stephen L. Kitay, recalled that the years 2013 and 2014 witnessed "a noticeable uptick" in the willingness of senior leaders in Washington to speak about the space threats, "as well as talking about resources . . . being driven towards space, to ensure that we're assuring [required] capabilities." At the start of 2014, Director of National Intelligence (DNI) James Clapper highlighted to the Senate Select Committee on Intelligence that Russia claimed openly to possess counter-space capabilities to include jamming and ASAT weapons. The Russians were working on an airborne laser as well. Two years later, a Lawrence Livermore National Laboratory (LLNL) report viewed Russia's renewed interest in ASAT weapons—coming after a long hiatus—to be "consistent with a strategy to strike at what it likely perceives as one of Washington's key vulnerabilities." Further, the LLNL report argued that both China and Russia "not only see space as a key military enabler, but [also] . . . as a Clausewitzian 'center of gravity' for space-enabled powers like the U.S." Space assets, then, were tempting targets at the outset of hostilities for wreaking havoc with the American command, control, communications, intelligence, surveillance, and reconnaissance (C3ISR) systems that enabled the U.S. military's long-range precision strike and missile defense capabilities. Developing ASAT weapons made perfect sense with such a strategy.[38]

It was perhaps surprising that even while U.S. analysts expressed increasing concern over Russia's intentions in space, the *Atlas V* medium-lift launch vehicle continued to depend on a Russian-made rocket engine, the RD-180. Air Force historian Robert D. Mulcahy wrote, "After the demise of the Soviet military industry, the low price of the RD-180 was a significant bargain." In 2014, Russia's illegal annexation of Crimea increased tensions between Moscow and Washington, and alongside economic sanctions levied against Russia, Washington determined to transition off the RD-180 and eliminate U.S. reliance on foreign rocket engines. Years earlier, the director of the Marshall Space Flight Center, J. Wayne Littles—near the end of his three-decade career with NASA—pointed out that U.S. competitors had "developed 25 new rocket engines to our one over the same period." Not much had changed since the late 1990s. Facing limited options, Congress allowed the Air Force to continue to use a small number of RD-180 rocket engines.[39]

During congressional budget testimony in early 2016, General Hyten spoke bluntly to the subcommittee chaired by Rep. Mike Rogers, stating, "Goodness knows we want off the Russian engine as fast as any human being on the planet." As historian Mulcahy explained, "You cannot just put a new rocket engine into the Atlas V and expect it to work. . . . A launch vehicle is built around its engine, not the other way around," the reason the *Atlas V* had to be replaced. Both Hyten and Rogers seemed cautiously optimistic about having the new engine within three to five years.[40]

In July 2014 another PRC test heightened U.S. concerns. Although the Chinese claimed they had tested a land-based missile interceptor—the same argument they had made in 2010, which, if true, constituted a defensive capability—the State Department announced that the United States had "high confidence" the test had been an ASAT weapon demonstration. Apparently mindful of the worldwide condemnation they had received in 2007 due to the unprecedented space debris threat to other nations' orbiting assets created by the explosion of their own defunct weather satellite, in 2014 China took care to conduct a nondestructive test in space.[41]

While no debris had been added to outer space by the most recent test, the mounting evidence of both Russian and Chinese counter-space capabilities under development soon contributed to strenuous efforts on the part of some U.S. military and congressional space leaders who believed the time had come for a U.S. space corps or space force. In 2001 the Rumsfeld Space Commission assessed, "The use of space in defense of U.S. interests may require the creation of a military department for space at some future date." While the commissioners felt the timetable was impossible to predict, they had gone on to say that such a decision "would be dictated by circumstances over the next five to ten years." It was now 2014. Time was up.[42]

Evidence that official Washington had been startled into activity appeared in the NDAA of 2015—enacted in December 2014—in which the Congress expressed its sense "that critical U.S. space systems face a growing foreign threat . . . both the [PRC] and the Russian Federation are developing capabilities to disrupt the use of space by the United States during a conflict." Congress called for a multifaceted approach "to deter and defeat any adversary's acts of aggression in outer space." This included a report to be completed by the secretary of defense in six months assessing the department's ability to deter and defeat such aggression. One Senate provision included in the NDAA directed the defense secretary to consult with the DNI "to update the space control and space superiority strategy" called for in the Space Posture Review from 2009. Another provision required the majority of the Space Security and Defense Program's funds to "be allocated to offensive space control and active defense strategies." It was congressional measures like those that helped set the stage—albeit unintentionally—for the movement toward a space corps/force two years later, led by two representatives: Mike Rogers of Alabama and Jim Cooper of Tennessee.[43]

In April 2015 at the annual space symposium in Colorado Springs, Air Force Secretary James stated, "We must prepare for the potentiality of conflict that might extend from Earth one day into space." Soon after that James acknowledged to the Senate Armed Services Committee that studies known as analysis of alternatives, with respect to next-generation satellite architectures, had taken "way longer than anticipated." The reason, as Douglas Loverro, the deputy assistant secretary of defense for space policy, explained, was that satellite "resiliency" had not been on the table to begin with. "It was not part of the lexicon." Due to the threat, now it was. Chirag Parikh, the NSC director of space policy, considered the change in thinking to be part of "a paradigm shift" within not only the Pentagon but in NSS circles as well.[44]

The Role of Air University, Maxwell AFB, Alabama

The intellectual center of the Air Force, the Air University (AU) was the home of the service's officer and senior noncommissioned officer professional military education programs in addition to several other research- and doctrine-oriented organizations. Even as a dawning occurred among more and more officials in Washington regarding developing and existing threats to U.S. assets in space, a tiny cadre of space-minded Air Force officers at AU were working with an eye toward an eventual space service. Especially between 2014 and 2017, under the leadership and career

70 CHAPTER 3

sheltering provided by the AU commander, Lt. Gen. Steven L. Kwast—protection for others, not for himself—at least four entrepreneurial and forward-thinking faculty members at the Air Command and Staff College collaborated and wrote on space—to include policy and draft legislation pieces. But unlike most U.S. government officials who came to recognize the dangers posed by China and Russia, the AU space advocates were "opportunity-driven," not "threat-driven." In a 2021 interview, one of the four, retired Lt. Col. Peter Garretson, described the view that "space is itself an independently important geographic theater of national power and that national power comes from the ability to access and control space resources."[45]

Another descriptor of that basic view was termed the "blue-water school," Garretson noted, bringing to mind a navy's role of protecting ocean-going trade on a 24/7 basis for the sake of national power. Another one of the four, whose deep thinking on space predated Garretson's, Dr. Michael V. Smith remarked that his preference was to see U.S. Naval Academy over other graduates coming into the Space Force because the Navy understood a 24/7 operations mindset and the need to protect a "carrying trade," which space is. The thing to be carried by our satellites is information, Smith said in 2020, of which the commercial value to the global economy continued to increase. Highlighting a basic distinction between air and space forces, he added, "Whereas the air forces are fielded forces, our space systems are organic essentials, national infrastructure. We are a global information grid that can't be managed, can't be penny-packeted into theater air support." And as many remarked, the United States was by far the nation most dependent on space, and so had the most to lose.[46]

2015–2016: Adversaries Reorganize Their Space Forces, and Russian ASAT Tests

At mid-decade, the United States was not alone in adjusting its thinking regarding military space—although its own restructuring of space was not to take place for several more years. In 2015 Russian defense minister Sergei Shoigu announced the creation of the "Aerospace Forces," a new military branch formed by the merging of air forces, antiair and antimissile defenses, and space forces, to function under a unified command structure. It was not the first time the country's military space forces had moved organizationally—for a decade and a half after 1982 the Soviet (later, Russian) "Military Space Forces" had comprised a separate branch of the armed forces. Between 2011 and 2015, its space forces—in addition to air defense forces—had been aligned under the Aerospace Defense Forces. That branch was "tasked with defending Russian airspace from airborne and space-borne attacks."[47]

One former Russian military officer and analyst at a Moscow-based think tank related the defense ministry's 2015 merger decision to what officials had observed during the 1999 U.S./NATO air campaign against Serbia. Maxim Shepovalenko said, "Based on what we saw, air and space attacks are the first stage of any conflict," regardless of the size, meaning that "the prime reason for the merger is to ensure a prompt response to any attack coming from the air or space with a streamlined and unified command." A quarter-century after the Soviet Union's dissolution, Russia was in the midst of a sweeping reorganization and modernization of its armed forces. While the Russian restructuring brought its forces into an alignment more closely resembling that of the U.S. Air Force, it differed in one key respect, Shepovalenko said. Russia's Aerospace Forces did not control the country's nuclear missiles. All of its nuclear missiles were controlled by a separate armed force, the Strategic Rocket Forces.[48]

Between May 2015 and December 2016, the Russian military's newly formed Aerospace Forces (a merger of the Russian Air Force and Aerospace Defense Forces) conducted three ASAT tests of its PL-19 Nudol missile. As the U.S. government had become accustomed to being told by Beijing regarding its surreptitious ASAT tests, Moscow claimed the Nudol was intended as a defensive weapon. American analysts reported the most recent test was the third successful flight "of a system Moscow has claimed is for use against enemy missiles." Analysts also noted that the "high rate of testing is an indication the program is a military priority and is progressing toward deployment."[49]

Other sources supported the threat assessment. A 2016 Defense Intelligence Agency report to Congress stated Russian leaders had openly asserted that their military possessed ASAT weapons and that ASAT research was ongoing. A former commander of Russia's space forces, Lt.

Gen. Oleg Ostapenko, claimed his country's S-500 antimissile system was capable of engaging satellites in low-Earth orbit. A Heritage Foundation defense analyst considered the 2016 test further proof that the space environment was "increasingly contested"—the United States no longer enjoyed guaranteed access to space as it had for decades. For some, if not many, U.S. space experts, the vulnerability of the nation's GPS satellites was a leading concern, if not a new one. If GPS was taken out, the effectiveness of many U.S. conventional forces—which depended on GPS-provided positioning and timing precision, such as joint direct attack munition weapons—must be seriously degraded, not to mention the myriad GPS-dependent civil and commercial enterprises.[50]

At the same time the Russians were reorganizing their space forces, the PRC did something similar. As part of a large-scale reorganization of the People's Liberation Army (PLA) initiated by China's President Xi Jinping, the Second Artillery Force, an independent branch that was treated as a service, was redesignated the PLA Rocket Force (PLARF). Formally elevated to service-level stature, the PLARF trained, equipped, and operated the PLA's land-based nuclear and conventional missiles. Xi Jinping has referred to the PLARF as the "core of strategic deterrence," and it has been upgrading from liquid-fueled, silo-based ballistic missiles to solid-fueled, road-mobile systems. The latter were more quickly fueled and more difficult to track and target. Clearly, the days were long gone when the "Chinese Reds" that comprised a delegation at the United Nations early in the Korean War "went on a shopping spree in a bookstore outside the Waldorf" and purchased "$88 worth of volumes on atomic energy," among other military-related subjects.[51]

At the close of 2015, the PLA established the Strategic Support Force (PLASSF). The PLASSF integrated the PLA's space, cyber, and electronic warfare capabilities. One U.S. Air Force AU study—produced by its China Aerospace Studies Institute—observed, "The creation of the PLASSF and the Space Systems Department in particular underscores the importance that China places on the space domain, and enables the PLA to carry out more effective military operations by leveraging space-based assets to disrupt or cripple the ability of adversary forces to use assets in space." A RAND study noted the PLASSF did "not appear to be a service" nor the equivalent to a "U.S.-styled unified command." The Strategic Support Force appeared to be composed of two departments—space systems and network systems—the former to handle satellite launch and operation, including "the co-orbital counterspace mission"; the latter responsible for cyber and electronic warfare. One senior fellow at the Center for a New American Security, Elsa B. Kania, wrote,

> [The PLASSF's] design and structure are meant to enable the integrated development of the battle networks that are critical to today's "informatized" warfare. In particular, the PLASSF is intended to enable the "information chain" that connects the initial intelligence, reconnaissance, and early warning capabilities with information transmission, processing, and distribution, and then, after an attack on an adversary, with the options for guidance, damage assessment, and follow-on strikes.[52]

The term "informatized" appeared in a Chinese defense white paper in 2015 that called for the PLA to become capable of "winning 'informatized' local war," thereby countering U.S. military intervention in a given region. The China Aerospace Studies Institute noted that some form of the term has been used to express the PLA's requirement to become "proficient in real-time collection, processing, and dissemination of battlefield information. The space domain plays a key role in informatization efforts because of the enormous quantity of data to be derived from and passed through C4ISR [command, control, communications, computers, intelligence, surveillance, and reconnaissance] space-based platforms."[53]

Although questions remained concerning the nature of, and intentions for, the new force, RAND concluded that the PLASSF's creation "suggests that information warfare, including space warfare, long identified by PLA analysts as a critical element of future military operations, appears to have entered a new phase of development in the PLA."[54]

The U.S. Commercial Space Launch Competitiveness Act of 2015

Five decades earlier, the OST declared, "The exploration and use of outer space, including the Moon and other celestial bodies, shall be carried out

74   CHAPTER 3

for the benefit and in the interests of all countries." Further, the treaty prohibited nations from claims of sovereignty in outer space by any means. But in the 1960s the commercialization of space was not yet in view, and the OST was unclear on matters surrounding extraction of space-based resources.[55]

By the Obama presidency, the potential for asteroid mining had become a legitimate, near-term issue, pursued by companies such as Planetary Resources, Deep Space Industries, and Shackleton Energy. Space scholar Namrata Goswami, writing in *Strategic Studies Quarterly*, stated, "Scientists infer that a small asteroid 200 meters in length and rich in platinum could be worth $30 billion." In July 2015, "Asteroid 2011 UW158, worth $5 trillion in platinum, sailed at a distance of 1.5 million miles from Earth." With such wild economic opportunities becoming available, in the 2015 legislation officially termed the U.S. Commercial Space Launch Competitiveness Act (Public Law 114-90), Congress provided the commercial space industry with added incentive to pursue the extraction of space-based resources by guaranteeing companies and investors of a relatively hands-off approach from Washington for the next eight years. An article in *Wired* envisioned the possibilities for "everything from asteroid-based gold mines to comet-collected rocket fuel." The co-founder of the space mining company Planetary Resources called the Spurring Private Aerospace Competitiveness and Entrepreneurship (SPACE) Act of 2015—the alternate title to PL 114-90—"the single greatest recognition of property rights in history."[56]

As welcome as the new SPACE Act was to space entrepreneurs, it was a double-edged sword. Taken in conjunction with the 1967 OST, the 2015 act also set the stage for conflict due to the ambiguities of "how space-based resources will be allocated." As Goswami queried insightfully in her 2018 article, "Will Chinese territorial assertion be replicated with regard to space resources? Once China reaches somewhere in space first—for instance, the far side of the moon or an asteroid—will it recreate a similar argument of owning a resource by being there first as it does with regard to the South China Sea and East China Sea?"[57]

Those were very good questions. In addition to its maritime claims, China's recent record of expanding its military presence in regions like

Africa, beginning with a base in Djibouti in 2016–17, argued for an affirmative response. In his Pulitzer-winning study, *The Heavens and the Earth: A Political History of the Space Age*, Walter A. McDougall suggested, "There is no reason to believe ... that [a future day's] space colonies would be free of greed, envy, politics, and war. Can the scientific knowledge or new perspectives gleaned from space exploration spawn a higher consciousness or wisdom and prepare a new, sublime culture?"[58]

2016: SpaceX and Air Force GPS III Contract

The degree to which the Merritt Island photo-op of President Obama with Elon Musk had motivated the innovative young company to even greater efforts was unknown, but in any case six years later, in 2016, SpaceX secured its first Air Force contract to fly NSS satellites into space. Considered a "huge victory" for the company, it came a year after SpaceX's monstrous Falcon 9 rocket had been certified as an NSS launch service provider.[59]

As if that was not enough, in December 2015, on a mission to fly eleven commercial communication satellites into orbit, Musk's company not only succeeded with the satellite mission, on the back end SpaceX managed to land the Falcon 9's first stage booster safely—the company's first-ever successful landing of a first stage rocket. It was only the second such landing, after Blue Origin did it one month earlier on a suborbital launch. Davenport described the scene at SpaceX's headquarters in California upon the announcement—in wording reminiscent of Apollo 11—"The Falcon 9 has landed." Davenport continued,

> It was pandemonium, with hundreds of employees hugging one another, and jumping up and down as if they had just won the Super Bowl. ... The throng of employees outside the glass-encased control room broke into spontaneous chants of "USA! USA!"
>
> It was perhaps an odd choice for a cheer—this was the feat of a single, private company, not a nation. But in the unbridled exuberance of the moment, it also felt right, as if what they had accomplished extended far beyond the company's headquarters.[60]

Differing Views on Great Power Adversaries and Threats

The years of the Obama presidency witnessed signs of increasing military capabilities in space on the part of China and Russia as well as their increasing aggressiveness. The degree to which the United States was responsible for the latter was open to debate. Regardless of where one fell on that argument, there were urgings at least within unofficial Pentagon circles for Washington to pursue more conciliatory relations with China. In January 2016 at an event hosted by the National Committee on U.S.-China Relations, four former U.S. defense secretaries—Harold Brown (1977–81), William Perry (1994–97), William Cohen (1997–2001), and Chuck Hagel (2013–15)—"agreed that the US needs to bolster the military exchanges of officers and information . . . to improve cultural understanding between the two nations," *Defense News* reported. The former Pentagon chiefs advocated for hosting PLA officers at DoD learning centers, among them West Point, and for inviting the Chinese to participate in more than just occasional military exercises in the Pacific region. The four also agreed that U.S. military leaders in the Pacific should have the lead in building closer relationships with the Chinese military.[61]

Those views were countered by others, including Elbridge Colby, a senior fellow at the Center for a New American Security, who argued, "The United States needs to prepare for war in space." The days are over when preparing to fight in space was viewed as provocative, Colby said. Russia and China "are gearing up to take any war with the United States into space." Acknowledging the anti-satellite capabilities of the United States' two great power competitors, in early 2016 Colby reported that in the last year a senior U.S. Air Force general had surmised, "We are quickly approaching the point where every satellite in every orbit can be threatened." Although the U.S. military relied on space assets for communications, precise positioning and navigation, intelligence collection, targeting, and more, Colby warned that its satellites offered "juicy targets" for adversaries because when they were built and placed into orbit, they were mostly beyond the reach of other countries. From the Chinese perspective, PLA strategists for years had considered U.S. space assets a "tempting and most irresistible choice"—which, in a less sobering context, might have been borrowed by a chef touting his daily special. Toward the end of

2016, a CNN production featuring General Hyten and other space leaders entitled, "War in Space: The Next Battlefield," ramped up the warnings of Colby and likeminded others concerning the threats U.S. space assets already faced.[62]

As evident from several of the recent ASAT tests, even the deterrent of producing massive debris from an explosion in space was no longer such a potential concern. Colby added, "Non-destructive, limitable and even reversible techniques" had become available, including blinding or dazzling with a laser, jamming, or cyberattacking.[63]

In April 2016 the commander of U.S. Northern Command and North American Aerospace Defense Command, Adm. William E. Gortney, testified before the House Armed Services Committee's Strategic Forces Subcommittee. Chairman Mike Rogers opened the hearing, which addressed "The Missile Defeat Posture" and U.S. strategy relative to the president's FY2017 budget request. Rogers seemed quite animated that afternoon, perhaps in part from the subject at hand, as well as the spring sunshine, with temperatures in the sixties. In opening remarks, the congressman noted that during 2015 there had been about three hundred foreign ballistic missile launches and seventy foreign space launches. Turning his attention to North Korea from which there had been "unprecedented [missile] activity" of late, he added, "If we have a policy to deal with the nut job in charge of that country, it can't be considered anything but a failure." The day prior, Rogers had spoken with Admiral Gortney. Now with the admiral before his subcommittee, Rogers added, "I'll just say you scared the Hell out of me in our conversation yesterday. The North Koreans now have, what, three different ICBMs, and two of them are road-mobile?"[64]

Shifting gears to Iran, Rogers complained of the terrorism sponsor's progress on what he called the Simorgh ICBM, apparently then sitting on a launch pad; the Iranians referred to it as a "space launch vehicle." Rogers asked those in the room, "If you believe the mullahs plan to go to the moon, please raise your hand. I didn't think so."[65]

Shortly it was Gortney's turn to speak, during which he addressed Russia and China each briefly. The admiral perceived Russia as "resurgent," whose "forays into Syria highlight Vladimir Putin's willingness to employ military power to advance his agenda outside Russia's near abroad." Gortney was concerned particularly with the country's capability to deploy "long-range, conventionally armed cruise missiles comparable to Western systems," some of which they had used in Syria one year earlier. Further, Russia remained the only nation possessing strategic nuclear forces "that could imperil our nation's existence," and Moscow continued its nuclear arsenal modernization efforts.[66]

China came next. Admiral Gortney assessed, "As part of its long-term, comprehensive military modernization program, China continues to modernize and expand its strategic forces with a focus on improving its ability to survive a first strike and penetrate United States missile defenses." Bringing up one of the specifics that had alarmed Rogers the day before, Gortney said China continued to upgrade its modest silo-based ICBM force "with a growing number of road-mobile ICBMs."[67]

Conclusion

While NSS held only a modest ranking among Obama administration priorities, nonetheless U.S. space capabilities increased between 2009 and 2016, perhaps most visibly the accomplishments of the young, innovative entrepreneurs known as NewSpace actors. The successful landings of commercial first stage boosters, first seen in 2015, promised unprecedented cost savings both for commercial space and NSS. Led by Musk and Bezos, NewSpace companies gained prominence and partnered more closely than before with NSS interests. Meanwhile, potential spacefaring adversaries, particularly China and Russia, continued their development of ASAT weapons and other capabilities, to include reorganizing their space forces. In his prepared remarks to Mike Rogers' Strategic Forces Subcommittee in March 2016, Douglas Loverro observed,

> Space services are inextricably woven throughout the fabric of our defense and national security infrastructure, and we do not intend to yield them. . . . Civil and commercial space capabilities add to this national security core and are part of our civilian critical infrastructure, creating opportunities to conduct business seamlessly across the planet. . . . These advantages go beyond purely U.S. national security interests

U.S. NATIONAL SECURITY SPACE

and remind us that while we will defend those U.S. interests, we remain fully committed to assuring the peaceful use of space by all nations.[68]

Loverro went on to state that today's adversaries perceived that "space is a weak-link in our deterrence calculus," and competitors viewed U.S. space forces "as the chink in [our] conventional armor—the place to gain an asymmetric advantage and reduce the likelihood of a U.S. response." General Hyten had already voiced his similar concerns to the subcommittee, stating, "Our ability to freely use these capabilities and maintain freedom of access to space is eroding as the space environment becomes more congested and contested." After years of observing adversaries' development of ASAT and other capabilities that might one day be employed against the United States—which ramped up during the Obama presidency—America's space leaders, both uniformed and civilian, were to gain the opportunity with the next administration to alter the deterrence calculus with a reorganizing of their own, culminating in the establishment of a new service—a space force.[69]

4

MIXED MOMENTUM FOR A SPACE SERVICE, 2017–2018

From his perch as the chair of the House Armed Services Strategic Forces Subcommittee, Mike D. Rogers had been beating the drum to awaken a slumbering Washington to the growing threats to the nation's interests in space. His warning was in conjunction with the need to put the military's space-house in order and nurture a cadre of space professionals that could lead the way in a new warfighting domain. Less than three months into the Donald J. Trump administration, in early April 2017 Representative Rogers addressed the 2017 Space Symposium, sponsored by the Space Foundation and held annually in the mecca of Air Force space activities, Colorado Springs, Colorado. Rogers enjoyed considerable assistance in his preparation for the symposium, including two papers and a seminal article entitled, "America Needs a Space Corps," by longtime space scholar Michael V. Smith of Maxwell AFB's Air University. Another space scholar said that Rogers' "push for a Space Corps [controlled the] narrative at [the] National Space Symposium."[1]

Rogers began his address by focusing on the Air Force's failure to demonstrate institutional commitment to growing a cadre of space professionals. Out of thirty-seven colonels who had just been nominated for promotion to brigadier general, none were space professionals. "This does not bode well for our ability to be ready for the threats we face in space," Rogers warned. "It is also telling as to the status and priority given to space in the current organizational construct of the Air Force."[2]

While Rogers bemoaned the dearth of space professionals among the one-star nominees, he referenced the foremost four-star space expert, John Hyten (commander of U.S. Strategic Command), who argued that without space assets, "you go back to World War II. You go back to industrial-age warfare." And that meant attrition and massive casualties. To Rogers, it was self-evident that the Air Force's current organizational structure was not what the nation required for its national security space (NSS) capabilities, requirements upped by the now-familiar 2007 Chinese ASAT test and the several subsequent tests by the PRC and Russia. His assessment was anything but new, however; the same shortcomings had been pointed out by high-level studies on multiple occasions, including the Rumsfeld and Allard space commissions.[3]

Mike Rogers had made the subject of space organization and management his "number one priority" for the 115th Congress that began in January 2017. Along with ranking member Jim Cooper (D-Tenn.), and the rest of their subcommittee, they devoted many hours to understanding the problems, beginning with the all-important question of "who was in charge [of NSS] below the level of the [defense] secretary and deputy secretary." According to Rogers, the GAO could not figure it out, but it offered the congressman's staff "a list of sixty offices that are involved in national security space." Rogers' staff continued the search on their own before agreeing with the GAO that no one was in charge. The conclusion harkened back to Air Force Chief of Staff T. Michael Moseley's description a decade earlier involving swinging a dead cat around the Pentagon "without [hitting] someone who thinks they're in charge of space." As Rogers told the symposium, "There are too many chiefs in the space camp." It was not an uncommon problem in large military organizations. In Lewis Sorley's *A Better War* on the final years of the Vietnam conflict, Gen. William

CHAPTER 4

Westmoreland's operations director, Maj. Gen. Charles Corcoran, summarized the divided command structure in Vietnam, stating, "Countrywide, there was really nobody in command. I don't think Westy ever really understood that he wasn't in command."[4]

Too many chiefs and not enough funding. Rogers compared the budget of the entire Air Force with that of military space after fiscal year 2013, the year the congressionally mandated "Defense sequester kicked in. As Secretary of the Air Force Heather Wilson put it several years later, looking back, "The budget collapsed in 2013." Rogers found that in fiscal year 2013, funding for space decreased by 28 percent while total Air Force funding declined 13 percent. Not good, but no foul—yet. But after 2013, space never recovered from the sequester cuts, according to the chairman, despite the rest of the Air Force's budget rising by an estimated 30 percent. Secretary Wilson noted that following 2013 and the rise of the Islamic State (ISIS) within a year, the Air Force—if not most of official Washington—remained "focused on violent extremism in the Middle East." No doubt, Mike Rogers and his subcommittee were among those who, in Wilson's words as she looked back, experienced "pent up frustration that the military as a whole didn't seem to be responding to the threat in space to develop the strategies and the programs to shift to a contested domain."[5]

Rogers' subcommittee had oversight of military satellites. Highlighting budgetary and management problems, fifteen months earlier an exasperated Rogers had blasted the Air Force over its handling of the legacy Defense Meteorological Satellite Program (DMSP), stating, "We could have saved the Air Force and the Congress a lot of aggravation if we put a half of a billion dollars in a parking lot and just burned it." For decades the Air Force had provided the Pentagon with weather capabilities from space, but its ambivalence over whether or not the final DMSP satellite was needed led Congress to shift to civil and international satellite sources rather than employ the DMSP-F20 (planned for a 2020 launch). As Rogers told the symposium in 2017, the Air Force "was willing to throw away a perfectly good weather satellite," which, if nothing else, he said, focused "me and my committee on the problems we're facing in [NSS] funding, organization, and management." In December 2017, Secretary Wilson made the best of a bad situation when she unveiled the $500 million satellite as the newest display piece at the Space and Missile Systems Center at Los Angeles AFB, California.[6]

While burning through half a billion dollars on a satellite was regrettable, it was not the only thing that Mike Rogers took issue with. The need for an Air Force cadre of space professionals had been highlighted in 1998–99 by Sen. Bob Smith of New Hampshire. Rogers noted the professional military education curricula at Maxwell AFB, Alabama—not in his district, but close by—did not prioritize space for the service's up-and-coming majors, lieutenant colonels, and colonels. An Air University official reported there were only two required curriculum hours for students at each of the two main schools, the Air Command and Staff College and Air War College. Rogers asked, "If space is meant to be integrated into the Air Force . . . how can that be done during only two hours of the [ten-month] professional development programs for future leaders?" The former acting secretary of the Air Force and undersecretary for most of 2017 through 2019, Matthew P. Donovan, recalled he had received only two hours devoted to space in the School of Advanced Airpower Studies curriculum in 1997–98.[7]

But the information Rogers had referenced was out of date and no longer even close to correct. One long-serving faculty member, a civilian PhD at ACSC, recalled that during his nearly fourteen years at the school the curriculum had always included far more than two hours devoted to space. In about 2008, ACSC had around sixteen to twenty hours on space, and more since then. In April 2017—three weeks after the Space Symposium in Colorado—the dean at ACSC wrote to Maj. Gen. David Thompson to explain the matter of space curriculum hours. Dr. James Forsyth stated that during the 2016–17 academic year, ACSC offered 38 hours focused on space out of 360 total hours of instruction. The next year's planned curriculum called for 60 hours on space out of 360 instructional hours. Four core courses were to have "a significant space emphasis." Forsyth added that "space is not always taught as a [stand-alone] topic, but it is integrated across multiple lessons to show space as [a] pervasive enabler." In 2021, Dr. John Terino of ACSC added that for a number of years "there [has been] definite space content in our wargames and exercises which is the [difficult] thing to quantify." Terino expanded on the difficulty of developing

84 CHAPTER 4

a curriculum with enough hours to please those in various niches of the Air Force stating, "We get critiqued a lot based on the predilections of various communities." Terino felt the real space advocates at ACSC were not unlike the air advocates in the 1930s, and for the former "we can't do enough regarding space." He added, "The reconciliation is the same as it would be for the Air Corps and the regular Army in the decade before the Second World War: we have two sides talking past each other because they have different agendas. The creation of the Space Force means they now have the opportunity to reconcile their differences or learn to appreciate each other more, but with high stakes. Just like the Air Corps in WWII."[8]

The space and cyber communities were not the only ones with predilections, but in some cases they did not help their own cause when they kept information helpful to the school's students at classified levels—an old problem with space data—or were reluctant to visit Maxwell AFB and brief the students in person. John Terino recalled that when it came to securing cutting-edge space lectures to present to the students, "Even at the 2 and 3 star level, we have had challenges getting stuff declassified to present to the students here. So, we have ... asked the right people to assist often. But there are just some things that are difficult to do." The maxim, "Space is Hard," used by author Christian Davenport in *The Space Barons*, rang true.[9]

Congress expected the space professionals to be among those to nurture a space culture within the Air Force. In 2001, the Rumsfeld Commission had stated the Air Force "must take steps to create a culture within the service dedicated to developing new space system concepts, doctrine, and operational capabilities." Wearing wings or badges on one's uniform was a big part of Air Force culture. Formerly, the Air Force had awarded the space badge—or space wings, known as "spings" for a time—to personnel in space acquisitions and space operations. But in later years, Rogers learned, the Air Force had ceased awarding the badge to those working in space acquisitions. Only space operations personnel were authorized the badge. "This situation leads to a lack of development of a 'tribe' mentality, for a unified group of space war-fighting professionals," said Rogers. "This is a cultural issue."[10]

In contrast, the Army had four thousand space professionals and all wore the career field's badge. Said Rogers, "It doesn't matter if you are doing planning or acquisitions or operations: a space professional is a space professional in the Army." He added that an Army officer told him, "'It is the ugliest badge in the Army, but every Soldier wants it.' The Army gets the significance of creating a culture behind key domains of war fighting." Within three years, the establishment of the U.S. Space Force again raised such concerns when a number of observers called for the new service to establish its own identity and define its own "cultural touchpoints and values" before others did it for them. Matters to address included what to call its members, uniforms, rank structure, nomenclature, and valued artifacts—the last no longer to be given away as gifts by the owning Air Force units that had no use for them.[11]

The U.S. Navy did not escape critique. The Navy managed a satellite program described in layman's terms as being similar to "a cell phone tower in space." Five satellites had been launched since 2012 and were on orbit, but Rogers reported that "for years, 90 percent of the capabilities for the satellite constellation could not be used because of delays with the ground terminals." And the Mobile User Objective System (MUOS) program came with a $7 billion price tag. It was an "unacceptable" situation of failed satellite-to-ground integration, exacerbated, in Rogers' view, by the fact that "no one is in charge."[12] Mike Rogers declared his objective in the clearest terms:

> My vision for the future is a separate Space Force within the Department of Defense, just like the Air Force, which had to be separated from the Army in order to be prioritized and become a world-class military service. Simply put, space must be a priority and it can't be one if you begin each morning thinking about fighters and bombers first. Don't get me wrong—I want planes and pilots to be priorities for the Air Force. At the same time, I want space to be as much of a priority for the professionals responsible for military space.[13]

Rogers sought not "radical surgery" but "bold reform . . . and it must start now."[14]

In closing, Rogers emphasized four guiding principles. First, the need to reduce the bureaucracy that continued to hinder military space, which—like the kudzu the Alabama representative was all-too familiar with—had to be ripped out "by the roots." Second, space must be "put on par" with the other warfighting domains of land, sea, air, and cyber, and until that happens, space funding needs to be protected from raiding by the other services. Third, "There must be a clearly identified cadre of space professionals," on which point Rogers sounded much like Sen. Bob Smith at Tufts University two decades earlier. Little had changed, it seemed. Both Smith and Rogers had chaired the Strategic Forces Subcommittee of their respective chamber's armed services committee. And fourth, Rogers pursued the goal of an integrated NSS program to ensure that military space and the NRO—while remaining separate and with differing cultures— nevertheless worked more closely together. While in April 2017 any serious, broad-based momentum in the Congress toward a Space Corps remained imperceptible, Rogers' Strategic Forces Subcommittee continued doing its part, and then some.[15]

Secretary of the Air Force Heather A. Wilson (2017–2019)

When Rogers addressed the Air Force's space problems at the symposium, Heather Wilson was not yet the Air Force secretary. In 1918, her grandfather had flown in the Royal Air Force looking for German U-boats in the Irish Sea, then came to America and flew as a barnstormer. Eventually, he became the fixed-base operator at Keene, New Hampshire, the reason the family settled there. Heather's father started working as a line boy at Keene's airport when he was thirteen and learned to fly at sixteen. Enlisting in the nascent U.S. Air Force, he served as a crew chief and later became a commercial pilot. During her school years at home, her father turned what might have been Heather's bedroom into the workshop for an experimental open-cockpit biplane—she moved into her brothers' bedroom. Needless to say, Heather Wilson had the DNA of flying in her blood.[16]

An Air Force Academy graduate with a doctorate from Oxford University, Wilson had served as an Air Force officer, NSC staff director, private sector entrepreneur-advisor, congresswoman from New Mexico, and college president. When secretary of defense-designate James Mattis first called her about becoming the secretary of the Air Force, it was both a shock and a tough decision for her—she loved her job of the last four years running a college. When over the Christmas holidays Mattis called again to offer her the job at the Pentagon, she replied, "Yes, sir, I will serve," but her confirmation was delayed and it was May before she was sworn in. In the meantime, the Senate Armed Services Committee (SASC) chairman, John McCain (R-Ariz.), wrote to the nominee, informing her of his committee's priorities. McCain charged her with "returning the culture of the Air Force to its core purpose of a warfighting force to fight and win our nation's wars and dispense with social experimentation that distracts your people from their primary purpose." The long-serving McCain's concern for social engineering in the services centered on transgender issues at that moment, including the maintaining of Air Force–required physical fitness standards during the transition period of transgender personnel.[17]

Wilson already had a connection with the Air Force chief of staff with whom she was to work closely: she and Gen. David Goldfein were Air Force Academy classmates from 1982. From their Academy days, she referred candidly to the pair as "the class geek and the class clown." She loved his sense of humor and they "hit it off really well." Wilson acknowledged Goldfein's storytelling ability in terms of promoting Air Force issues, saying, "He does stories, I do math," smilingly admitting to stealing his stories at times. "I don't think I ever made a major decision without asking for his advice," she said. In the prior administration there had been "some tension" between the secretary's and chief's offices. Wilson and Goldfein determined to restore closer relations, and they typically communicated with one another seven or eight times a day. Instead of the standard practice of holding separate staff meetings, they combined them into a single staff meeting, which helped perhaps in more ways than one. In particular, the combined meetings facilitated rewriting or rescinding more than seven hundred Air Force instructions of a total of fourteen hundred or more—40 percent were out of date—a huge improvement to a bureaucratic nightmare the chief had brought to the new secretary's attention. Perhaps just as important as halving the number of instructions, Wilson emphasized getting those that remained into "clear English that an 18-year-old can understand." One lieutenant colonel recalled that during his time working on strategy issues for the air staff from 2018 to 2019, staff

88 CHAPTER 4

officers' trust in the Air Force department's senior leadership was "high." It was evident to the majors, lieutenant colonels, and colonels that Wilson, Goldfein, vice chief of staff Gen. Stephen W. "Seve" Wilson (no relation), and Undersecretary Donovan worked well together and seemed to enjoy one another's company, providing a worthy model and promoting high morale among their team.[18]

Perhaps most of all, Secretary Wilson admired Goldfein's respect for the Constitution's deference to civilian control of the military: not once did the chief call her by her first name in her two years as the secretary. In her outgoing interview in 2019, she looked forward to being "Heather" once again with her classmate.[19]

In the meantime, in her first few months as the Air Force secretary, Wilson found herself of one mind with her superiors—Secretary of Defense Mattis and President Trump—both of whom were yet to be convinced of the need for a separate military branch for space. Influenced by her years in Congress and aware that members often could not wait for a week or more for a reply, Wilson prioritized her office's responsiveness to congressional inquiries. Although certain offices on Capitol Hill had devoted considerable time and effort to the problem of how best to leverage space for the national security, Stephen L. Kitay, the deputy assistant secretary of defense for space policy during the Trump administration, recalled that in mid-2017 the idea of a sixth armed service was a "fairly newer concept" to the administration. In any case, by year's end, due to the heavy lifting of Strategic Forces Subcommittee chairman Mike Rogers and ranking member Jim Cooper, and the work of the conferees from both chambers, the 2018 National Defense Authorization Act included language calling for a federally funded research effort "to develop a plan to establish a separate military department" responsible for NSS under the Pentagon.[20]

The timeline was not entirely clear, but between the summer of 2017 and the spring of 2018, Secretary Wilson found herself on the opposite side of the Space service issue, first, with the House of Representatives, and later, the Trump White House. Exactly when Trump first considered the idea of the Space Force was a mystery, but several Washington insiders with knowledge of space issues were convinced the president had "never warmed to the 'Space Corps' term." While the president's space policy directive

(SPD) in early 2019 calling on the Pentagon to develop a legislative proposal "to establish a United States Space Force" as a sixth armed service appeared to be the primary reason for Wilson's leaving Washington three months later—after two years on the job—there was more to her decision.[21]

One noted defense writer asked why she was leaving, declaring, "No political appointee has ever been more qualified to lead the Air Force than Heather Wilson." In March 2019, Loren Thompson penned that Wilson "repeatedly found herself crosswise with the White House on matters of policy," then offered the example of what he considered her opposing "a half-baked idea to fashion a Space Force . . . that even now [lacks] a clear rationale." Thompson concluded that probably Wilson wearied of "a very stressful work environment," not the least of which was keeping apace with presidential policies that were not always coordinated beforehand with the departments they affected.[22]

In addition, Wilson held Mattis in high regard and they worked well together, but that was not the case with his successor, she acknowledged. Secretary Mattis left the Pentagon at the end of 2018 over policy differences with the Trump White House, of which a U.S. withdrawal from Syria appeared to be the last straw. The Air Force secretary recalled from her last meeting with her boss on the day he resigned that as a young officer, Mattis had been forced to leave allies in the field. As Mattis expressed, he simply could not live through that experience again. (Unknown at the time, his resignation was to slow the American withdrawal.) Moreover, Wilson relished the role of a college president. At her swearing-in ceremony, Secretary Mattis had quoted a former student at the South Dakota School of Mines and Technology who said, "She was much more than just a president to us . . . she was a role model, a friend to us all, and, above all, an inspiration." As she departed from office at the end of May 2019, Dr. Wilson had the opportunity to return to those and other important roles as the president of the University of Texas at El Paso.[23]

In any case, few space proponents shed tears at her departure. Some attributed to her, at least in part, what they called a "malign effect" of the Air Force department's influence upon the process of adding a space service. For that reason, by 2019 some proponents had changed their mind from favoring a Space Corps under the Department of the Air Force to

90   CHAPTER 4

preferring a Space Force under its own department and civilian chief. In the end, their glass was half full.[24]

Pushback to the 2018 NDAA

At the Space Symposium, Mike Rogers' vision of a separate Space Force foreshadowed his intent for the upcoming defense budget. Soon after, as committees crafted the House version of the 2018 defense bill, Rogers inserted language into it to "authorize the creation of a Space Corps within the Department of the Air Force," to be established by January 1, 2019.[25]

Over the next few months, the White House, Pentagon, and Air Force appeared to push back. The Space Corps language in the House's version was among the NDAA provisions the Trump White House was unprepared to accept at that point, calling the measure "premature." In late August 2017, *Air Force* magazine emphasized the Trump administration's public opposition to the legislation's Space Corps language. Emphasizing the defense department's need for an integrated rather than a parochial approach to space, Mattis—at Wilson's urging—took the unusual step of writing a letter to a key House Armed Services Subcommittee chairman, stating, "I strongly urge Congress to reconsider the proposal of a separate service Space Corps."[26]

Mattis' letter was not the only unusual feature of the developing space corps/force controversy. The day after being sworn-in as the secretary of the Air Force, Wilson had found herself at the deep end of the pool, testifying with CSAF Goldfein before the SASC in its hearing on military space organization, policy, and programs. Wilson found some of the materials intended to prepare her for the hearing to be unhelpful, calling one Air Force strategic master plan "rubbish," another paper among "the worst planning/operating concept documents I have ever read," and a third one too long and "not clear," leading her to conclude, "we have a process problem on testimony." Moreover, the SASC's majority policy director, Matthew P. Donovan—three months later to become the undersecretary of the Air Force—recalled it was very unusual for a service secretary and chief to attend a SASC subcommittee meeting.[27]

May and June were busy months for Wilson and Goldfein in terms of congressional appearances. In late June, in one of his more memorable remarks pertaining to the space corps proposal that was building momentum in the House, Goldfein told the House Armed Services Committee (HASC), "If you're saying the word 'separate' and 'space' in the same sentence, I would offer you're moving us in the wrong direction.... Every mission that we perform in the United States military is dependent on space. Now's not the time to build seams and segregate and separate, now's the time to further integrate."[28]

A month earlier, the CSAF had said nearly the same thing to the Senate Armed Services Committee.[29]

As she had been doing since her confirmation as the Air Force secretary, Wilson again spoke unhesitatingly against the Space Corps proposal, saying such a move must increase the Pentagon's complexity, "add more boxes to the organization chart, and cost more money. . . . I don't need another chief of staff and another six deputy chiefs of staff." The CSAF added, "The secretary and I are focused [on] how do we *integrate* space" [emphasis in original].[30]

Goldfein's focus was on operational matters. He advocated multi-domain operations, bringing networks, doctrine, and training together, as seamlessly as possible, across the domains of air, sea, land, space, and cyberspace in order to overwhelm the enemy. Both Wilson and Goldfein were convinced it was not the time to create a Space Corps for reasons including the ongoing transition in space from a benign environment to a warfighting domain as well as recent organizational changes affecting military space—especially the position of the new deputy chief of staff for space—and a hefty 20 percent Air Force space budget increase after the damage of sequester in 2013. Low readiness levels among USAF fighter squadrons were also a concern. In April 2017 the Heritage Foundation stated, "Average sortie per aircraft/month and total flying time, point to a readiness level not witnessed by the Air Force since the Carter Administration." In those days, the U.S. military rightly was known as the hollow force.[31]

But Mike Rogers was having none of it. While the eight-term representative was not easily provoked, he was "outraged" at the Air Force position, perhaps especially at Wilson's seemingly gratuitous reference to six more deputy chiefs of staff. "The Pentagon always resists change," he opined in response to Wilson in particular, as well as Goldfein. At the opening of his subcommittee's markup of the 2018 NDAA, Rogers said, "They [the Air Force] just need a few more years to rearrange the deck chairs: I don't think so. This is the same Air Force that got us into the situation where the Russians and the Chinese are near-peers to us in space"—both of which had reorganized their military's space forces within the last two to three years. While the still-fresh Air Force secretary was not the one to blame for the service's arguably mixed-bag approach to military space since 2001, she was the one in the seat at a critical moment and could hardly avoid angering one side or the other. Incensed at Wilson's comments—even though the current proposal called for the Space Corps to report to the Air Force secretary—Rogers threw down the gauntlet, saying, "Maybe we need a Space Corps Secretary instead of an Air Force Secretary leading space." Having let off some steam, Rogers toned it down by expressing his willingness to work with the Air Force "to reform the national security space enterprise." He insisted, nonetheless, "The Department cannot fix itself on this issue. . . . Congress has to step in." Rogers' subcommittee approved the entire mark, including the Space Corps provision, and it went to the full HASC.[32]

Rogers had an ally in Rep. Mac Thornberry (R-Tex.), who chaired the HASC. Pushing back on the argument of certain opponents that the Space Corps proposal had not been fully vetted, Thornberry stated, "There are times when an issue becomes developed and ripe and it is our responsibility to act. . . . This is the time for us to act." Democrat Jim Cooper of Tennessee added, "Whether we like it or not, space is the new warfighting domain," and it had not been granted the requisite priority by the Air Force. The HASC voted 60–1 to pass the NDAA as a whole.[33]

Steve Kitay, for six years a professional staffer on the HASC supporting the Strategic Forces Subcommittee before he moved to the Pentagon to do space policy in 2017, later stated, "The HASC started with studying the problem. And the problem was our eroding advantage in space. It was assessed that a Space Force, then called a Space Corps, was a key element to addressing that challenge." The deputy assistant secretary believed it was the congressional action regarding space that "energized the topic" and got the "broader community and Executive branch" more deeply engaged in studying the problem. Kitay continued, "In addition to Congress,

President Trump's vision and support was essential to the creation of the Space Force." In Kitay's view, "At the end of the day [the act during 2019 to establish the U.S. Space Force] was a bipartisan piece of legislation across both executive and legislative branches. . . . This was a strategic move for our nation, to prioritize space, to prioritize the people, the education, the training, the doctrine development, and the equipment and resources necessary for the US to [lead] in this critical domain."[34] But that was yet to come, in 2019.

Two years earlier when Rogers and Cooper appeared before the House Rules Committee to answer its questions, Cooper spoke his mind, explaining that classified briefings had convinced him that failing to solve the well-known problems in NSS decision-making risked "another 9/11 or Pearl Harbor." In response to the committee's query on why the Space Corps had generated such opposition from the Pentagon, Rogers replied, "They don't like Congress meddling in their business." Alluding to the long-running practice of the Air Force taking funds intended for military space and using them for its high priority aircraft programs, Rogers emphasized, "If we [organize] space . . . into a separate corps, that money goes with that corps." He offered years of data to the committee to support his claim that the Air Force not infrequently diverted space dollars to its fighters and bombers. The Rules Committee sided with Rogers and, following two-and-a-half days of floor debate and dealing with two hundred other amendments, on 14 July 2017 the full House passed the NDAA by 344–81, with the Space Corps provision intact.[35]

Secretary Wilson remained unimpressed with the idea of a Space Corps, and in September she focused elsewhere with a *Politico*-hosted space panel, telling them, "Space will become more congested," if not also "more contested." At the first National Space Forum held in 1997, one speaker had begun with the words, "Space is the New High Seas." The space and maritime domains often were compared with one another, and Wilson anticipated space becoming "more like the ocean. There will be more players—some of them private." She viewed the decline of launch costs and the miniaturization of payloads as the biggest factors likely to promote increased congestion and competition in space. Her predecessor as Air Force secretary, Deborah Lee James, expected "enormous upheaval" with creating the proposed new corps. James put it succinctly, "Sometimes the juice is not worth the squeeze." Days later, Wilson addressed the Air Force Association's Air, Space & Cyber conference, insisting the Air Force had been—and remained—a strong advocate for space, again touting the anticipated deputy chief of staff for space operations and an expected 20 percent boost for space in the Air Force's 2018 budget.[36]

The Senate's version of the NDAA had not merely lacked a Space Corps provision—which Matt Donovan attributed in part to the traditional "tension" between intelligence committees and the Pentagon regarding space— it included language to "prohibit the establishment" of any new "military department or corps ... including a Space Corps." In the summer of 2017, Donovan was transitioning from the SASC's majority policy director to becoming undersecretary of the Air Force, so he enjoyed a unique perspective on the NDAA process. When the Senate took up the bill in September after the August recess, the upper chamber remained somewhere between the House's proposal and the Air Force's reliance on organizational change and increased funding alone to preclude the need for anything more drastic. The Senate version of the bill—a lighter squeeze using James' metaphor— called for a "high-level chief information warfare officer" responsible for space, cyberspace, and electronic warfare (the proposal did not survive). Maj. Gen. Clinton E. Crosier, who in 2019 led the Pentagon's planning for the Space Force, stated plainly that in his view, "The Air Force worked hard to ensure the Senate didn't support the House version of the bill [in 2017]." In the fall, conferees from both legislative chambers finished crafting the collaborative NDAA bill. While they dropped the Space Corps provision, conferees stated in a summary of the bill their intent to "begin fixing the broken national security space enterprise," a harsh criticism of the Air Force. Although the service was not specifically named, all knew that the Air Force controlled at least 80 percent of the NSS budget.[37]

The House and Senate negotiators made sure the Air Force felt their displeasure by eliminating three entities or positions, reducing the Air Force's influence over military space: 1) the Defense Space Council; 2) the brand-new billet of Air Force deputy chief of staff for space operations (A11); and 3) the office of Principal Department of Defense Space Advisor (PDSA), which since its creation in 2015 had been filled by the secretary of the Air

Force. As Lt. Gen. David D. Thompson (in 2020 the U.S. Space Force vice commander) recalled, no small amount of study by the Air Force on space stewardship went by the wayside when the A11 was canned. Thompson had the unusual experience of being confirmed by the Congress as the A11 by about the first of November 2017 and then, only one week later—as he put it wryly—"fired . . . by Act of Congress" with the passage of the NDAA. Six months later, Thompson was confirmed by Congress in a position that supported the Air Force Space Command vice commander.[38]

Perhaps perceived unfairly by some as twisting the knife, Congress required the PDSA office's duties and personnel to be assigned to an official selected by the deputy defense secretary, "except the Deputy Secretary may not select the Secretary of the Air Force nor the Under Secretary of Defense for Intelligence." In any event, in January 2018 the deputy defense secretary, Patrick Shanahan, took over the duties of principal space adviser on an interim basis.[39]

Not all independent space advocates agreed on every matter impinging on NSS. In mid-2017, just before Matt Donovan began the confirmation process for undersecretary, he argued in a paper prepared for SASC chairman John McCain that eliminating the PDSA office and Defense Space Council were not in the best interests of a Space Corps. Doing away with either or both entities was, in his view, to "weaken space governance rather than strengthen the [Air Force] Secretary's position." Perhaps there was room for debate over what weakened space governance, but it seemed clear enough that Rogers' subcommittee did not wish to strengthen the secretary's position at the moment.[40]

More fundamentally, from his position as SASC majority policy director, Donovan perceived the Air Force's senior leaders as "digging in their heels for a battle with Congress" over the Space Corps rather than seeking collaboration, which he considered more prudent. Even though it had been a decade and a half since CSAF General Jumper ended the Air Force's mantra of air-space seamlessness, either the old doctrine survived in certain corners or it resurfaced. Logically, Donovan viewed part of the service's intransigence in 2017 as being linked to its reluctance to accept that "no capabilities currently fielded can transit the physical seam between air and space efficiently, or even physically affect one from the other."[41]

96   CHAPTER 4

The conferees took a dual track that appeared likely to lead to a separate space service in the foreseeable future. They required the deputy defense secretary, by 1 March 2018, to submit to the congressional defense committees an interim report "on the review and recommended organizational and management structure for the [NSS] components of the Department of Defense, including the Air Force Space Command," and the final report by 1 August. The final report was to include a proposed implementation plan. In addition, the deputy secretary was to "enter into a contract with a federally funded research and development center that is not closely affiliated with the Department of the Air Force to develop a plan to establish a separate military department responsible for the [NSS] activities of the Department of Defense," with the final report due to the congressional defense committees by 31 December 2018.[42]

Despite the favorable prospects, Mike Rogers remained unsatisfied. He vowed to continue the fight for the Space Corps' establishment even if it took several more years. The congenial but—when sufficiently provoked—fiery congressman was convinced that "dramatic organizational change" was required for NSS to meet its challenges. If one thought otherwise, he stated plainly, "you're fooling yourself."[43]

Rogers' and other space advocates' anxieties aside, in mid-November the House agreed to the NDAA conference report by 356–70 and the Senate approved it by voice vote. On 12 December 2017, President Trump signed the 2018 NDAA into effect as Public Law 115-91.[44]

Space Policy Directives and Trump's Call for a Space Force, 2017–18

Only the president was empowered to set national space policy; for decades the issuance of presidential SPDs—or simply, presidential directives (each bore a number) as during the Carter administration—was the usual mechanism for disseminating major policy changes. The Trump White House, led by the president's point man, Vice President Mike Pence, was extremely active in that arena, issuing three SPDs between December 2017 and June 2018.[45]

In early December 2017, Space Policy Directive-1 replaced one of the civil space guidelines from Obama's fourteen-page National Space Policy (2010) regarding NASA's manned spaceflight program. Trump refocused on returning humans to the moon "for long-term exploration and utilization, followed by human missions to Mars and other destinations." His predecessor's human spaceflight policy had been to bypass the moon, and instead aim for "crewed missions beyond the moon, including sending humans to an asteroid" by 2025 and orbiting Mars by the 2030s.[46]

President Trump's second and third space policy directives, issued in May and June 2018 respectively, addressed commercial space matters (SPD-2) and space situational awareness and traffic management (SPD-3). SPD-2 aimed to promote economic growth, protect national security and public safety, and "encourage American leadership in space commerce" by reforming commercial space regulations and creating what SpacePolicy Online.com called a "one-stop shop" for the commercial space sector at the Department of Commerce. Specifically, SPD-2 called for the reform of licensing requirements regarding commercial space flight launch and reentry operations as well as commercial remote sensing activities. The commercial space directive went hand-in-hand with space scholar Everett Dolman's *Astropolitik: Classical Geopolitics in the Space Age*, in which he wrote, "Athens, Britain, and the United States were powerful trading states before they became world military powers. The opening of the seas accomplished for ... [them] what the true opening of space will in the future," for those states that pursue "exploration and exploitation of the vast riches there."[47]

Further, NASA administrator Jim Bridenstine viewed SPD-2 as another way for the National Space Council—which in June 2017 the president revived from long dormancy by executive order—to offer "much-needed direction for the many different aspects of our nation's activity in space." Former Rep. Robert S. Walker, the 2016 Trump Campaign's chief space adviser, recalled that Trump had promised to bring back the National Space Council, which both Walker and former speaker of the House Newt Gingrich supported. As Walker said of President Trump: "Once he committed to something, he did it." Moreover, the council's roughly quarterly meetings—chaired by the vice president—pressured the members to ensure their departments actually were working on the president's space program. Dr. Scott Pace, the National Space Council's executive secretary from 2017 to 2020, recalled, "I don't know that the existence of the [National Space Council] per se pushed the Space Force idea. But the idea space was important to the nation and that a whole of government approach was needed provided what might be called a 'conducive environment' with knowledgeable senior leaders." The point had been made by commissions and study groups for two decades. Finally, it seemed to be taking hold at the White House.[48]

Trump's third directive, National Space Traffic Management Policy, included measures to mitigate the effects of orbital debris on space activities. Noting that space was becoming "increasingly congested and contested," the SPD-3 policy directive stated,

> As the number of space objects increases [20,000-plus trackable objects] ... [the current] limited traffic management activity and architecture will become inadequate. At the same time, the contested nature of space is increasing the demand for DoD focus on protecting and defending U.S. space assets and interests.
>
> Emerging commercial ventures such as satellite servicing, debris removal, in-space manufacturing, and tourism ... are increasingly outpacing efforts to develop and implement government policies and processes to address these new activities.[49]

Space Force Questions

President Trump's most significant space policy announcement came not by means of an official, written directive, but informally—and quite unexpectedly—by word of mouth in a presidential address. Given Trump's signature on SPD-1 three months earlier, one assumed that certain key individuals including space experts had enjoyed the president's ear regarding the space domain. Vice President Pence certainly did and, through him, former speaker Gingrich as well. Rep. Mike Rogers was a likely candidate, but there may have been others, including Bob Walker, during the 2016 campaign. During his visits to Maxwell AFB during this period, Mike Rogers referred to "Trump whisperers" who had the president's ear on space, but he did not name names. Another space insider named Gingrich as one of the whisperers, although when interviewed the speaker stated his main inputs took the form of papers he submitted to Pence's office. Among the several visits by Gingrich and Rogers to Maxwell that included discussions on space, in February 2015 Gingrich spoke in person to Air University students, and six months later Rogers attended an AU cyber meeting hosted by Lt. Gen. Steven L. Kwast, the AU commander. In August 2017, Kwast and two of his leading AU space proponents—Michael V. Smith and Peter Garretson—visited Gingrich in Washington, DC. In July 2018, Smith and Garretson met with Rogers at an event in Montgomery, Alabama, and five months later Gingrich attended the first Schriever Space Scholars symposium held at Maxwell. In short, there was plenty of interaction by several AU space proponents with at least two Washington insiders who engaged with President Trump (or more precisely, Vice President Pence) on space.[50]

At least beyond a very small circle, the degree to which the whisperers had influenced Trump's thinking was unknown at the time (and has remained largely opaque to this study). In any case, on 13 March 2018 during a speech before a Marine air wing at Marine Corps Air Station Miramar in San Diego, California, the president announced, "My new national strategy for space recognizes that space is a war-fighting domain just like the land, air, and sea. . . . We may even have a Space Force." He went on to say, "Maybe we'll have to do that." It was far from a direct order from the president transmitted through the chain of command. The president's words appeared to be off-the-cuff and were in fact contrary to the current policy of his administration and the DoD. One day earlier at a joint appearance of the three service secretaries (Army, Navy, Air Force) at the Center for Strategic and International Studies, Secretary Wilson had talked up the Air Force's emphasis on defending space and enabling multi-domain military operations. "There is not a military mission that doesn't rely in some way on space," she said, but her words offered no clue of an impending sixth branch of the armed forces. If the Air Force secretary knew nothing of the new policy, perhaps the entire Pentagon was in the dark. Under the circumstances, at a HASC hearing two days later, 14 March—the day after the president's announcement—Wilson might have been excused for dodging a question about the call for a space force, saying politely, "We look forward to the conversation."[51]

Several days later, Secretary Wilson returned to some of the same themes during congressional testimony on the USAF's fiscal year 2019 budget. She assured the HASC that the Air Force's budget aligned with the national defense strategy, which highlighted China and Russia as strategic competitors, but without mentioning space in that context. She referred to "two bold moves" on the part of the Air Force, the first "the acceleration of a defendable space," and the second the shift to multi-domain operations especially with respect to command and control. At that time, the Air Force operated seventy-six satellites, including thirty GPS and twenty-five providing communications. Noting that the Air Force was "investing in jam-resistant satellite technology" for both of the above capabilities, the secretary emphasized that the 2019 budget was "accelerating our ability to defend our assets on orbit." Through the use of multiple 90-day reviews involving the Army, Navy, Air Force, and NRO, participants examined architectures and strategies, engaged in wargaming, and reached agreements on probability of kill, and of survival, for U.S. assets on orbit as well as threat assets.[52]

But regardless of its genesis, Trump's advocacy of a new military branch dedicated to space was music to the ears of some in Congress and the Air Force, although it probably was some time before most of the latter felt at ease to voice their approbation in public. Later that day (13 March), Mike Rogers gushed to *The Atlantic*, "I am so proud of President Trump's support of this important and historic initiative to create an independent space force." His colleague Jim Cooper added, "While I have not seen anything beyond President Trump's comments today, his remarks seem encouraging."[53]

The president's words had been fuzzy enough to allow some, perhaps most space insiders including Steve Kitay, to consider the president's directive to build a space force to date not from 13 March, but three months later. Kitay viewed the presidential order as stemming from the 18 June meeting of the National Space Council at which Trump signed SPD-3 (on space traffic management). That afternoon in the East Room of the White House, the president said, "Very importantly, I'm [hereby] directing the Department of Defense . . . to immediately begin the process necessary to establish a space force as the sixth branch of the armed forces. . . . We are going to have the Air Force and we are going to have the Space Force." Kitay had not been aware of what the president was going to announce that day, but he also pointed out that the president was under no obligation to inform him. While others in attendance may have been taken aback—reportedly among them were Secretary Wilson and Joint Chiefs Chairman Gen. Joseph F. Dunford Jr.—Sandra Erwin of *Space News* wrote that the president's remarks "were not off-the-cuff" and had been planned for weeks. Trump had spoken of his desire for the Space Force "at four different events in recent months," presumably one of which was at Miramar.[54]

In any case, the Pentagon's leading space policy official viewed Trump's announcement as extremely important. "That was direction from the President of the United States to the Pentagon," Kitay said, and the president used "very precise wording" to begin the planning for a new branch of the armed forces. Kitay added, "That was a very important strategic direction to take for our nation."[55]

The day after Trump's announcement on 18 June, Wilson issued a one-page memorandum to all airmen acknowledging that the president had directed the Pentagon to begin the planning "to establish a space force as a new military service within the [defense] department." While not striking an enthusiastic tone with her airmen so as to encourage expectations of rapid change that could not be met, nonetheless, the secretary's message was accurate and measured. There were big questions to be answered. A number of space insiders, including Kitay, acknowledged there were different ideas "'of what the Space Force is' when it was first put out there." Prudently, Wilson's choice of words left open the question of whether the Space Force was to have its own military department, or—similar to the Marine Corps within the Department of the Navy—would become the smaller service within the Department of the Air Force. A week later, NASA administrator Jim Bridenstine came out strongly in favor of a Space Force. While some space advocates viewed the contrasting responses of Wilson and Bridenstine in stark, if not dark, terms, the president's decision did not add to NASA's to-do list for national security space, to include force restructuring. It did for the Department of the Air Force.[56]

Two months later, on 9 August, Vice President Pence spoke at the Pentagon on the future of the U.S. military in space. Pence noted that "President Trump [has] stated clearly and forcefully that space is, in his words, 'a warfighting domain, just like . . . land, [and] air, and sea.'" Highlighting

102   CHAPTER 4

the Defense Department report that was produced in response to the president's directive to begin the planning to create the Space Force, Pence stated that the report "identifies concrete steps that our administration will take to lay the foundation for a new Department of the Space Force." Later in his address, the vice president twice referred to "the United States Department of the Space Force." It was apparent the president's point man for space did not envision the new service as being created within the Department of the Air Force; rather, it was to have its own department. Scott Pace, who ran the National Space Council meetings, considered that Pence "played a critical role in translating the President's direction into reality," not only through his 9 August speech, but also by working with Pentagon leaders and on the Hill—especially the Senate—and, in the months that followed, "his presentation of options on placing the Space Force within the [Department of the Air Force]."[57]

Beginning in late August, a space governance committee began a series of meetings to turn the concept into something concrete. Deputy Secretary of Defense Shanahan—soon to be the acting defense secretary—led many of the meetings, recalled Col. Casey Beard, who at that time worked in space policy at the Pentagon. Perhaps unsurprisingly, Kitay recalled someone saying to him, "You know, Steve, everybody between you and the President has a different idea of what the Space Force is." Maj. Gen. Stephen N. Whiting, later the U.S. Space Force's deputy commander, saw it this way: "When the President started talking [about] a separate Department of the Space Force, he stretched the debate even further, and all of a sudden the Space Corps seemed like a reasonable alternative, and essentially that's . . . where we landed. The Space Force is a separate service within the Department of the Air Force. I think that's the right answer. I think the President really stretched the debate to make that the reasonable alternative."[58]

Whiting referred to the fact that a space corps (or force) within the Department of the Air Force—similar to the Marine Corps within the Navy department—seemed less radical than the creation of an entirely new military department. One Air Force space professional interviewed for this work indicated that as far as he knew, the president never mentioned a space corps in public, only a space force. In a 2022 interview, Newt

Gingrich recalled a conversation he had with Vice President Pence. He told Pence that if the Space Corps could get through, maybe he should adopt it. The vice president replied along the lines of, "Well, the guy down the hall will not accept it." Gingrich took that to mean the term "Space Force" was not open for further discussion, whatever the organizational construct might look like.[59]

The Gag Order Controversy

By the summer of 2018, Air Force restrictions placed on public communications by airmen about current service matters raised fears of a gag order in some quarters. In March 2018 a Military.com article whose title mentioned an Air Force "Gag Order on Press Engagements" highlighted Secretary Wilson's concern for operations security in a period of renewed near-peer competition. The memorandum also called for a "Public Engagement Reset." The wording was typical of an official reemphasis for airmen to "avoid giving insights to our adversaries which could erode our military advantage." For those unsuspicious of any ulterior motive, the memo was unspectacular and seemed quite reasonable at a time when potential adversaries China and Russia were becoming more aggressive. But a few months later when some space advocates noticed the memo, it began to take on a darker meaning. During the summer, several incidents in which academic freedom, mainly on the part of several Air University students and faculty, appeared to be restricted reinforced the view of space proponents that a gag order on space was in effect. Matt Donovan, the Air Force undersecretary at the time, commented that a "'gag order' of sorts [was] not unwarranted." He continued,

> We had some space folks that started getting out in front of leadership's headlights on this issue before we had a chance to assess the situation and the [Air Force] way forward. Heather Wilson certainly did not want this playing out in the press until we could consider and solidify a position based on written guidance from the [White House]. . . . There was no doubt both [Wilson] and Dave Goldfein at that time opposed the formation of a separate Space Force, but both saluted smartly and (reluctantly) complied when we got the official guidance.[60]

104   CHAPTER 4

The gag order controversy peaked with respect to the career of Lt. Gen. Steven Kwast, the AU commander from 2014 to 2017. A 1986 Air Force Academy graduate, Kwast earned a master's degree in public policy from Harvard University before attending flight training at Williams AFB, Arizona. He spent the next seven years as an F-15E pilot, graduated from Air Command and Staff College at Maxwell in 1997—in the same class as Matt Donovan—then served as military aide to the vice president for the next two years. A lieutenant colonel in thirteen years, Kwast was clearly on the fast track. Following three years in a fighter squadron in which his final job was as commander, he returned from England for a year as a national defense fellow at Boston University. For the next six years, he alternated between command tours, at group and wing level, and staff duty at the Pentagon and Langley AFB, Virginia. Following a year-long deployment to Afghanistan where he commanded the air expeditionary wing at Bagram Air Base (2009–10), over the next four years he served a joint staff and two headquarters assignments, including at Air Combat Command and U.S. Air Force headquarters. In early 2014, Kwast moved to Maxwell where he was dual-hatted initially as the doctrine center commander and the vice commander of Air University. In November, he pinned on his third star and took command of Air University, in which capacity he was to think deeply on space, promote the Space Force, and offer career protection for several of his field grade officers who were doing the same.[61]

An interview in the fall of 2017—two full years before the Space Force and not long before Kwast left Maxwell—shed light on his thinking and strategy focus for the previous three years. In response to a question on strategy-related projects at Air University, the commander said,

> One project is with regard to our grand strategy as an Air Force in this age of networks, and I will specifically say space. Our strategy for space is evolving based on China and the threat. As China is building a navy in space where the shoreline of America will now be over all of our heads. The Air Force is still just building buoys in space that can see and hear it, but can't do much about a battleship or an aircraft carrier in space that is maneuvering and taking action. This University provided the research that is guiding not only our Secretary as the primary

defense space advisor to the Secretary of Defense and to the Vice-President, but also the administration's ability to bring together all of the different departments to create the statutory and regulatory environment for us to move forward. . . . So, we have made a huge impact on the strategy of space for the nation.[62]

Kwast's naval theme, characteristic of nearly all the serious space advocates, was reminiscent of *Astropolitik*, in which Dolman wrote, "Just as the major trading states of history had to establish strong military forces to patrol the seas, providing a safe operating environment for . . . commerce to prosper, the top spacefaring states would see it in their own best interests to establish a space force capable of dominating the major space trade routes, point locations of commercial and military value, and decisive regions of strategic control . . . to maximize space power."[63]

Another of the several space advocates at ACSC who lauded Lieutenant General Kwast's leadership as well as his sheltering those under him, credited Kwast with "the most far-reaching thinking to advance U.S. space power," including initiatives at Air University such as the Fast Space study (which set the stage for partnering with commercial space), the Space Horizons Task Force, and the Schriever Space Scholars for developing space strategists. Addressing the period of what Donovan called the "'gag order' of sorts," from spring 2018 to roughly the following spring, Peter Garretson wrote that during that time, "Only one Air Force officer, Lt. Gen. Steve Kwast, spoke publicly in favor of [the Space Force]. Air Force officers who hope to maintain our proud tradition of conscience over career owe him a debt of gratitude." When Kwast's tour at Maxwell ended in late 2017, he went on to lead the Air Education and Training Command (AETC) at San Antonio, Texas, until 2019. In early May his successor at AETC was named and Kwast retired that summer. One senior officer acknowledged that especially after the facts surrounding an incident of unprofessional behavior on the part of flight instructors that occurred in 2018 at Laughlin AFB, Texas—a major AETC flying training base—came to light, to include an alcohol-indulging culture at the remote base, Air Force senior leaders "wanted change." While the story was complex and there were at least two sides to it, some space proponents felt that

Kwast had lost his career "over his advocacy for the Space Force." For the forward-thinking space advocates at Maxwell's Air University—the predecessor of which had been the Air Corps Tactical School where the air doctrine for the next world war was developed in the 1930s—rightly or wrongly, they could not help but equate Kwast with Billy Mitchell and his career-ending advocacy of airpower in an earlier era.[64]

Newt Gingrich, who had been constantly in touch with Kwast—especially while he commanded Air University—estimated he had spent twenty or more hours with him and his staff discussing space issues in person. The speaker considered the general to be "the most aggressive innovator in doctrine and in thinking about the world that's emerging that I had met in the Air Force." Gingrich agreed with Air University's space proponents, stating, "Yeah, I would say that his parallel is Billy Mitchell."[65]

Lt. Gen. David D. Thompson and the Changing Views on a Space Force

Perhaps Lieutenant General Thompson—in mid-2018 the Air Force Space Command's vice commander who would become vice commander of the U.S. Space Force within eighteen months—was not the only career space officer to undergo a change of heart regarding the advisability of a space force. In 2016 and 2017, while Mike Rogers led the charge in the lower chamber for a space corps, Thompson recalled thinking, "Please do not do this; please do not inflict this on us." His rationale at the time was that China and Russia "have really upped their game" in space and he considered the United States unprepared: "All the time and energy we focus on things like a Space Force or a Space Corps is time, and energy, and resources that we're not going to spend worrying about Russia and China and what we have to do to face down the threat. . . . So, at the time, I absolutely was not a fan."[66]

One of the ways in which China and Russia were upping their game was with worker-bee satellites, spacecraft expected to be deployed within five years that were ostensibly intended for space debris removal and the refueling and servicing of satellites. But such dual-use satellites might also be employed to degrade or neutralize adversaries' satellites. Physicist and independent policy analyst Brian Chow wrote, "A Chinese spacecraft that has been bustling around snagging debris or providing tune-ups can be

MIXED MOMENTUM FOR A SPACE SERVICE, 2017–2018   107

readily diverted to stay arbitrarily close to one of our critical satellites." There was no space arms control agreement against tailgating or stalking. "An adversary could set up multiple space stalkers and, at a time of its choosing, move in and destroy multiple critical satellites ... far faster than we could activate our defenses." Chow viewed President Trump's directive on the Space Force as an opportunity to mitigate the chances of adversaries' worker-bee satellites "from turning into killer bees." Gone were the Cold War days when a tacit agreement existed between the two superpowers, described by Lt. Gen. Forrest S. McCartney as, "You don't tinker with my satellites and I don't tinker with yours." (Earlier in his career, McCartney served as a satellite controller; he later worked for General Schriever at Air Force Systems Command.)[67]

By the middle of 2018, Thompson was at the Pentagon in a newly confirmed position looking out for the interests of Air Force space. In his first assignment to the Pentagon in a thirty-three-year career to that point, Thompson began seeing problems there regarding space. He was "in the Pentagon, every single day, seeing the vacuum at the highest levels with respect to space knowledge, space expertise, and the way the conversations related to space just weren't happening." There was plenty of expertise in the air, land, maritime, and special operations realms, and cyber was increasing, but the three-star observed "a total vacuum" of space competency that affected conversations and decisions at the senior level on a daily basis.[68]

The experience pushed Thompson "to the point where I knew a Space Force was the right thing, because of what I had seen. . . . The only way to get space into the conversation, to get the focus and the advocacy it truly needed, was some form of the Space Force." In eighteen months, said Thompson, he had come all the way around on the Space Force. More than likely he was not alone, especially among those senior leaders who took heart at the serious planning efforts to minimize bureaucracy in the new service. Looking back from 2020, Stephen Whiting had been excited to learn of the attempt "to flatten the organization."[69]

Space Culture and Warfighting

For years, many in the space community and official Washington had recognized the importance of developing a distinctive space culture. While the

108 CHAPTER 4

two senior leaders in the Office of the Secretary of the Air Force between 2017 and 2019—Secretary Wilson and Undersecretary Donovan—did not see eye-to-eye on the need for a separate space service, they agreed largely on space culture. In an outgoing interview in 2019, Wilson shared her thoughts on culture: "I do think that there are cultural issues around space warfighting, but it doesn't have to do with it being a separate service. It has to do with this shift from being a utility provider to being a war fighter. And that cultural shift we're going to have to navigate no matter whether there is a space force as a separate service under the [Department of the] Air Force or whether it continues to be just a category within."[70]

One of the challenges Wilson perceived dealt with the space architecture the Air Force was building. A critical question to her was, "How do we change that architecture to account for the fact that this will be a contested domain? How can [space assets] protect themselves? I think chaff and flares. What is the threat?" Secretary Wilson viewed the new Space Development Agency's predilection for a system of unprotected, low-Earth orbiting satellites—useful for communications but not for other missions—as an example of failing to design "for a contested domain. . . . That's been one of my concerns."[71]

Wilson described a shift at Schriever AFB (later, Schriever Space Force Base) in which space operators spent four months on the operations floor followed by four months in upgrade training for warfighting. The latter, employing simulation and modeling, provided opportunities for operators to develop "the skills, abilities, [and] tactics to protect your asset on orbit from whatever . . . threat is coming at you." The mindset was much different from a peaceful domain in which "I'm not going to do something with my satellite that burns fuel or whatever."[72]

After moving from the Pentagon to the Mitchell Institute Space Power Advantage Research Center—which he led—former undersecretary Donovan reflected on space culture. Similar to Secretary Wilson's view, he was convinced the Space Force needed to put "the *arms* into the newest armed force [emphasis in original]." While there were pockets in the space community working to become an armed force, most space personnel still viewed themselves as enabling forces in support of warfighters in the other domains. The former F-15 fighter pilot and Air Force

MIXED MOMENTUM FOR A SPACE SERVICE, 2017-2018   109

undersecretary perceived the intelligence community's outsized influence in space in addition to the high classification of space matters as contributors to the reluctance to transition from enabling to warfighting. Donovan recalled the Air Force redesignation of air operations groups to air and space operations centers (2006–8), although dated, as having been a step in the right direction.[73]

From the beginning of the space era, the U.S. government studiously avoided publicizing the idea of outer space as an arena of potential armed conflict. In the 1950s, while President Dwight D. Eisenhower's administration publicly sought to preserve space for peaceful purposes, Eisenhower openly pursued a civilian satellite for scientific purposes and at the same time discreetly sought a military satellite under a classified program for strategic reconnaissance of Soviet intercontinental ballistic missile development. Following the downing of Francis Gary Powers' U-2 reconnaissance aircraft and the subsequent cessation of manned overflights of the Soviet Union's interior, the classified NRO launched its first spy satellite in 1962. With the end of the Cold War, the NRO was declassified in 1996, but the subject of space as a warfighting domain remained forbidden in public. The sentiment had continued as late as Heather Wilson's preparation for her confirmation hearing in May 2017. As she recalled,

> When I actually edited my opening statement for my confirmation hearing, I was not allowed to have *space* and *warfighting* in the same sentence. The previous administration did not want to publicly acknowledge that that was an issue—[a view that] came from the State Department [so they] kind of scratched it out of my draft statement. [They] passed it back to me through [the administrative assistant office] and I said, "Well, they're going to have to find somebody more senior to tell me I have to take it out," and . . . I kept it in.[74]

A career space officer, Major General Crosier seconded the incoming secretary's observation when he stated that in prior years, "We weren't allowed to say 'Warfighting' in any connection with anything about space. You couldn't have the word warfighting and the word space on the same page, let alone in the same paragraph." In 2017, warfighting was such a

CHAPTER 4

new, or radical, concept for the space domain that when the new secretary and General Goldfein testified together before the SASC the day after her swearing-in, the chief stated in no less than three similar phrases to the senators that the Air Force was "in this transition from a benign environment to a warfighting domain." A year later the *Congressional Research Service* remarked that some, both in and out of the military, "now increasingly refer to space as a 'warfighting domain.'" Likewise, Steve Kwast, a strong advocate for establishing a "civilizational foothold in space" as a means of promoting national prosperity, wrote in 2018 of approaching space "as an active warfighting domain—an arena of competition and conflict."[75]

It seemed that up to 2017, in the context of space as a warfighting domain, things had barely improved since 1957, when Bernard Schriever exhorted the Air Force to "move forward rapidly into space." The next day, Secretary of Defense Charles Wilson directed Schriever to avoid the word space "in all future speeches." As detailed by space historian David Spires, the defense policy voiced in that era was "not to consider satellites as weapon platforms." It had taken six decades to move beyond that official stance.[76]

Conclusion

By 2017 it had been more than a decade-and-a-half since the Rumsfeld Commission had sounded the tocsin on the potential for a space Pearl Harbor. The Russians and Chinese appeared to have gained ground on the United States by reorganizing their space and rocket forces in addition to demonstrating new capabilities in space, causing alarm amid national security space circles. For the fiscal 2018 defense bill, congressman Mike Rogers' subcommittee worked hard to insert language that advanced the cause of military space and set the conditions for a space corps or space force decision in the not-too-distant future. Within a year, an unconventional President Donald Trump unexpectedly reversed the course of his administration and the Pentagon, suddenly advocating for a Space Force; perhaps he had just completed his assessment in collaboration with the vice president and concluded the Space Force was the right answer for leveraging space in the nation's interests. In the spring and early summer of 2018 the president directed the Defense Department to begin planning for the Space Force, the details of which remained unknown—beginning with whether the sixth branch of the armed forces was to be established within the Department of the Air Force or in its own department. While presidential advocacy and Pentagon planning gained momentum for the new service, Congress had yet to act as the Constitution required. Meanwhile, after six decades of not speaking publicly of space as a warfighting domain, the Air Force and official Washington—perhaps led by the White House—began doing just that. This change in vocabulary and mindset was one element of an evolving change in space culture that space proponents had longed for.

5

STANDING UP, 2019—2020

In June of 2018 the president directed the DoD "to immediately begin the process necessary to establish a space force as the sixth branch of the armed forces." At the time, and for much of the next year, ideas and proposals abounded as to what a space force, or the space corps favored by the House of Representatives, meant, but the essential point was that Congress had to act in order to bring a new service into existence. As Lt. Gen. David D. Thompson—soon to be promoted to full general and to serve as vice chief of space operations, USSF—expressed, "Whatever members of Congress said was interesting, unless it was in law—then it was law." By the close of 2019, the White House, Department of Defense, and Congress were all to play their parts in establishing the new service, the USSF. By the end of 2020, although many important questions remained unanswered, there was modest progress toward consolidating the sixth branch.[1]

Part I: 2019

On 19 February 2019 the White House issued President Donald Trump's fourth space policy directive (SPD), "Establishment of the United States

Space Force" (see Appendix). Continuing the theme of SPD-3 from the previous June, the text stated,

> The Department of Defense shall take actions under existing authority to marshal its space resources to deter and counter threats in space, and to develop a legislative proposal to establish a United States Space Force as a sixth branch of the United States Armed Forces within the Department of the Air Force. This is an important step toward a future military department for space. Under this proposal, the [USSF] would be authorized to organize, train, and equip military space forces of the United States.[2]

Aside from the advocacy for a sixth armed force—responsible for the domain of space—SPD-4 clarified what had been murky for some months: initially, the Space Force was intended to be organized within the Department of the Air Force but with a view toward "a future military department for space," to be known as the Department of the Space Force. The initial arrangement was similar to the U.S. Marine Corps within the Department of the Navy. The text also made clear that, like the other services, USSF was to be responsible for supplying mission-ready space forces and capabilities to the combatant commands, particularly the U.S. Space Command, reestablished in August 2019 as the unified combatant command for space.[3] Although SPD-4 envisioned the senior officer of the USSF as "a Chief of Staff of the Space Force," the designation that was later applied to Gen. John W. Raymond's position was "Chief of Space Operations, United States Space Force."[4]

PLANNING FOR THE SPACE FORCE

With the release of Trump's SPD-4, the Pentagon went into high gear for the planning required to turn vision into reality. Two days later, Acting Secretary of Defense Patrick Shanahan issued a memorandum to the military department secretaries, the chairman of the Joint Chiefs of Staff (CJCS), and other senior leaders directing the secretary of the Air Force "to organize and lead a team of civilian and military subject matter experts from across the DoD to conduct the detailed planning

114 CHAPTER 5

necessary to establish the U.S. Space Force." All addressees were to support this effort.[5]

ENTER MAJ. GEN. CLINT CROSIER

Clinton E. Crosier, a 1987 aerospace engineering graduate of Iowa State University, had command experience at the space squadron, group, and wing levels. Crosier led the implementation of the Air Force Warfighting Integration Capability (AFWIC) in 2018 at Chief Goldfein's request. As Major General Crosier recalled in a 2020 interview, in December 2018 the new organization "stood up" and he returned to his job as "the Deputy A5" (strategic plans/requirements). Shortly thereafter, he secured General Goldfein's approval for a highly anticipated June 2019 retirement date. It was not to be.[6]

At the end of a staff meeting in February, Goldfein asked to see Crosier in his office for a minute. The conversation, according to Crosier, went something like this:

> Goldfein: "Clint, you've probably heard the President talking about the Space Force, right? . . . And he's . . . getting closer . . . to directing the DOD to establish a legislative proposal to submit to Capitol Hill for consideration of authorization of the U.S. Space Force."
>
> Crosier: "And I'm taking all this in and I say, 'Okay, yes, Chief, I understand. I've been watching the news.'"
>
> Goldfein: "Congress has talked about let's study this for a year, then let's implement part of it for a year."
>
> Crosier: "He said the President was so concerned about the threat and the timing. The President doesn't want to wait for all that to take place. Again, this is February of 2019. The President wants a plan for how we would stand up the Space Force. And he wants it in 30 days."[7]

For a second Clint Crosier thought to himself, *Wow, Chief, you got quite a problem on your hands!* A moment later, "I realized this is exactly why I'm standing here in the Chief's office. So, the Chief said to me, 'The Secretary and I have talked, and given the success in standing up the

AFWIC, given that you're a career space officer, we think there's really nobody to take on this planning effort but you.'"

At that point, the major general felt the need to gently remind his chief that just forty days earlier he had approved Crosier's retirement request. Goldfein had not forgotten, but Crosier's well-deserved retirement was eventually pushed back by more than a year.[8]

THE U.S. SPACE FORCE PLANNING TASK FORCE

Within about a week of his conversation in the chief's office, on 22 February, Secretary Heather A. Wilson formally appointed Crosier as the director, Space Force Planning Task Force. Quickly, Crosier pulled together a team. Officially, they had thirty days, although Crosier considered he actually had about thirty-six days if one counted from his impromptu meeting in the chief's office. In response to Acting Secretary Shanahan's directive on 21 February, the next day Wilson had followed with her own memorandum to her fellow secretaries, the CJCS, and other Pentagon leaders, which stated: "I am establishing a Space Force Planning Task Force to begin conducting the detailed planning necessary to establish the [USSF] when the legislation proposed by the President is enacted." Crosier's task force had until 22 March to deliver an Initial Work Plan "that lays out key phases of transition from Pre-establishment through Full Operational Capability," as well as key decisions in each phase, associated actions, timelines, and milestones. Further, Wilson wanted the team to identify "critical actions required to stand up an initial Space Force Staff by 1 October 2019." A tall order.[9]

Over the next four weeks, Crosier's team of roughly eighteen full-time members took a macro-level approach to the requirement "to declare [full operational capability] of a space force five years out," likening it, in a sense, to the acquisition of a new satellite. As Crosier described in 2020, "If I'm going to launch the satellite five years from now, then . . . here's where I need to have the design phase complete, here's where I need to have the systems integration phase complete, here's where I'm going to start bending metal, here's where I'm going to start doing integration and testing. And we took the same approach." The task force's director continued, providing an overview of how in less than thirty pages his team had walked through and identified for each phase "the entry and exit criteria," key conditions, decisions to be made, and "who owns this particular phase." The task force put it together and coordinated it through the joint staff and the services. Secretary Wilson gave it her initial approval "literally on day 30." She then transmitted it to the acting defense secretary; Shanahan concurred.[10]

In the heady days of late winter and early spring in Washington, it was never as though space force issues were the only thing on the agenda of the Air Force secretary or the Pentagon. In mid-March, a week prior to the completion of the Initial Work Plan for the Space Force, while the Air Force's senior leaders addressed the impact of the president's FY2020 budget on the force, the issue of "Military Service by Transgender Persons and Persons with Gender Dysphoria" made the list of the department's top public affairs issues. In March 2017, Senate Armed Services Committee (SASC) chairman John McCain (R-Ariz.) had written to Heather Wilson—then the nominee for secretary of the Air Force—charging her with focusing on warfighting and dispensing with "social experimentation that distracts your people from their primary purpose." By 2019 the venerable senator was gone, but even the priorities of Space Force planning and the budget, plus the drawing down of U.S. combat operations in central-southwest Asia, could not preclude matters of social experimentation from requiring senior Pentagon leaders' attention to some degree. Such distractions from warfighting and readiness were all too common.[11]

TASK FORCE TANGO

Major General Crosier's planning task force was not the only one initiated in early 2019 in support of the proposed Space Force. While Crosier was tapped by the CSAF and the secretary for his planning effort, Task Force Tango—so named simply because the preceding task force at AFSPC had used the designation Sierra—was an Air Force Space Command initiative. The two began at nearly the same time, just after SPD-4's issuance: Crosier on about 22 February, Tango on the 28th. Maj. Gen. John E. Shaw, the AFSPC deputy commander, planned to lead Tango initially, but his duties and those of the command's strategic requirements director, Brig. Gen. William J. Liquori, required a handoff. They looked to Col. Jack Fischer, the vice commander of the 50th Space Wing, situated at nearby Schriever AFB. For the next month, Fischer led a team of space planners who did their best to envision what the structure of the Space Force should look like. Given little guidance at the outset, he expressed later, "It's exciting to see [what] an empty white board and 20–30 folks" can come up with for the foundation of something new. While Fischer counted his part-time task force members, there were only about ten to twelve full-timers. For at least part of the year, three colonels (O-5 or O-6) comprised the core of a "smaller Tango," as physicist and career space officer Lt. Col. Charles Cooper recalled. Cooper viewed Colonel Fischer as a great motivator with a deep sense of the historic nature of the opportunity before them, who provided broad guidance and then allowed his team to do the job—which included "dreaming big and building a new Service from scratch."[12]

Fischer offered his view on the differences between Tango and Crosier's planning: first, Crosier's team had "very little space operator input," something that Fischer's team enjoyed; and second, Crosier's team, working in Washington, had "the tougher job of navigating a political minefield." Lieutenant Colonel Cooper added that, from his perspective, Crosier's Pentagon team was "under much more tightly constrained direction," apparently to keep the Space Force as small as possible, which was part and parcel of Washington politics. In any case, Cooper felt that the individual relationships between the players on both teams were strong and supportive. As a NASA astronaut, Colonel Fischer's perspective was different than many, perhaps facilitating his opinion that they were "not just reorganizing Air Force Space Command. You are building the foundation for a future force that is going to change humanity." If Crosier had a tall order, Fischer's self-assigned order was taller.[13]

The only other full colonel on the team was Col. Anthony Lujan, who took the handoff from Fischer in mid-March. An air guardsman from New York who served on the AFSPC staff, Lujan also provided his perspective on the role of Tango and Crosier's task force. In a May 2019 interview, Lujan recalled that initially, "there was a lot of flail, a lot of who's doing what" with both efforts, in Washington and Colorado—perhaps to no one's surprise. Some, if not many, issues overlapped between the work of both teams. But generally speaking, Tango focused on the field command structure, including roles and responsibilities; Crosier's team dealt mainly with the macro-organizational piece. Tango also handled tasks from Headquarters Air Force pertaining to various staff functions such as intelligence and operations. Colonel Lujan felt the significance of Tango, including the give-and-take discussions and adjudications on certain matters was "actually making it easier for our respective staffs at [Headquarters Air Force] and here at [AFSPC]" as they coordinated on building the not-yet-authorized Space Force. Tango's lone Army member, Maj. Jerry Drew—a space operations officer and graduate of the Army's highly respected School of Advanced Military Studies program—expected it should take at least four years to reach a full-size Space Force staff. He also felt "this little group of planners will probably have . . . a disproportionate say in the future of the Service."[14]

In the end, Tango and Crosier's planners dovetailed. As Lieutenant General Thompson summarized, "Clint was the overall lead, but his primary focus was up here in the Pentagon in the macro sense, and basically subbed out the task of figuring out the field designs to Task Force Tango. . . . It was a great arrangement."[15]

GARRISON SUPPORT

A field command structure for the Space Force also required planning for base operating support (BOS) functions, or garrison support. In the short term, USSF expected the Air Force to provide "more than 75 percent of its enabling functions to significantly reduce cost and avoid duplication." The Space Force was to "leverage" the Air Force for support with logistics, BOS, civilian personnel management, business systems, information technology, and other functions.[16]

In early 2020, the chief of the civil engineer division at Headquarters USSF weighed in on BOS. Michelle Linn, with twenty-four years' experience on the AFSPC engineering staff, noted that SPD-4 called for combat support elements to transfer to the Space Force.[17] General Raymond's intent was to keep USSF as lean and agile as possible and to avoid a large bureaucracy. Linn observed that "there was always this term that the Space Force would leverage the Air Force. But nobody ever defined 'leverage,'" before adding, "BOS is kind of a squishy term," plus it encompassed many different programs. People "would throw around the term BOS," as well as leverage, which some interpreted as, "We're going to be completely hands-off and the Air Force is going to do that for us, and we're going to just focus on operations," a dreamy expectation. Moreover, when the National Defense Authorization Act was signed in December 2019, "It was pretty much silent on BOS," Linn said; a surprise to many including herself. For those and other reasons, much work remained to be done in terms of settling on garrison support at USSF installations.[18]

Space Force leaders commented on the significance of the new service having its own bases. "From a culture perspective," voiced civil engineer chief Linn, "owning real property and saying 'this is a Space Force base' is huge." Major General Whiting brought up a related issue, adding, "As we transition to our new installation commands, for example, at Patrick AFB, we're going to have a black-suited Space Force commander of that installation." But aside from that officer, "virtually every other person that works running that installation will be an Airman [USAF]," mainly under the medical or mission support group. "But we want those Airmen to feel like they're not just people providing support, they are a part of Space Force." Perhaps, mused Whiting, the Navy-Marine Corps model might prove useful, as he reflected on the case that Navy corpsmen assigned to Marine Corps units wore the Marine uniform.[19]

One tangible cultural issue at Peterson AFB involved the collocation of Air Force Space Command headquarters and the Army's component, the U.S. Army Space and Missile Defense Command. The two headquarters buildings were not far apart, but they existed as worlds unto themselves. As it occurred to Army space officer Jerry Drew in 2019, "There's no direct sidewalk from the front door of Air Force Space Command to Army Space [and Missile Defense] Command. You have to go out, [and walk] all around to the edges of the diagonal." It was a chore to get from one building to the other. Major Drew had assisted in the planning for the U.S. Space Command (USSPACECOM), which, on 29 August 2019 was established as the eleventh unified combatant command in the force structure by Secretary of Defense Mark T. Esper's signature at a White House ceremony. Later, Drew recalled, "Not all combatant commands have the luxury of having their service components a hundred yards from one another." If he

120 CHAPTER 5

might have recommended two things to the new USSPACECOM commander, it seemed likely that one was the sidewalk, and the other was to "get your people badge access to both buildings, so you can just walk in and talk to each other."[20]

Space Force bases posed other issues that required deft handling. One concern was of promotion or career advancement, generally, for Air Force uniformed personnel assigned to a base where the Space Force commanded the installation. A legitimate question was, will they be taken care of when it comes to promotion? One idea considered was to civilianize the majority of support personnel at USSF bases so as not to hurt the careers of uniformed members who belonged to a different branch. As in the Patrick example, Space Force planners wanted certain support units to belong to USSF while consisting, to a large degree in some cases, of Air Force personnel. Again, the Navy-Marine Corps model seemed a hopeful alternative, without resorting to civilianization.[21]

OTHER SPACE-RELATED MATTERS, SPRING 2019

India's ASAT Test, March 2019

The growing space threat provided much of the strategic context for the U.S. Space Force's establishment. Sometimes even an ally's actions in space highlighted the dangers, if indirectly. Ever since the Chinese ASAT test of 2007, that alarming incident—both for the space debris it produced and for its demonstration of an offensive weapons capability—became part of the standard argument for a fundamental shift in viewing space as no longer benign but, rather, as a warfighting domain. The United States was not the only Western nation to undergo strategic and policy changes stemming largely from the destruction of a defunct Chinese weather satellite that had shocked many, but not all, space organizations and observers around the world. Such changes required long years to be realized, however. On 27 March 2019, in a test that appeared to have been approved two years earlier, the Indian government announced the successful test of an ASAT weapon that hit and destroyed an Indian Microsat-R satellite earlier that day. One scholar with the Carnegie Endowment for International Peace underscored the basis for the test, which was dubbed Mission Shakti: "It was precipitated entirely by the Chinese demonstration of its ASAT capabilities over a decade ago . . . that China was the intended audience of the Indian demonstration was perhaps New Delhi's worst kept secret."[22]

While demonstrating that India was capable of responding in kind to any potential ASAT attack from Beijing, the Indians were careful not to antagonize their Western allies in the process. The Indians launched the target satellite into a low altitude, sun-synchronous orbit, weeks before the test. Further, the satellite was smaller than other Indian communications satellites. Those two factors ensured the space debris created by the strike must deteriorate quickly, in weeks or a few months, in contrast with the decades or even centuries from China's 2007 test; and there was not much of it, some 400 trackable pieces compared with 3,000 in 2007. Most space analysts, Ashley Tellis argued, "are agreed that the Indian test, however undesirable, did not compare with the Chinese test in terms of the damage done to the space environment." The Indian Space Research Organization (ISRO), one of the world's six largest space agencies, with "huge stakes" in the peaceful use of space—including distance education and telemedicine—was by no means unconcerned with the test's consequences. But the ISRO's as well as the government's greater interest, most likely, was to ensure New Delhi could protect its space assets that China might otherwise hold at risk, if not to deter Beijing.[23]

Although the Indian demonstration certainly met its technical objective, which offered its government the option of holding Chinese satellites at risk, New Delhi's newfound capability was unlikely to neutralize China's growing space threat. Since facing worldwide opprobrium for its kinetic test in 2007, Beijing had developed an array of non-kinetic counter-space capabilities, including sophisticated cyber attacks against ground stations to corrupt or hijack the telemetry and tracking of spacecraft on orbit; and ground-, air-, and space-based radio frequency jamming that targeted the up-, down-, and cross-links that control space systems or the transmission of data from space. Such capabilities could be considered a twenty-first century example of Sun Tzu's timeless counsel on warfare: "Subtle and insubstantial, the expert leaves no trace; divinely mysterious, he is inaudible." The above realities, and others beyond the scope of this work, were what Carnegie author Ashley Tellis called, "Hard Pills to Swallow," for the

122   CHAPTER 5

Indians. The degree to which other Western space powers, including the United States, were perhaps at risk for some unpleasant pill-swallowing of their own, seemed a legitimate question.[24]

Follow-on Duties for Space Force Planners

In early April, Clint Crosier's planning task force completed the formal coordination of its Initial Work Plan across the defense department. By 22 April, all critical comments had been resolved; Secretary Wilson approved the plan, but that was not all. As Crosier recalled, she said, "I think your task force is not just [to] build me a 30-day plan and turn it in and now we're done. It's [to] continue on with all necessary and required planning to preserve the ability to implement rapidly, if authorized." That became the task force's guidance that Crosier gave to the team and that he repeated in writing to Wilson and the deputy secretary of defense, both of whom approved. Crosier translated that into a plan that said "if Congress authorizes we will be prepared to stand up an Initial Space Force [Staff, or ISFS] headquarters within 90 days. 200 people within 90 days."[25]

One of the next functions was to determine the roles and billets for the 200-member ISFS. By mid-April, Crosier's task force completed its coordination with the Air Staff "2-Letters" regarding the ISFS. Unfortunately, Major General Crosier acknowledged there was a single 2-Letter who, exhibiting what Crosier called "standard organizational behavior . . . non-concurred with every single product we put out in coordination. . . . We were ultimately able to adjudicate it all, even though it sometimes had to go to the three- or four-star level." In at least the case of one Air Staff directorate, going to the top was Crosier's only recourse for securing a commitment for much-needed personnel, billets, and funds should the Space Force stand up. It was perhaps amusing in hindsight that Crosier recalled other Air Staff officers that took the alternate view, "Yeah, this'll never happen and where do I sign?" Meanwhile, Crosier's original retirement date came and went. He kept quiet. He and his team pressed on with their work.[26]

The initial staff was planned as a provisional headquarters and planning element that, upon the service's establishment, was, first, to "take over all planning and execution activity from USSF Planning Task Force"; and,

Sen. Robert C. "Bob" Smith (R-NH)
Official portrait, U.S. Senate

Gen. Michael E. Ryan, Air Force chief of staff (1997–2001) *Official Air Force photo*

Secretary of Defense Donald H. Rumsfeld (2001–2006) *Official DoD photo*

Gen. John P. Jumper, Air Force chief of staff (2001–2005), praised the military members in harm's way fighting the war on terrorism, during keynote speech at the Armed Services YMCA's annual recognition luncheon at Capitol Hill, 12 May 2005. Jumper also praised those volunteers who support ASYMCA programs that show young service members there are those who care and want to help. *Official DoD photo by Rudi Williams*

The USS *Lake Erie* (CG 70) launched a Standard Missile-3 at a nonfunctioning National Reconnaissance Office satellite as it traveled in space at more than 17,000 mph over the Pacific Ocean on 20 February 2008. The objective was to rupture the satellite's fuel tank to dissipate the approximately 1,000 pounds of hydrazine, a hazardous material, before it entered Earth's atmosphere. *Lake Erie* is an Aegis-class guided missile cruiser. *Official U.S. Navy photo*

President Barack Obama toured the commercial rocket processing facility of Space Exploration Technologies, known as SpaceX, along with Elon Musk, SpaceX CEO, at Cape Canaveral Air Force Station, Florida, on 15 April 2010. Obama also visited the NASA Kennedy Space Center to deliver remarks on the new course intended by the administration to maintain U.S. leadership in human space flight. *Official NASA photo by Bill Ingalls*

Gen. John E. Hyten, Commander, U.S. Strategic Command at Minot AFB, North Dakota, 6 June 2017. Hyten presented the 5th Bomb Wing with the 2017 Omaha Trophy in the Strategic Bomber category and recognized multiple Team Minot airmen for their mission contributions. *Official Air Force photo by SrA J. T. Armstrong*

Congressman Mike Rogers (R-Ala.) *(left)* arriving at Air University to discuss the new Cyber University initiative with Lt. Gen. Steven Kwast, Commander and President, Air University, Maxwell AFB, Alabama, on 21 August 2015. *Official Air Force photo by Melanie Rodgers Cox*

Launch of *New Shepard* reusable launch vehicle, 19 June 2016 *Courtesy of Blue Origin*

Left to right: Lt. Col. Peter Garretson, Rep. Mike Rogers, and Dr. Michael V. Smith met at an event in Montgomery, Alabama, 31 July 2018. Garretson and Smith served on the faculty at nearby Maxwell AFB's Air Command and Staff College. Lieutenant General Kwast brought Garretson and Smith with him to discuss their ongoing efforts to help lay the groundwork for a space service and to answer the congressman's questions. *Courtesy of Peter Garretson*

Rep. Jim Cooper (D-Tenn.)
Official portrait, U.S. House of Representatives

Dr. Heather A. Wilson, President, University of Texas at El Paso, 25 May 2021. Wilson served as the secretary of the Air Force from May 2017 to May 2019. *Courtesy of Heather A. Wilson*

Acting Secretary of the Air Force Matthew P. Donovan spoke to Air Force Ball attendees at South Point Hotel and Casino in Las Vegas, Nevada, 21 September 2019. Donovan spoke about the Air Force's past, present, and future and recognized airmen from Nellis and Creech Air Force bases. *Official Air Force photo by SrA Olivia Grooms*

Vice President Mike Pence congratulated Gen. John W. "Jay" Raymond after swearing him in as the first chief of space operations during a ceremony in Washington, DC, 14 January 2020. *Official Air Force photo by Andy Morataya*

Maj. Gen. Clinton E. "Clint" Crosier *Official Air Force photo*

The Indian Defence Research and Development Organisation successfully launched the Ballistic Missile Defence Interceptor missile in an antisatellite (A-SAT) missile test code named Mission Shakti from the Dr. A. P. J. Abdul Kalam Island, Odisha, 27 March 2019. The missile engaged an Indian orbiting target satellite in low-Earth orbit (LEO) in a "hit to kill" mode. *Official photo, courtesy of the Indian Ministry of Defence*

Lt. Gen. Stephen N. Whiting, commander of Space Operations Command, officiated at a ceremony in which Delta 6 airmen at Peterson AFB, Colorado, were inducted into the U.S. Space Force, 3 February 2021. *Official U.S. Space Force photo by SSgt J. T. Armstrong*

Lt. Gen. David T. Thompson, U.S. Space Force vice commander, talked about the future of the Space Force at the Air Force Association's Air Warfare Symposium in Orlando, Florida, 27 February 2020. The Air Warfare Symposium is a premier event for the aerospace and defense industry geared toward the professional development of Air Force officers and enlisted members, civilians, retirees, and veterans. *Official Air Force photo by TSgt Jonathan Snyder*

Secretary of the Air Force Barbara M. Barrett (October 2019–January 2021) *Official Air Force photo*

Left to right: Gen. John Raymond, Commander, U.S. Space Command and Air Force Space Command, Secretary of the Air Force Barbara Barrett, and U.S. Air Force Chief of Staff Gen. David Goldfein signed memoranda related to the authorization of the U.S. Space Force on 20 December 2019. Later that day, the president appointed Raymond as chief of space operations for the newest branch of service. *Official Air Force photo by TSgt Robert Barnett*

President Donald Trump signed S.1790, the National Defense Authorization Act for Fiscal Year 2020, as the First Lady and senior leaders looked on, 20 December 2019, at Joint Base Andrews, Maryland. The act authorized a budget that supported the U.S. armed forces and postured the Air Force to meet the requirements of the National Defense Strategy. *Official Air Force photo by A1C Spencer Slocum*

CMSgt of the Space Force Roger A. Towberman spoke at the Air Force Association's Air, Space & Cyber Conference at National Harbor, Maryland, 21 September 2021. The ASC conference is a professional development seminar open to DoD personnel and features forums, speeches, workshops, and a technology exposition. *Official Air Force photo by SSgt Jeremy L. Mosier*

STANDING UP, 2019–2020 123

second, to develop the processes and expertise to assume the organize-train-equip functions "from the Air Staff notionally one year later." Of the first 200 personnel, the Air Force was to provide 150; the Army, 24; Navy, 14; Office of the Secretary of Defense, 8; and 3 others from the Joint Staff or other defense department agencies. There were three general officer (GO) billets and one senior executive service (SES), a civilian position.[27]

Air Chiefs Confer on Space

Also in April, in a one-day gathering at Colorado Springs, CSAF General Goldfein hosted the air chiefs from eleven other nations to discuss space matters. Air Force Public Affairs noted the event was "the first time air chiefs from other countries had come together in such numbers, at the same time, to talk about space." Australia, Canada, Denmark, France, Germany, Italy, Japan, Netherlands, New Zealand, Norway, and the United Kingdom, were represented. General John W. "Jay" Raymond, the Air Force Space Command commander, also attended. After the meeting, Goldfein stated, "Our focus really was to get a common understanding of where each of us is on this journey and leave with a sense of the way ahead." In addition to hearing a presentation by each of the air chiefs, the leaders discussed topics such as defining "norms" for space activities, normalizing space situational awareness and intelligence sharing, and ideas for better partnering among allies. At the same time, General Goldfein was careful to emphasize the U.S. Air Force's commitment to the peaceful and responsible use of space, which he considered "part of the global commons." Perhaps in part encouraged by the partnering among allies, three months later French president Emmanuel Macron announced the establishment of a space command within the French Air Force with the primary mission of defense of the nation's satellites. In September 2020, the country's air force was redesignated the French Air and Space Force. Meanwhile, in November 2019, the North Atlantic Treaty Organization—according to the *UK Space Power Joint Doctrine Publication 0-40*, released in September 2022—"formally announced it considered space to be an operational domain." The UK endorsed that approach.[28]

On the very day the air chiefs conferred, in Washington the SASC held its first major hearing on the proposed Space Force. Secretary Wilson

124   CHAPTER 5

voiced her support for the proposal, acknowledging her earlier opposition. While the lame-duck status of both Wilson and Gen. Joseph F. Dunford Jr., the outgoing JCS chairman, may not have helped the cause, the senators had no shortage of legitimate questions about the Space Force. According to Air Force Public Affairs, "Senators were skeptical whether a Space Force is the answer." The two events that day made for an interesting juxtaposition.[29]

CONGRESS ACTS ON THE SPACE FORCE

In 2017, the House Armed Services Committee's Strategic Forces Subcommittee had led the way in the NDAA process that lifted the hopes of many for a future space corps. That year, Rep. Mike Rogers (R-Ala.) was the chairman, Rep. Jim Cooper (D-Tenn.) the ranking member. Two years later, the results of the 2018 congressional election had reversed their roles. But it was still the same two men running the same subcommittee that was leading the way on space. Between 2014 and 2016, at least two events deepened Congress' concern of U.S. potential adversaries in space, particularly China and Russia. One was a classified briefing that President Obama directed be given to Congress, to which Mike Rogers confessed, "It scared the ---- out of us!" The other was a classified tabletop exercise (known as TTX) in which things went badly for the Blue Team's satellites. Since that time, the congressional duo had worked long and hard toward a space corps. In May–June 2019, both chambers' armed services committees agreed to support an independent space service—the House still referred to a space corps, the Senate to a space force. The upper chamber favored disestablishing Air Force Space Command and redesignating it as the U.S. Space Force, which in the end was essentially what happened.[30]

While Cooper made it known that the Space Force had not been "a Trump idea" to begin with—which was true enough—his colleague, Rogers, credited the president with having "re-energized" the idea of the Space Force, providing "a second wind." Rogers gratefully acknowledged Vice President Pence for bringing around the SASC to support the new branch of service. Both Matthew Donovan—from June to October 2019, the acting secretary of the Air Force—and Barbara M. Barrett, since

STANDING UP, 2019–2020

October the Air Force secretary, had lent their considerable influence in support, said Rogers. At the outset of his four-month stint, Donovan—who had favored a space force for two decades—published an opinion piece on *Fox News*, stating the best way to "secure the final frontier for our citizens, friends, and allies" was through the Space Force, "because it's the best way to protect America and dominate future warfare." Retired Lt. Col. Peter Garretson considered that piece had facilitated the "sea-change" in terms of Air Force support for the Space Force. Six weeks later, in an article posted at the War on the Rocks foreign policy and national security platform, the acting secretary argued strenuously and at greater length for the Space Force.[31]

As the 2020 defense budget wound its way through both legislative chambers, it seemed for a time to many advocates of a space branch that it was unlikely to happen that year. In 2019, Col. Stuart Pettis, a career space officer—who commanded an air expeditionary support squadron in Iraq during the surge (2007–8)—worked at the Pentagon doing force development and career field management for space. He was keeping up with Space Force "but wasn't knee deep in it," Pettis recalled. Then in September, Major General Crosier said basically, "It's going to happen and we need to get serious." Immediately, Pettis acquired a second job, "doing Space Force full-time." But then Washington politics kicked in and the likelihood of getting the Space Force appeared to dim. "But if you didn't do it this year . . . you go into an election cycle and nobody's going to want to do it. So, we thought we were pretty much done in early November," Pettis recounted. At almost the same time, Lt. Gen. David Thompson, who felt like he was on a rollercoaster all year regarding the chances of getting the Space Force, remembered hearing the chances of an NDAA had dropped—impeachment hearings began in November—or if it happened, it was expected to be "a skinny NDAA, which isn't going to have a Space Force . . . there's no way this is going to happen." Between Thanksgiving and early December, Maj. Gen. Stephen Whiting recalled having the same sinking feeling.[32]

But to the surprise of many both in and outside of Washington, it happened. As *Space News* reported, in the end, "The language in this year's NDAA is very similar to the Space Corps bill from two years ago. The only

126   CHAPTER 5

difference between the Space Corps of 2017 and the Space Force of 2019 is," as Representative Jim Cooper put it, "'just one word.'" On 11 December, the full House gave its approval to the fiscal 2020 NDAA—with the U.S. Space Force included—by a vote of 377–48. Six days later, the Senate followed suit, 86–8. All that remained was for President Trump to sign the legislation into law.[33]

SECRETARY OF THE AIR FORCE BARBARA M. BARRETT (2019–2021)

Barbara Barrett had established roots in Arizona. In the 1970s she earned three degrees from Arizona State University: bachelor's, master's, and juris doctor. Following her education, Barrett's commercial and civil U.S. government sector, as well as her personal experience, was as varied as one could imagine, ranging from corporate law in the Southwest to senior positions with the U.S. Civil Aeronautics board and the Federal Aviation Administration, in addition to private law practice. During the George W. Bush administration, she served as senior adviser to the U.S. Mission to the United Nations in New York (2006), and, later, as ambassador to Finland (2008–9). From 2013 to 2017 Barrett served four terms as chairman of the board for the Aerospace Corporation in El Segundo, California. As an aviator, she was instrument-rated and was trained and certified for space flight.[34]

Her path to becoming the secretary of the Air Force was no less unique than her career. After stepping down from the Aerospace Corporation, Barbara Barrett was not looking for another senior government job. Far from it. But in early March 2019, when Heather Wilson announced her impending departure as the Air Force Secretary, slated for 31 May, Barrett quickly received communications from two prominent fellow Arizonans: retired Maj. Gen. Donald W. Shepperd, former director of the Air National Guard, and serving U.S. Senator Martha McSally (R-Ariz.). Both vigorously exhorted her to pursue the Secretary's job. However, Barrett was "pretty disinclined" to do so, she recalled. Secretary Wilson also contacted Barrett and encouraged her to pursue the office.[35]

At that point, one of her many previous leadership roles entered the picture. During the second half of George W. Bush's tenure, Barrett had joined Laura Bush and the wife of Afghan president Hamid Karzai in

STANDING UP, 2019–2020

establishing the U.S.-Afghan Women's Council, which sought to increase opportunities for Afghan women in healthcare and education and to provide them economic empowerment and civil sphere participation options as well. Under the women's council, Barrett developed a program for Afghan businesswomen that later became affiliated with Arizona State University. Goldman Sachs of New York picked up on her curriculum, committed $100 million, and initiated its own program for the advancement of 10,000 women worldwide. Needless to say, when Barrett received word from Secretary Wilson that Ivanka Trump, the president's daughter, also was involved and wanted to hear about Barrett's program—called Project Artemis—Barrett was all in. On the Thursday prior to their scheduled meeting on Monday, 20 May, Barrett was told offhandedly that following her meeting with Ivanka, "her father would like to see you right after." "I was then a bit suspicious," she confessed.[36]

On the 20th, Barrett had back-to-back meetings in the West Wing of the White House. First, she met with Ivanka Trump to discuss Project Artemis and other women's programs. Then Barrett met with President Trump. When that conversation ended, the president extended his hand and said, "Congratulations," because he would nominate her as the next Secretary of the Air Force. The next day, 21 May, was Secretary Wilson's farewell at Andrews AFB, Maryland. Shortly after Secretary Wilson's farewell—which Barrett attended—the Secretary-designate received a congratulatory call from Governor Doug Ducey of Arizona who had seen a White House tweet announcing the president's intent to nominate her. Barrett appreciated that President Trump had waited until after Wilson's farewell event to announce his intention: it was "a great courtesy on the part of the White House," she said. A White House announcement prior to completion of the requisite and time-consuming background checks was unusual. Despite having been through about a dozen confirmations in her career, this U.S. Senate confirmation was no less time-consuming, and on 18 October 2019 Barbara Barrett was administratively sworn in as the Secretary of the Air Force.[37]

As events transpired, there were only two months before the U.S. Space Force was to be established, but no one yet knew if it was going to happen. Congress had not passed the national defense authorization act and the

128 CHAPTER 5

Space Force's status remained uncertain. Wanting to be prepared, Barrett exhorted Clint Crosier's planning team to "sharpen your pencil on the timeframe," and "expedite, expedite." Back in the spring, Secretary Wilson asked for a plan for a 200-member Initial Space Force Staff within 90 days. Now prudence called for a plan for an initial staff, not months after the NDAA was signed but weeks or even days after the Space Force's establishment.[38]

SIDE-BY-SIDE WITH GENERAL RAYMOND

A U.S. Army aviator-turned-space officer, Col. Brian Bolio viewed his year-and-a-half with General Raymond as an extraordinary leadership lab. A West Pointer who flew Blackhawk helicopters before moving into the Army's space command, Bolio became the four-star's executive officer following a phone interview with him at the start of 2019. Colonel Bolio recalled his boss dealt with him as well as with his personal security detail like family, and despite the long work hours they often exercised and went out to eat together. On one of the first trips Bolio took with his boss, they visited Boston, where Raymond met with top-tier scientists and engineers at MIT and the Lincoln Laboratories. Years earlier, Raymond had attended the Naval War College in Newport, Rhode Island, and there developed a taste for seafood. When Raymond asked Bolio to find them a good place for some seafood, Bolio knew just where to go. Calling his mother who lived nearby in historic Concord, Massachusetts, Bolio picked up about fifteen lobsters and ten pounds of clams and led the general's entourage to his mom's home. She was thrilled to work her magic in the kitchen for General Raymond, his security detail, and her son. It was a win and helped Bolio to earn even more trust with his boss.[39]

20 DECEMBER SIGNING CEREMONY FOR NDAA AND U.S. SPACE FORCE

Months later, when it became clear there was to be a U.S. Space Force, Bolio remembered his and the staff's uncertainty whether General Raymond was to be named the chief of space operations (CSO). Clearly, he had the inside track but nothing official had been announced. As the NDAA worked its way through Congress and finally arrived at the president's desk for signature, Raymond and Bolio were among the throng expected to attend the signing ceremony. Not only was the NDAA's signing a big event in itself but on this occasion, when the president signed and thereby enacted the next year's defense bill, his signature also established the U.S. Space Force—which took center stage.[40]

Bolio recalled, "The morning of December 20th, we didn't know who the CSO was. [Raymond] didn't know he was going to be on stage that night." When they arrived and Bolio inquired of a Pentagon protocol staffer where his boss was to sit, he was directed to the seat between Ivanka Trump and the vice president. Bolio turned to Raymond: "Well, hey, sir, I guess you're going to be the Chief of Space Operations."[41]

Being inside the hangar "felt like a rock concert, music blaring," according to Bolio. Clint Crosier—who shook hands with the vice president before the ceremony and with the president afterward—described that night's event as "electricity in the air," and among the crowd "was a bunch of space geeks, all of whom had worked [toward] this for the last year." Lieutenant General Thompson likened the evening to "the day I got married, the day my daughter got married. . . . You kind of feel numb and tingly, and it just whizzes by . . . and you just wish you could crystallize in your mind the memories of that day." Everyone who was there seemed to remember vividly the once-in-a-lifetime experience. And with the stroke of a pen, President Trump not only signed into law the $738 billion defense bill; the United States Space Force was born. Whether or not it was a commentary on the seriousness—or the lack thereof—of what had transpired nearby at the Capitol two days earlier, amid the excitement of the signing ceremony if any attendees were distressed over the president of the United States having been impeached by the U.S. House of Representatives . . . it did not show.[42]

The night was exciting for many space professionals who were unable to be there. While General Raymond was in Washington, the AFSPC deputy commander, Maj. Gen. Stephen Whiting, remained at Peterson AFB, Colorado. Someone came up with the idea to open the headquarters building and invite the families to join in the event, having it piped in to watch on television. The protocol office got a sheet cake, which was a great idea, but the "baby cake"—as Col. Suzanne Streeter called it— was not nearly enough for the several hundred that turned out.[43] The U.S.

130 CHAPTER 5

Army Space and Missile Defense Command, whose headquarters was next door to the AFSPC headquarters building, joined as well, including its commanding general, James H. Dickinson, and several other senior leaders. Most important, though, the evening became an informal celebration for space professionals and their spouses and children. General Raymond's wife, Molly, brought balloons. Major General Whiting made a few remarks, conveying the historic nature of the event and "how proud we were of our legacy." Then he cut the cake. Several months later he recounted,

> We were standing in what, up to that very moment had been the headquarters of Air Force Space Command for 30 years, and I was in my [tactical field uniform] wearing my AFSPC patch . . . and I just wanted to make the point that as proud as we are of that, we're going to build on that legacy . . . [AFSPC] wasn't our organization anymore. So, we took off the patch and highlighted that we're something new and different now.[44]

Later that night, many of the former AFSPC staff—now, they were assigned to the U.S. Space Force—went out to the flight line to greet the boss' plane when it arrived. "We all brought our drink of choice and we just toasted the new Chief as he landed." After deplaning on the cold December night, Raymond came into base operations, and as Whiting said, "He told us some stories about what the President had said. Just a moment to let him know how proud we were." As David Thompson put it, the long-anticipated U.S. Space Force was now—on day one of the NDAA's signing—"a thing."[45]

Part II: 2020

PRIORITIZING THE U.S. SPACE FORCE

As 2019 drew to a close, for the first time in seventy-two years the United States had established a new armed force. It was the culmination of more than two decades of significant effort on the part of dedicated space professionals, depending on how far back one wished to trace them. Formal establishment on 20 December—which included 16,000 airmen now assigned to the Space Force from Air Force Space Command but not yet transferred—was only a small beginning, however, to the work that lay ahead. Two months later, in February 2020, Secretary of the Air Force Barbara Barrett and her two chiefs—Air Force Chief of Staff Goldfein and Space Force Chief of Space Operations Raymond—issued a one-page memorandum "To the Men and Women of the Department of the Air Force." Secretary Barrett said, "We are now a Department with two distinct services, yet we remain singularly focused on implementing the National Defense Strategy." She named four priorities: first, to "Build the United States Space Force"; second, to modernize the department's air and space forces; third, to "Grow Strong Leaders and Resilient Families"; and fourth, to strengthen our partnerships with U.S. allies. Significantly, Barrett made clear her intent was to "Prioritize and field the newest branch of the Armed Services to protect, defend, and fight in, through, and from the ultimate high ground."[46]

At the same time the secretary's memorandum came out, she participated in the Air Force Association's (AFA) Air Warfare Symposium in Orlando, Florida. There she emphasized the same four priorities. Barrett elaborated, "Modernization requires updates that are equal parts cultural and operational," and she mentioned the example of what was called Joint All Domain Command and Control, a battle network intended to provide commanders with vast amounts of data across the spectrum of air, land, sea, space, and cyber domains. The current parlance for that concept was connecting "all shooters to all sensors." To some degree, Barrett viewed the challenge as "trading short term titanium for long term electrons," part of a mindset or cultural transformation. "We still need titanium, but it's also about electrons," she told the AFA audience, "being able to have instant access to usable information."[47]

SPACE DEVELOPMENT AGENCY

For years, the acquisition of new space systems took far too long and involved far too many players for U.S. national security space planners and leaders alike. In 2000 the defense department attempted to streamline the DoD-wide satellite acquisition process by making it similar to that practiced by the National Reconnaissance Office, but problems persisted. Two decades later, the likelihood of establishing a space service spurred renewed efforts within the department to develop a less bureaucratic approach to satellite acquisitions. In 2019 Acting Secretary of Defense Shanahan directed the establishment of an organization called the Space Development Agency (SDA). Officially, the SDA was established in March 2019, falling under the oversight of the undersecretary of defense for research and engineering. Shanahan wrote, "The SDA will define and monitor the Department's future threat-driven space architecture and will accelerate the development and fielding of new military space capabilities necessary" for national defense. Three months later—on the verge of returning to DARPA from which he had come—Fred G. Kennedy III, the SDA acting director, put recent congressional "skepticism" in a positive light and interpreted the ongoing discussions on SDA's potential value and the assigning of tasks to the agency as "a good sign." For fiscal 2020, the Pentagon sought and was granted funding for fifty personnel, thirty of them new civilians and twenty military personnel transferring from other positions.[48]

For SDA's first year of existence, its "driving force" was aerospace engineer Michael D. Griffin, then undersecretary of defense for research and engineering. His director of defense research and engineering, Mark J. Lewis, credited Griffin with making significant headway in battling "the bloated bureaucracy of space acquisition." The agency's task was described in *Defense News* as "creating a proliferated architecture of hundreds or potentially thousands of small satellites . . . organized in different 'layers' specializing in operations ranging from deep space situational awareness to providing an alternative to GPS." That many Pentagon space advocates were excited about the prospect of moving from dependence upon current satellites in higher orbits to smaller proliferated satellites in low-Earth orbit, by tapping into the best commercial technology available, reflected Griffin's leadership and his team's technical expertise and resourcefulness, stated Dr. Lewis.[49]

But with Griffin's departure in July 2020 for the private sector, some expressed concern that SDA's "main champion is leaving the Pentagon." That concern may have been somewhat overblown, as after Griffin left Lewis moved up to the front office and continued to advocate for SDA. Todd Harrison, director of an aerospace project at the Center for Strategic and International Studies, felt that Griffin's departure might actually hasten SDA's transition under the Space Force. In any case, not all air and space leaders agreed on SDA. The Air Force secretary from 2017 to 2019, Heather Wilson, felt clarity was lacking in SDA's mission and remained unconvinced that its establishment was likely to improve the convoluted space acquisition process. Others criticized the likelihood of SDA's overlap with the work of DARPA and the Space and Missile Systems Center (later, Space Systems Command). In 2021 the SDA strategic engagement cell summarized, "Much work has been done since the establishment of the Space Force in December 2019 to ensure collaboration and planned competition while avoiding unintentional overlap."[50]

In late 2020, under the leadership of Derek M. Tournear, an SDA fact sheet stated the agency's charge "is to define and deliver the [DoD's] future resilient, threat-driven, and affordable military space architecture for the joint warfighter at or ahead of the speed of need." The last phrase addressed what General Raymond and General Hyten considered a critical requirement for the United States: responding much more quickly than before to the threats, including space-based, of peer competitors China and Russia. As Hyten recommended a year earlier, "Put some sensors on some satellites, fly them cheap, fly them fast, see what they can do and then figure out what you need to actually go build. If you do that we'll go infinitely faster, save enormous amounts of . . . money, and you'll get the capability faster. But that's not the way we do it. We try to study the heck out of it to get a perfect answer before we start something. I think that's crazy."[51]

Dr. Tournear's SDA was committed to ending such craziness and delivering capabilities into the hands of the warfighter in *semper citius* fashion. The SDA engagement cell continued,

> SDA capitalizes on a unique business model that values speed and lowers costs by harnessing commercial development to achieve a proliferated architecture and enhance resilience. SDA will deliver a minimum viable product—on time, every two years—by employing spiral development methods, adding capabilities to future generations as the threat evolves. . . . By December 2020, SDA delivered its first two satellites carrying experimental communication terminals to the launch provider

just nine months after receiving the agency's initial appropriated funds. Between June and August 2020, the agency launched four experiments on six satellites on two different shared launches. SDA quickly followed up . . . in September 2021 by publishing its second major call for proposals for space vehicle acquisition to be delivered [fiscal] 2024—the Tranche 1 Transport Layer consisting of almost 150 satellites.[52]

PROMOTING THE SPACE FORCE

The formal establishment of the nation's newest armed force nearly coincided with the onset of a strange and deadly virus that originated in Wuhan, China, and that, for at least the next year, dramatically changed everyday life for billions worldwide. In the midst of the COVID-19 pandemic restrictions implemented across the United States, which precluded the opportunity for normal travel and traditional in-person gatherings, in early May 2020 Secretary of the Air Force Barrett and General Raymond teamed up for a webinar to promote the Space Force. Sponsored by the Space Foundation, the webinar allowed the two senior leaders to address current issues affecting the Space Force and to field questions from the listening audience.[53]

Barrett and Raymond emphasized several key areas, one of which was international partnerships in space. In the early decades of space activity, neither the benign nature of space nor the technical challenges of getting there—which only a few nations met—lent themselves to partnerships. But that had changed, and, as General Raymond stated, space partnerships were "absolutely critical today." He mentioned Norway and Japan as two nations with whom the U.S. Space Command was pursuing a relatively new partnership that called for at least one satellite of each country to host American surveillance capabilities deemed of mutual benefit. Further, security cooperation had been increasing for the last several years. A prime example was the Combined [multinational] Space Operations Center's establishment at Vandenberg AFB, California, which provided command and control of space forces.[54] The designation Combined Space Operations Center was one example of what then–brigadier general Dale Meyerrose had in mind two decades earlier when he emphasized the need of Air Force space and cyber professionals to use terminology that the

STANDING UP, 2019–2020   135

rated Air Force could relate to, in this case wording similar to a combined *air* operations center.

To a degree, the other side of the partnership coin could be seen in the transition from the U.S. government's practice of buying seats on Russian *Soyuz* rockets to restoring America's ability to launch her own astronauts from U.S. soil. As others had noted with chagrin, since 2011 American astronauts rocketing to space had been forced to rely on the Russians to get them there. At the end of May 2020—the same month as the senior leaders' webinar—NASA astronauts for the first time "launched from American soil in a commercially built and operated American crew spacecraft on its way to the International Space Station [ISS]," NASA reported. The mission served as an end-to-end test flight to validate SpaceX's launch, in-orbit, docking, and landing operations. Launched from Complex 39A at Cape Canaveral, it was the second spaceflight test of the SpaceX *Crew Dragon* spacecraft, powered by its Falcon 9 rocket. The crew of Robert Behnken and Douglas Hurley, both NASA astronauts, were military veterans: Behnken an Air Force flight test engineer, Hurley a Marine Corps fighter pilot and test pilot. Secretary Barrett viewed the SpaceX launch as "a metaphor for America's leadership" in space—a return, that is, to its former leadership.[55]

Addressing the current state of space, Secretary Barrett and General Raymond made clear that America's dependence on space was at an all-time high. They pegged the global marketplace value of space at $415 billion. Even the most recent months witnessed mounting evidence of space threats, including incidents in which Russia maneuvered a satellite possessing the characteristics of a weapon system in proximity to an American satellite and Iran attempted to launch an operational satellite. Under the circumstances, Raymond viewed the present moment as "a strategic inflection point," one that the activation of a combatant command for space and a new service for space anticipated.[56]

For any doubters, General Raymond also made clear that the much-preferred scenario was for deterrence to prove effective in space, just as on earth. Should deterrence fail, however, "Space fuels our American way of life; space also fuels our American way of war," he said, perhaps an echo of Air Force Chief of Staff Goldfein's emphasis on integrated operations across all domains. Further, the Space Force chief of space operations pointed out that when it came to tracking objects in space, it was standard practice for U.S. military space officials to warn adversaries when their spacecraft were in danger of a collision, sometimes even with space debris they had created. Not only was it an example of going the proverbial extra mile, the practice minimized the chances of creating even more space debris that threatened other satellites. Like the COVID virus, space debris cared not for the identity of what lay in its path.[57]

In terms of building the Space Force cadre, Raymond pointed encouragingly to the commissioning at the Air Force Academy, three weeks earlier, of eighty-six officers into the U.S. Space Force. Of the group, two were to attend Harvard University and one MIT for advanced degrees. At least fifty, however, went directly into space operations, while others headed to acquisitions, intelligence, cyber or engineering jobs. Raymond affirmed there was to be a Space Force reserve component, and he fully expected to open it to members of other services besides the Air Force. It should also be an option for members of other services to serve a joint assignment with U.S. Space Force and then return to their own branch.[58]

On the lighter side, Raymond was well aware of the new comedy streaming television series called *Space Force*. Its first of ten episodes was scheduled for the end of May 2020. When curious webinar participants asked what he thought of the series, General Raymond replied good-naturedly that Steve Carell, who was to play the general, was "looking a little too shaggy if he wants to play the Space Force chief." He needed a haircut. The real chief of space ops had preferred Bruce Willis—for whom many fans voted—adding, "But Steve Carell's a great actor, and, I tell you, I love his shows. So, we're looking forward [to the new series]."[59]

PROMOTING THE INTELLIGENCE CAREER FIELD

While Secretary Barrett and General Raymond were promoting the USSF on top-tier issues with a little help from streaming television comedy, the Space Force director of Intelligence, Surveillance, and Reconnaissance did her part for the intelligence profession. Most of Col. Suzanne Streeter's twenty-eight years on active duty had been in signals intelligence, but her more recent years were in space intelligence. Streeter arrived at Peterson

AFB in the summer of 2017 as AFSPC's senior intelligence officer, and she conducted her first threat briefing that fall. Later, when planning began for a revitalized USSPACECOM, she helped stand up the command's J2 (intelligence) directorate. In a 2020 interview, while addressing up-and-coming adversary threats, she noted, "Things that were far-fetched [in 2017] are now becoming reality."[60]

That realization made the Space Force's establishment seem all the more timely. Only two weeks after the excitement of 20 December—to which she contributed some champagne for the celebration at Peterson before taking part in the flight line welcome for General Raymond later that night—Streeter participated in field design workshops for fleshing out the new service. One overarching reality was that, because for so long the space domain had been considered benign, intelligence "hasn't always been part of the sight picture for space operations," she said. There was much education to be done, starting with the seemingly simplistic question of "what is intelligence" in a space context? Some of the issues to be hammered out included determining the intelligence support required at the unit, air operations center, and combat support agency levels—the latter included the National Geospatial-Intelligence Agency and National Security Agency (NSA).[61]

In Colonel Streeter's view, one of the top near-term priorities for USSF intelligence involved the sensitive matter of cryptologic authorities from the NSA for the purpose of collection, keeping in mind that the U.S. Constitution's 4th Amendment prohibited "unreasonable searches and seizures."[62]

Although not nearly as dramatic, another immediate priority was how best to sell the Space Force to uniformed personnel in the intelligence fields of the other services, encouraging transfers into the USSF. While the Space Force's relatively small size and correspondingly few general officer positions in intelligence, a limited number of bases for assignment, and fewer intelligence mission sets than those available in the sister services appeared as disincentives to many professionals, they also could be turned on their head, Streeter observed. While the chances in Space Force intelligence for promotion to general officer were indeed minuscule, on the other hand, if one made it to lieutenant colonel (O-5) there was a pretty good chance for promotion to full colonel (O-6). Fewer bases from which to choose also meant opportunities for long-term stability for families, and limited intelligence mission sets meant that one who wanted to specialize could do so more easily than in a job with a much broader portfolio. At the end of the day, as Colonel Streeter put it, those who came into the Space Force were part of something new, and "you're going to be a plankholder."[63]

LOCATING THE HEADQUARTERS, UNITED STATES SPACE COMMAND

The USSPACECOM had been established four months prior to the stand-up of the U.S. Space Force. As the sixth armed force, the USSF was to provide combat-ready forces to its primary customer, U.S. Space Command, the combatant command whose job it was to employ space forces to meet U.S. national security objectives. While the U.S. Space Force was to be headquartered at the Pentagon as were the other branches of service, there was considerable political boil regarding the location of USSPACE-COM's headquarters. Secretary Barrett called it one of her most hotly contested issues, exacerbated by the "false start" on the selection process that occurred prior to her arrival in Washington. Leaked information, regardless of whether accurate or not, only made things worse. She had to "back up and start again," emphasizing to all concerned that the process—analytical and quantitative—was to be done by the book, adhering precisely with all relevant guidelines.[64]

In May 2020 the Department of the Air Force, in coordination with the defense secretary's office, announced its approach for determining the permanent location of USSPACECOM's headquarters. "[The department's] revised approach considers the newly established U.S. Space [Force's] emerging organizational structure and analyzes its effects on the limited number of highly specialized personnel and infrastructure required to support both the Space Force and Space Command. Additionally, the approach expands the number of locations eligible for consideration to host the permanent U.S. Space Command headquarters, and provides a comprehensive and transparent analysis before selecting a final location."[65]

In the meantime—and probably until about 2026—Colorado Springs was to remain the locale of the provisional headquarters for U.S. Space Command. In the following months of 2020, however, no fewer than twenty-four states nominated municipalities within their borders as potential host locales for the command. The six finalists were, alphabetically by city: Albuquerque (N.M.), Bellevue (Neb.), Cape Canaveral (Fla.), Colorado Springs (Colo.), Huntsville (Ala.), and San Antonio (Tex.). In January 2021—within days of the end of the Trump administration—the Air Force announced Redstone Arsenal in Huntsville, Alabama, as the selection. To no one's surprise, the decision generated renewed political thrash, the results of which could only be known over time. In April 2022 the Government Accountability Office completed its investigation of the location decision but did not immediately release the results to the public.[66]

SPACE FORCE CULTURE AND IDENTITY

Air Force space professionals had long talked about the importance of nurturing a space culture distinct from that of the USAF, but with the Space Force's formal establishment it was time to get serious about it. While myriad issues of importance to the service needed resolution, in some cases requiring several more years, other matters called for quicker action in order to minimize unnecessary confusion as well as to begin new traditions and thinking.

One such matter was the question of how to address the USSF's boss, General Raymond. After everyone had returned to work in early January following the holidays, Maj. Gen. Stephen Whiting emailed the staff, "Now that Gen Raymond is a Service Chief, many of us (myself included) have started to refer to him as 'Chief.' Through dialogue with senior [Office of the Chief of Space Operations] staff and [Raymond] himself, we want to begin a tradition of referring to him as 'the CSO' [chief of Space Operations] when talking about him in his USSF Service Chief hat. This will differentiate the CSO from CSAF (who is referred to as 'Chief') and all the CMSgts [chief master sergeants] in our Service."[67]

Whiting mentioned that the U.S. Navy practiced a similar form of reference to their service chief (the Chief of Naval Operations) under certain circumstances, before concluding, "Let's start the new tradition of referring to our new Service Chief as 'the CSO.'"[68]

While Major General Whiting's guidance seemed logical, two weeks later he reported to the staff that "guidance today from the senior levels of the Pentagon" directed that General Raymond "will be referred to as 'Chief' in his Chief of Space Operations (CSO) hat. The term 'CSO' can be used just as we use the term 'CSAF,' but just as the tradition is to refer to CSAF as 'Chief' when talking to him or writing to him, we will also adopt this same term when referring to the CSO. Thanks for your agility as we are still charting new traditions and norms." So the term "Chief" was to be used when addressing both the USAF and USSF chiefs, a practice General Goldfein insisted on to help drive home that his Space Force counterpart was a full-fledged member of the JCS.[69]

Whiting—the Space Force's first deputy commander—could have empathized with John Adams, the nation's first vice president, who in 1789 found himself at the forefront of a month-long debate in the Senate over how to address George Washington. In his Pulitzer Prize-winning biography, *John Adams*, David McCullough wrote, "In the Senate, the issue of titles, and particularly the question of how the President was to be addressed, superceded [*sic*] all other business." Some discussions were heated, "with Adams taking part more than the members deemed appropriate." Some of his political opponents thought Adams deserved his own title, and they gave him the mocking sobriquet of "His Rotundity." Thankfully, the athletically built Whiting appeared to be spared Adams'—or any other—indignity over the present-day question of a similar nature.[70]

There were other pressing cultural and identity issues, such as what to call the members of the Space Force and its units, establishing unit heraldry, and the renaming of bases. One peculiarity was that as of January 2020, of about 16,000 airmen assigned to the U.S. Space Force, General Raymond was the only one who had been formally transferred from the Air Force into the USSF; he was followed by CMSgt. Roger A. Towberman in April.[71] In February Major General Whiting again ventured into the cultural arena, seeking input from USSF-assigned personnel "on the name we will collectively call ourselves as US Space Force members, what we will call our junior ranks and what we will potentially call [our] operational units. The effort is part of a deliberate effort to ensure Space Force member titles and ranks appropriately convey the nature of the mission and vision of [our] force and the domain in which we operate." One news release added that USSF officials especially sought ideas from personnel currently assigned to the Space Force or those who expected to join in the future, including the space professionals of the sister services. On the first anniversary of the Space Force's establishment, 19 December 2020, Vice President Pence announced, on behalf of the president, "Henceforth, the men and women of the United States Space Force will be known as 'Guardians.'" By that time, there were about four thousand guardians in the USSF.[72]

During 2020, Space Force leaders adopted two basic terms for their units. Dr. Gregory W. Ball, the USSF command historian, explained the evolution:

> The efforts to name the O-6 and O-5 level organizations had initially been tackled by Task Force Tango in March of 2019. . . . By the end of January [2020], USSF planners had settled on two Courses of Action (COA). The first identified the term Vanguard as the O-6 equivalent, with the O-5 level retaining the USAF name of Squadron. The second COA recommended the O-6 level use the term Delta while the O-5 level would use Vanguard. . . . As it turned out, the term Vanguard was eventually discarded and the final naming convention for USSF units at the O-6 and O-5 level was Delta and Squadron, respectively.[73]

Major General Whiting noted that the term "delta" was perceived as a "new term for a unit, but it links us to our seal and the arrows in the USSPACECOM emblem and provides a distinctive unit name," while the use of squadron retained the USAF's term for the traditional O-5 level of command.[74]

Traditionally, heraldry in the military was among the issues most likely to affect the morale of individuals and their unit, organization, or service. Often it was a love-hate relationship between service members and their heraldry. Moreover, the White House was quite interested in the matter, and in mid-January 2020 the Defense and Air Force secretaries—Mark Esper and Barbara Barrett—and CSO General Raymond met with President Trump to discuss the official Space Force seal. On 24 January the president took to Twitter to release the official USSF seal. The new seal, similar to the emblem of the former AFSPC, featured in part an oval globe that resembled the earth as seen from space; lines of latitude and longitude to represent the global nature of space operations; an ellipse to symbolize the orbital path traced by satellites; and the delta symbol representing the upward thrust into space and the launch vehicles needed to place satellites into orbit.[75]

Four months later at an Oval Office ceremony with senior military leaders, President Trump unveiled the official flag of the Space Force. The flag was nearly identical to the seal except for the flag's black background. The three large stars near the orbital ellipse were to symbolize the service functions of organizing, training, and equipping space forces for employment by combatant commanders. Another cultural piece was the official Space Force logo and motto. On 22 July 2020 Secretary Barrett presented the USSF logo to the Department of the Air Force: "The Delta with an embedded North Star [will] serve as our guiding light as we build a new Service to secure the space domain." The Space Force's official motto is *Semper Supra* ("Always Above"); Barrett viewed it as a reminder of "the strategic imperative to ensure that our space capabilities and the advantages they provide the nation and our Joint and Coalition partners are always there. We can accept nothing less."[76]

There had been no shortage of service culture suggestions—some serious, others mocking—from the naming of Space Force members and units to their uniforms to their heraldry elements. Popular culture influenced a number of ideas, especially the *Star Trek* movies decades earlier that featured Captain James T. Kirk as commander of the USS *Enterprise*. In October 2021, the actor who portrayed Captain Kirk—ninety-year-old William Shatner—participated in a launch with Jeff Bezos' Blue Origin, flying on a suborbital mission with three other crew members. Upon landing, Shatner, filled with emotion, expressed his appreciation for "the most profound experience I can imagine."[77]

The redesignating of Air Force bases to Space Force installations was another high-visibility concern, which Secretary Barrett stated was "critical to establishing a distinct culture and identity for the Space Force." On 16 March 2020 Barrett approved, under Title 10 U.S. Code authority, the first such redesignation—Patrick AFB to Patrick Space Force Base. In doing so, she made clear that the new designation was not to affect existing base operating support, funding, or other agreements at Patrick. In part due to COVID-19 virus concerns, the actual ceremony redesignating Patrick and Cape Canaveral—to Patrick Space Force Base and Cape Canaveral Space Force Station—did not take place until December. Those were the first two installations to be so redesignated. While their renaming appeared fairly straightforward, Thule Air Base presented a more complicated situation. One Space Force paper noted that renaming Thule AB to Thule Space Base required the State Department to seek approval from the Kingdom of Denmark because "Thule Air Base is a part of the autonomous territory of Greenland under the Kingdom of Denmark." Sometimes the phrase "Space is Hard" had unexpected relevance.[78]

While the aforementioned matters of service culture and identity were highly unlikely to change, the same could not be said regarding many other issues, including those of organization, management, and accessioning. To no one's surprise, a number of them remained in flux during 2020 and beyond.

Terminology, heraldry, and base designations were among the tangible elements of service culture, but there were deeper, intangible elements as well. The Air University at Maxwell AFB, Alabama, was home to several professional military education programs. The Air Command and Staff College was the school that mid-career officers, generally in the grade of major (O-4), attended, where students focused on air campaign planning and the operational art of war. Certain outdated information on the space curriculum notwithstanding, since at least 2016 or 2017 ACSC had devoted considerable attention to space issues. The AU commander from 2014 to 2017, Lt. Gen. Steven Kwast, was a space advocate and encouraged space-mindedness in AU's schools. There were a handful of space scholars on the ACSC faculty, and due to the academic climate and the fact that their evaluations did not run through more traditional Air Force channels, they enjoyed greater liberty to share their views than did some other military space professionals. That was the case particularly under Kwast's command. In a 2021 interview, Dr. Brent Ziarnick, an associate professor in the Department of Spacepower, highlighted the contrast between the Space Force's branding and the reality. In his view, "If you take a look at what the Space Force does, it's no different than what Air Force Space

144   CHAPTER 5

Command used to do....The problem with the culture now ... is that the Space Force has branded itself as something new and something innovative, but has really not changed at all."

His former ACSC colleague, Peter Garretson, agreed with that assessment. In an op-ed, Ziarnick said, "Aggressiveness and innovation in space is owned entirely by the civilian space community," epitomized by SpaceX. In terms of the satellites being flown and operated by the U.S. Space Force, however, the ones in orbit were nearly identical to those AFSPC had operated for years. If the ambition of the 50th Space Wing's Colonel Fischer, having a Space Force that is "not just reorganizing Air Force Space Command ... [but] that is going to change humanity" was to make any headway, the observations of Ziarnick, Garretson, and certain others deserved serious attention. It was also the sort of cultural issue that required greater effort and much more time to change than names, logos, and base designations.[79]

Conclusion

Even with considerable political support especially from Congress and the White House, until the final weeks of 2019 few, if any, Air Force Space Command or U.S. Space Command leaders seem to have expected the U.S. Space Force to be formally established by the end of the year. Two extensive planning efforts that began in February—one at the Pentagon, the other at Peterson AFB in Colorado—accomplished important work toward standing up a space service, but even those two teams anticipated their plans to be placed on the shelf, to be pulled off at a later time. The establishment of U.S. Space Force on 20 December in conjunction with the president's signing of the NDAA into law was, for many, the rewarding, dramatic culmination of a long and often frustrating drive to advance the interests of U.S. national security space. Perhaps Lt. Gen. David Thompson, the first U.S. Space Force vice commander, was not the only senior leader to feel that it was kind of "like the dog that [finally] caught the car"—now what?[80]

Thankfully, the considerable effort begun earlier in the year was available to help jump-start the process of standing up the Space Force. Major General Crosier's Space Force Planning Task Force in Washington, DC, did most of the macro-level planning, while AFSPC's Task Force Tango in Colorado Springs handled the bulk of the service field structure plans. At long last, by year's end the Department of the Air Force had two distinct services, and the process of determining the relationship between the two and transferring from the USAF those space entities and personnel that needed to go into the USSF was bound to take time. Meanwhile, many issues had to be addressed: from base operating support at Air Force installations that housed Space Force interests to satellite acquisitions; from keeping up with real-world threats in space to nurturing a culture and identity for the members of the nation's new service. There was much to be done.

EPILOGUE

SERVICE FUNDAMENTALS, 2021

To state that 2021 was a tumultuous year is to acknowledge the painfully obvious. Yet through it all, the nation's youngest armed forces branch, the U.S. Space Force, made headway in a number of areas foundational to a new service, while in others it experienced modest progress in growing and stabilizing the force. One sticking point was that a permanent basing decision for U.S. Space Command remained unresolved as of this writing, although in any case the command was expected to remain in place at Peterson AFB, Colorado, for several more years.

Redesignation of Air Force Installations to the Space Force

By the close of 2020, only Patrick and Cape Canaveral had been formally redesignated as Space Force installations. In April 2021 Acting Secretary of the Air Force John Roth emphasized that the redesignating of installations was "critical to establishing a distinct culture and identity for the Space Force." In a memorandum to the department, Roth approved nine additional installations for redesignation, three of them as Space Force bases, six as Space Force stations. The Space Force bases were Buckley, Peterson, and Schriever, all in the vicinity of Colorado Springs. Roth directed both of the service chiefs in the Department of the Air Force to jointly determine the effective dates for the redesignations and for the

USSF to coordinate with local leadership (military and local community) to mark each event with an appropriate ceremony. On 26 July Lieutenant General Whiting and Col. Shay Warakomski, the Peterson-Schriever garrison commander, presided over the renaming ceremony for Peterson and Schriever Space Force bases and for Cheyenne Mountain Space Force Station. Peterson provided mission support to Space Operations Command including the space domain awareness, space electronic warfare, and space intelligence-surveillance-reconnaissance missions. Schriever Space Force Base's current mission set focuses on cyberspace operations, satellite communications and navigational warfare, and orbital warfare, conducted under Joint Task Force-Space Defense. Cheyenne Mountain served as the North American Aerospace Defense Command and U.S. Northern Command's Alternate Command Center and as a crew qualification training site.[1]

A Polarized Society Impacts the Space Force

The conduct and aftermath of a controversial 2020 U.S. presidential election fueled an already polarized electorate and stressed the country's fragile civil sphere even more. Amid that volatile cultural climate, a U.S. Space Force officer, Lt. Col. Matthew Lohmeier, added his voice to the mix. In May 2021, Lohmeier—who had served as General Raymond's aide before attending the ACSC, where he excelled as a Schriever Scholar—commanded the 11th Space Warning Squadron at Buckley AFB, Colorado. His self-published book that addressed his views on neo- or quasi-Marxist influences in the U.S. military had just been released. Shortly after its publication, Lohmeier appeared on a podcast to promote the book, in which he stated that Secretary of Defense Lloyd Austin was promoting "diversity, inclusion, and equity," which are "rooted in critical race theory [CRT], which is rooted in Marxism." Lohmeier's comments quickly reached Lt. Gen. Stephen Whiting, commander of the Space Operations Command. It did not take long for the Space Force to announce that Whiting had relieved Lieutenant Colonel Lohmeier of his command "due to loss of trust and confidence in his ability to lead." Whiting also initiated an investigation into whether Lohmeier's comments amounted to "prohibited partisan political activity." Following Lohmeier's firing, Sen. Roger Wicker

148   EPILOGUE

(R-Miss.) wrote a letter to Secretary Austin to express his concerns, beginning with the fact that Lohmeier had been relieved prior to any investigation. Wicker declared,

> If the Department of Defense finds that Lt. Col. Lohmeier's statements on CRT qualify as a "partisan cause," it would then follow that the Department recognizes CRT itself as reflecting one side in a partisan debate. Yet if CRT is partisan, it must be asked why this ideology is increasingly being pushed on U.S. service members. It has become increasingly clear that the Department is actively pushing CRT through "diversity and inclusion" trainings, recommended reading materials, and cadet instruction. The Department therefore cannot call Lt. Col. Lohmeier's statements on CRT "partisan" without being implicated in the same partisan advocacy.[2]

Wicker's point notwithstanding, in September 2021 Lohmeier separated from the service, yet another scenario harkening to Senator McCain's admonition to the Air Force in 2017 to focus on "returning the culture of the Air Force to its core purpose of a warfighting force to fight and win our nation's wars and dispense with social experimentation." While the Space Force was in a season of considerable media attention, the Lohmeier incident certainly was not the kind of publicity the USSF, nor the USAF, desired.[3]

The First Soldiers, Sailors, and Marines Transfer into USSF

From early on, planners expected the Space Force to provide interservice transfer opportunities for selected personnel, but to ease the new service's stand-up only Air Force members were allowed to do so for the first year. In July 2021 the USSF announced that the first fifty active-duty volunteers from outside the USAF were in the process of transferring permanently into the Pentagon's sixth branch of service. The vice chief of space operations, Gen. David Thompson, said he was "overwhelmed by the number of applicants, and [by] the outpouring of support our sister services have provided." Some 3,700 officers and enlisted members had applied for the 50 slots. Of those chosen—in what officials considered to be the first test bed for matching individuals' skill sets with Space Force unit requirements—40 came from the Army, 7 from the Navy, and 3 from the Marine Corps. Another 350 transfers were expected soon, to enter specialties including space operations, intelligence, cyber, engineering, and acquisition. The Space Force expected a larger batch of transfers during fiscal 2022.[4]

In addition to some 3,600 airmen who began transferring into USSF earlier in the year, plus about 100 newly-commissioned Air Force Academy graduates who went directly into the Space Force, and 300 new recruits, the USSF anticipated having approximately 6,400 guardians in its permanent ranks by year's end. Of the total, the vast majority originated in the Air Force. By the fall of 2022 USSF expected to boast 8,000 to 9,000 guardians.[5]

Acquisition Reform, Space Systems Command

In 2020 the Space Force requested the help of Congress with certain acquisition reforms, one of the most important of which was to allow the service to "consolidate budget line items along mission portfolios rather than by platform." Air Force Secretary Barbara Barrett argued the change was needed to allow USSF to realign funds more easily for specific programs based on changing threat assessments. As of mid-2021, the Space Force needed to submit reprogramming requests to Congress, which has criticized the military's use of such requests in order to quicken the development of a missile warning satellite constellation. Shawn Barnes, the deputy assistant Air Force secretary for space acquisition and integration, agreed that the USSF could benefit by "thinking in terms of portfolios rather than single platforms" or programs of record. He envisioned the Space Force being able to draw from the Space Development Agency, the NRO, and the Space Rapid Capabilities Office "to create a portfolio of capabilities" for a particular mission. While the USSF request was unusual, it was not unprecedented—both the NRO and Space Rapid Capabilities Office managed their budgets by portfolio.[6]

In August 2021, the redesignation of the SMC as the Space Systems Command (SSC) at Los Angeles AFB (El Segundo, California) represented the most far-reaching reorganization of the SMC since its

150 EPILOGUE

inception in 1954 when Bernard Schriever was setting up the Western Development Division. The center's commander, Lt. Gen. John Thompson, considered the location a "very unique space acquisition ecosystem," as much of the "nation's space industrial base ... is right here in the L.A. area." One of the Space Force's three field commands (USSF's equivalent to a major command in the Air Force), the SSC was responsible for "developing and acquiring space capabilities, including launch services." The SSC's first commander was Lt. Gen. Michael Guetlein, with responsibility for a $9 billon annual budget and some 6,300, mostly civilian, personnel.[7]

Space Training and Readiness Command (STARCOM)

Space Training and Readiness Command was the third and final U.S. Space Force field command to be established. Its mission set included the training of new guardians. As of 2021, recruits underwent Air Force Basic Military Training in San Antonio, Texas, before attending Undergraduate Space Training at Vandenberg SFB, California. While new enlisted personnel took advanced classes in space, cyber, or intelligence operations, newly accessioned officers were eligible for engineering or acquisitions programs in addition to the others. The command was also responsible for doctrine development and wargaming, including the well-established Schriever Wargame, which tested new space systems.[8]

The command was not merely the Space Force counterpart to the Air Force's Air Education and Training Command, however. For starters, as Col. Niki J. Lindhorst (who in 2022 was STARCOM's Delta 13 commander at Maxwell AFB) explained, unlike the Air Force the Space Force has separated training from education. In another dissimilarity from the Air Force, the Space Force's training command portfolio—under its readiness piece—included the testing of new hardware prior to its being made available for operational use. The command's "operational test authority evaluates the system capabilities after launch," similar to the Air Force's operational tests at Edwards AFB. As Brig. Gen. Shawn Bratton—the first Air National Guardsman to attend the Space Weapons Instructor Course and STARCOM's first commander—explained, "So the acquirers ... work with industry to get us the best stuff, [then] STARCOM will wring that out and make sure that it's ready to go for operations before

EPILOGUE   151

Space Operations Command takes it over." One difference from traditional Air Force test ranges was that although satellites could not be tested there, the corresponding ground stations could. For space-based systems, Bratton's command planned to rely on "digital engineering and modeling to simulate testing."[9]

Professional Military Education for Space at Air University

From 2017 to 2021, Colonel Lindhorst served as the space chair to the Air University commander, (initially) Lt. Gen. Steve Kwast. Lindhorst also taught at the Air War College, where she was passionate in wanting to "bring space to life here at AU in such a way that . . . not just our space professionals at the time—now, Guardians—[got] excited about what they were doing, but [to] get my joint brothers and sisters excited about what space brings to their fight." Looking back from 2022, Lindhorst had seen an increase in the understanding of space by students at AU. She did not necessarily want them to learn orbital mechanics, but rather to appreciate that, depending on whether a space asset was in place, there were times when guardians might not be able to provide the joint warfighter with a particularly desirable photograph, for example. She also wanted them to understand the impacts on their own operational capabilities should friendly space assets be lost for any reason. Seeing joint warfighters "encompassing [space] in their own missions" was hugely rewarding for her. The learning went both ways of course, and Lindhorst emphasized also the importance of Space Force members understanding the basics of their sister services' operational missions.[10]

Colonel Lindhorst explained that beginning with the 2023–24 academic year, the Space Force planned to implement its own version of both intermediate- and senior-level professional military education. The names of the Space Force's staff college and war college were yet to be decided. Perhaps more important, the location of both schools was undetermined, but it was not going to be at Maxwell. As of mid-2022, a search was ongoing for civilian universities interested in partnering with the Space Force to implement the required military education programs, and a contract was awarded in the fall of 2022 to the Johns Hopkins University School of Advanced International Studies..[11]

The Uncertainty of a Space Force Reserve Component: A Space National Guard?

Beginning with General Raymond, a number of Space Force officials anticipated a Space National Guard, but as with certain other programs and capabilities, they were hesitant to take that step at the outset of the new service. Not surprisingly, their Guard counterparts in space-friendly states agreed on the Space Guard's desirability, if not on its timing. In 2020, at least two major generals—Michael Loh, the Colorado National Guard's adjutant general, and his Florida counterpart, James Eifert—had backed the idea of a Space Guard. Loh, who went on to a third star as the director of the ANG, said, "I don't see how we have a Space Force without a Space Guard," while Eifert opined, "We are the perfect partner for the newly formed [USSF]." Moreover, Gen. Joseph Lengyel, then the chief of the National Guard Bureau, stated that establishing a Space National Guard "is one of my top priorities." His successor, Gen. Daniel Hokanson, considered it "among my most pressing concerns."[12]

Colorado had more Guard members performing space missions than any other state, and in 2021 the Colorado House of Representatives passed a bill that allowed the state's ANG space units to transition into the Space National Guard upon the federal government's establishment of the Space Guard—which they hoped to see in the fiscal 2022 defense budget. The bill was signed into law by Governor Jared Polis. In Washington, two Colorado congressmen, Jason Crow (D) and Doug Lamborn (R), introduced bipartisan legislation to create a "Space Force Reserve and National Guard," evidence of support for the concept. Historically, one of the reserve component's best-selling points was that members with specialized skills, whose civilian jobs were in fields the military also required, could perform excellent service in reserve status (whether state or federal) with a minimum of training, and they might easily flow between active duty and reserve status. Especially since 2001, many congressmen and reserve leaders promoted this "continuum of service" concept.[13]

As crisper fall air returned to Washington, the degree of congressional support for a Space Guard in the very near term remained murky. The House Armed Services Committee (HASC) continued its traditional support for military space, passing its version of the 2022 NDAA that included an amendment approving the establishment of "a Space Guard as

EPILOGUE 153

a reserve component of the U.S. Space Force." But the Senate Armed Services Committee did not include language on creating a Space National Guard. Instead, the Senate's version of the bill called simply for renaming the Air National Guard "the Air and Space National Guard." Three weeks later, the full House passed its version of the NDAA, but the Senate was yet to complete its work on the bill. For the twelfth time in thirteen years, the Defense Department began the new fiscal year on 1 October 2021 with a continuing resolution in effect. Meanwhile, the White House strongly opposed the House's Space Guard measure, voicing fears of creating "new government bureaucracy." Unstated, however, was the degree to which the Space Force's affiliation with former president Trump—actual or perceived—may have influenced some political players either in the White House or congressional circles to oppose the Space Guard.[14]

A Space Force Reserve?

As of fall 2021, USSF senior leaders publicly supported a Space Force Reserve component, but the details were not forthcoming. One new talent management planning document, called "Guardian Ideal," laid the groundwork for the USSF's hiring, development, and retention of its guardians. The document addressed the service's military and civilian personnel, and while it sought "to maximize opportunities for [full-] and part-time Guardians," it failed to mention a reserve component. Some wondered if part-time members might end up serving as individuals rather than in reserve units, similar to traditional U.S. Air Force individual mobilization augmentees who served in active component units and organizations. Under that construct, command opportunities might be almost nonexistent for reservists. Earlier in the year, Brent Ziarnick—an Air Force Reserve lieutenant colonel in the 310th Space Wing when he was not teaching space power at ACSC—opined that many reservists in space jobs remained anxious as long as rumors abounded concerning the prospects for their part-time careers. He wrote that "rumors that Space Force leaders favored a 'single component' Space Force that absorbed the reservists but eliminated any reserve organization itself, [had] spread."[15]

Compounding the situation, the planning done to date at the USSF on how to incorporate reservists into the service "apparently did not include

154   EPILOGUE

any space reservists." Ziarnick's warning that Space Force leaders presumed "to know reserve affairs better than reservists" echoed the experiences of earlier generations of the Reserve and Guard. In the aftermath of the Persian Gulf conflict three decades prior, an Army War College faculty member who had served in all three Army components (active-duty, Guard, and Reserve) stated, "For an RC [reserve component] officer, the AC [active component] officer seems to possess an *arrogance toward*, and an *ignorance of*, the RC" [emphasis in original]. The post-2001 experience demonstrated that mobilizing the RC "on a judicious but regular basis," for operational duty, side-by-side with the active component, was the best antidote to such unhelpful perceptions.[16]

Space Force Enlisted Grade Insignia, Service Ranks, and Uniforms

In September 2021, Chief Master Sergeant of the Space Force Roger Towberman took to social media to unveil what the USSF's grade insignia was to look like for enlisted personnel. The USSF's insignia borrowed from the Air Force's white and blue color scheme. All nine grades employed the familiar ascending Delta, and, for E-1 through E-4 the Delta was placed vertically in the middle of the insignia; for E-5 through E-9, it was at the top of the insignia. Modifying the traditional Air Force usage of stripes, grades E-2 through E-4 featured "Vandenberg Stripes" that honored General Hoyt Vandenberg's idea decades earlier, which the Air Force had not adopted; E-2 had one stripe, E-3 two stripes, and E-4 three. The NCO grades, E-5 and E-6, had three or four "Sergeant Chevrons" below the Delta, respectively. Those two grades also employed the "Delta, Globe, and Orbit" in the insignia's upper portion, in which the delta was superimposed on the globe, with a single orbit arcing around the delta and globe. It was intentionally reminiscent of the U.S. Marine Corps' eagle, globe, and anchor. For the top three grades (E-7 through E-9), in addition to the four sergeant chevrons in the insignia's lower portion, one, two, or three "Orbital Chevrons" were situated at the top, with the delta ascending through the middle of them. For E-7 through E-9, the globe and orbital was positioned vertically between the delta and the sergeant chevrons.[17]

Earlier in the year the official names of Space Force ranks, enlisted and officer, were announced, much to the chagrin of many *Star Trek* fans.

EPILOGUE

William Shatner of *Star Trek* fame had taken up their cause in a commentary that argued for the USSF to adopt Navy ranks "because they are the ones the public is most used to being heroes." A year before reaching space as a Blue Origin passenger in real life, Hollywood's Captain Kirk pointed out that entertainment heroes including Buck Rogers and Flash Gordon from an earlier era had been known as captains—the Navy grade of O-6—in contrast with a number of Hollywood colonels and majors who portrayed less than heroic or bumbling characters. The latter included Maj. Anthony Nelson (Larry Hagman), the lead Air Force officer in the long-running television series, *I Dream of Jeannie*. The Space Force's delta logo was viewed by many as "an homage to 'Star Trek,'" Shatner said, so why not borrow again from the iconic movie series and use the Navy ranks that *Star Trek* had employed, he suggested. "They made better sense when talking about a [space] ship." Instead, the Space Force was going to use traditional Air Force names for its ranks.[18]

The decision on Space Force rank names perhaps seemed incongruous to some in part because the USSF had adopted the delta as its logo—popularized by *Star Trek*—and was using it for enlisted rank insignias. Most likely, the Space Force's release of its service dress uniform in September 2021 only heightened those sentiments. Military.com called it a uniform "worthy of the Starship *Enterprise*," while others were reminded of the *Battlestar Galactica* series. The uniform had a dark navy coat with six buttons on the right side, and gray pants. The dark blue represents "the vastness of outer space," explained a USSF colonel, and the buttons containing a delta, globe, orbit, and stars are elements of the service's flag and seal. General Raymond noted that "the coat's six buttons . . . are meant to represent its status as the military's sixth service." The same theme is represented in the six-sided nametag and six-sided enlisted insignia. The uniform released was only a prototype, however, and the service planned to modify it based on feedback from the field. That was fortunate, as one of the more polite comments on social media was, "The fit for pants and jacket is ridiculous. It looks like they put both on backwards." A Space Force official responded, "We heard your feedback. New pants, new fit coming soon."[19]

156   EPILOGUE

Continued Provocative Behaviors of U.S. Adversaries in Space

The United States' chief competitors in space, Russia and China, continued with certain actions that were at best irresponsible, or at worst unacceptable, by those nations that pursued space for nonaggressive purposes. In November the five astronauts and two cosmonauts on board the ISS were forced to take refuge for two hours in the two emergency-return spacecraft, *Crew Dragon* and *Soyuz*, when a Russian ASAT "hit an old satellite precisely," as Russian defense minister Sergei Shoigu told reporters. The strike against *Cosmos 1408* produced some fifteen hundred pieces of space debris, roughly one-half that of the Chinese test in 2007. But even one piece that impacted a spacecraft or satellite in just the wrong spot could render it inoperable and endanger the lives of astronauts or cosmonauts. Since the 2007 incident, the deliberate creation of space debris had come to be considered one of the most offensive, disruptive, and dangerous behaviors in the space domain. One writer at *National Review* opined that the Russian ASAT indicated that "Vladimir Putin is willing to risk his own citizens' lives to demonstrate Russia's prowess in space warfare," not to mention the lives of five astronauts—four Americans and one German. Andrew Follett, a space and science researcher-writer with experience at NASA and several other enterprises, concluded that the Russians had demonstrated that the Americans' "current level of satellite protection is inadequate." The danger was heightened by the fact that the United States continued to be inordinately reliant upon satellites for everyday life and so had far more to lose in a space war than did any other spacefaring nation. Topping off the Russian government's provocative behavior, its state news service, TASS, continued to divert accountability from the country's space program woes by promoting a false narrative that three years earlier an American astronaut had drilled a hole in a *Soyuz* spacecraft when it was docked to the ISS in order to force an early return to earth.[20]

Although Russian activities in space were exasperating if not always dangerous, China posed the greatest threat. In April 2021 the commander of USSPACECOM, Gen. James H. Dickinson, presented prepared remarks before the SASC on the priorities and posture of his command. General Dickinson noted, "China and Russia each weaponized space to deter and counter U.S. and allied intervention and military effectiveness in future conflicts. Today, space is a warfighting domain not because we desired it to be . . . [but] because our competitors made it so." General Dickinson's concerns encompassed a wide array of Chinese capabilities in or from space, which included at least four hundred satellites on orbit—second in number only to the United States. In comparison, Russia operated about two hundred satellites. Perhaps the most striking specific threat Dickinson mentioned was a new Chinese satellite with a robotic arm, the *Shijian-17*, which might be used "in a future system for grappling other satellites." The arm was ten meters in length and capable of lifting objects and disabling them. In addition, by 2021 China had "multiple ground-based laser systems of varying power levels that could blind or damage" U.S. satellites—one of the threats that Air Force officers Dino Lorenzini and Charles Fox had warned about forty years earlier, except the adversary in those days was the Soviet Union. In short, the USSPACECOM commander expected that "China will attempt to hold U.S. space assets at risk while using its own space capabilities to support its military objectives and overall national security goals." In November 2021, in his "Parting Shot," the vice chairman of the Joint Chiefs of Staff, Gen. John Hyten, admonished the Pentagon for its "unbelievably bureaucratic and slow" response to China's rapid upgrading of its space arsenal.[21]

Ongoing Controversy on U.S. Space Command's Permanent Basing

The question of a permanent home for USSPACECOM—reestablished in 2019—was a hot-button issue. That was bound to be the case regardless of the circumstances, but because the decision involved a mercurial president Donald Trump, it was all the more so. In the waning days of the Trump administration, the Air Force announced that Redstone Arsenal in Huntsville, Alabama, had been selected as the future base for USSPACECOM. Naturally, many Coloradans including elected officials were disappointed, if not enraged, that the state that had served as the home to both the Air Force Space Command and the Army Space and Missile Defense Command had been passed over. Some—perhaps many—had assumed Colorado's selection was a foregone conclusion. It was not the first time the disappointed had charged politics rather than rational criteria as the reason for a basing or closure decision. After the 1964 presidential election,

158   EPILOGUE

residents of Savannah, Georgia, and others in the state charged President Lyndon Johnson with "political recrimination" when his administration decided to close a major military airlift base, Hunter AFB. Savannah had voted for Johnson's opponent, Barry Goldwater.[22]

At the start of 2021 both of Colorado's U.S. senators "pledged to get the incoming [Joseph R.] Biden administration to review the decision." By late summer, as the HASC worked on the fiscal 2022 defense bill, two investigations—one led by the Pentagon's inspector general, the other by the Government Accountability Office (GAO)—were ongoing. The HASC amended the defense bill to prevent any expenditure of funds for the designing, planning, or constructing of a new headquarters building for Space Command until both investigations of the site selection decision were completed. While Trump was visiting Alabama in August, he issued a statement that complicated matters. During a radio interview just prior to a rally at Cullman, Trump said he had "single-handedly" decided to bring Space Command's headquarters to Alabama. That claim ran counter to the Air Force's previous statement, although the documented scoring of eleven categories favoring Alabama and ten favoring Colorado was close enough to reasonably allow for presidential discretion in the decision. The mayor of Colorado Springs, John Suthers, was not alone in using the off-the-cuff boast to buttress his claim that the basing decision announced in January "was not made on merit."[23]

In May 2022 the DoD released its inspector general report. Its stated objective was "to review the basis for selecting Huntsville, Alabama, as the preferred permanent location of the U.S. Space Command headquarters." The inspector general concluded the selection process "complied with law and policy, and was reasonable in identifying Huntsville as the preferred location." Of the "21 associated criteria Basing Office officials used in the process, we determined that 10 criteria were reasonable and accurate." Eight other criteria "were reasonable," although the lack of supporting documentation did not allow for full verification of their accuracy. For the remaining three criteria, neither reasonableness nor accuracy could be determined because either the Basing Office personnel or experts were unavailable to discuss them or the supporting documentation was lacking. The secretary of the Air Force, however, "placed less importance on these three criteria" in the selection process. As of March 2023, no final decision on the permanent home for the command had been announced. In any case, Space Command headquarters was expected to remain at Peterson Space Force Base, Colorado, until about 2026.[24]

Also in November 2022, the nation's first chief space officer, General Raymond, passed the torch to the next leader, Gen. B. Chance Saltzman. Capping a thirty-eight-year military career, Raymond had led the Space Force for nearly three years since its creation in 2019, during which period he oversaw the service's growth from one member—himself—to some fifteen thousand guardians. For some months, Raymond navigated "a charged political landscape" in which many viewed the Space Force "as a vanity project" of President Trump. Raymond's vision for the Space Force was that of an agile, lean service with a "flattened bureaucracy," which made sense for a very small service formed "largely out of existing resources." Nearing his retirement, Raymond expressed his desire that the service continue to build on its links with the commercial space industry as a feasible means of increasing the U.S. space architecture's capabilities and resilience in the face of emerging threats. Given that perspective, it was appropriate that Elon Musk was among the high-profile attendees at Raymond's retirement ceremony at Joint Base Andrews, Maryland, over which Secretary of Defense Lloyd Austin presided. As space writer Sandra Erwin expressed, Raymond's retirement marked "the end of an era."[25]

Former Air Force secretary Barbara Barrett offered her thoughts as well on Raymond's service: "Cometh the Hour; Cometh the Man. Success for the United States space program and especially the fledgling Space Force demanded a seminal leader who could keep existing assets functioning smoothly. At the same time, we needed to envision, build and field new capabilities and stand up an enduring new military service. With his wisdom and steady hand, General Jay Raymond was the leader for this monumental task at a precarious time in American history."[26]

Conclusion

Since the 1950s, the United States publicly referred to the domain of outer space in peaceful, rather than warfighting, terms. That public image had a profound impact on the evolution of the thinking and objectives, the

160   EPILOGUE

structure and management, and the funding and culture of U.S. military space. Meanwhile, the era of a binary spacefaring universe consisting of the United States and the USSR gave way to a multiplicity of players. By the twenty-first century, a few of them began to demonstrate space-based capabilities that threatened the interests of law-abiding nations. Presidential administrations with, at best, middling interest in space—those of Bill Clinton, George W. Bush, and Barack Obama—came and went, as did space-focused commissions and reports with their warnings and recommendations. Then, beginning in 2017, the stars seemed to align. The unlikely combination of a revived National Space Council by an unconventional president, heavy-lifting on Capitol Hill led by congressmen Mike Rogers and Jim Cooper (following in the footsteps of Sen. Bob Smith and Rep. Bob Walker), and growing concern in Washington that long-assumed American superiority in space was being increasingly diminished by challengers China and Russia, somehow broke things loose. With the signing of the fiscal 2020 National Defense Authorization Act on 20 December 2019, the U.S. Space Force was established. Whether it was called Space Corps or Space Force or had its own department was less important than the basic decision to establish a branch of service dedicated to space. It was the right call at roughly the right time, albeit coming several years after China and Russia had reorganized their space forces. Only time could tell whether that call at that moment was to be fleshed out in a way that increased U.S./allied national security, including economic advancement and increased well-being for many, perhaps even to a degree irrespective of nationality.

Steve Kitay, who went from the House's Strategic Forces Subcommittee (chaired by Rogers) to serving as the Trump administration's senior space policy official at the Pentagon, provided a big picture view of the accomplishment of establishing the United States Space Force. To Kitay, it was "the power of an idea, and the power of a team. . . . It took a team of people in the Executive branch, in the Pentagon, in the White House, in Capitol Hill, across both chambers, across both parties, and it took industry and independent experts . . . weighing in on this." After all the false starts, and the bumps and detours along the way over the course of several decades, in the end the road to establishing the Space Force was an effort truly national, strategic, and bipartisan; in Kitay's words, it was "how our system is meant to work."[27]

As a still-maturing United States Space Force completed its second full year as a service branch under the Department of the Air Force, perhaps a return to the words of the recognized father of Air Force space and missiles, Bernard Schriever, is apropos. In October 1965, General Schriever, then commander of Air Force Systems Command, spoke at a National Space Club luncheon in Washington, DC. His topic was "The Spectrum of Deterrence." Schriever addressed current research and development in connection with limited war and counterinsurgency, and he alluded to the command's "hundreds of programs, projects and tasks directed towards improving Air Force limited war and special air warfare capabilities." Affirming that limited war and counterinsurgency were "fully as important as our many other responsibilities," he pointed out that there were other important tasks facing the United States "and its partners in freedom around the world." General Schriever closed with a message that, slightly modified, still applies today:

> For this reason, the continual objective in the Systems Command [read: U.S. Space Force today] is to achieve the proper balance in all that we do. The challenges confronting our nation encompass a very wide range and they exist at every level of possible conflict. Our planning obviously must take them all into account. It would be wrong to think that we should become exclusively concerned with one or two of these challenges and thereby risk neglecting some of the others.
>
> I think that our present range of activities in the Systems Command [U.S. Space Force] enables us to avoid this mistake. With research and experimental activities ... we are addressing ourselves to our responsibilities across the entire spectrum of deterrence. This total effort is the best guarantee that we shall be prepared to meet whatever threats may emerge in the years ahead.[28]

While Bernard Schriever had addressed a broad array of concerns, his Air Force Systems Command's official stationery bore these concise and focused words: "Forging Military Spacepower." With allowances for today's challenges, activities, and responsibilities—and those that lie ahead—may General Schriever's words serve to guide those guardians who follow in his storied steps.[29]

APPENDIX

SPACE POLICY DIRECTIVE-4, 19 FEBRUARY 2019

Presidential Documents

Space Policy Directive–4 of February 19, 2019

Establishment of the United States Space Force

Memorandum for the Vice President[,] the Secretary of State[,] the Secretary of Defense[,] the Secretary of Commerce[,] the Secretary of Labor[,] the Secretary of Transportation[,] the Secretary of Homeland Security[,] the Director of the Office of Management and Budget[,] the Director of National Intelligence[,] the Assistant to the President for National Security Affairs[,] the Director of the Office of Science and Technology Policy[,] the Chairman of the Joint Chiefs of Staff[,] the Administrator of the National Aeronautics and Space Administration[, and] the Deputy Assistant to the President for Homeland Security and Counterterrorism

Section 1. *Introduction.* Space is integral to our way of life, our national security, and modern warfare. Although United States space systems have historically maintained a technological advantage over those of our potential adversaries, those potential adversaries are now advancing their space capabilities and actively developing ways to deny our use of space in a crisis or conflict. It is imperative that the United States adapt its national security organizations, policies, doctrine, and capabilities to deter aggression and protect our interests. Toward that end, the Department of Defense shall take actions under existing authority to marshal its space resources to deter and counter threats in space, and to develop a legislative proposal to establish a United States Space Force as a sixth branch of the United States Armed Forces within the Department of the Air Force. This is an important step toward a future military department for space. Under this proposal, the United States Space Force would be authorized to organize, train, and equip military space forces of the United States to ensure unfettered access to, and freedom to operate in, space, and to provide vital capabilities to joint and coalition forces in peacetime and across the spectrum of conflict.

Sec. 2. *Definitions.* For the purposes of this memorandum and the legislative proposal directed by section 3 of this memorandum, the following definitions shall apply:

(a) The term "United States Space Force" refers to a new branch of the United States Armed Forces to be initially placed by statute within the Department of the Air Force.

(b) The term "Department of the Space Force" refers to a future military department within the Department of Defense that will be responsible for organizing, training, and equipping the United States Space Force.

(c) The term "United States Space Command" refers to a Unified Combatant Command to be established pursuant to the Presidential memorandum of December 18, 2018 (Establishment of United States Space Command as a Unified Combatant Command), that will be responsible for Joint Force space operations as will be assigned in the Unified Command Plan.

Sec. 3. *Legislative Proposal and Purpose.* The Secretary of Defense shall submit a legislative proposal to the President through the Office of Management and Budget that would establish the United States Space Force as a new armed service within the Department of the Air Force.

The legislative proposal would, if enacted, establish the United States Space Force to organize, train, and equip forces to provide for freedom of operation in, from, and to the space domain; to provide independent military options for national leadership; and to enhance the lethality and effectiveness of the Joint Force. The United States Space Force should include both combat and combat support functions to enable prompt and sustained offensive and defensive space operations, and joint operations in all domains. The United States Space Force shall be organized, trained, and equipped to meet the following priorities:

(a) Protecting the Nation's interests in space and the peaceful use of space for all responsible actors, consistent with applicable law, including international law;

(b) Ensuring unfettered use of space for United States national security purposes, the United States economy, and United States persons, partners, and allies;

(c) Deterring aggression and defending the Nation, United States allies, and United States interests from hostile acts in and from space;

(d) Ensuring that needed space capabilities are integrated and available to all United States Combatant Commands;

(e) Projecting military power in, from, and to space in support of our Nation's interests; and

(f) Developing, maintaining, and improving a community of professionals focused on the national security demands of the space domain.

Sec. 4. *Scope.* (a) The legislative proposal required by section 3 of this memorandum shall, in addition to the provisions required under section 3 of this memorandum, include provisions that would, if enacted:

(i) consolidate existing forces and authorities for military space activities, as appropriate, in order to minimize duplication of effort and eliminate bureaucratic inefficiencies; and

(ii) not include the National Aeronautics and Space Administration, the National Oceanic and Atmospheric Administration, the National Reconnaissance Office, or other non-military space organizations or missions of the United States Government.

(b) The proposed United States Space Force should:

(i) include, as determined by the Secretary of Defense in consultation with the Secretaries of the military departments, the uniformed and civilian personnel conducting and directly supporting space operations from all Department of Defense Armed Forces;

(ii) assume responsibilities for all major military space acquisition programs; and

(iii) create the appropriate career tracks for military and civilian space personnel across all relevant specialties, including operations, intelligence, engineering, science, acquisition, and cyber.

Sec. 5. *United States Space Force Budget.* In accordance with the Department of Defense budget process, the Secretary of Defense shall submit to the Director of the Office of Management and Budget a proposed budget for the United States Space Force to be included in the President's Fiscal Year 2020 Budget Request.

Sec. 6. *United States Space Force Organization and Leadership.* (a) The legislative proposal required by section 3 of this memorandum shall create a civilian Under Secretary of the Air Force for Space, to be known as the Under Secretary for Space, appointed by the President by and with the advice and consent of the Senate.

(b) The legislative proposal shall establish a Chief of Staff of the Space Force, who will be a senior military officer in the grade of General or Admiral, and who shall serve as a member of the Joint Chiefs of Staff.

Sec. 7. *Associated Elements.* (a) A Unified Combatant Command for space, to be known as the United States Space Command, will be established consistent with law, as directed on December 18, 2018. This command will have all of the responsibilities of a Unified Combatant Command in addition to the space-related responsibilities previously assigned to United

Federal Register / Vol. 84, No. 37 / Monday, February 25, 2019 / Presidential Documents **6051**

States Strategic Command. It will also have the responsibilities of the Joint Force provider and Joint Force training for space operations forces. Moving expeditiously toward a Unified Combatant Command reflects the importance of warfighting in space to the Joint Force. The commander of this command will lead space warfighting through global space operations that may occur in the space domain, the terrestrial domains, or through the electromagnetic spectrum.

(b) With forces provided by the United States Space Force and other United States Armed Forces, the United States Space Command shall ensure unfettered access to, and freedom to operate in, space and provide vital effects and capabilities to joint and coalition forces during peacetime and across the spectrum of conflict.

Sec. 8. *Relationship with National Intelligence.* The Secretary of Defense and the Director of National Intelligence shall create and enhance mechanisms for collaboration between the Department of Defense and the United States Intelligence Community in order to increase unity of effort and the effectiveness of space operations. The Secretary of Defense and the Director of National Intelligence shall provide a report to the President within 180 days of the date of this memorandum on steps they have taken and are planning to take toward these ends, including legislative proposals as necessary and appropriate.

Sec. 9. *Operational Authorities.* In order to ensure that the United States Space Force and United States Space Command have the necessary operational authorities, the National Space Council and the National Security Council shall coordinate an accelerated review of space operational authorities. Within 90 days of the date of this memorandum, the Secretary of Defense shall present to the National Space Council and the National Security Council proposed relevant authority changes for the President's approval. The National Space Council and the National Security Council shall then conduct an interagency review of the Secretary's proposal and make recommendations to the President on appropriate authorities, to be completed no later than 60 days from the date the Secretary of Defense presents his proposal to the councils.

Sec. 10. *Periodic Review.* As the United States Space Force matures, and as national security requires, it will become necessary to create a separate military department, to be known as the Department of the Space Force. This department will take over some or all responsibilities for the United States Space Force from the Department of the Air Force. The Secretary of Defense will conduct periodic reviews to determine when to recommend that the President seek legislation to establish such a department.

Sec. 11. *General Provisions.* (a) Nothing in this memorandum shall be construed to impair or otherwise affect:

(i) the authority granted by law to an executive department or agency, or the head thereof; or

(ii) the functions of the Director of the Office of Management and Budget relating to budgetary, administrative, or legislative proposals.

(b) This memorandum shall be implemented consistent with applicable law and United States national and homeland security requirements, and subject to the availability of appropriations.

(c) This memorandum is not intended to, and does not, create any right or benefit, substantive or procedural, enforceable at law or in equity by any party against the United States, its departments, agencies, or entities, its officers, employees, or agents, or any other person.

6052   **Federal Register** / Vol. 84, No. 37 / Monday, February 25, 2019 / Presidential Documents

(d) The Secretary of Defense is authorized and directed to publish this memorandum in the *Federal Register*.

THE WHITE HOUSE,
Washington, February 19, 2019

[FR Doc. 2019–03345
Filed 2–22–19; 11:15 am]
Billing code 5001–06–P

NOTES

Foreword

1. For the record, the present author was one of the panelists, speaking in favor of establishing a space force, and was also, at the time, a senior consultant to the Science and Technology Policy Institute.
2. Richard P. Hallion, "Space Force: The Time is Now," panel presentation at the IDA-STPI/SI-NASM Space History Department Symposium on a Possible Space Force, Science and Technology Policy Institute of the Institute for Defense Analyses, Washington, DC, 23 Aug 2018.
3. Lt. Gen. David A. Deptula, USAF (Ret.), and Col. Mark Gunzinger, USAF (Ret.), "Decades of Air Force Underfunding Threaten America's Ability to Win," *Mitchell Institute Policy Paper* 37 (Sep 2022): 1–29.
4. Gen. Michael E. Ryan, CSAF, "High Stakes in the High Ground," in *Guideposts for the United States Military in the 21st Century*, ed. Jacob Neufeld (Washington, DC: Air Force History and Museums Program, 2000), 39.
5. Ryan, "High Stakes," 39.
6. Gen. Donald J. Kutyna USAF (Ret.), "Indispensable: Space Systems in the Persian Gulf War," in R. Cargill Hall and Jacob Neufeld (eds.), *The USAF in Space: 1945 to the 21st Century* (Washington, DC: Air Force History and Museums Program, 1998), 102–27.
7. In the wake of Desert Storm, Gen. Merrill A. "Tony" McPeak called the operation "The First Space War"; despite that, the circumstances of National Security Space at the time—highly compartmentalized and highly classified, as it still is today, and with the National Reconnaissance Office (NRO) then still deep in the black—mitigated against a full appreciation of what space had brought to the first Gulf War, something that really annoyed the then–commander of Air Force Space Command, Gen. Thomas A. Moorman. The compilation of doctrinal papers was Col. Bruce M. DeBlois, USAF (ed.), *Beyond the Paths of Heaven: The Emergence of Space Power Thought* (Maxwell AFB, AL: School of Advanced Airpower Studies/Air University Press, 1999).
8. The author was privileged to know the late Gen. Bernard Schriever; for a fine and incisive biographical treatment, see the late Neil Sheehan's *A Fiery Peace*

170　　　　　NOTES TO PAGES xxiii–xxx

in a Cold War: Bernard Schriever and the Ultimate Weapon (New York: Random House, 2009).

Preface

1. Jerry B. Marion, *Physics, The Foundation of Modern Science* (John Wiley and Sons: New York and London, 1973), 3, including quote (emphasis in original).
2. Marion, *Physics, The Foundation of Modern Science*, 1, including quote.
3. Patricia Kime, "210 US evacuees fleeing China's coronavirus outbreak land at California air reserve base," *Military Times*, 29 Jan 20.

Prologue

1. David N. Spires, *Beyond Horizons: A History of the Air Force in Space, 1947–2007* (Peterson AFB, CO: Air Force Space Command, 2nd ed., 2007), 174–76, including quotes; History, Lineage and Honors, Space Operations Command (USSF), Air Force Historical Research Agency (AFHRA), as of October 2021.
2. The second call for a space force came from David E. Lupton, *On Space Warfare: A Space Power Doctrine* (Maxwell AFB, AL: Air University Press, Jun 1988), 142–45. Although Lupton's book did not appear until 1988, the bulk of his work was completed by 1983 (Lupton, xi).
3. Dino A. Lorenzini and Charles L. Fox, "2001: A U.S. Space Force," *Naval War College Review*, vol. 34, no. 2 (Mar–Apr 1981): 48, 64, including quote 1; E-mail, Lt. Col. Edward V. Lorenzini (USAF, Ret.), to Marion, Subj: "RE: Greetings from Forrest Marion," 8 Jan 22, including quotes 2–3. In the fall of 1996, providentially the author and Ed Lorenzini shared the same Air Command and Staff College seminar at Maxwell AFB, Alabama, along with Matt Donovan, two decades later, the undersecretary (and acting secretary) of the Air Force.
4. *Report of the Commission to Assess United States National Security Space Management and Organization* [Pursuant to Public Law 106–65] (Washington, DC: 11 Jan 01).
5. Lorenzini and Fox, "2001: A U.S. Space Force," *Naval War College Review* (cited hereafter as *NWCR*), Mar–Apr 1981, 49, including quote 1; Daniel O. Graham, *High Frontier: A New National Strategy* (Washington, DC: High Frontier, 1982), 21, 51, including quotes 2–3; Graham, *We Must Defend America: A New Strategy for National Survival* (Chicago: Regnery Gateway, 1983), 25, 47–53, 107, 111–13. After his retirement from the U.S. Army in 1976, Graham served as military adviser to Ronald W. Reagan in the 1976 and 1980 presidential campaigns. In 1982–83, Graham's High Frontier project was influential in President Reagan's Strategic Defense Initiative (SDI, also known as Star Wars); see Louie Estrada, "Gen. Daniel Graham Dies," *Washington Post*, 3 Jan

NOTES TO PAGES xxxii–xxxiv   171

96; "Lieutenant General Daniel O. Graham, US Army, Retired (Deceased)," pdf biographical sketch, accessed at https://www.ikn.army.mil/apps/MIHOF/biographies/Graham,%20Daniel.pdf.

6. The authors could not have known that in the end, the shuttle was to be much more expensive than anticipated.

7. Lorenzini and Fox, "2001: A U.S. Space Force," *NWCR*, Mar–Apr 1981, 49–52, 60, including quote; Graham, *We Must Defend America*, 53–58; Lupton, *On Space Warfare*, 68; chap. 2, present work, discusses the Chinese 2007 ASAT test.

8. William Leavitt, "How Much of a Spurt SINCE SPUTNIK," *Air Force Magazine*, vol. 42, no. 1 (Jan 1959): 63, including quote 1; Lee V. Gossick, "The Implications of Space in Global Power Relationships," Air War College Thesis No. 1595, Maxwell AFB, AL, 1959, 48, including quote 2; Ford Eastman, "Defense Officials Concede Missile Lag," *Aviation Week Including Space Technology*, vol. 70, no. 6 (9 Feb 59): 26–27, including quote 3; *USAF Historical Study No. 85, USAF Credits for the Destruction of Enemy Aircraft, World War II* (Washington, DC: Office of Air Force History, Headquarters USAF, 1978), 74; Maj. Gen. Lee V. Gossick, *U.S. Air Force*, Biographies, accessed at https://www.af.mil/About-Us/Biographies/Display/Article/104960/major-general-lee-v-gossick/ (5 Oct 22). Gossick's aerial victories took place on 7 Apr 43 and 10 Jun 43. The "missile lag" stated in the above article, and which was the general consensus of Americans at the time, was later proven erroneous.

9. Edgar Ulsamer, "Space Shuttle Mired In Bureaucratic Feud," *Air Force Magazine*, vol. 63, no. 9 (Sep 1980): 72, including quotes 1, 4; Richard E. Hansen, "Freedom Of Passage On The High Seas Of Space," *Strategic Review*, Fall 1977, 85, including quotes 2–3 (quote 2, Smart quoted by Hansen); Lorenzini and Fox, "2001: A U.S. Space Force," *NWCR*, Mar–Apr 1981, 51, 61 (they also quoted Smart); David N. Spires, *Beyond Horizons: A History of the Air Force in Space, 1947–2007* (Peterson AFB, CO: Air Force Space Command, 2nd ed., 2007), 38–41. Lorenzini and Fox referred to U.S. Sen. Malcolm Wallop, who warned that with only four space-based laser stations, the Soviets could shoot down most of the strategic bomber fleet of the Strategic Air Command (51).

10. Lorenzini and Fox, "2001: A U.S. Space Force," *NWCR*, Mar–Apr 1981, 52–53, including quotes. In the present work, Chapter 5's discussion of the Space Development Agency includes General Hyten's concern of over-studying certain space problems.

11. Lorenzini and Fox, "2001: A U.S. Space Force," *NWCR*, Mar–Apr 1981, 53–54, including quote; Draft (Prologue) (comments provided by Dr. Dino A. Lorenzini), attached to E-mail, Edward V. Lorenzini to Marion, Subj: "Fwd: Space Force Prologue," 29 Mar 22 (copy at AFHRA).

172 NOTES TO PAGES xxxiv–2

12. Lorenzini and Fox, "2001: A U.S. Space Force," *NWCR*, Mar.–Apr. 1981, 54–55, including quotes (quote 4, William J. Beane quoted by authors).

13. Lorenzini and Fox, "2001: A U.S. Space Force," *NWCR*, Mar.–Apr. 1981, 55–59, 61, including quotes.

14. Rex Warner, trans., Thucydides, *History of the Peloponnesian War* (London, New York, and Victoria, Australia: Penguin Books, 1954 [1972, introduction, appendices]), 49, including quote; Lorenzini and Fox, "2001: A U.S. Space Force," *NWCR*, Mar.–Apr. 1981, 60; personal conversation, Dr. Richard P. Hallion with Marion, Shalimar, Fla., 15 Dec 21.

15. [John F. Kennedy], "The Moon Decision," *Smithsonian National Air and Space Museum*, May 25, 1961, including quote 1; Lorenzini and Fox, "2001: A U.S. Space Force," *NWCR*, Mar.–Apr. 1981, 61–64, including quotes 2–5.

16. Lupton, *On Space Warfare*, 4, 14–15, 33, 51, 63, 143, including quote; History, Lineage and Honors, Space Operations Command (USSF), AFHRA, October 2021. Note that one official document, "Air Force Space Command History," Air Force Space Command (Archived), accessed at https://www.afspc.af.mil/About-Us/AFSPC-History/ (5 Oct 22), erroneously stated that, "On Sept. 1, 1982, the Air Force established Air Force Space Command." In fact, the Air Force established "Space Command" in 1982, which three years later was redesignated "Air Force Space Command."

17. Lupton, *On Space Warfare*, xiv, 1, 4, 7, 15, 43, 51, including quotes; Everett C. Dolman, *Astropolitik: Classical Geopolitics in the Space Age* (London and Portland, Ore.: Frank Cass, 2002), 166 (note 31). Lupton noted that in the 1981–82 AWC curriculum, "security classification of space-related topics was a major hindrance" (15). The issue continued for decades at Maxwell's Air University professional military education organizations, if not elsewhere; see chap. 4, present work.

18. Lupton, *On Space Warfare*, 142–45, including quotes (emphasis in original).

Chapter 1. Survey of U.S. National Security Space, 1996–2000

1. "President Clinton Issues New National Space Policy," The White House, Office of the Press Secretary, 19 Sep 96, including quote 1, accessed at https://clinton whitehouse4.archives.gov/WH/EOP/OSTP/html/spacepol-press.html (5 Oct 22); John E. Hyten, *A Sea of Peace or a Theater of War: Dealing with the Inevitable Conflict in Space* (University of Illinois at Urbana-Champaign: ACDIS [Occasional Paper], Apr 2000), 63, 69, including quote 2, accessed at https://www .ideals.illinois.edu/bitstream/handle/2142/102028/ASeaofPeaceoraTheaterof WarDealingwiththeInevitableConflictinSpace.pdf?sequence=1&isAllowed=y (16 Nov 21); Oral History Interview (cited herafter as OHI), Hon. Robert S. Walker (U.S. House of Representatives), conducted by Marion, Maxwell

NOTES TO PAGES 2-4   173

AFB, AL (remote), 19 Apr 22, including quotes 3–4 (AFHRA, call number S239.0512–2850, audio only); Peter L. Hays, James M. Smith, Alan R. Van Tassel, and Guy M. Walsh, eds., *Spacepower for a New Millennium: Space and U.S. National Security* (New York and St. Louis: McGraw-Hill, 2000), 7–8; Matthew Mowthorpe, *The Militarization and Weaponization of Space* (New York and Toronto: Lexington Books, 2004), 195; Everett C. Dolman, *Astropolitik: Classical Geopolitics in the Space Age* (London and Portland, OR: Frank Cass, 2002), 153.

2. Hyten, *A Sea of Peace or a Theater of War*, 63, including quote (James Hackett paraphrased or quoted by Hyten).

3. Hyten, *A Sea of Peace or a Theater of War*, 67, including quote.

4. "Reviving the National Space Council," Executive Order 13803, *Federal Register*, 30 Jun 17; Heather Bloemhard, "National Space Council Reestablished," *American Astronomical Society*, 11 Jul 17. The NDAA in view was the fiscal 2018; see chap. 4, present study.

5. OHI, Walker, 19 Apr 22.

6. "President Clinton Issues New National Space Policy," 19 Sep 96, including quote; "Fact Sheet, National Space Policy," The White House, 19 Sep 96; Roelof L. Schuiling, "STS-95: 'The John Glenn Flight,'" *Spaceflight* 41 (Feb 1999): 60–62; "John Glenn, The Come-Back Astronaut," *Spaceflight* 40 (Nov 1998): 413.

7. [Michael P. C. Carns], "National Security Industrial Association: SPACE-CAST 2020 Symposium Held in Washington, DC on 9–10 November 1994," report dated 1994, p. 26, including quote 1; "Looking Into The Aviation Future," *Plane News*, 25 Jan 1919, including quote 2 (AFHRA call number 167.612–3); "Fact Sheet, National Space Policy," The White House, National Science and Technology Council, 19 Sep 96, including quote 3, accessed at https://clintonwhitehouse4.archives.gov/WH/EOP/OSTP/NSTC/html/fs/fs-5.html (5 Oct 22); Michael E. O'Hanlon, *Neither Star Wars Nor Sanctuary: Constraining the Military Uses of Space* (Washington, DC: Brookings Institution Press, 2004), 38; David N. Spires, *Beyond Horizons: A History of the Air Force in Space, 1947–2007* (Peterson AFB, CO: Air Force Space Command, 2nd ed., 2007), 277. Interest in commercial space outside the United States was high: although most commercial satellites were built domestically, less than one-half were launched by American companies. One study counted some eleven hundred companies in fifty-three countries that were exploiting space by the late 1990s; Tim Furniss, "Space News Round-Up," *Spaceflight* 41 (Sep 1999): 355; Hyten, *A Sea of Peace or a Theater of War*, 7. In 2011, a multi-authored space power essay concluded, "The commercial, communication, and military uses of space have become less separable"; Michael Krepon, Theresa Hitchens, and

174 NOTES TO PAGES 4-5

Michael Katz-Hyman, "Preserving Freedom of Action in Space: Realizing the Potential and Limits of U.S. Spacepower," chap. 6 in Charles D. Lutes and Peter L. Hays, eds., with Vincent A. Manzo, Lisa M. Yambrick, and M. Elaine Bunn, *Toward a Theory of Spacepower, Selected Essays* (Washington, DC: Institute for National Strategic Studies, National Defense University, 2011), 119.

8. "President Opens Door to Commercial GPS Markets; Move Could Add 100,000 New Jobs to Economy by Year 2000," The White House, Office of the Press Secretary, 29 Mar 96, including quotes, accessed at https://clinton whitehouse4.archives.gov/WH/EOP/OSTP/html/gps-pressrel.html (5 Oct 22); Hyten, *A Sea of Peace or a Theater of War*, 59.

9. "Fact Sheet, National Space Policy," 19 Sep 96, including quotes 1–3; Dolman, *Astropolitik*, 153–54, including quotes 4–5; O'Hanlon, *Neither Star Wars nor Sanctuary*, 12–13, including quote 6; Mowthorpe, *Militarization and Weaponization of Space*, 205, 217. In accord with détente, in late 1999 the Air Force began imploding Minuteman III missile silos at Grand Forks AFB, North Dakota, in keeping with the Strategic Arms Reduction Treaty (START); History, Air Force Space Command (AFSPC), Jan 1994–Dec 2003, vol. 1, 54–55 (held at AFHRA, Maxwell AFB, AL). Note that NSS included the satellites and systems of the armed forces as well as the National Reconnaissance Office, but not those that served U.S. government civil functions.

10. Jacob Neufeld, *Bernard A. Schriever, Challenging the Unknown* (Washington, DC: Office of Air Force History, 2005), 1, including quote (by Neufeld, on unnumbered page preceding page 1); Neil Sheehan, *A Fiery Peace in a Cold War: Bernard Schriever and the Ultimate Weapon* (New York: Random House, 2009), 474.

11. The 1998 Rumsfeld Commission stirred the passage in Congress of the National Missile Defense Act of 1999. It passed with a veto-proof majority, but a failed national missile defense test in 2000 led President Clinton to delay any further decisions until the George W. Bush administration took over; Mowthorpe, *Militarization and Weaponization of Space*, 190–91.

12. Mowthorpe, *Militarization and Weaponization of Space*, 87, 99, 190–91; Dwayne A. Day, "Recon for the Rising Sun," *Spaceflight* 41 (Oct 1999): 420; Hays et al., *Spacepower for a New Millennium*, 34. Prior to the Taepo Dong 1, the North Koreans had launched only a single-stage missile; Taepo Dong 1 was a three-stage booster, and the third stage failed in-flight (Mowthorpe, 191). Note that for years the North had pursued nuclear programs that many U.S./allied analysts suspected were a cover for the development of nuclear weapons that might be delivered by such a missile.

13. Furniss, "Space News Round-Up," *Spaceflight* 41 (Jul 1999): 267–68; "US Air Force Loses Early Warning Satellite," *Spaceflight* 41 (Jun 1999): 224; "Boeing

NOTES TO PAGES 6–8   175

Inertial Upper Stage Mock-up," Museum of Flight, Boeing, accessed at https://www.museumofflight.org/spacecraft/boeing-inertial-upper-stage-mock (5 Oct 22). Typically, when launched from a Titan IVB rocket the IUS separated from the second-stage booster about nine minutes into the flight, powering the spacecraft the rest of its way into orbit. Note that the first Boeing IUS failure occurred with the loss of the *Challenger* in 1986.

14. Spires, *Beyond Horizons*, 283, 286–87, 289, including quotes 1–3; L. Parker Temple III, *Implosion: Lessons from National Security, High Reliability Spacecraft, Electronics, and the Forces Which Changed Them* (Hoboken, N.J.: John Wiley and Sons, 2013), 266–67, including quote 4; Furniss, "Space News Round-Up," *Spaceflight* 41 (July 1999): 267–68.

15. Spires, *Beyond Horizons*, 85; Mowthorpe, *Militarization and Weaponization of Space*, 192, 205. In late May 1999, Lockheed Martin succeeded in launching a Titan IVB booster (without an upper stage) that carried an unidentified NRO satellite (this was the previously delayed mission referenced in the text); see Furniss, "Space News Round-Up," *Spaceflight* 41 (Aug 1999): 310. Note that the NRO was established in the early 1960s at the height of the Cold War, and its existence remained classified until 1996; "First 'Announced' NRO Payload," *Spaceflight* 39 (Mar 1997): 77.

16. United States Air Force Scientific Advisory Board, *Report on A Space Roadmap for the 21st Century Aerospace Force, Volume 3: Appendices F-J* [SAB-TR-98–01], Dec 2000, G-78–82, including quotes; Mowthorpe, *Militarization and Weaponization of Space*, 92–93, 98, 102–104; O'Hanlon, *Neither Star Wars Nor Sanctuary*, 38–39, 86–87, 109, 130.

17. Hyten, *A Sea of Peace or a Theater of War*, 23, 60–62, 73, including quotes (quote 2 quoted by Hyten); Mowthorpe, *Militarization and Weaponization of Space*, 98–100. In the fiscal 1999 national defense authorization act (signed in October 1998), Congress transferred authority for the licensing of satellites from Commerce back to the State Department.

18. Furniss, "Space News Round-Up," *Spaceflight* 41 (Jul 1999): 269, including quote; Mowthorpe, *Militarization and Weaponization of Space*, 100, 173; Hyten, *A Sea of Peace or a Theater of War*, 61–62.

19. "Military Affairs," *Current Digest of the Post-Soviet Press* 48, no. 43 (20 Nov 96): 18, including quote 1; "Rodionov Proposes Changes in Military Doctrine," *Current Digest of the Post-Soviet Press* 48, no. 50 (8 Jan 97): 1, including quote 2; Benjamin S. Lambeth, *Russia's Air Power in Crisis* (Washington, DC and London: Smithsonian Institution Press, 1999), 158, including quote 3 (Arbatov quoted by Lambeth); "Army Reform Launched With Lebed on Sidelines," *Current Digest of the Post-Soviet Press* 48, no. 40 (30 Oct 96): 6; "Main Staff of Strategic Missile Forces Gets New Chief," *Current Digest of the*

176   NOTES TO PAGES 8–9

Post-Soviet Press 49, no. 2 (12 Feb 97): 18; "Russian Space Future Dims," *Space-flight* 39 (Mar 1997): 95; Rodric Braithwaite, *Afgantsy: The Russians In Afghanistan, 1979–89* (Oxford and New York: Oxford University Press, 2011), 84–85, 309. By early 1997, Russian officials announced their military reform plan "for the creation of missile and space forces (to be made up of the Strategic Missile Forces, military space forces and missile and space defense forces), with the prospect of their being reconstituted as the Russian Federation Strategic Deterrent Forces (SDF) by 2000"; see above 12 Feb 97 article, p. 19.

20. Mowthorpe, in his *Militarization and Weaponization of Space* (166), wrote: "The war in the Persian Gulf was the first circumstance in which a wide range of military space systems were used in a conflict. It was the first real test under war conditions of the sixty or so Western military satellites that were involved. Space added a fourth dimension to the war. It allowed a communications network to support a 400,000-strong army to be established in theater in a few weeks. It provided images of Iraqi forces and the reconnaissance photographs for the Allied air attacks. Satellites provided a navigation system which provided accurate information for combat soldiers, on missiles, tanks, aircraft, and ships. It is for these principal reasons that the Gulf War is being described as the first space war."

21. Michael E. Ryan, "On Becoming a Space and Air Force," Air Force Association (AFA) National Symposia, 14 Nov 97, including quotes 1, 3, and 4 (quote 1 quoted by Ryan); Hyten, *A Sea of Peace or a Theater of War*, 28, including quote 2 (Moorman quoted by Hyten); Hays et al., *Spacepower for a New Millennium*, 17–18. In 1999, former Air Force chief of staff Mike Dugan commented that a familiar photograph from Operation Desert Storm known as "The Highway of Death" should have been called, "Air and Space Inferiority"; see Michael J. Dugan, "Forgotten, But Not Gone . . . Thinking About Air & Space Power," AFA National Symposia, 5 Feb 99.

22. John A. Tirpak, "Future Engagement," *Air Force Magazine* 80, no. 1 (Jan 1997): 19–20, including quote 1; Hays et al., *Spacepower for a New Millennium*, 18, including quote 2; Ryan, "On Becoming a Space and Air Force," including quotes 3–6; Benjamin S. Lambeth, *Mastering the Ultimate High Ground: Next Steps in the Military Uses of Space* (Santa Monica, CA; Arlington, VA; and Pittsburgh, PA: RAND, 2003), 52. In 1998, the Air Force's Scientific Advisory Board wrote, "The United States Air Force is today an air and space force whose core competencies, as articulated in Global Engagement, entail the integrated employment of weapons and support systems across the physical media of air and space. But that force is largely a legacy of the Cold War, it often treats air and space operations as separate activities, and it faces wrenching changes in evolving to deal with the very different world of the 21st century"; see John M.

Borky (study chairman), *Report on a Space Roadmap for the 21st Century Aerospace Force, Volume 1 [SAB-TR-98-01]* (Washington, DC: United States Air Force Scientific Advisory Board, Nov 1998), vii.

23. Howell M. Estes III, "The Air Force at a Crossroad," AFA National Symposia, 14 Nov 97, including quote.

24. Hyten, *A Sea of Peace or a Theater of War*, 39, 49; Spires, *Beyond Horizons*, 279–80, 295; History, AFSPC, Jan 2009–Dec 2010, chap. 1 (Mission), 4 (held at AFHRA). Spires listed the Air Force share of the DoD space budget at 85 percent; Hyten, more than 90 percent. The Air Force Space Command was by far the largest component of U.S. Space Command.

25. Estes, "The Air Force at a Crossroad," including quote; Lambeth, *Mastering the Ultimate High Ground*, 53–54.

26. Estes, "The Air Force at a Crossroad," including quotes.

27. Estes, "The Air Force at a Crossroad," including quotes 1–2; Jeffrey J. Smith, *Tomorrow's Air Force: Tracing the Past, Shaping the Future* (Bloomington and Indianapolis: Indiana University Press, 2014), chap. 16, especially 214–20, including quotes 3–5.

28. Smith, *Tomorrow's Air Force*, 190–91, 220, including quote.

29. William S. Cohen, *Annual Report to the President and the Congress* (Washington, DC: 1998), 68–71, including quotes 1–2; Memorandum, Secretary of Defense [Cohen] to Secretaries of the Military Departments et al., Subj: "Department of Defense Space Policy," 9 Jul 99, including quote 3; [Cohen], *Space Policy*, Department of Defense Directive (DoDD) 3100.10 (Washington, DC, 9 Jul 99), 3–9.

30. Bob Smith, "The Challenge of Space Power," *Airpower Journal* 13, no. 1 (Spring 1999): 32, including quote. In the House of Representatives in the 1980s, Smith served on the Space Subcommittee of the Science and Technology Committee.

31. Smith, "Challenge of Space Power," *Airpower Journal*, 33, 37, including quote 1; E-mail, Dr. Michael V. Smith (Air Command and Staff College (ACSC), Maxwell AFB, AL) to Marion, Subj: "RE: USSF Book Project," 23 Jan 20, including quote 2 (DeKok quoted by M. V. Smith); Shawn P. Rife, "On Space-Power Separatism," *Airpower Journal* 13, no. 1 (Spring 1999): 21, including quote 3 (Horner quoted by Rife); OHI, Dr. Michael V. Smith (ACSC), conducted by Marion, Maxwell AFB, AL, 3 Aug, 12–13 Aug 20 (AFHRA, call number S239.0512–2837, audio only); Lt. Gen. Roger G. DeKok, *U.S. Air Force*, Biographies, accessed at https://www.af.mil/About-Us/Biographies/Display/Article/107256/lieutenant-general-roger-g-dekok/ (5 Oct 22). Michael V. Smith retired in 2016 as a USAF colonel with many years in missiles as well as space.

NOTES TO PAGES 13–16

32. Smith, "Challenge of Space Power," *Airpower Journal*, 33, including quotes 1–3; Julian S. Corbett, *Principles of Maritime Strategy* (Mineola, N.Y.: Dover, 2004 [1911]), 284, including quote 4.

33. Hyten, *A Sea of Peace or a Theater of War*, 67–68, including quote. A near-contemporary of Corbett, Alfred Thayer Mahan was cited by space scholars as well, for his highly influential 1890 work, *The Influence of Sea Power Upon History, 1660–1783*; see Dolman, *Astropolitik*, 32–39.

34. Krepon, Hitchens, and Katz-Hyman, "Preserving Freedom of Action in Space," 123, including quotes.

35. Smith, "Challenge of Space Power," *Airpower Journal*, 33–35, including quotes; Lambeth, *Mastering the Ultimate High Ground*, 57–58.

36. Smith, "Challenge of Space Power," *Airpower Journal*, 35, including quotes; OHI, M. V. Smith, 3 Aug, 12–13 Aug 20; Hyten, *A Sea of Peace or a Theater of War*, 54. One objection voiced by space proponents to the tendency to combine space and missile personnel was rooted in the fact that ICBMs did not operate from space, but merely passed through space en route to the target.

37. OHI, Hon. Speaker Newton L. Gingrich, conducted by Marion (via telephone), 21 Mar 22, including quote [1] (AFHRA, call number S239.0512–2846); OHI, Lt. Gen. William T. Lord (USAF, Ret), conducted by Daniel P. Williams and F. L. Marion, Peterson SFB, Colo., 6 Mar 23, including quote 2 (AFHRA, call number K239.0512-2872, audio only); Smith, "Challenge of Space Power," *Airpower Journal*, 35–36; Spires, *Beyond Horizons*, 8. Originally, the board's designation was the Army Air Forces Scientific Advisory Group.

38. Smith, "Challenge of Space Power," *Airpower Journal*, 35–36, including quote.

39. Smith, "Challenge of Space Power," *Airpower Journal*, 37–38, including quotes; *Report of the Commission to Assess United States National Security Space Management and Organization* [Pursuant to Public Law 106-65] (Washington, DC: 11 Jan 01), xxxv, 76, 82, 96–97; Hays et al., *Spacepower for a New Millennium*, 18. Although Smith's article used the subtitling, "Two Options," three options were presented in the text. Differing somewhat from Senator Smith, the Rumsfeld Commission recommended establishing an undersecretary of defense for space, intelligence, and information (xxxii–xxxiii, 81–82, 85–87).

40. Dwight R. Messimer, *An Incipient Mutiny: The Story of the U.S. Army Signal Corps Pilot Revolt* (Lincoln, Neb.: Potomac Books, 2020), 1–3, including quote (chief signal officer's report quoted by Messimer); Smith, "Challenge of Space Power," *Airpower Journal*, 38.

41. Smith, "Challenge of Space Power," *Airpower Journal*, 38–39, including quote.

42. *Report of the Commission . . . National Security Space Management and Organization*, xxxiii, 93–94, including quote, accessed at https://aerospace.csis.org/

NOTES TO PAGES 16–20   179

wp-content/uploads/2018/09/RumsfeldCommission.pdf (5 Oct 22); Lambeth, *Mastering the Ultimate High Ground*, 72–74.

43. Richard B. Myers, "Achieving the Promise of Space—The Next Step," AFA National Symposia, 4 Feb 99, including quote 1; Spires, *Beyond Horizons*, 294, including quote 2 (proponents quoted by Spires).

44. Myers, "Achieving the Promise of Space," 4 Feb 99, including quote 1; Spires, *Beyond Horizons*, 328–29, including quote 2; Hyten, *A Sea of Peace or a Theater of War*, 73, including quote 3. For Horner's quote, see paragraph for citation 31.

45. Myers, "Achieving the Promise of Space," 4 Feb 99, including quote 1; Cynthia A.S. McKinley, "The Guardians of Space: Organizing America's Space Assets for the Twenty-First Century," *Aerospace Power Journal*, Spr. 2000, 40–41, including quotes 2–5.

46. Myers, "Achieving the Promise of Space," 4 Feb 99, including quote 1; Bryant Jordan, "Will the Air Force lose its space program?" *Air Force Times*, 8 Feb 99, 26, including quote 2; Hays et al., *Spacepower for a New Millennium*, 18; Lambeth, *Mastering the Ultimate High Ground*, 147.

47. Michael E. Ryan, "From Above and Beyond," AFA National Symposia, 4 Feb 99, including quote.

48. Michael E. Ryan, untitled address to AFA National Symposia, 17 Nov 2000; Lambeth, *Mastering the Ultimate High Ground*, 58–59.

49. Dugan, "Forgotten, But Not Gone," AFA National Symposia, 5 Feb 99, including quote 1; Michael P. C. Carns [closing remarks], *National Security Industrial Association SPACECAST 2020 Symposium, Washington, D.C., 9–10 November 1994* (Maxwell AFB, AL: Air Education and Training Command, 1994?), 3–5, including quotes 2–3; Spires, *Beyond Horizons*, 281. The author served on the faculty of the Squadron Officer School from 1988 to 1991, and in that capacity recalled numerous discussions and curriculum readings that addressed the tendency of USAF flight-rated officers to identify more closely with their aircraft type than with the profession of arms.

50. Dugan, "Forgotten, But Not Gone," AFA National Symposia, 5 Feb 99; Smith, *Tomorrow's Air Force*, 187–91; OHI, M. V. Smith, 3 Aug, 12–13 Aug 20; see Carl H. Builder, *The Icarus Syndrome: The Role of Air Power Theory and the Evolution of the U.S. Air Force* (New Brunswick, NJ, and London: Transaction Publishers, 1994), xvi, 6–7, 179–82, 285.

51. Richard B. (Dick) Myers, untitled address to AFA National Symposium and Annual Air Force Ball, 19 Nov 99, including quotes 1–2, 4–5; O'Hanlon, *Neither Star Wars nor Sanctuary*, 109, including quote 3; Krepon, Hitchens, and Katz-Hyman, "Preserving Freedom of Action in Space," 124, including quote 6.

52. Myers, untitled address to AFA National Symposium, 19 Nov 99, including quotes 1–2; Lambeth, *Mastering the Ultimate High Ground*, 102–103, including

180   NOTES TO PAGES 21–24

quote 3; William B. Scott, "Innovation Is Currency of USAF Space Battlelab," *Aviation Week & Space Technology* 152, no. 14 (3 Apr 00), including quotes 4–5 (quote 4, Maj. Tim Marceau quoted by Scott).

53. Myers, untitled address to AFA National Symposium, 19 Nov 99, including quotes 1–2; Lambeth, *Mastering the Ultimate High Ground*, 103, including quote 3; Hyten, *A Sea of Peace or a Theater of War*, 73; O'Hanlon, *Neither Star Wars nor Sanctuary*, 127.

54. Hays et al., *Spacepower for a New Millennium*, 228, including quotes; Brig. Gen. Simon P. Worden, *U.S. Air Force*, Biographies, accessed at https://www.af.mil/About-Us/Biographies/Display/Article/105213/brigadier-general-simon-p-worden/ (5 Oct 22). Worden's chapter was entitled, "Space Control for the 21st Century: A Space 'Navy' Protecting the Commercial Basis of America's Wealth."

55. Hays et al., *Spacepower for a New Millennium*, 228, including quote; OHI, Lt. Col. Peter A. Garretson, USAF (Ret.), conducted by Marion, Maxwell AFB, AL, 29 Oct 21 (AFHRA, call number S239.0512–2840, audio only).

56. Michael E. Ryan, "Aerospace Domain," AFA National Symposium and Annual Air Force Ball, 19 Nov 99, including quotes.

57. Spires, *Beyond Horizons*, 82, including quote.

58. Lambeth, *Mastering the Ultimate High Ground*, 43–44, 46–47, including quotes. When I queried Dr. M. V. Smith whether he was Lambeth's unidentified source, Smith confirmed that he was, indeed: E-mail, Smith to Marion, Subj: "RE: Lambeth's 2003 book," 1 Dec 21, 10 Dec 21 (copy at AFHRA).

59. Ryan, "Aerospace Domain," AFA National Symposium, 19 Nov 99, including quote 1 (Mike Ryan quoted his father in this address); *The Aerospace Force: Defending America in the 21st Century* (Washington, DC, 2000 [white paper]), i, including quote 2; McKinley, "Guardians of Space," *Aerospace Power Journal*, Spring 2000, 39, including quote 3; Lambeth, *Mastering the Ultimate High Ground*, 39–40; Spires, *Beyond Horizons*, 54, 191, 288.

60. Ryan, "Aerospace Domain," AFA National Symposium, 19 Nov 99, including quote; Neville Kidger, "Early orbital operations," *Spaceflight* 42 (Nov. 2000), 462.

61. Michael E. Ryan, untitled address to AFA National Symposium, 17 Nov 2000, including quotes 1, 3; Spires, *Beyond Horizons*, 300, including quote 2; Ralph E. Eberhart, untitled address to AFA National Symposium, 17 Nov 2000. Eberhart agreed with Ryan on Kosovo/Serbia as a good example of air-space integration.

62. Ryan, untitled address to AFA National Symposium, 17 Nov 2000, including quote; Eberhart, untitled address to AFA National Symposium, 17 Nov 2000. From February 2000 to April 2002, Eberhart was commander in chief

NOTES TO PAGES 24–27 181

of U.S. Space Command and North American Aerospace Defense Command (NORAD); and commander, Air Force Space Command (AFSPC); Gen. Ralph E. "Ed" Eberhart, *U.S. Air Force*, Biographies, accessed at https://www.af.mil/About-Us/Biographies/Display/Article/105056/general-ralph-e-ed-eberhart/ (5 Oct 22).

63. F. Whitten Peters, untitled address to AFA National Symposium, 17 Nov 2000, including quotes; Hyten, *A Sea of Peace or a Theater of War*, 50.

64. Lambeth, *Mastering the Ultimate High Ground*, 58–59, including quote (Maj. Gen. William E. Jones, USAF (Ret.), quoted by Lambeth); Hyten, *A Sea of Peace or a Theater of War*, 49–50. Rumsfeld had chaired the 1998 ballistic missile threat commission.

Chapter 2. U.S. National Security Space: The Bush Years, 2001–2008

1. *Report of the Commission to Assess United States National Security Space Management and Organization* [Pursuant to Public Law 106-65] (Washington, DC: 11 Jan 01), vii, xxii, including quote 1; Michael E. Ryan, untitled address to the Air Force Association (AFA) National Symposium, 17 Nov 2000, including quote 2; Oral History Interview (OHI), Gen. Lance W. Lord (USAF, Ret.), conducted by George Bradley and Rick Sturdevant, AFSPC/HO, Peterson AFB, CO, 29 Jan 07, including quote 3 (copy at AFHRA); F. Whitten Peters, untitled address to the AFA National Symposium, 17 Nov 00; Bob Smith, "The Challenge of Space Power," *Airpower Journal* 13, no. 1 (Spring 1999): 35–36.

2. *Report of the Commission . . . National Security Space Management and Organization*, unnumbered page following title page, Attachment A, Resumes of Commission Members, A-1–A-4, and Attachment C, Commission Meetings, C-1–C-7, accessed at https://aerospace.csis.org/wp-content/uploads/2018/09/RumsfeldCommission.pdf (5 Oct 22); Benjamin S. Lambeth, *Mastering the Ultimate High Ground: Next Steps in the Military Uses of Space* (Santa Monica, Calif., and Arlington, Va.: RAND, 2003), 81. Rumsfeld resigned from the commission on 28 Dec 2000, the day he was nominated as the incoming secretary of defense. Although the report was delivered directly to those legislators who had helped select the commissioners, the NDAA of 2001 required the defense secretary, by April 2001, to provide Congress with his assessment of the commission's recommendations. Note Lambeth erred in the timing of two statements by USAF senior leaders (Secretary Peters, General Eberhart) relative to the space commission, whose statements were made in November 2000—prior to the release of the commission's report in January 2001—rather than following its release (p. 79). Peters' statement is addressed in Chapter 1, present work.

182 NOTES TO PAGES 27-30

3. Tom Bowman, "Tough Pentagon To-Do List Awaits Cold War Veteran," *Baltimore Sun*, 11 Jan 01, including quote. Rumsfeld's involvement with space in the Ford administration is covered by David N. Spires, *Beyond Horizons: A History of the Air Force in Space, 1947–2007*, 2nd. ed. (Peterson AFB, CO.: Air Force Space Command, 2007), 189.

4. Charles Hutzler, "Rocket Launch Advances China's Space Program," *Washington Times*, 11 Jan 01, including quote; "Yang Liwei," *Encyclopedia Britannica*, 17 Jun 20, accessed at https://www.britannica.com/biography/Yang-Liwei (5 Oct 22); *Report of the Commission . . . National Security Space Management and Organization*, 10; Michael E. O'Hanlon, *Neither Star Wars nor Sanctuary: Constraining the Military Uses of Space* (Washington, DC: Brookings Institution Press, 2004), 54.

5. *Report of the Commission . . . National Security Space Management and Organization*, ii, vii, 1, A-1–A-4; Lambeth, *Mastering the Ultimate High Ground*, 61.

6. *Report of the Commission . . . National Security Space Management and Organization*, xxii–xxiii, 57, including quotes; Lambeth, *Mastering the Ultimate High Ground*, 63–65; Spires, *Beyond Horizons*, 292.

7. Spires, *Beyond Horizons*, 299–306, including quote 1; Michael E. Ryan, "Aerospace Domain," AFA National Symposium and Annual Air Force Ball, 19 Nov 99, including quote 2.

8. *Report of the Commission . . . National Security Space Management and Organization*, xxii–xxiii, 57, including quote 1; Tom Clancy with General Chuck Horner, *Every Man a Tiger* (New York: G. P. Putnam's Sons, 1999), 520, including quote 2; OHI, Dr. Michael V. Smith (Col., USAF, Ret.), conducted by Marion, Maxwell AFB, AL, 3 Aug, 12–13 Aug 20.

9. OHI, M. V. Smith, 3 Aug, 12–13 Aug 20; E-mail, Dr. Michael V. Smith (Air Command and Staff College (ACSC), Maxwell AFB, AL), to Marion, Subj: "RE: Para. on space culture," 6 Jan 21.

10. *Report of the Commission . . . National Security Space Management and Organization*, 42–46, 89, including quotes; Smith, "Challenge of Space Power," *Airpower Journal*, 35; Lambeth, *Mastering the Ultimate High Ground*, 63–64; History, Air Force Space Command (AFSPC), Jan 1994–Dec 2003, vol. 1, 109. In 1998, Sen. Bob Smith reported that of eleven general officers in AFSPC, none were career space officers.

11. *Report of the Commission . . . National Security Space Management and Organization*, xxxi, 17–18, 22, including quotes.

12. For more on Lorenzini's career, see the prologue, present work.

13. *Report of the Commission . . . National Security Space Management and Organization*, 23, including quote; George W. Bradley III, "The Navstar Global Positioning System: Origins and Development," *Space Times*, Nov–Dec 1997,

NOTES TO PAGES 31–33   183

9–13; Aarthi Ravikumar, "History of GPS satellites and commercial GPS tracking," *GEOTAB*, 23 Jun 20. As of May 2020, there were 29 operational GPS satellites.

14. Everett C. Dolman, *Astropolitik: Classical Geopolitics in the Space Age* (London and Portland, OR: Frank Cass Publishers, 2002), 32–39, including quote.

15. *Report of the Commission . . . National Security Space Management and Organization*, viii, xiii–xv, 22, 25, including quotes 1–2, 4; James M. Gavin, *War and Peace in the Space Age* (New York: Harper and Brothers, 1958), 16, including quote 3; OHI, Hon. Speaker Newton L. Gingrich (1995–99), conducted by Marion (via telephone), 21 Mar 22, including quote 5; Dolman, *Astropolitik*, 32–29. Among space scholars that took issue with the "Space Pearl Harbor" warning were Joan Johnson-Freese and Michael O'Hanlon; see Johnson-Freese, *Heavenly Ambitions: America's Quest to Dominate Space* (Philadelphia: University of Pennsylvania Press, 2009), 24, 56; Johnson-Freese, *Space Warfare in the 21st Century: Arming the Heavens* (London and New York: Routledge, 2017), 59, 69; and O'Hanlon, *Neither Star Wars nor Sanctuary*, 93, 120.

16. *Report of the Commission . . . National Security Space Management and Organization*, xxv–xxvi, xxxi–xxxiii, 50–51, 59, 64–65, 82–87, including quotes; History, AFSPC, Jan 1994–Dec 2003, vol. 1, 122, 124; Spires, *Beyond Horizons*, 296.

17. *Report of the Commission . . . National Security Space Management and Organization*, xxxiii, 87–89, including quotes; *Defense Space Activities: Status of Reorganization, GAO-02-772R* (Washington, DC: US General Accounting Office, Jun 2002), 4; History, AFSPC, Jan 1994–Dec 2003, vol. 1, 108, 114–15, 122–24; Lambeth, *Mastering the Ultimate High Ground*, 65–66. The GAO report was included as Supporting Document (SD) I-486 in History, AFSPC, Jan 1994–Dec 2003, vol. 15. Because GAO reports are available to the public, I elected to cite the report, *GAO-02-772R*. In 2002, General Lord became the first four-star AFSPC commander to be selected under the new guidelines implemented by Secretary Rumsfeld. A decade earlier, the author served under then–Brig. Gen. (select) Lord at the USAF's Squadron Officer School.

18. *Report of the Commission . . . National Security Space Management and Organization*, xxxiii–xxxiv, 89–90, including quotes; Spires, *Beyond Horizons*, 298.

19. "Fact Sheet, National Space Policy," The White House, National Science and Technology Council, 19 Sep 96, including quote 1, accessed at https://clinton whitehouse4.archives.gov/textonly/WH/EOP/OSTP/NSTC/html/fs/fs-5 .html (5 Oct 22); "First 'Announced' NRO Payload," *Spaceflight*, vol. 39 (Mar 1997): 77, including quote 2 (press release quoted by *Spaceflight*); Matthew Mowthorpe, *The Militarization and Weaponization of Space* (New York and Toronto: Lexington Books, 2004), 192, 205; Spires, *Beyond Horizons*, 85.

184 NOTES TO PAGES 33–37

20. *Report of the Commission . . . National Security Space Management and Organization*, xxiii, xxvi, xxxiv, 59, 65–68, 90–93, including quote (p. 68); Spires, *Beyond Horizons*, 296.

21. *Report of the Commission . . . National Security Space Management and Organization*, xxvi, 67–68, including quote.

22. E-mail, Dr. Michael V. Smith (ACSC, Maxwell AFB, AL), to Marion, Subj: "Coyote Feedback Re: draft para.," 23 Feb 21, including quotes 1–2; Dwayne A. Day, "The Air Force in Space: Past, Present and Future," *Space Times*, Mar–Apr 1996, 16–17, including quotes 3–4. It was unclear from *Space Times* whether or not Schriever intended to include the Apollo program in his comment on excessive secrecy.

23. *Report of the Commission . . . National Security Space Management and Organization*, xxxiv–xxxv, 95–96, including quote.

24. *Report of the Commission . . . National Security Space Management and Organization*, xxxv, 96–97, including quote; Lambeth, *Mastering the Ultimate High Ground*, 75–78; Spires, *Beyond Horizons*, 296. In 1998, Sen. Bob Smith (R-N.H.) suggested an MFP for space similarly applied as was MFP-11 for U.S. Special Operations Command, in addition to the creation of an assistant secretary of defense for space; see Smith, "Challenge of Space Power," *Airpower Journal*, 37–38. The 2001 commission favored a more powerful undersecretary of defense for space, intelligence, and information in lieu of an assistant secretary of defense for space (pp. 81–82, 85–87).

25. *Report of the Commission . . . National Security Space Management and Organization*, xxx, 1–2, 5, 80–81, 89, including quotes; Lambeth, *Mastering the Ultimate High Ground*, 67–69, 74–75.

26. *Report of the Commission . . . National Security Space Management and Organization*, 93–94, including quote.

27. History, AFSPC, Jan 1994–Dec 2003, vol. 13, SD I-422, E-mail, Unknown Sender ("Bill") to Roger G. DeKok (Lt. Gen., USAF), Subj: "Commission feedback," 24 Jan 01, including quotes; Donald H. Rumsfeld, "Transforming the Military," *Foreign Affairs* 81 (May/Jun 2002): 20–32.

28. History, AFSPC, Jan 1994–Dec 2003, vol. 13, SD I-422, E-mail, DeKok to Unknown Recipient ("Bill"), Subj: "RE: Commission feedback," 25 Jan 01, including quotes; History, AFSPC, Jan 1994–Dec 2003, vol. 1, 110, 113; E-mail, Wade A. Scrogham (USSF/HO) to Marion, Subj: "RE: SAE acronym," 19 Jan 21.

29. History, AFSPC, Jan 1994–Dec 2003, vol. 1, 110–13, including quote (Allard quoted by AFSPC historian).

30. "Ryan says Space Force unwarranted for next 50 years," *Aerospace Daily* 197, no. 26 (9 Feb 01): 217, including quote; Spires, *Beyond Horizons*, 297; Lambeth,

NOTES TO PAGES 37–39   185

Mastering the Ultimate High Ground, 72–75, 79; *Report of the Commission . . .*
National Security Space Management and Organization, 94; Dwight R. Mes-
simer, *An Incipient Mutiny: The Story of the U.S. Army Signal Corps Pilot Revolt*
(Lincoln, Neb.: Potomac Books, 2020), 1.

31. History, AFSPC, Jan 1994–Dec 2003, vol. 1, 113, 120, including quotes 1–2;
*Report of the Commission . . . National Security Space Management and Orga-
nization*, xxii, 56, 90, including quotes 3–4; History, AFSPC, Jan 1994–Dec
2003, vol. 14, SD I-470, "Space and Missile Systems Center becomes part of
Air Force Space Command," *News Release United States Air Force*, 2 Oct 01,
including quote 5; Spires, *Beyond Horizons*, 298; Lambeth, *Mastering the Ultimate High Ground*, 80. With realignment, the Air Force expected no changes
to SMC's mission of "acquiring and sustaining America's quality space
systems."

32. History, AFSPC, Jan 1994–Dec 2003, vol. 14, SD I-451, Ltr, SecDef Rumsfeld
to Sen. John Warner (chair, SASC), (date stamp smudged, other sources indi-
cate 8 or 9 May 01), including quotes 1–2; Lambeth, *Mastering the Ultimate
High Ground*, xi, including quote 3; History, AFSPC, Jan 1994–Dec 2003, vol.
1, 114–17. Using GAO-02–772R's enumeration, realignment of headquarters
and field commands was #5, which also encompassed the organize-train-equip
function (as did #7, which was not to be implemented, presumably due to its
redundancy with #5 in terms of space operations). There was a lack of con-
sistency in the enumeration or listing of the commission's recommendations,
the tasks directed by Secretary Rumsfeld in his letter to Sen. Warner, and the
GAO's report. For simplicity and accessibility, I elected to follow the GAO's
enumeration above. RAND's Benjamin Lambeth called the decision "not only
appropriate but arguably a generation late in coming." Note the SMC was the
most significant field command.

33. Roelof Schuiling, "Discovery delivers second crew to Space Station," *Spaceflight* 43 (Jun 2001): 232, including quote 1; "Space tourist Tito touches down,"
Spaceflight 43 (Jul 2001): 270, including quotes 2–3; Neville Kidger, "Tito
recalls historic 'tourist' flight," *Spaceflight* 43 (Sep 2001): 371; "US companies
gloomy about space work," *Spaceflight* 43 (Jun 2001): 226, including quote 4.
Efforts to engage U.S. Government officials in promoting space tourism began
at least by 1995; see Rick W. Sturdevant, "Report on the AAS 42nd Annual
Meeting 'Beyond the Adventure: The Development and Utilization of Space,'"
Space Times, Jan–Feb 1996, 12.

34. History, AFSPC, Jan 1994–Dec 2003, vol. 1, 120–21, 123–24, including quote.

35. OHI, Lord, 29 Jan 07, including quotes 1–3; Neil Sheehan, *A Fiery Peace in
a Cold War: Bernard Schriever and the Ultimate Weapon* (New York: Random
House, 2009), 474–75, including quote 4; Gen. Lance W. Lord, *U.S. Air Force*,

186   NOTES TO PAGES 40–43

Biographies, accessed at https://www.af.mil/About-Us/Biographies/Display/Article/105049/general-lance-w-lord/ (5 Oct 22).

36. *Defense Space Activities: Status of Reorganization, GAO-02–772R*, 2–5, including quote; History, AFSPC, Jan 2009–Dec 2010, chap. 1 (Mission), 30.

37. History, AFSPC, Jan 1994–Dec 2003, vol. 1, 124–25; Department of Defense Directive 5101.2, DoD Executive Agent for Space, 3 Jun 03, 1, 3, 5 (also SD I-488).

38. *Report of the Commission . . . National Security Space Management and Organization*, 14, 18, 33–34, including quote; Alfred Goldberg, Sarandis Papadopoulos, Diane Putney et al., *Pentagon 9/11* [Defense Studies Series] (Washington, DC: Historical Office, Office of the Secretary of Defense, 2007), 2–10.

39. Spires, *Beyond Horizons*, 306–7, including quote.

40. Spires, *Beyond Horizons*, 307–8, including quote. For an excellent unclassified discussion of space support during OEF, see pp. 307–14. Note that O'Hanlon listed the number of satellites used for OEF as "More than fifty"; see O'Hanlon, *Neither Star Wars nor Sanctuary*, 4.

41. Spires, *Beyond Horizons*, 309; History, AFSPC, Jan 1994–Dec 2003, vol. 1, 435; O'Hanlon, *Neither Star Wars nor Sanctuary*, 4; Maj. Gen. Richard E. Webber, *U.S. Air Force*, Biographies, accessed at https://www.af.mil/About-Us/Biographies/Display/Article/105106/major-general-richard-e-webber/ (5 Oct 22). O'Hanlon mentions a space team on duty "in the Persian Gulf in late 2002 to plan operations against Iraq"; see p. 5. While O'Hanlon estimated OEF required five times the bandwidth of the 1991 conflict, Spires estimated the requirement at seven times.

42. Spires, *Beyond Horizons*, 309–11, including quote.

43. Spires, *Beyond Horizons*, 311–12. O'Hanlon points out, in April 2003, "The Bush administration directed all government agencies, including the military, to look first to the commercial sector to meet their imaging needs"; see his *Neither Star Wars nor Sanctuary*, 46.

44. Spires, *Beyond Horizons*, 314, including quote (Marine general quoted by Spires).

45. Lambeth, *Mastering the Ultimate High Ground*, 90–91, 127–28, including quotes 1–2 [emphasis added by Lambeth, quote 2, Jumper quoted by Lambeth]; Amy Butler, "Departing from Ryan's Rhetoric, Jumper Notes Unique Space Needs," *Inside the Air Force* 12, no. 42 (19 Oct 01): 15–16, including quote 3 (Jumper quoted by Butler).

46. Spires, *Beyond Horizons*, 54, including quote (White quoted by Spires).

47. Butler, "Departing from Ryan's Rhetoric," *Inside the Air Force*, including quote 1 (Butler's paraphrase of Jumper); Day, "The Air Force in Space: Past, Present and Future," *Space Times*, Mar–Apr 1996, 20–21, including quotes 2–3 (quote 2, Day's paraphrase of Dickman).

NOTES TO PAGES 44–47

48. History, AFSPC, Jan 1994–Dec 2003, vol. 1, 436–37, including quotes 1, 3 (quote 3, quoted by AFSPC); O'Hanlon, *Neither Star Wars nor Sanctuary*, 4, including quote 2. I am grateful to my longtime AFHRA colleague and friend, archivist Barry Spink, for his help with this paragraph. For an excellent unclassified discussion of space support during OIF, see Spires, *Beyond Horizons*, 314–21.

49. History, AFSPC, Jan 1994–Dec 2003, vol. 1, 437, including quote.

50. History, AFSPC, Jan 1994–Dec 2003, vol. 1, 438, including quote; O'Hanlon, *Neither Star Wars nor Sanctuary*, 46–47.

51. Spires, *Beyond Horizons*, 321, including quotes 1–2 (James quoted by Spires); Day, "The Air Force in Space: Past, Present and Future," *Space Times*, Mar–Apr 1996, 18, including quote 3 (Kutyna quoted by Day); History, AFSPC, Jan 1994–Dec 2003, vol. 1, 439.

52. *Report of the Commission . . . National Security Space Management and Organization*, ix, xxxi, 82, 99, including quotes.

53. Johnson-Freese, *Heavenly Ambitions*, 58–59, including quote. For extended discussion of the G. W. Bush national space policy, see pp. 58–61 and 101–7.

54. [George W. Bush], "U.S. National Space Policy," Aug–Oct 2006, [NASA, Key Documents in the History of Space Policy], 1–4, 9, including quotes 1–3, 5, accessed at https://history.nasa.gov/ostp_space_policy06.pdf (5 Oct 22); Leonard David, "New Bush Space Policy Unveiled, Stresses U.S. Freedom of Action," Space.com, 7 Oct 06, including quote 4; Johnson-Freese, *Heavenly Ambitions*, 103.

55. Johnson-Freese, *Heavenly Ambitions*, xi, 103–4, including quotes [emphasis added by Johnson-Freese]; "Fact Sheet, National Space Policy," The White House, National Science and Technology Council, 19 Sep 96.

56. "Fact Sheet, National Space Policy," The White House, National Science and Technology Council, 19 Sep 96; [George W. Bush], "U.S. National Space Policy," Aug–Oct 2006.

57. Spires, *Beyond Horizons*, 338–39, including quotes.

58. Robert M. Gates, *Duty: Memoirs of a Secretary at War* (New York: Alfred A. Knopf, 2014), 414, 527.

59. T. Michael Moseley, *The Nation's Guardians, America's 21st Century Air Force* [CSAF White Paper], 29 Dec 07, 5, including quote 1 (copy at AFHRA); Anthony J. Mastalir, *The US Response to China's ASAT Test: An International Security Space Alliance for the Future* (Maxwell AFB, AL: Air University Press, August 2009, Drew Paper No. 8), 1–2, 98, including quote 2; Paul Glenshaw, "The First Space Ace," *Air & Space Magazine*, Apr 2018, 22–27; Carin Zissis, "China's Anti-Satellite Test," [backgrounder by] *Council on Foreign Relations*, 22 Feb 07; Johnson-Freese, *Heavenly Ambitions*, 9–14. Dr. Michael V. Smith,

188 NOTES TO PAGES 47–48

a retired USAF colonel who has taught for years at ACSC, Maxwell AFB, Alabama, wrote: "Actually, we were not surprised by the Chinese ASAT test. [National Air and Space Intelligence Center] was on top of this event. We had paid close attention to at least three previous tests, which the Chinese conducted quite openly. Regarding the test in January 2007 that hit the target, we even knew the date and time of the test and had our sensors focused in advance to collect as much data as possible"; see E-mail, M. V. Smith to Marion, Subj: "Re: 2007 Chinese ASAT test," 13 Feb 21. The Chinese weather satellite was designated Feng-Yun 1C.

60. Dave Baiocchi and William Welser IV, *Confronting Space Debris: Strategies and Warnings from Comparable Examples Including Deepwater Horizon* (Santa Monica, Calif.: RAND Corporation, 2010), 2, including quote; Mastalir, *US Response to China's ASAT Test*, 98; Johnson-Freese, *Heavenly Ambitions*, 9–10. In a September 1985 ASAT test, a USAF F-15–launched missile destroyed a defunct U.S. weather satellite, creating 285 pieces of measurable space debris. It took nearly 19 years for the debris pieces to disintegrate or reenter the atmosphere.

61. Tim Furniss, "Space News Round-Up," *Spaceflight* 42 (Jan 2000): 3, including quote.

62. Glenshaw, "The First Space Ace," *Air & Space Magazine*, 26–27.

63. Space scholars were divided on how to interpret the Chinese ASAT test. Johnson-Freese viewed the test as likely the natural outcome of Chinese engineers wanting to see the fruits of their prolonged labors; see her *Space Warfare in the 21st Century*, 71. Her argument was buttressed somewhat by Gates' suggestion (based on unidentified sources) that the Chinese People's Liberation Army leadership probably acted on its own "without the knowledge of the civilian leadership in Beijing"; see his *Duty: Memoirs of a Secretary at War*, 414.

64. Jon Kyl, "China's Anti-Satellite Weapons and American National Security," [address delivered to U.S. Senate, 29 Jan 07], [report by] *The Heritage Foundation*, 1 Feb 07, including quotes (quote 3, Biden quoted by Kyl), accessed at https://www.heritage.org/defense/report/chinas-anti-satellite-weapons-and-american-national-security (5 Oct 22); Johnson-Freese, *Heavenly Ambitions*, 7, 13, 63; Johnson-Freese, *Space Warfare in the 21st Century*, 71.

65. Kyl, "China's Anti-Satellite Weapons and American National Security," including quotes.

66. Kyl, "China's Anti-Satellite Weapons and American National Security," including quote. Note that although the commission referred to space as "*a top national security priority*" (emphasis added) both in the executive summary and conclusion, the recommendation for the president in the body of the report was

NOTES TO PAGES 49–51   189

that he should establish space as "*a* national security priority" (emphasis added); see *Report of the* [2001] *Commission . . . National Security Space Management and Organization*, ix, xxxi, 82, 99. If President Bush's 470-page memoir, *Decision Points* (New York: Crown Publishers, 2010), contained more than a passing reference to space, I missed it.

67. Richard P. Hallion, Roger Cliff, and Phillip C. Saunders, eds., *The Chinese Air Force: Evolving Concepts, Roles, and Capabilities* (Washington, DC: National Defense University Press, 2012), 165–66, 174–75, 179, including quotes (quotes 2–3 quoted by Kevin Pollpeter, author of this chapter). For more on U.S. experience with net-centric warfare, see Chapter 2, present work.

68. Hallion, Cliff, and Saunders, eds., *The Chinese Air Force*, 180–82, including quotes 1–3 (quote 1 quoted by Pollpeter); J. F. C. Fuller, *The Conduct of War, 1789–1961: A Study of the Impact of the French, Industrial, and Russian Revolutions on War and Its Conduct* (New Brunswick, N.J.: Rutgers University Press, 1961), 211–12, including quotes 4–5.

69. "Allard Commission: Executive Summary of Independent Assessment Panel on the Organization and Management of National Security Space," *Army Space Journal* 8, no. 2 (Sum. 2009): 14, including quotes. The Rumsfeld commission's designation had rendered *management* prior to *organization* in its title.

70. "Allard Commission," *Army Space Journal*, 15–16, including quotes.

71. President Clinton never formally disestablished the National Space Council, but it effectively ceased to function by 1993; see "Reviving the National Space Council," Executive Order 13803, *Federal Register*, 30 Jun 17, accessed at https://www.federalregister.gov/documents/2017/07/07/2017–14378/reviving-the-national-space-council (5 Oct 22).

72. "Allard Commission," *Army Space Journal*, 16; Bush, *Decision Points*, chaps. 6–8, 12.

73. "Allard Commission," *Army Space Journal*, 16, including quotes 1, 4; "Our National Space Effort," *Air Force Magazine* no. 2 (Feb 1959): 67, including quotes 2–3; Smith, "Challenge of Space Power," *Airpower Journal*, 32–39; David E. Lupton, *On Space Warfare: A Space Power Doctrine* (Maxwell AFB, AL: Air University Press, Jun. 1988), 143–44.

74. George Luker, "Army Space: Schriever IV," *Army Space Journal* 7, no. 2 (Spring 2008): 34–35, 40, including quote 1; History, Headquarters, United States Air Force, 2 Sep 05–1 Aug 08, chap. 2: Air Force Mission and Organization, 71, including quotes 2–3 (copy at AFHRA, call number K168.01); *Report of the* [2001] *Commission . . . National Security Space Management and Organization*, xvi, xxii, xxix, 29, 55, 77–78; Mowthorpe, *Militarization and Weaponization of Space*, 193–94; Johnson-Freese, *Space Warfare in the 21st Century*, 62, 98. Johnson-Freese wrote, "If the Schriever wargames have demonstrated

190   NOTES TO PAGES 53-57

anything, it is that when things start to go poorly in the space battlefield, rapid escalation occurs. The chances of maintaining a space war at a limited level appear similar to those of fighting a limited nuclear war: not good." The wargame was planned before the report's release, perhaps anticipating a push for the testing of space capabilities and strategies through military exercises.

Chapter 3. U.S. National Security Space: The Obama Years, 2009–2016

1. Christian Davenport, *The Space Barons: Elon Musk, Jeff Bezos, and the Quest to Colonize the Cosmos* (New York: Public Affairs, 2018), 117, 121, 156–59. The *Challenger* crew perished on the spacecraft's tenth mission; *Columbia*'s crew on its twenty-eighth.

2. Davenport, *The Space Barons*, 156–59, 172–73, including quote ("unexecutable" memo quoted by Davenport).

3. Davenport, *The Space Barons*, 159–60, including quote 1; Valerie Insinna, "Air Force Launches Space Consortium That Puts Startups to Work on Prototypes," DefenseNews.com, 18 Oct 16, including quotes 2–3.

4. Davenport, *The Space Barons*, 160–61, including quote; Sam Jones, "Barack Obama to drop Nasa moon mission in budget cutbacks," *Guardian*, 1 Feb 10.

5. *Public Papers of the Presidents of the United States, Barack Obama, 2010 (In Two Books), Book 1—January 1 to June 30, 2010* (Washington, DC: U.S. GPO, 2013), 497–99, including quotes; Davenport, *The Space Barons*, 161.

6. *Public Papers, Barack Obama, 2010, Book 1—January 1 to June 30, 2010*, 499, including quote 1; "How NASA Helped 'The 33' Chilean Miners," nasa.gov, 13 Nov 15, including quote 2, accessed at https://www.nasa.gov/feature/how-nasa -helped-the-33-chilean-miners (5 Oct 22); Mannix Porterfield, "Explosion kills 29 in worst mine tragedy in 40 years," *Register-Herald* [Beckley, W.Va.], 31 Dec 10, updated 30 Sep 15. On 25 April 2010, Obama addressed the gathering at a memorial service for the victims of the Upper Big Branch Mine Accident (*Public Papers*, 538–39).

7. *Public Papers, Barack Obama, 2010, Book 1—January 1 to June 30, 2010*, 499 including quote 1; Joan Johnson-Freese, *Space Warfare in the 21st Century: Arming the Heavens* (London and New York: Routledge, 2017), 110–12, including quotes 2–3; Davenport, *The Space Barons*, 142–43.

8. *Public Papers, Barack Obama, 2010, Book 1—January 1 to June 30, 2010*, 499 including quotes.

9. Amy Thompson, "SpaceX launches 60 new Starlink internet satellites, nails latest rocket landing at sea," Space.com, 24 Mar 21, including quote, accessed at https://www.space.com/spacex-starlink-22-satellites-launch-rocket-landing -success (5 Oct 22); Davenport, *The Space Barons*, 1–3, 221–30. The SpaceX mission was the sixth landing for that particular booster and, overall, the 78th

NOTES TO PAGES 57–59   191

successful landing of a first stage booster for the company—a revolutionary, money-saving feat first accomplished barely five years earlier, in late 2015 by Blue Origin, and a month later by SpaceX with the first "orbital-class rocket landing—with control room excitement reminiscent of the Apollo days"; see Johnson-Freese, *Space Warfare in the 21st Century*, 138. Note the 24 March launch was "the 112th overall flight for Falcon 9, and the 58th reflight of a booster" by SpaceX (Thompson).

10. Johnson-Freese, *Space Warfare in the 21st Century*, 110–12, including quote 1; Oral History Interview (OHI), Hon. Speaker Newton L. Gingrich (1995–99), conducted by Marion (via telephone), 21 Mar 22, including quote 2; *Public Papers, Barack Obama, 2010, Book 1—January 1 to June 30, 2010*, 499–500; "SpaceX Head Musk Visits Pentagon," *Defense News*, 13 Jun 16, 4.

11. *Public Papers, Barack Obama, 2010, Book 1—January 1 to June 30, 2010*, 500, including quotes. Prior to Obama's presidency, George W. Bush had made "a bold bet" that private space companies could provide "a taxi-like delivery service" to the ISS, thereby freeing NASA "to do the hard stuff, to explore in deep space"; see Davenport, *The Space Barons*, 133.

12. Scott Pace, "American space strategy: Choose to steer, not drift," *Space Policy*, vol. 30, no. 1 (Feb 2014): 1–2, including quotes; Marcia Smith, "Scott Pace Departing White House National Space Council Today," SpacePolicyOnline .com, 31 Dec 20.

13. Davenport, *The Space Barons*, 162–64, including quotes (quote 1, Musk quoted by Davenport).

14. Michelle Spitzer, "NASA Chief Bolden's Muslim Remark to Al-Jazeera Causes Stir," Space.com, 7 Jul 10, including quote, accessed at https://www .space.com/8725-nasa-chief-bolden-muslim-remark-al-jazeera-stir.html (5 Oct 22); Jim Wilson, ed., "Former Administrator Charles F. Bolden," Nasa. gov, March 2016 (updated 3 Aug 17), accessed at https://www.nasa.gov/about/ highlights/bolden_bio.html (5 Oct 22); Mark R. Whittington, "Was NASA's Charles Bolden right all along about Muslim outreach?" *Foreign Policy Journal*, 23 Sep 16. Whittington focused on the United Arab Emirates Mars Mission and the prospects for changing the youth culture in the Middle East by offering science- and math-oriented alternatives to jihad/terrorism.

15. Spitzer, "NASA Chief Bolden's Muslim Remark," 7 Jul 10, including quote 1; Victor Davis Hanson, "Why Is Our Military Choosing New Enemies?" *National Review*, 18 Mar 21, including quote 2; Clara Moskowitz, "NASA chief says agency's goal is Muslim outreach, forgets to mention space," *Christian Science Monitor*, 14 Jul 10, accessed at https://www.csmonitor.com/ Science/2010/0714/NASA-chief-says-agency-s-goal-is-Muslim-outreach-forgets-to-mention-space (5 Oct 22).

192   NOTES TO PAGES 59–62

16. T. Michael Moseley, *The Nation's Guardians, America's 21st Century Air Force* [CSAF White Paper], 29 Dec 07, 2, including quote 1 (copy at AFHRA); History, Air Force Space Command (AFSPC), Jan 2009–Dec 2010, chap. 1 (Mission), 21, and chap. 7 (Cyberspace), 5–6, including quote 2 (CD held at AFHRA). Prior to the resignations of Secretary of the Air Force Michael W. Wynne and CSAF T. Michael Moseley in June–July 2008—in part over problems with the USAF's nuclear enterprise—the USAF had expected to activate Air Force Cyber Command later that year; see History, Headquarters, United States Air Force, 2 Sep 05–1 Aug 08, chap. 2: Air Force Mission and Organization, 84–85 (copy at AFHRA, call number K168.01).

17. *Hearing on [NDAA] for Fiscal Year 2017 . . . Before the Committee on Armed Services, House of Representatives, One Hundred Fourteenth Congress, Second Session, Subcommittee on Strategic Forces Hearing on Fiscal Year 2017 Budget Request for National Security Space . . . March 15, 2016* (Washington, DC: GPO, 2017), 8–9, including quotes; *Guardians of the High Frontier: The Heritage of Air Force Space Command* (Peterson AFB, CO: AFSPC History Office, Apr 2018), 14, 15, 21 (of seventy-seven pages, unnumbered).

18. Kevin P. Chilton, "Cyberspace Leadership: Towards New Culture, Conduct, and Capabilities," *Air & Space Power Journal* no. 3 (Fall 2009): 7, including quote; "Kennedy Space Center, NASA Orbiter Fleet, Space Shuttle Overview: Atlantis (OV-104)," 12 Apr 13, Nasa.gov, accessed at https://www.nasa.gov/centers/kennedy/shuttleoperations/orbiters/atlantis-info.html (5 Oct 22); Gen. Kevin P. Chilton, *U.S. Air Force*, Biographies, accessed at https://www.af.mil/About-Us/Biographies/Display/Article/1316843/kevin-p-chilton/ (5 Oct 22). Note that in 2002, USSTRATCOM had assumed the combatant command mission of U.S. Space Command upon its disestablishment.

19. Chilton, "Cyberspace Leadership," *Air & Space Power Journal*, 7–8, including quotes.

20. Chilton, "Cyberspace Leadership," *Air & Space Power Journal*, 8, including quote.

21. *Hearing on [NDAA] for Fiscal Year 2017 . . . Budget Request for National Security Space . . . March 15, 2016*, 38; Comment on draft, Dr. Paul J. Springer (ACSC) to Marion, Sep. 2021.

22. *Hearing on [NDAA] for Fiscal Year 2017 . . . Budget Request for National Security Space . . . March 15, 2016*, 9, including quote; Forrest L. Marion and Jon T. Hoffman, *Forging A Total Force: The Evolution of the Guard and Reserve* (Washington, DC: Historical Office, Office of the Secretary of Defense, 2018), xiii–xiv, 97, 123, 187. Note that the Air Force had a long history of its reserves serving periodically in the conduct and support of operational missions.

23. Davis Winkie and Rachel S. Cohen, "Do we need a Space National Guard? Colorado says yes, but Congress is not so sure," *Air Force Times*, 13 Apr 21,

NOTES TO PAGES 62–64 193

accessed at https://www.airforcetimes.com/news/your-air-force/2021/04/13/do-we-need-a-space-national-guard-colorado-says-yes-but-congress-is-not-so-sure/ (5 Oct 22); History, Air Force Space Command, Jan 1994–Dec 2003, vol. 1, xvii (copy at AFHRA).

24. For details, see chap. 2, present work. Note that General Kehler was not triple-hatted during his command of AFSPC (2007–11). General Chilton also recalled the phrase, "Rodney Dangerfield command"; Telephone conversation, Chilton with Marion, 22 Sep 21.

25. OHI, Gen. C. Robert Kehler, AFSPC/CC, conducted by George W. Bradley III, AFSPC/HO, Peterson AFB, CO, 22 Dec 10, iv–vi, 2, including quotes (copy at AFHRA); Peter L. Hays, James M. Smith, Alan R. Van Tassel, and Guy M. Walsh, eds., *Spacepower for a New Millennium: Space and U.S. National Security* (New York and St. Louis: McGraw-Hill, 2000), 10. The authors of the chapter in *Spacepower* that referred to U.S. Space Command suffering from "'Rodney Dangerfield Syndrome'" were of the opinion the command "does not believe it receives the respect it deserves as a unified command." Note that while *Spacepower* referred to the U.S. Space Command, General Kehler referred to the *Air Force* Space Command as the Dangerfield command. Perhaps some in both commands felt that way at times.

26. OHI, Gen. C. Robert Kehler, AFSPC/CC, 22 Dec 10, 2–3, including quotes (quotes 1–2, Moseley quoted by Kehler).

27. The Bush White House issued four narrowly focused space policies prior to 2006; see Joan Johnson-Freese, *Heavenly Ambitions: America's Quest to Dominate Space* (Philadelphia: University of Pennsylvania Press, 2009), 59.

28. Jeff Foust, "A change in tone in national space policy," *Space Review*, 6 Jul 10, including quote, accessed at https://www.thespacereview.com/article/1660/1 (5 Oct 22); George W. Bush, *Decision Points* (New York: Crown, 2010).

29. Foust, "A change in tone in national space policy," *Space Review*, 6 Jul 10, including quotes.

30. Foust, "A change in tone in national space policy," *Space Review*, 6 Jul 10, including quote 1; [Barack H. Obama] *National Space Policy of the United States of America, Jun. 28, 2010*, 2–3, including quotes 2–4, accessed at https://history.nasa.gov/national_space_policy_6–28–10.pdf (5 Oct 22). Note that peaceful purposes allowed "for space to be used for national and homeland security activities."

31. [Obama] *National Space Policy of the United States of America, Jun. 28, 2010*, 3, including quotes 1–2; [George W. Bush], "U.S. National Space Policy," Aug–Oct 2006, [NASA, Key Documents in the History of Space Policy], 1, including quote 3, accessed at https://history.nasa.gov/ostp_space_policy06.pdf (5 Oct 22).

194   NOTES TO PAGES 65–66

32. [Bush], "U.S. National Space Policy," Aug–Oct 2006, 1, including quotes 1, 3–4; [Obama] *National Space Policy of the United States of America, Jun. 28, 2010*, 3, including quotes 2, 5; Todd Barnet, "United States National Space Policy, 2006 & 2010," *Florida Journal of International Law* 23 (2011): 278, 286, including quotes 6–8.

33. E-mails (2), Dr. John G. Terino (ACSC) to Marion, Subj: "RE: Recent NSS books," 7 Oct 21, including quote 1 (copy at AFHRA); Johnson-Freese, *Heavenly Ambitions*, 4–5, 32–33, 101–106, 143, including quotes 2–3; [Obama] *National Space Policy of the United States of America, Jun. 28, 2010*, 6–14, including quote 4; William J. Broad and Kenneth Chang, "Obama Reverses Bush's Space Policy," *New York Times*, 28 Jun 10; [Bush], "U.S. National Space Policy," Aug–Oct 2006, 3–7.

34. Foust, "A change in tone in national space policy," *Space Review*, 6 Jul 10, including quotes. Note that the Clinton policy had forbidden the use of direct federal subsidies.

35. Foust, "A change in tone in national space policy," *Space Review*, 6 Jul 10, including quote 1; "Fact Sheet, National Space Policy," The White House, National Science and Technology Council, 19 Sep 1996, 1, including quote 2, accessed at https://clintonwhitehouse4.archives.gov/textonly/WH/EOP/OSTP/NSTC/html/fs/fs-5.html (5 Oct 22); [Barack H. Obama] *National Space Policy of the United States of America, Jun. 28, 2010*, 3.

36. "Fact Sheet, National Space Policy," The White House, 19 Sep 1996, 1, including quote 1; [Obama] *National Space Policy of the United States of America, Jun. 28, 2010*, 3, including quote 2; [Bush], "U.S. National Space Policy," Aug–Oct 2006, 1.

37. Mike Gruss, "Pentagon Says 2013 Chinese Launch May Have Tested Antisatellite Technology," *Space News*, 14 May 15, including quote (Weeden quoted by Gruss), accessed at https://spacenews.com/pentagon-says-2013-chinese-launch-may-have-tested-antisatellite-technology/ (5 Oct 22); Brian Weeden, "Anti-Satellite Tests in Space—The Case of China," *Secure World Foundation*, 16 Aug 13; Mike Wall, "China Launches High-Altitude Rocket on Apparent Science Mission: Reports," Space.com, 15 May 13; Andrea Shalal, "Analysis points to China's work on new anti-satellite weapon," *Reuters*, 18 Mar 14; Zachary Keck, "China Secretly Tested an Anti-Satellite Missile," *Diplomat*, 19 Mar 14; Johnson-Freese, *Space Warfare in the 21st Century*, xiv, 12–13, 168, 180, 182. Not only had China tested an anti-satellite missile in 2007, U.S. analysts concluded that a 2010 Chinese test purportedly of missile interception technology—which if true, was defensive in nature and thereby acceptable—was actually a test of their SC-19 ASAT missile; they also conducted a similar test of the SC-19 in January 2013.

NOTES TO PAGES 67–68 195

38. OHI, Stephen L. Kitay, DASD (Space Policy), and Col. Casey M. Beard, OSD/
SP, conducted by Gregory W. Ball and Wade A. Scrogham, USSF/HO, Peterson AFB, CO, 13 Feb 20, 5, including quotes 1–2 (copy at AFHRA); B.W.
Bahney, J. J. Pearl, and M. A. Markey, "Grounded: The Logic of Anti-Satellite
Threats to Military Space Systems," Lawrence Livermore National Laboratory
(LLNL)-JRNL-689357, 18 Apr 16, pp. 8–9, including quotes 3–4, accessed
at https://www.osti.gov/servlets/purl/1513834 (5 Oct 22). The reference was
to the early nineteenth-century Prussian military thinker, Carl von Clausewitz, whose treatise, *On War*, is considered by many the foremost work on the
nature of war and the relationship between politics and war, recognizing war
as a political phenomenon or as an instrument of policy; he also believed that
victory came from massing one's forces at the enemy's "center of gravity"; see
Hew Strachan, *Clausewitz's On War: A Biography* (New York: Atlantic Monthly
Press, 2007), 4, 6, 69, 178.

39. E-mail, Robert D. Mulcahy Jr., SMC/HO, to Gregory W. Ball, USSF/HO,
Subj: "RE: Rocket Engine Transition & Russian RD-180," 13 Apr 21, including quote 1; Rick W. Sturdevant, "Report on the AAS National Conference
'Space Exploration and Development: Beyond the Space Station,'" *Space Times*,
Jan–Feb 1997, 7, including quote 2 (Littles paraphrased by Sturdevant); "Dr. J.
Wayne Littles," Smithsonian *National Air & Space Museum*, accessed at https://
airandspace.si.edu/support/wall-of-honor/dr-j-wayne-littles (5 Oct 22); "Russian Rocket Engines," *Spaceflight* (Feb 1996): 64; *Public Law 113-291, 113th
Congress, [NDAA] for Fiscal Year 2015*, 918; *Hearing on [NDAA] for Fiscal Year
2017 . . . Budget Request for National Security Space . . . March 15, 2016*, 2–3,
15–17, 19, 33–35; *Historical Overview of the Space and Missile Systems Center,
1954–2016* (Los Angeles: History Office, Space and Missile Systems Center, 23 Oct 17 [revised]), 45–46. Similarly, tensions over Russia's actions in
Crimea also led the U.S. government gradually to move away from supplying the Afghan Air Force with Mi-17 helicopters in favor of the American-manufactured UH-60 Blackhawks.

40. *Hearing on [NDAA] for Fiscal Year 2017 . . . Budget Request for National Security
Space . . . March 15, 2016*, 2–3, 15–17, 19, 33–35, including quote 1; E-mail, Robert D. Mulcahy Jr., SMC/HO, to Marion, Subj: "RE: DRAFT para's," 14 Apr 21,
including quote 2; *Historical Overview of the Space and Missile Systems Center*, 46.

41. Mike Gruss, "U.S. State Department: China Tested Anti-satellite Weapon,"
Space News, 28 Jul 14, including quote (State Department spokesman quoted
by Gruss).

42. *Report of the Commission to Assess United States National Security Space Management and Organization* [Pursuant to Public Law 106–65] (Washington, DC: 11
Jan 01), 80–81, 89, 93–94, including quotes.

196   NOTES TO PAGES 69–72

43. *Public Law 113-291, 113th Congress, [NDAA] for Fiscal Year 2015*, 915, 917–18, including quotes. Note an earlier example of secretary of defense and DNI cooperation, in line with the 2001 Space Commission, when in 2011 the two officials released the first-ever NSS strategy document; see "Aligning with the Space Enterprise Vision: Overcoming the Threat to Space Systems," *MITRE Corporation*, 27 January 2017, accessed at https://apps.dtic.mil/sti/pdfs/AD1107865.pdf (5 Oct 22). Note the two provisions mentioned in the text originated in the Senate rather than in the soon to be more space-service-minded House of Representatives.

44. Theresa Hitchens, "A Pause Button for Militarizing Space," *Center for International & Strategic Studies at [University of] Maryland*, 1 Apr 16, including quote 1 (James quoted by Hitchens), accessed at https://cissm.umd.edu/research-impact/publications/pause-button-militarizing-space (5 Oct 22); Gruss, "Delays in U.S. Military Satellite Studies Could Be Limiting," *Space News*, 7 May 15, including quotes 2–5 (James, Loverro, and Parikh quoted by Gruss), accessed at https://spacenews.com/delays-in-u-s-military-satellite-studies-could-be-limiting/ (5 Oct 22). Prior to the requirement for satellite resiliency, cost and capability were the primary considerations.

45. OHI, Lt. Col. Peter A. Garretson, USAF (Ret.), conducted by Marion, Maxwell AFB, AL, 29 Oct 21, including quotes.

46. OHI, Garretson, 29 Oct 21, including quote 1; OHI, Col. Michael V. Smith, USAF (Ret.), conducted by Marion, Maxwell AFB, AL, 3 Aug, 12–13 Aug 20, including quotes 2–3 (from 3 Aug 20).

47. Matthew Bodner, "Russian Military Merges Air Force and Space Command," *Moscow Times*, 3 Aug 2015, including quotes 1, 3, accessed at https://www.themoscowtimes.com/2015/08/03/russian-military-merges-air-force-and-space-command-a48710 (5 Oct 22); "Russian Space Future Dims," *Spaceflight* 39 (Mar 1997): 95, including quote 2; Johnson-Freese, *Space Warfare in the 21st Century*, 47–48.

48. Bodner, "Russian Military Merges," *Moscow Times*, 3 Aug 2015, including quotes.

49. Bill Gertz, "Russia Conducts Fifth Test of New Anti-Satellite Missile," *Washington Free Beacon*, 21 Dec 16, including quotes, accessed at https://freebeacon.com/national-security/russia-conducts-fifth-test-new-anti-satellite-missile/ (5 Oct 22); Johnson-Freese, *Space Warfare in the 21st Century*, 65. Note that the second of the three ASAT tests referred to above took place in November 2015. As in the case of the Chinese test in 2014, the second and third Russian tests were non-destructive; I have not seen a source that stated whether or not the first test was nondestructive.

50. Gertz, "Russia Conducts . . . New Anti-Satellite Missile," *Washington Free Beacon*, 21 Dec 16, including quote; *Hearing on [NDAA] for Fiscal Year 2017 . . . Budget Request for National Security Space . . . March 15, 2016*, 11.

NOTES TO PAGES 72–75

51. *PLA Aerospace Power: A Primer on Trends in China's Military Air, Space, and Missile Forces*, 2nd ed. (Maxwell AFB, AL: China Aerospace Studies Institute, 2017 [2018?]), 45–46, 48, including quote 1 (Xi Jinping quoted by China Aerospace Studies Institute); "United Nations: Who's Wu," *Newsweek*, 25 Dec 1950, pp. 26, 28, including quotes 2–4; Johnson-Freese, *Space Warfare in the 21st Century*, 48.

52. *PLA Aerospace Power*, 54, including quote 1; Kevin L. Pollpeter, Michael S. Chase, and Eric Heginbotham, *The Creation of the PLA Strategic Support Force and Its Implications for Chinese Military Space Operations* (Santa Monica, Calif.: RAND, 2017), ix, including quotes 2–4; Elsa B. Kania, "China Has a 'Space Force.' What Are Its Lessons for the Pentagon?" *Defense One*, 29 Sep 18, including quote 5, accessed at https://www.defenseone.com/ideas/2018/09/china-has-space-force-what-are-its-lessons-pentagon/151665/ (5 Oct 22).

53. *PLA Aerospace Power*, 57, including quotes; Pollpeter, *Creation of the PLA Strategic Support Force and Its Implications*, ix.

54. Pollpeter, *Creation of the PLA Strategic Support Force*, x, including quote.

55. *United Nations Treaties and Principles on Outer Space* (New York: United Nations, 2002), 4, including quote.

56. Namrata Goswami, "China in Space: Ambitions and Possible Conflict," *Strategic Studies Quarterly* 12, no. 1 (Spring 2018): 75, including quotes 1–2; Nick Stockton, "Congress Says Yes to Space Mining, No to Rocket Regulations," *Wired*, 18 Nov 15, including quote 3, accessed at https://www.wired.com/2015/11/congress-says-yes-to-space-mining-no-to-rocket-regulations/ (5 Oct 22); "President Obama Signs Bill Recognizing Asteroid Resource Property Rights into Law," press release, *Planetary Resources*, 25 Nov 15, including quote 4 (Eric Anderson quoted by *Planetary Resources*), accessed at http://www.spaceref.com/news/viewpr.html?pid=47408 (5 Oct 22); Johnson-Freese, *Space Warfare in the 21st Century*, 143–45; Sarah Fecht, "Senate Votes to Legalize Space Mining," *Popular Science*, 12 Nov 15. The alternate title of P.L. 114-90 was the Spurring Private Aerospace Competitiveness and Entrepreneurship (SPACE) Act of 2015, often dubbed simply the SPACE Act of 2015.

57. Goswami, "China in Space: Ambitions and Possible Conflict," *Strategic Studies Quarterly*, 75, 89–90, including quotes.

58. Walter A. McDougall, *The Heavens and the Earth: A Political History of the Space Age* (Baltimore and London: Johns Hopkins University Press, 1985 [1997]), 451, including quote; "China eyes more military bases in Africa," *ANInews*, 18 May 21.

59. Lara Seligman, "SpaceX Wins US Air Force Contract For GPS III Launch," *Defense News*, 2 May 16, 13, including quote; *Hearing on [NDAA] for Fiscal Year 2017 . . . Budget Request for National Security Space . . . March 15, 2016*, 34; *Historical Overview of the Space and Missile Systems Center*, 47.

NOTES TO PAGES 75-80

60. Davenport, *The Space Barons*, 225–30, including quotes; Loren Grush, "SpaceX successfully landed its Falcon 9 rocket after launching it to space," *Verge*, 21 Dec 15, accessed at https://www.theverge.com/2015/12/21/10640306/spacex-elon-musk-rocket-landing-success (5 Oct 22).

61. Aaron Mehta, "Former US SecDefs: Stronger Military Ties with China Key to Peace," Defensenews.com, 14 Jan 16, including quote.

62. Elbridge Colby, "US Needs to Prepare for Space War," *Defense News*, 22 Feb 16, 21, including quotes 1–4 (quote 3, Air Force general quoted by Colby); "Overcoming the Threat to Space Systems," *MITRE Corporation*, January 2017, including quote 5 (Chinese sources quoted by *MITRE*); "War in Space: The Next Battlefield," CNN.com, 23 Nov 16, including quote 6 (production title). Note that the "tempting . . . choice" quote was also found in congressional testimony; see *Hearing on [NDAA] for Fiscal Year 2017 . . . Budget Request for National Security Space . . . March 15, 2016*, 52.

63. Colby, "US Needs To Prepare for Space War," *Defense News*, 22 Feb 16, 21, including quote.

64. *Hearing on [NDAA] for Fiscal Year 2017 . . . Before the Committee on Armed Services, House of Representatives, One Hundred Fourteenth Congress, Second Session, Subcommittee on Strategic Forces Hearing on The Missile Defeat Posture and Strategy of the United States—The Fiscal Year 2017 President's Budget Request . . . April 14, 2016* (Washington, DC: GPO, 2017), 27–28, including quotes.

65. *Hearing on [NDAA] for Fiscal Year 2017 . . . Missile Defeat Posture and Strategy of the United States . . . April 14, 2016*, 28, including quotes.

66. *Hearing on [NDAA] for Fiscal Year 2017 . . . Missile Defeat Posture and Strategy of the United States . . . April 14, 2016*, 42, including quotes.

67. *Hearing on [NDAA] for Fiscal Year 2017 . . . Missile Defeat Posture and Strategy of the United States . . . April 14, 2016*, 42–43, including quotes. Note that more than likely, the North Koreans shared to some degree in the operational advances that stemmed from closest-ally China's road-mobile ICBM development.

68. *Hearing on [NDAA] for Fiscal Year 2017 . . . Budget Request for National Security Space . . . March 15, 2016*, 50, including quote.

69. *Hearing on [NDAA] for Fiscal Year 2017 . . . Budget Request for National Security Space . . . March 15, 2016*, 39, 50–52, including quotes.

Chapter 4. Mixed Momentum for a Space Service, 2017–2018

1. M. V. Smith, "America needs a space corps," *Space Review*, 13 Mar 17, including quote 1, accessed at https://www.thespacereview.com/article/3193/1 (5 Oct 22); E-mail, Dr. Peter L. Hays (George Washington University) to Marion, Subj: "Re: Support for Book, 'Standing Up Space Force,'" 28 Apr 22, including

NOTES TO PAGES 81–83 199

quote 2 (copy at AFHRA); Talking Paper, M. V. Smith, "CSAF Position Regarding US Space Corps," 31 Mar 17 (provided by Smith, copy at AFHRA); Talking Paper, M. V. Smith, "Ten Myths Regarding The US Space Corps," 31 Mar 17 (provided by Smith, copy at AFHRA).

2. "Remarks of Congressman Mike Rogers, Chairman, House Armed Services Strategic Forces Subcommittee, Presented to the 2017 Space Symposium," *Strategic Studies Quarterly (SSQ)*, Summer 2017, 3, including quotes; Wilson Brissett, "The Space Corps Question," *Air Force Magazine*, 29 Aug 17, accessed at https://www.airforcemag.com/article/the-space-corps-question/ (5 Oct 22).

3. "Remarks of Congressman Mike Rogers . . . 2017 Space Symposium," *SSQ*, Summer 2017, 4, including quote.

4. "Remarks of Congressman Mike Rogers . . . 2017 Space Symposium," *SSQ*, Summer 2017, 4–5, including quotes 1–3, 6; Oral History Interview (OHI), Gen C. Robert Kehler, AFSPC/CC, conducted by George W. Bradley III, AFSPC/HO, Peterson AFB, CO, 22 Dec 10, 2–3, including quotes 4–5 (Moseley quoted by Kehler) (copy at AFHRA); Lewis Sorley, *A Better War: The Unexamined Victories and Final Tragedy of America's Last Years in Vietnam* (Orlando, Austin, and New York: Harcourt, 1999), 19, 32, including quote 6 (Corcoran quoted by Sorley).

5. "Remarks of Congressman Mike Rogers . . . 2017 Space Symposium," *SSQ*, Summer 2017, 6–7, including quote 1; OHI, Hon. Dr. Heather A. Wilson, SecAF, conducted by Dr. James Malachowski and Ms. Aungelic Nelson, AF/HO, Pentagon, 8 May 19, 13–14, including quotes 2–4 (copy at AFHRA). Note that sources varied in stating the USAF controlled between 80 and 90 percent of the defense department's space budget; for two references of "about 80%," see Hon. Heather Wilson Papers, [single typed page], Notes from Congressional Testimony, [date unspecified] May 2017, AFHRA, call number 168.7768–8, and Document, "SECAF, Rep. Mike Rogers (R-AL-3) and Rep. Jim Cooper (D-TN-3), 19 May 2017," AFHRA, call number 168.7768–21.

6. Mike Gruss, "Rogers: U.S. Air Force Wasted $518 Million on Weather Satellite," *Space News*, 7 Jan 16, including quote 1, accessed at https://spacenews.com/rogers-u-s-air-force-wasted-518-million-on-weather-satellite/ (5 Oct 22); "Remarks of Congressman Mike Rogers . . . 2017 Space Symposium," *SSQ*, Summer 2017, 7, including quotes 2–3; Amber Corrin, "Air Force unveils $500M satellite museum piece," *C4ISRNET*, 22 Dec 17.

7. "Remarks of Congressman Mike Rogers . . . 2017 Space Symposium," *SSQ*, Summer 2017, 7, including quote; Telephone conversation, Hon. Matthew P. Donovan with author, 27 May 21. For more on Sen. Smith's views on space, see chap. 1, present work. It was 2002 when the School of Advanced Airpower Studies was redesignated to include "Space."

NOTES TO PAGES 84–86

8. Memorandum, Dr. James W. Forsyth (dean, ACSC) to Major General Thompson, Subj: "Space Content in ACSC Curriculum," 25 Apr 17, including quotes 1–2 (copy at AFHRA); E-mail, Dr. John G. Terino (ACSC) to Marion, Subj: "RE: ACSC curriculum data," 24 Aug 21 and 7 Sep 21, including quotes 3–4 (both from 7 Sep 21) (copy at AFHRA); E-mail (1 of 2), Terino to Marion, Subj: "RE: draft para on Space in ACSC curriculum," 25 Oct 21, including quotes 5–6 (copy at AFHRA). At least one ACSC faculty member seriously disagreed with Terino's version of the school's space curriculum (copy of email at AFHRA), perhaps an illustration that where one stood among the several schools of thought regarding space could be reflected in space sub-topics such as curriculum as well as one's perspective, as Terino stated, of the "context on what we are required to have in our curriculum and what the goals are regarding the students we graduate."

9. E-mail (2 of 2), Terino to Marion, Subj: "RE: draft para on Space in ACSC curriculum," 25 Oct 21, including quote 1 (copy at AFHRA); Christian Davenport, *The Space Barons: Elon Musk, Jeff Bezos, and the Quest to Colonize the Cosmos* (New York: Public Affairs, 2018), 203, including quote 2.

10. *Report of the Commission to Assess United States National Security Space Management and Organization* [Pursuant to Public Law 106-65] (Washington, DC: 11 Jan 01), xxii–xxiii, 42, 57, including quote 1; OHI, Dr. Michael V. Smith (ACSC), conducted by Marion, Maxwell AFB, AL, 3 Aug, 12–13 Aug 20, including quote 2; "Remarks of Congressman Mike Rogers . . . 2017 Space Symposium," *SSQ*, Summer 2017, 8, including quotes 3–4. Note the Air Force had no formal space career field outside of space operations.

11. "Remarks of Congressman Mike Rogers . . . 2017 Space Symposium," *SSQ*, Summer 2017, 8, including quotes 1–2; Tobias Naegele, "Launching the Space Force," *Air Force Magazine* 103, no. 1 & 2 (Jan/Feb 2020): 2, including quote 3. On the disposition of space artifacts in earlier years, see chap. 2, present work.

12. "Remarks of Congressman Mike Rogers . . . 2017 Space Symposium," *SSQ*, Summer 2017, 8–9, including quotes. The formal designation of the Navy program was the Mobile User Objective System, or MUOS.

13. "Remarks of Congressman Mike Rogers . . . 2017 Space Symposium," *SSQ*, Summer 2017, 10–11, including quote.

14. "Remarks of Congressman Mike Rogers . . . 2017 Space Symposium," *SSQ*, Summer 2017, 10–11, including quotes.

15. "Remarks of Congressman Mike Rogers . . . 2017 Space Symposium," *SSQ*, Summer 2017, 11, including quotes; Bob Smith, "The Challenge of Space Power," *Airpower Journal* 13, no. 1 (Spring 1999): 32–39; Telephone conversation, Hon. Matthew P. Donovan with author, 27 May 21. Note the House

NOTES TO PAGES 86–89   201

Armed Services Committee, or HASC, subcommittees were much more powerful than their Senate counterparts (Donovan conversation). Over the years, a number of others agreed on the need for a cadre of space professionals in the USAF, from the Rumsfeld and Allard commissions to Air Force senior generals such as Robert Dickman, John Jumper, and David Thompson.

16. OHI, Hon. Dr. Heather A. Wilson, SecAF, conducted by Marion, El Paso, Tex., 8 Aug 22 (AFHRA, call number S239.0512–2854).

17. OHI, Wilson, 8 May 19, 3–5, including quote 1; Hon. Heather Wilson Papers, Ltr, Sen. John McCain to Wilson, 30 Mar 17, including quote 2, AFHRA, call number 168.7768–2; Heather Wilson, *U.S. Air Force*, Biographies, accessed at https:// www.af.mil/About-Us/Biographies/Display/Article/1183103/dr-heather -wilson/ (5 Oct 22).

18. OHI, Wilson, 8 Aug 22, 6, 31–34, including quotes 1, 4–5; OHI, Wilson, 8 May 19, 8–9, 11, including quotes 2–3, 6; Personal discussion, Lt. Col. Michael M. Trimble (USAF), with Marion, Maxwell AFB, AL, 29 Jun 22, including quote 7; Hon. Heather Wilson Papers, Memorandum, Subj: "Air Force Directive Publication Reduction," 3 Aug 17, AFHRA, call number 168.7768–115.

19. OHI, Wilson, 8 May 19, 8, including quote.

20. OHI, Mr. Stephen L. Kitay (former deputy assistant secretary of defense— space policy), conducted by Marion (via telephone), 16 May 22, including quote 1 (AFHRA, call number S239.0512–2852, audio only); *Public Law 115-91, 115th Congress, National Defense Authorization Act for Fiscal Year 2018* (Washington, DC: GPO, 12 Dec 17), 439, including quote 2; OHI, Wilson, 8 Aug 22, 33.

21. E-mail, Dr. Scott Pace (George Washington University) to Marion, Subj: "Re: Support for Book, 'Standing Up Space Force,'" 27 Apr 22, including quote 1 (copy at AFHRA); "Presidential Documents, Space Policy Directive-4 of February 19, 2019, Establishment of the United States Space Force," *Federal Register* 84, no. 37 (25 Feb 19), including quote 2, accessed at https://www .govinfo.gov/content/pkg/FR-2019-02-25/pdf/2019-03345.pdf (5 Oct 22); Travis J. Tritten, "Mattis urges House to abandon Space Corps proposal," *Real Clear Defense*, 13 Jul 17; Joe Gould, "Trump, Mattis lose as 'Space Corps' proposal survives in defense policy bill," *Defense News*, 13 Jul 17; Sydney J. Freedberg Jr., "Space Corps, What Is It Good For? Not Much: Air Force Leaders," *Breaking Defense*, 21 Jun 17, accessed at https://breakingdefense.com/2017/06/ space-corps-what-is-it-good-for-not-much-air-force-leaders/ (5 Oct 22); Marcia Smith, "Trump Talks Mars, Rockets, Space Force—But Not The Moon," SpacePolicyOnline.com, 13 Mar 18; Lara Seligman, "Before Resigning, Air Force Secretary Heather Wilson Irked Trump," *Foreign Policy*, 8 Mar 19; Michael Ray, "James Mattis," *Encyclopedia Britannica*, 4 Sep 20, accessed at

202   NOTES TO PAGES 89–91

https://www.britannica.com/biography/James-Mattis (5 Oct 22); "Military/ National Security Space Activities," SpacePolicyOnline.com, updated 25 May 21, accessed at https://spacepolicyonline.com/topics/militarynational-secu rity-space-activities/ (5 Oct 22); Telephone conversation, Hon. Matthew P. Donovan with author, 27 May 21.

22. Loren Thompson, "Heather Wilson Was Uniquely Qualified to Be Air Force Secretary. So Why Is She Leaving?" Forbes.com, 8 Mar 19, including quotes, accessed at https://www.forbes.com/sites/lorenthompson/2019/03/08/heather -wilson-was-uniquely-qualified-to-be-air-force-secretary-so-why-is-she-leav ing/?sh=47fab440ef9d_(5 Oct 22).

23. Hon. Heather Wilson Papers, SecAF Swearing-In Ceremony, Remarks by Secretary of Defense James Mattis, 16 May 2017, including quote, AFHRA, call number 168.7768–76; OHI, Wilson, 8 May 19, 3–4; OHI, Wilson, 8 Aug 22, 38–39.

24. OHI, Lt. Col. Peter A. Garretson USAF (Ret.), conducted by Marion, Maxwell AFB, AL, 29 Oct 21, including quote; OHI, M. V. Smith, 13 Aug 20.

25. *National Defense Authorization Act for Fiscal Year 2018, Conference Report to Accompany H.R. 2810* [115th Congress, 1st Session, House of Representatives, Report 115–404] (Washington, DC: GPO, 9 Nov 17), 1008, including quote.

26. Brissett, "The Space Corps Question," *Air Force Magazine*, 29 Aug 17, including quote 1 (Trump administration quoted by Brissett); Tritten, "Mattis urges House to abandon Space Corps proposal," *Real Clear Defense*, 13 Jul 17, including quote 2 (Mattis quoted by Tritten); Gould, "Trump, Mattis lose as 'Space Corps' proposal survives," *Defense News*, 13 Jul 17; Telephone conversation, Hon. Matthew P. Donovan with author, 27 May 21. The National Space Council had languished in 1992–93.

27. Hon. Heather Wilson Papers, [Wilson's handwritten note on title page], *USAF Strategic Master Plan*, May 2015, including quote 1, AFHRA, call number 168.7768–3; Hon. Heather Wilson Papers, [Wilson's handwritten note on table of contents page], *Air Force Future Operating Concept, A View of the Air Force in 2035*, Sep 2015, including quote 2, AFHRA, call number 168.7768–3; Hon. Heather Wilson Papers, [Wilson's handwritten notes, separate page], Draft of Suggested Testimony for SASC on 17 May 17, including quotes 3–4, AFHRA, call number 168.7768–6; E-mail, Donovan to author, Subj: "RE: draft para's—USSF, chap. 4 (2017–2018)," 2 Jun 21.

28. Phillip Swarts, "Space Corps proposal becoming flashpoint in DoD budget negotiations," *Space News*, 22 Jun 17, including quote (Goldfein quoted by Swarts), accessed at https://spacenews.com/space-corps-proposal-becoming -flashpoint-in-dod-budget-negotiations/ (5 Oct 22).

NOTES TO PAGES 91–93   203

29. On 17 May 2017, Goldfein, testifying with the new Air Force secretary before the SASC, said something similar to the above quote ("I would just offer to you that any move that actually ends up separating space as opposed to integrating space . . . is a move in the wrong direction."); see "Stenographic Transcript Before the Subcommittee on Strategic Forces, Committee on Armed Services, United States Senate, Military Space Organization, Policy, and Programs," [Alderson Court Reporting], Washington DC, 17 May 17.

30. Swarts, "Space Corps proposal becoming flashpoint," *Space News*, 22 Jun 17, including quote 1; Freedberg, "Space Corps, What Is It Good For?" *Breaking Defense*, 21 Jun 17, including quote 2.

31. John Venable, "Backgrounder: Independent Capability Assessment of U.S. Air Force Reveals Readiness Level Below Carter Administration Hollow Force," *Heritage Foundation*, no. 3208, 17 Apr 17, including quote; Freedberg, "Space Corps, What Is It Good For?" *Breaking Defense*, 21 Jun 17; Swarts, "Space Corps proposal becoming flashpoint," *Space News*, 22 Jun 17; Brissett, "The Space Corps Question," *Air Force Magazine*, 29 Aug 17. The new three-star billet, the deputy chief of staff for space, was designated the air staff's A11. It functioned informally for three months (Aug–Nov 2017) before being eliminated by Congress in the 2018 NDAA.

32. Sydney J. Freedberg Jr., "Rogers 'Pissed' At Air Force Opposition To Space Corps," *Breaking Defense*, 22 Jun 17, including quotes 1–5 (Rogers quoted by Freedberg), accessed at https://breakingdefense.com/2017/06/rogers-pissed-at-air-force-opposition-to-space-corps/ (5 Oct 22); "Rogers Says Air Force Cannot Fix Space, so Congress Must," *Air Force Magazine*, 22 Jun 17, including quote 6 (Rogers quoted by *AFM*), accessed at https://www.airforcemag.com/rogers-says-air-force-cannot-fix-space-so-congress-must/ (5 Oct 22); Swarts, "Space Corps proposal becoming flashpoint," *Space News*, 22 Jun 17; Brissett, "The Space Corps Question," *Air Force Magazine*, 29 Aug 17. Rogers was first elected to Congress in November 2002. For the reorganizing of Russian and Chinese space forces, see chap. 3, present work. The current proposal for the Space Corps-Air Force secretary arrangement was similar to the Marine Corps in the Department of the Navy.

33. Brissett, "The Space Corps Question," *Air Force Magazine*, 29 Aug 17, including quotes (Thornberry, Cooper quoted by Brissett).

34. OHI, Kitay, 16 May 22; E-mail, Mr. Stephen L. Kitay to Marion, Subj: "RE: Space Force: DRAFT section, 2017–2018," 16 May 22 (copy at AFHRA). Quotes in this paragraph resulted from blending the above interview and e-mail.

35. Brissett, "The Space Corps Question," *Air Force Magazine*, 29 Aug 17, including quotes (Cooper, Rogers quoted by Brissett); "Actions—H.R. 2810—115th

204 NOTES TO PAGES 94-95

Congress (2017–18): National Defense Authorization Act for Fiscal Year 2018," Congress.gov (Library of Congress), accessed at https://www.congress .gov/search?q={%22search%22:%22cite:PL115–91%22}&searchResultView Type=expanded (5 Oct 22).

36. Mike Fabey, "Space Corps proposal will 'figure' itself out, Wilson says," *Space News*, 13 Sep 17, including quotes 1–2, 4 (Wilson quoted by Fabey), accessed at https://spacenews.com/space-corps-proposal-will-fizzle-wilson-says/ (5 Oct 22) (Note the word "fizzle" in the URL; if Wilson used that word, it did not appear in the article); Michael Bjorklund, "A Report on the First National Space Forum," *Space Times*, July–Aug 1997, 4–5, including quote 3 (Marc Johansen quoted by Bjorklund); Christian Davenport, "Some in Congress are pushing for a 'Space Corps,' dedicated to fighting wars in the cosmos," *Washington Post*, 15 Sep 17, including quotes 5–6 (James quoted by Davenport), accessed at https://www.washingtonpost.com/news/checkpoint/wp/2017/09/15/some-in -congress-are-pushing-for-a-space-corps-dedicated-to-fighting-wars-in-the -cosmos/ (5 Oct 22); Brissett, "The Space Corps Question," *Air Force Magazine*, 29 Aug 17; Sandra Erwin, "Secretary Wilson: Air Force to step up advocacy of space," *Space News*, 18 Sep 17.

37. Telephone conversation, Hon. Matthew P. Donovan with author, 27 May 21, including quote 1; *National Defense Authorization Act for Fiscal Year 2018, Conference Report to Accompany H.R. 2810* [115th Congress, 1st Session, House of Representatives, Report 115–404] (Washington, DC: GPO, 9 Nov 17), 1008, including quotes 2–3; Davenport, "Some in Congress are pushing for a 'Space Corps,'" *Washington Post*, 15 Sep 17, including quote 4; OHI, Maj. Gen. Clinton E. Crosier, Deputy, Deputy CoS, Strategy, Integration and Requirements, Hq USAF, Arlington, Va., conducted by Greg Ball and Wade Scrogham, USSF/ HO, Peterson AFB, CO, 12 Feb 20, including quote 5 (copy at AFHRA); Zachary Cohen, "Lawmakers scrap 'Space Corps' proposal," CNN, 8 Nov 17, including quote 6 (summary quoted by Cohen); Sandra Erwin, "Space reforms coming: 2018 NDAA drops legislative bombshells on U.S. Air Force," *Space News*, 9 Nov 17, accessed at https://spacenews.com/space-reforms-coming -2018-ndaa-drops-legislative-bombshells-on-u-s-air-force/ (5 Oct 22); "Military/National Security Space Activities," SpacePolicyOnline.com, updated 25 May 21. According to Donovan, typically much of the collaborative work that resulted in the conference report was accomplished during the August recess.

38. OHI, Lt. Gen. David D. Thompson, USSF/CV, conducted by Greg Ball and Wade Scrogham, USSF/HO, Peterson AFB, CO, 13 Feb 20, including quote (copy at AFHRA); *National Defense Authorization Act . . . 2018, Conference Report*, 439–40; Marcia Smith, "No Space Corps In Final FY2018 NDAA," SpacePolicyOnline.com, 8 Nov 17, accessed at https://spacepolicyonline.com/

NOTES TO PAGES 95–96 205

news/no-space-corps-in-final-fy2018-ndaa/ (5 Oct 22); Erwin, "Space reforms coming: 2018 NDAA drops legislative bombshells," *Space News*, 9 Nov 17. The NDAA also designated the AFSPC commander the service acquisition executive for defense space acquisitions (*NDAA Conference Report*, 440). Upon the president's signing the bill into law in December, the corresponding portions in the NDAA were found in *Public Law 115-91, 115th Congress, National Defense Authorization Act for Fiscal Year 2018*, 436–37. The A11 office was unofficially in operation for three months (Aug–Nov 2017). In April 2018, the new entity's designation was the Air Force Space Command Forward Element. Although Thompson's official Air Force biography does not reflect this duty, it is covered in the AFSPC history for the period; see E-mail, Gregory W. Ball, USSF/HO, to author, Subj: "RE: draft para (chap. 4)," 16 Jun 21 (copy at AFHRA).

39. *National Defense Authorization Act . . . 2018, Conference Report*, 439–40, including quote; Sandra Erwin, "Deputy Defense Secretary Shanahan to take over duties of principal space adviser," SpaceNews.com, 18 Jan 18.

40. Document (draft), Matthew P. Donovan, "Toward an Independent Space Force: Is It Time for a Space Corps?" Jun–Jul 2017, including quote (provided by Donovan to author, copy at AFHRA).

41. Document (draft), Donovan, "Toward an Independent Space Force: Is It Time for a Space Corps?" Jun–Jul 2017, including quotes; Benjamin S. Lambeth, *Mastering the Ultimate High Ground: Next Steps in the Military Uses of Space* (Santa Monica, Calif.; Arlington, Va.; and Pittsburgh, Pa.: RAND, 2003), 43–44.

42. *National Defense Authorization Act . . . 2018, Conference Report*, 439–42, including quotes; Smith, "No Space Corps in Final FY2018 NDAA," SpacePolicy Online.com, 8 Nov 17; Erwin, "Space reforms coming: 2018 NDAA drops legislative bombshells," *Space News*, 9 Nov 17. The corresponding portions in the NDAA were found in *Public Law 115-91, 115th Congress, National Defense Authorization Act for Fiscal Year 2018*, 438–39. The 2018 NDAA upgraded Air Force Space Command's command billet to a six-year appointment in the grade of general and granted the commander full authority for the organize/train/equip functions for Air Force space forces.

43. Valerie Insinna, "Key lawmaker vows to continue Space Corps fight," *Defense News*, 2 Dec 17, including quotes (Rogers quoted by Insinna).

44. "Actions—H.R. 2810—115th Congress (2017–2018): National Defense Authorization Act for Fiscal Year 2018," Congress.gov.

45. David N. Spires, *Beyond Horizons: A History of the Air Force in Space, 1947–2007* (Peterson AFB, CO: Air Force Space Command, 2nd ed., 2007), 190–91, 200. *SpacePolicyOnline* observed, "When the Obama Administration released its 2010 National Space Policy, it stated it would release additional specific space policies on other topics as previous Presidents had done. . . . Obama did not,

206 NOTES TO PAGES 97–99

however, release updated versions of the others." (See "Military/National Security Space Activities," SpacePolicyOnline.com, updated 25 May 21.) Trump issued four other SPDs between February 2019 and January 2021; see chap. 5, present work.

46. "Presidential Documents, Space Policy Directive-1 of December 11, 2017, Reinvigorating America's Human Space Exploration Program," *Federal Register* 82, no. 239 (11 Dec 17), including quote 1; [Barack H. Obama] *National Spcace Policy of the United States of America, Jun. 28, 2010,* 11, including quote 2.

47. Marcia Smith, "Text of President Trump's Space Policy Directive 2, May 24, 2018," SpacePolicyOnline.com, 24 May 18, including quotes 1–2 (quote 2, quoted by Smith), accessed at https://spacepolicyonline.com/news/text-of-president-trumps-space-policy-directive-2-may-24–2018/ (5 Oct 22); Everett C. Dolman, *Astropolitik: Classical Geopolitics in the Space Age* (London and Portland, Ore.: Frank Cass, 2002), 176, including quotes 3–4.

48. "NASA Administrator Statement on Space Policy Directive-2," NASA Release 18–042, 24 May 18, including quote 1; OHI, Hon. Robert S. Walker (U.S. House of Representatives), conducted by Marion, Maxwell AFB, AL (remote), 19 Apr 22, including quote 2; E-mail, Pace to Marion, Subj: "Re: Support for Book, 'Standing Up Space Force,'" 27 Apr 22, including quote 3; Heather Bloemhard, "National Space Council Reestablished," *American Astronomical Society,* 11 Jul 17.

49. "Presidential Documents, Space Policy Directive-3 of June 18, 2018, National Space Traffic Management Policy," *Federal Register* 83, no. 120, 21 Jun 18, including quotes, accessed at https://www.federalregister.gov/documents/2018/06/21/2018–13521/national-space-traffic-management-policy (5 Oct 22); *National Security Strategy of the United States of America* (Washington, DC: Dec 2017), 31, accessed at https://trumpwhitehouse.archives.gov/wp-content/uploads/2017/12/NSS-Final-12–18–2017–0905.pdf (5 Oct 22); "Remarks by President Trump at a Meeting with the National Space Council and Signing of Space Policy Directive-3," TrumpWhiteHouse.Archives.gov, 18 Jun 18.

50. OHI, Garretson, 29 Oct 21, including quote; OHI, Hon. Speaker Newton L. Gingrich (1995–99), conducted by Marion (via telephone), 21 Mar 22; E-mail, Dr. Michael V. Smith (ACSC) to Marion, Subj: "RE: USSF Book Project," 23 Jan 20 (copy at AFHRA); E-mail, Garretson to Marion, Subj: "Re: 2 Questions for USSF Book," 15 Nov 21 (copy at AFHRA); E-mail, Roland L. Dukes (AU/CCP) to Marion, Subj: "RE: Speaker Gingrich visits with Lt Gen Kwast," 3 Dec 21, with attachments (copy at AFHRA); E-mail, Garretson to Marion, Subj: "Re: Historic Pictures . . . 2017," 2 Dec 21 (copy at AFHRA). Apart from several visits to Maxwell AFB to discuss space issues, Gingrich also attended exercises at the Air Force Wargaming Center on base.

NOTES TO PAGES 99–101

51. Mike Wall, "Trump Says US May Need a 'Space Force,'" Space.com, 13 Mar 18, including quote 1 (Trump quoted by Wall), accessed at https://www.space.com/39966-trump-space-force-for-us.html (5 Oct 22); "Trump introduces idea of 'Space Force,'" CNBC.com, 13 Mar 18, including quote 2, (video) accessed at https://www.cnbc.com/video/2018/03/13/trump-introduces-idea-of-space-force.html (5 Oct 22); Sandra Erwin, "Air Force secretary raises space awareness inside Pentagon; Startups grab spotlight at satellite industry's annual DC trade show," *Space News*, 13 Mar 18, including quote 3 (Wilson quoted by Erwin); Sandra Erwin, "House members energized by Trump's sudden attention to space warfare," *Space News*, 14 Mar 18, including quote 4 (Wilson quoted by Erwin). In a similar scenario former undersecretary of the Air Force Matt Donovan commented that when the president tweeted a statement that appeared to set a new policy on transgenderism in the military, Secretary of Defense Mattis calmly stated something to the effect that the department doesn't react to posts on social media but rather to official directives from the president transmitted through the chain of command; see e-mail, Hon. Matthew P. Donovan (Mitchell Institute for Aerospace Studies), to Marion, Subj: "Re: Insight on SecAF 'Gag Order' & POTUS 'Order' to Start Space Force—2018," 2 Nov 21 (copy at AFHRA).

52. "SECAF: Accelerating defendable space, multi-domain operations key to future readiness," *Secretary of the Air Force Public Affairs Office*, 21 Mar 18, including quotes, accessed at https://www.afspc.af.mil/News/Article-Display/Article/1472471/secaf-accelerating-defendable-space-multi-domain-opera tions-key-to-future-readi/ (5 Oct 22); OHI, Wilson, 8 May 19, 14; *Summary of the 2018 National Defense Strategy of the United States of America* (Washington, DC, 2018), 1.

53. Marina Koren, "What Does Trump Mean By 'Space Force'?" *Atlantic*, 13 Mar 18, including quotes (Rogers, Cooper quoted by Koren), accessed at https://www.theatlantic.com/science/archive/2018/03/trump-space-force-nasa/555560/ (5 Oct 22).

54. "Remarks by President Trump . . . Signing of Space Policy Directive-3," Whitehouse.gov, 18 Jun 18, including quote 1; Sandra Erwin, "Trump: 'We are going to have the Space Force,'" SpaceNews.com, 18 Jun 18, including quotes 2–3; OHI, Mr Stephen L. Kitay, Deputy Assistant Secretary of Defense for Space Policy, and Col. Casey M. Beard, OSD/SP, conducted by Greg Ball and Wade Scrogham, USSF/HO, Peterson AFB, CO, 13 Feb 20 (copy at AFHRA); OHI, Kitay, 16 May 22; E-mail, Kitay to Marion, "RE: Space Force: DRAFT section, 2017–2018," 16 May 22; E-mail, Hays to Marion, Subj: "Re: Support for Book, 'Standing Up Space Force,'" 28 Apr 22.

55. OHI, Kitay, 16 May 22, including quotes.

208 NOTES TO PAGES 101–106

56. "Letter to Airmen on Space—19 Jun 18.pdf," *Military News*, 20 Jun 18, including quote, accessed at https://www.militarynews.com/letter-to-airmen-on-space-19-june-18-pdf/pdf_59eafcda-74b7–11e8-b617-b7c9162cc0cd.html (5 Oct 22); OHI, Kitay, 13 Feb 20, including quote 2; "NASA Administrator Jim Bridenstine explains Trump's Space Force," *Politico*, 27 Jun 18, (video) accessed at https://www.politico.com/video/2018/06/27/nasa-on-space-force-066971 (5 Oct 22).

57. "Remarks by Vice President Pence on the Future of the U.S. Military in Space," press release from White House, SpaceRef.com, 9 Aug 18, including quotes 1–3, accessed at http://spaceref.com/news/viewpr.html?pid=52955 (5 Oct 22); Pace to Marion, Subj: "Re: Support for Book, 'Standing Up Space Force,'" 27 Apr 22, including quotes 4–5.

58. OHI, Kitay, 13 Feb 20, including quote 1; OHI, Maj. Gen. Stephen N. Whiting, USSF/CD, conducted by Greg Ball, USSF/HO, Peterson AFB, CO, 18 Mar 20, including quote 2 (copy at AFHRA).

59. OHI, Gingrich, 21 Mar 22, including quote; OHI, Whiting, 18 Mar 20; OHI, Garretson, 29 Oct 21.

60. Oriana Pawlyk, "Air Force Issues Gag Order on Press Engagements: Memo," Military.com, 13 Mar 18, including quotes 1–3 (quotes 2–3, quoted by Pawlyk), accessed at https://www.military.com/daily-news/2018/03/13/air-force-issues-gag-order-press-engagements-memo.html (5 Oct 22); E-mail, Donovan to Marion, Subj: "Re: Insight on SecAF 'Gag Order' & POTUS 'Order' to Start Space Force—2018," 2 Nov 21, including quote 4; OHI, Garretson, 29 Oct 21 (and personal documentation provided to the author, copy at AFHRA); OHI, M. V. Smith, 13 Aug 20.

61. Lt. Gen. Steven L. Kwast, *U.S. Air Force*, Biographies, accessed at https://www.af.mil/About-Us/Biographies/Display/Article/108470/lieutenant-general-steven-l-kwast/ (5 Oct 22).

62. OHI, Lt. Gen. Steven L. Kwast (AU/CC), conducted by Dr. Robert Kane (AU/HO), Maxwell AFB, AL, 18 Sep 17, including quote (AFHRA call number 239.01, 1 Oct 2016–30 Sep 2017).

63. Dolman, *Astropolitik*, 179, 183, including quote.

64. Peter Garretson, "Air Force Suppressed Space Force Debate; Lt. Gen. Kwast Spoke Truth To Power," *Breaking Defense*, 8 Aug 19, including quotes 1, 3, accessed at https://breakingdefense.com/2019/08/air-force-suppressed-space-force-debate-lt-gen-kwast-spoke-truth-to-power/ (5 Oct 22); E-mail, Donovan to Marion, Subj: "Re: Insight on SecAF 'Gag Order' & POTUS 'Order' to Start Space Force—2018," 2 Nov 21, including quote 2; OHI, Anonymous, Randolph AFB, TX, xx Sep 22, including quote 4; OHI, Garretson, 29 Oct 21, including quote 5; E-mail, Donovan to Marion, Subj: "Re: Quick Rewrite—But

NOTES TO PAGES 106–109   209

Leaves Unanswered Questions," 4 Nov 21 (copy at AFHRA); Stephen Losey, "Laughlin misconduct included vulgar call sign for female student pilot," *Air Force Times*, 6 Nov 18, accessed at https://www.airforcetimes.com/news/your -air-force/2018/11/06/laughlin-misconduct-included-vulgar-call-sign-for -female-student-pilot/ (5 Oct 22). On 7 May 19, Lt. Gen. Marshall B. Webb was announced by the Air Force as the next commander of AETC ([Air Force] "General Officer Assignments 2019," Release No. NR-110–19, 7 May 19). Webb took command in July. Meanwhile, Lt. Gen. Kwast retired, officially on 1 Sep 19.

65. OHI, Gingrich, 21 Mar 22, including quotes.
66. OHI, Thompson, 13 Feb 20, including quotes.
67. Brian G. Chow, "Worker-Bee Satellites Will Weaponize Space—and Help Us Keep the Peace," DefenseOne.com, 5 Jun 18, including quotes 1–2, accessed at https://www.defenseone.com/ideas/2018/06/worker-bee-satellites-will-wea ponize-space-we-can-still-keep-peace/148746/ (5 Oct 22); Brian G. Chow, "Trump's Space Force announcement could propel us to deal with space 'Pearl Harbor,'" *Space News*, 20 Jun 18, including quote 3; Neil Sheehan, *A Fiery Peace in a Cold War: Bernard Schriever and the Ultimate Weapon* (New York: Random House, 2009), 435, including quote 4; Lt. Gen. Forrest S. McCartney, *U.S. Air Force*, Biographies, accessed at https://www.af.mil/About-Us/Biographies/Dis play/Article/106313/lieutenant-general-forrest-s-mccartney/ (5 Oct 22); Sandra Erwin, "On-orbit satellite servicing: The next big thing in space?" *Space News*, 17 Nov 17; John E. Hyten, *A Sea of Peace or a Theater of War: Dealing with the Inevitable Conflict in Space* (University of Illinois at Urbana-Champaign: ACDIS [Occasional Paper], Apr 2000), 67–68.
68. OHI, Thompson, 13 Feb 20, including quotes.
69. OHI, Thompson, 13 Feb 20, including quote 1; OHI, Whiting, 18 Mar 20, including quote 2.
70. OHI, Wilson, 8 May 19, 15, including quote.
71. OHI, Wilson, 8 May 19, 16–17, including quotes 1–2; "Remarks by Vice President Pence on the Future of the U.S. Military in Space," White House, SpaceRef .com, 9 Aug 18, including quote. A 2018 Pentagon report called for the creation of the Space Development Agency, which Vice President Pence said was to provide space force personnel with "cutting-edge warfighting capabilities."
72. OHI, Wilson, 8 May 19, 16, including quotes.
73. Telephone conversation, Donovan with author, 27 May 21, including quote. The author is indebted to Ms. Peggy Ream, longtime AFHRA colleague, for her timely researching of the lineage of air and space operations centers.
74. OHI, Wilson, 8 May 19, 14, including quote—emphasis in original; Spires, *Beyond Horizons*, 41–47, 55, 85; Dwayne A. Day, "The Air Force in Space: Past,

210   NOTES TO PAGES 110–114

Present and Future," *Space Times*, Mar–Apr 1996, 16–17; "First 'Announced' NRO Payload," *Spaceflight* 39 (Mar 1997): 77.

75. OHI, Crosier, 12 Feb 20, including quote 1; "Stenographic Transcript Before the . . . United States Senate," [Alderson Court Reporting], Washington, DC, 17 May 2017, 15, 18, 22, including quote 2; "Toward the Creation of a U.S. 'Space Force,'" *Congressional Research Service*, 16 Aug 18, including quote 3; Steve Kwast, "Opinion: 'There won't be many prizes for second place,'" *Politico*, 10 Aug 18, including quotes 4–5.

76. Spires, *Beyond Horizons*, 47, including quotes (quote 1, quoted by Spires).

Chapter 5. Standing Up, 2019–2020

1. "Remarks by President Trump . . . Signing of Space Policy Directive-3," White-house.gov, 18 Jun 18, including quote 1; Oral History Interview (OHI), Lt. Gen. David D. Thompson, USSF/CV, conducted by Greg Ball and Wade Scrogham, USSF/HO, Peterson AFB, CO, 13 Feb 20, including quote 2 (copy at AFHRA).

2. "Text of Space Policy Directive-4: Establishment of the United States Space Force," including quotes.

3. In 2002, Secretary of Defense Donald Rumsfeld disestablished the first U.S. Space Command, reorganizing it under the U.S. Strategic Command.

4. "Text . . . Establishment of the United States Space Force," including quotes 1–2; Gen. John W. "Jay" Raymond, *U.S. Space Force*, Leadership, including quote 3, accessed at https://www.spaceforce.mil/SFB/Display/Article/2040592/john-w-jay-raymond/ (5 Oct 22). In May 2019, retired Air Force Lt. Gen. David Deptula wrote that in order to maintain U.S. national security in the space domain, "The solution path to the first priority objective [viewing space as a warfighting domain] . . . is establishing a new combatant command focused on warfighting in space—U.S. Space Command"; see Dave Deptula, "A Space Force That Would Make A Difference," *Forbes*, 5 May 19, accessed at https://www.forbes.com/sites/davedeptula/2019/05/05/a-space-force-that-would-make-a-difference/?sh=17c6117f737c (5 Oct 22). Two weeks earlier, Rep. Doug Lamborn (R-Colo.) argued that Colorado Springs was the only serious option for U.S. Space Command's location; see Doug Lamborn, "Reestablishing U.S. Space Command in Colorado Springs is the only serious option," *Space News*, 23 Apr 19.

5. Memorandum, Acting SecDef Patrick M. Shanahan to Chief Management Officer of the Department of Defense, Secretaries of the Military Departments et al., Subj: "U.S. Space Force Planning Team," 21 Feb 19, including quote (copy at AFHRA).

NOTES TO PAGES 114–118 211

6. OHI, Maj. Gen. Clinton E. Crosier, Deputy, Deputy CoS, Strategy, Integration and Requirements, Hq USAF, Arlington, Va., conducted by Greg Ball and Wade Scrogham, USSF/HO, Peterson AFB, CO, 12 Feb 20, including quotes (copy at AFHRA); Maj. Gen. Clinton E. Crosier, *U.S. Air Force*, Biographies, accessed at https://www.af.mil/About-Us/Biographies/Display/Article/108783/major-general-clinton-e-crosier/ (5 Oct 22).

7. OHI, Crosier, 12 Feb 20, including quote.

8. OHI, Crosier, 12 Feb 20, including quotes; Crosier, *U.S. Air Force*, Biographies.

9. Memorandum, SecAF Wilson to Chief Management Officer of the Department of Defense, Secretaries of the Military Departments et al., Subj: "Establishment of the US Space Force Planning Task Force," 22 Feb 19, including quotes (copy at AFHRA); OHI, Crosier, 12 Feb 20.

10. OHI, Crosier, 12 Feb 20, including quotes; Memorandum, SecAF Wilson to Acting Secretary of Defense, Subj: "Completion of a U.S. Space Force Initial Work Plan (U.S. Space Force Planning Team Memorandum, 21 February 2019)," 22 Mar 19 (copy at AFHRA).

11. E-mail, Brig. Gen. Edward W. Thomas Jr. (SAF-PA), to Hon. Heather Wilson, Gen. David Goldfein, Subj: "Message Summary & Weekend Reads 9–15 Mar 19," 15 Mar 19, including quote 1 (copy at AFHRA); Hon. Heather Wilson Papers, Ltr, Sen. John McCain to Wilson, 30 Mar 17, including quote 2, AFHRA, call number 168.7768–2.

12. OHI, Col. Jack Fischer, USAF, conducted by Greg Ball, USSF/HO, Schriever AFB, Colo., 3 Jan 20, including quote 1 (copy at AFHRA); OHI, Lt. Col. Charles J. Cooper, USSF, conducted by Greg Ball, USSF/HO, 4 Jun 20, including quotes 2–3 (copy at AFHRA, audio only); Lt. Gen. John E. Shaw, *U.S. Space Force*, Leadership, accessed at https://www.spaceforce.mil/SFB/Display/Article/2830935/john-e-shaw/ (5 Oct 22); Lt. Gen. William J. Liquori, *U.S. Space Force*, Leadership, at https://www.spaceforce.mil/SFB/Display/Article/2358653/william-j-liquori/ (5 Oct 22).

13. OHI, Fischer, 3 Jan 20, including quotes 1–2, 4; OHI, Cooper, 4 Jun 20, including quote 3; OHI, Maj. Jerry Drew, USA, conducted by Greg Ball, USSF/HO, Peterson AFB, CO, 3 May 19 (copy at AFHRA).

14. OHI, Col. Anthony Lujan, USAF, conducted by Greg Ball, USSF/HO, Peterson AFB, Colo., 31 May 19, including quotes 1–2 (copy at AFHRA); OHI, Drew, 3 May 19, including quote 3; OHI, Thompson, 13 Feb 20.

15. OHI, Thompson, 13 Feb 20, including quote; Briefing slides, "USSF HQ Staff Macro-Organizational Design Preliminary Options," (DRAFT—Pre-Decisional Working Papers), Space Force Planning Task Force (SFPTF), 18 Jun 19, slides 1, 5 (copy at AFHRA). Slide 5 stated, "The design for Field

212 NOTES TO PAGES 118–122

Organizations and [Direct Reporting Units/Field Operating Agencies] are being coordinated separately," to which Thompson alluded.

16. "USSF Organization," *United States Space Force Organization*, including quotes, accessed at https://www.spaceforce.mil/About-Us/About-Space-Force/Space -Force-Organization/ (5 Oct 22).

17. In Section 3, SPD-4 stated, "The United States Space Force should include both combat and combat support functions to enable prompt and sustained offensive and defensive space operations, and joint operations in all domains." SPD-4 did not specify the source, but Linn's logical assumption was that combat support elements must come to USSF from the Air Force. Note that some Pentagon, USAF, and USSF leaders including General Raymond may have been hesitant to bring them in, however, because they sought to minimize bureaucracy in the new service.

18. OHI, Michelle Linn, Hq USSF/S4, conducted by Greg Ball, USSF/HO, Peterson AFB, Colo., 28 Feb 20, including quotes (copy at AFHRA); OHI, Maj. Gen. Stephen N. Whiting, USSF/CD, conducted by Greg Ball, USSF/HO, Peterson AFB, CO, 18 Mar 20 (copy at AFHRA).

19. OHI, Linn, 28 Feb 20, including quotes 1–2; OHI, Whiting, 18 Mar 20, including quotes 3–5.

20. OHI, Drew, 3 May 19, including quotes; Rachel S. Cohen, "US Space Command Takes Reins on Space Ops," *Air Force Magazine*, Oct 2019, 20. AFSPC was the Air Force component to U.S. Space Command.

21. OHI, Linn, 28 Feb 20.

22. Ashley J. Tellis, "India's ASAT Test: An Incomplete Success," *Carnegie Endowment for International Peace*, 15 Apr 19, including quote, accessed at https:// carnegieendowment.org/2019/04/15/india-s-asat-test-incomplete-success -pub-78884 (15 Jul 21).

23. Tellis, "India's ASAT Test," *Carnegie Endowment for International Peace*, 15 Apr 19, including quotes.

24. Mark R. McNeilly, *Sun Tzu and the Art of Modern Warfare* (Oxford and New York: Oxford University Press, 2015), 255, including quote 1; Tellis, "India's ASAT Test," *Carnegie Endowment for International Peace*, 15 Apr 19, including quote 2.

25. OHI, Crosier, 12 Feb 20, including quotes; Memorandum, HAF/DS (Lt. Gen. Jacqueline D. Van Ovost) to AFSPC/CD, Subj: "U.S. Space Force Macro-Organizational Design Structure," 2 May 19 (SD 4133, Space Studies folder, CD provided by AF/HOH to AFHRA).

26. Document, "Read Ahead, U.S. Space Force Planning Task Force Phase 1 Deliverables, Vector Check with SecAF and CSAF, Mon., 6 May 2019, 1400," Maj. Gen. Clint Crosier (USSF PTF [Planning Task Force]), 2 May 19 (copy at AFHRA), including quote 1; OHI, Crosier, 12 Feb 20, including quotes 2–3.

NOTES TO PAGES 123-125 213

27. Document, "Read Ahead, U.S. Space Force Planning Task Force . . . 6 May 2019, 1400," Crosier, 2 May 19, including quotes; OHI, Crosier, 12 Feb 20; Briefing Slides, "Initial Space Force Staff (ISFS) Billet Allocation" (DRAFT-Pre-Decisional Working Papers), Maj. Gen. Clint Crosier (USSF PTF), 6 May 19, slide 2 (copy at AFHRA). Note the numbers given in the "Read Ahead" document totaled to 199, not 200.

28. Charles Pope, "Gen Goldfein hosts inaugural space conference for US, partner nations," Secretary of the Air Force Public Affairs, 17 Apr 19, including quotes 1–4; *UK Space Power Joint Doctrine Publication 0-40* (Bristol: UK Ministry of Defence), 5, including quote 5; Hanneke Weitering, "France Is Launching a 'Space Force' with Weaponized Satellites," Space.com, 2 Aug 19; Christina Mackenzie, "French Air Force changes name as it looks to the stars," *Defense News*, 15 Sep 20.

29. Pope, "Gen Goldfein hosts inaugural space conference," Secretary of the Air Force Public Affairs, 17 Apr 19, including quote; B. J. Altvater, Samantha Clark, and Jeff Bozman, "Senators Question the Administration's Space Force Proposal," *Covington Global Watch Policy*, 15 Apr 19.

30. E-mail, Dr. Michael V. Smith (Air Command and Staff College [ACSC]) to Marion, Subj: "RE: Space Threat Question," 23 Oct 21, including quote (Rogers quoted by Smith) (copy at AFHRA); OHI, Dr. Brent D. Ziarnick (ACSC, Maxwell AFB, AL), conducted by Marion, Maxwell AFB, AL, 14 Oct 21 (AFHRA, call number S239.0512–2839, audio only); Sandra Erwin, "Senate Armed Services bill shakes up management of Air Force space acquisitions," *Space News*, 12 Jun 19; Sandra Erwin, "House Armed Services Committee votes to create a U.S. Space Corps," *Space News*, 13 Jun 19. I am greatly indebted to Peggy Ream, AFHRA Organizational Histories Branch chief, for the following information regarding the lineage of the Space Force: According to AFHRA's official lineage records, the Department of the Air Force redesignated "Air Force Space Command, Hq," as "United States Space Force, Hq," on 20 Dec 2019. On 21 Oct 2020, "United States Space Force, Hq," was redesignated as "Space Operations Command, Hq," and concurrently assigned to the "United States Space Force (Service)." As a consequence, since 21 Oct 2020, no organization now carries the designation as "U.S. Space Force, Hq." See Air Force Organizational Lineage and Honors Archive, Organizational Details—Actions, "Space Operations Command, Hq." E-mail, Ream to Marion, Subj: "RE: USSF," 21 Oct 21 (copy at AFHRA).

31. Sandra Erwin, "Space Force proponents in Congress warn Air Force: 'We will watch you like a hawk,'" *Space News*, 11 Dec 19, including quotes 1–3 (Cooper, Rogers quoted by Erwin), accessed at https://spacenews.com/space-force-proponents-in-congress-warn-air-force-we-will-watch-you-like-a-hawk/ (5 Oct

214 NOTES TO PAGES 125-129

22); Matthew Donovan, "Acting Air Force Secretary Donovan: America needs a Space Force—Here's why," *Fox News*, 21 Jun 19, including quotes 4–5, accessed at https://www.foxnews.com/opinion/acting-air-force-secretary-matthew-donovan-space-force (5 Oct 22); OHI, Lt. Col. Peter A. Garretson, USAF (Ret.), conducted by Marion, Maxwell AFB, AL, 29 Oct 21, including quote 6; Donovan, "Unleashing the Power of Space: the Case for a Separate U.S. Space Force," *War on the Rocks*, 1 Aug 19, accessed at https://warontherocks.com/2019/08/unleashing-the-power-of-space-the-case-for-a-separate-u-s-space-force/ (5 Oct 22); Pope, "Gen Goldfein hosts inaugural space conference," Secretary of the Air Force Public Affairs, 17 Apr 19. Maj. Gen. Crosier stated, "My understanding is the Vice President started calling members of the Senate Armed Services Committee personally and lobbying on behalf of the greater need, for national security, for the U.S. Space Force"; see OHI, Crosier, 12 Feb 20.

32. OHI, Col. Stuart Pettis, USAF, conducted by Greg Ball and Wade Scrogham, USSF/HO, Pentagon, Va., 11 Feb 20, including quotes 1–4 (copy at AFHRA); OHI, Thompson, 13 Feb 20, including quote 5; OHI, Whiting, 18 Mar 20.

33. Erwin, "Space Force proponents in Congress warn Air Force,'" *Space News*, 11 Dec 19, including quotes (quote 2, Cooper quoted by Erwin); "Roll Call Vote 116th Congress—1st Session," *United States Senate*, accessed at https://www.senate.gov/legislative/LIS/roll_call_lists/roll_call_vote_cfm.cfm?congress=116&session=1&vote=00400 (5 Oct 22).

34. Barbara M. Barrett, *U.S. Air Force*, Biographies.

35. OHI, Ambassador Barbara M. Barrett (former secretary of the Air Force), conducted by Marion (via telephone), 13 Apr 22 (AFHRA, call number S239.0512–2848, audio only), including quote.

36. OHI, Barrett, 13 Apr 22, including quotes.

37. OHI, Barrett, 13 Apr 22, including quotes; E-mail, Barrett to Marion, Subj: "FW: ACTION: Review paragraph," 16 Jun 22; Charles Pope, "Barrett publicly sworn in as secretary of the Air Force," Secretary of the Air Force Public Affairs, 2 Nov 19. Her public swearing-in was on 2 Nov.

38. OHI, Barrett, 13 Apr 22, including quotes.

39. OHI, Col. Brian Bolio, USA, conducted by Greg Ball (USSF/HO) (via telephone), 23 Apr 20 (copy at AFHRA, audio only).

40. OHI, Bolio, 23 Apr 20.

41. OHI, Bolio, 23 Apr 20, including quotes.

42. OHI, Bolio, 23 Apr 20, including quote 1; OHI, Crosier, 12 Feb 20, including quotes 2–3; OHI, Thompson, 13 Feb 20, including quote 4; OHI, Pettis, 11 Feb 20; "With the stroke of a pen, U.S. Space Force becomes a reality," Secretary of the Air Force Public Affairs, 20 Dec 19; "President Donald Trump impeached," History.com ("This Day in History," December 18, 2019). Note that on 20 Dec

NOTES TO PAGES 129-132 215

19, SecAF Barrett also redesignated Fourteenth Air Force as Space Operations Command (located at Vandenberg AFB, CA); see Cody Chiles, "14th Air Force Redesignated as Space Operations Command," Space Operations Command Public Affairs, 27 Dec 19.

43. Estimates varied widely on how many attended this event. Maj. Gen. Whiting estimated two to three hundred, but the USSF historian estimated at least twice that number (no wonder the cake ran out!); see OHI, Whiting, 18 Mar 20; OHI, Linn, 28 Feb 20.

44. OHI, Col. Suzanne M. Streeter, USSF, conducted by Greg Ball, USSF/HO, 26 Feb 20, including quote 1 (copy at AFHRA, audio only); OHI, Whiting, 18 Mar 20, including quotes 2–3; OHI, Drew, 3 May 19; History, Headquarters AFSC [2019], "Essay 2.1—Space Force Planning," 39–40.

45. OHI, Whiting, 18 Mar 20, including quotes 1–2; OHI, Thompson, 13 Feb 20, including quote 3. Up to about 10 Dec, AFSPC senior leaders did not expect that the U.S. Space Force was to be established at the very time the president signed the NDAA into law (Whiting OHI). Upon establishment of the U.S. Space Force, the former AFSPC personnel were assigned to the new service, but they were not yet transferred into the Space Force. They remained U.S. Air Force members for a time.

46. Memorandum, SecAF [Barbara Barrett] to Department of the Air Force, Subj: "Department of the Air Force Priorities," 27 Feb 20, including quotes (copy at AFHRA); Valerie Insinna, "Air Force Secretary Barbara Barrett chats about her top four priorities," *Defense News*, 27 Feb 20; Memorandum, SecAF Barrett to ALMAJCOM-FOA-DRU/CC, Subj: "Redesignation of Air Force Space Command to United States Space Force," 20 Dec 19 (copy at AFHRA).

47. Charles Pope, "Barrett highlights space, modernization, alliances, people as pressing priorities," *Secretary of the Air Force Public Affairs*, 27 Feb 20, including quotes 1–2; Insinna, "Air Force Secretary Barbara Barrett chats about her top four priorities," *Defense News*, 27 Feb 20, including quotes 3–5.

48. Aaron Mehta and Valerie Insinna, "Pentagon officially stands up Space Development Agency, names first director," *Defense News*, 13 Mar 19, including quote 1 (Shanahan quoted by Mehta/Insinna), accessed at https://www .defensenews.com/space/2019/03/13/pentagon-officially-stands-up-space -development-agency-names-first-director/ (5 Oct 22); Sandra Erwin, "Kennedy sees growing congressional support for Space Development Agency," *Space News*, 11 Jun 19, including quotes 2–3, accessed at https://spacenews.com/ken nedy-sees-growing-congressional-support-for-space-development-agency/ (5 Oct 22); *Report of the Commission to Assess United States National Security Space Management and Organization* [Pursuant to Public Law 106-65] (Washington: 11 Jan 01), 66; Rachel S. Cohen, "Appropriators: No Space Development

216 NOTES TO PAGES 132–135

Agency Funds Until We Get More Info," *Air Force Magazine*, 14 May 19; Nathan Strout, "The Space Development Agency's first director is already out," *Military Times*, 21 Jun 19; Yasmin Tadjdeh, "Future of Space Development Agency Debated," *National Defense*, 23 Jul 20.

49. E-mail, Dr. Mark J. Lewis (former DoD director of defense research and engineering), to Marion, Subj: "RE: Air Staff-tasked book on USSF," 26 Aug 21, including quotes 1–2 (copy at AFHRA); Valerie Insinna, "Space Development Agency on track to become part of Space Force in 2022, director says," *Defense News*, 21 Jan 20, including quote 3, accessed at https://www.defensenews.com/space/2020/01/21/space-development-agency-on-track-to-become-part-of-space-force-in-2022-director-says/ (5 Oct 22).

50. Tadjdeh, "Future of Space Development Agency Debated," *National Defense*, 23 Jul 20, including quote 1, accessed at https://www.nationaldefensemagazine.org/articles/2020/7/23/future-of-space-development-agency-debated (5 Oct 22); E-mail, Jonathan B. Withington (SDA Public Affairs) to Marion, Subj: "RE: AF History Program book—"Standing Up Space Force," 17 Nov 21, with attachment (copy at AFHRA), including quote 2; OHI, Hon. Dr. Heather A. Wilson, SecAF, conducted by Dr. James Malachowski and Ms. Aungelic Nelson, AF/HO, Pentagon, 8 May 19, 16–7 (copy at AFHRA); Theresa Hitchens, "Space Force Nears Year Mark, Acquisition Remains A Quagmire," *Breaking Defense*, 2 Oct 20; Sandra Erwin, "End of an era: Space and Missile Systems Center is now Space Systems Command," *Space News*, 13 Aug 21; E-mail, Dr. Mark J. Lewis to Marion, Subj: "Re: SDA Section for USSF Book," 18 Nov 21 (copy at AFHRA).

51. [SDA] Fact Sheet, "Space Development Agency: What You Need to Know," ca. late 2020, including quotes (copy at AFHRA).

52. E-mail, Withington to Marion, "RE: AF History Program book—'Standing Up Space Force,'" 17 Nov 21, with attachment, including quotes.

53. Webinar, SecAF Barrett and General Raymond, conducted by Thomas Dorame, *Space Foundation*, 6 May 20 (copy at AFHRA, audio only). Note that one of USSF's COVID responses was to optimize the bandwidth for the U.S. Navy's hospital ship stationed off the coast of California.

54. Webinar, Barrett and Raymond, 6 May 20, including quote; Pope, "Gen Goldfein hosts inaugural space conference," Secretary of the Air Force Public Affairs, 17 Apr 19; E-mail, Lt. Gen. William T. Lord, USAF (Ret.) to Marion, Subj: "Re: Quick RFI re: Space Force book," 21 Mar 23 (copy at AFHRA).

55. "NASA Astronauts Launch from America in Historic Test Flight of SpaceX Crew Dragon," NASA Release 20–057, 30 May 20, including quote 1, accessed at https://www.nasa.gov/press-release/nasa-astronauts-launch-from-america-in-historic-test-flight-of-spacex-crew-dragon (5 Oct 22); Webinar, Barrett

NOTES TO PAGES 135–140 217

and Raymond, 6 May 20, including quote 2. The Behnken-Hurley mission on board *Crew Dragon* was "the first crewed test flight for the Commercial Crew Program (CCP)"; see "NASA Astronauts Robert Behnken and Douglas Hurley's Scientific Journeys on board the Space Station," NASA.gov, 30 Jul 20.

56. Webinar, Barrett and Raymond, 6 May 20, including quote.

57. Webinar, Barrett and Raymond, 6 May 20, including quote.

58. Webinar, Barrett and Raymond, 6 May 20.

59. Mike Wall, "'Get a haircut,' real Space Force chief tells Netflix 'Space Force' star Steve Carell," Space.com, 7 May 20, including quotes (Raymond quoted by Wall); Webinar, Barrett and Raymond, 6 May 20; "*Space Force* (TV series)," Wikipedia, updated 9 Jul 21.

60. OHI, Streeter, 26 Feb 20, including quote; Col. Suzanne M. Streeter, *U.S. Air Force*, Biographies (copy at AFHRA).

61. OHI, Streeter, 26 Feb 20, including quotes; OHI, Thompson, 13 Feb 20.

62. *U.S. Constitution*, Amendment IV, including quote; OHI, Streeter, 26 Feb 20. The Foreign Intelligence Surveillance Act of 1978 (FISA) established the Foreign Intelligence Surveillance Court, whose purpose was to oversee requests by federal law enforcement for warrants to conduct surveillance of foreign spies on U.S. soil.

63. OHI, Streeter, 26 Feb 20, including quote.

64. OHI, Barrett, 13 Apr 22, including quotes.

65. "Department of the Air Force expands potential basing locations for U.S. Space Command Headquarters," *Space Force News*, 15 May 20, including quote, accessed at https://www.spaceforce.mil/News/Article/2188763/depart ment-of-the-air-force-expands-potential-basing-locations-for-u-s-space-co/ (5 Oct 22).

66. Rachel S. Cohen, "Colorado Pushes Back on Decision to Base U.S. Space Command in Alabama," *Air Force Magazine*, 13 Jan 21, accessed at https://www.airforcemag.com/air-force-picks-alabama-to-host-space-command-hq/ (5 Oct 22); Dustin Jones, "U.S. Space Command Headquarters May Land in Alabama," National Public Radio (NPR.org), 13 Jan 21; Sandra Erwin, "GAO completes investigation of the decision to relocate U.S. Space Command," *Space News*, 12 Apr 22.

67. E-mail, Maj. Gen. Stephen N. Whiting, USSF/CD, to Staff, Subj: "Building a new tradition—CSO," 10 Jan 20, including quote (copy at AFHRA).

68. E-mail, Whiting to Staff, "Building a new tradition—CSO," 10 Jan 20, including quote.

69. E-mail, Whiting to Staff, "Building a new tradition—CSO," 10 Jan 20, including quotes; E-mail, Dr. Paul J. Springer (ACSC) to Marion, Subj: "Manuscript draft review," 24 Sep 21 (copy at AFHRA).

NOTES TO PAGES 140–143

70. David McCullough, *John Adams* (New York, London, Toronto: Simon & Schuster, 2001), 404, including quotes.

71. "Chief Master Sergeant of the Space Force Roger A. Towberman," *United States Space Force*, Leadership, accessed at https://www.spaceforce.mil/SFB/Display/Article/2136021/chief-master-sergeant-roger-a-towberman/ (5 Oct 22). Towberman was transferred into the Space Force on 3 April 2020.

72. E-mail, Whiting to Staff, Subj: "USSF Naming Initiative," 13 Feb 20, including quote 1 (copy at AFHRA); Jim Garamone, "Space Force Personnel to Be Called Guardians," *DOD News*, 19 Dec 20, including quote 2, accessed at https://www.defense.gov/Explore/News/Article/Article/2452910/space-force-personnel-to-be-called-guardians/ (5 Oct 22); Sandra Erwin, "U.S. Space Force nameplates introduced for camouflage uniforms," *Space News*, 18 Jan 20.

73. E-mail, Gregory W. Ball, USSF/HO, to Marion, Subj: "RE: Delta & Vanguard terms," 13 Aug 21, including quote (copy at AFHRA).

74. E-mail, Ball to Marion, Subj: "RE: Delta & Vanguard terms," 13 Aug 21, including quote.

75. Erwin, "U.S. Space Force nameplates introduced," *Space News*, 18 Jan 20; E-mail, Lt. Col. Sean M. Lindsay, USSF/S2F, Subj: "POTUS released the USSF Logo via Twitter," 24 Jan 20 (copy at AFHRA); Rebecca Kheel, "Trump unveils Space Force logo," *The Hill*, 24 Jan 20; Case File, "Space Badge Heraldry," labeled OCSO-Space Staff, KA6 Culture and Identity (copy at AFHRA). The U.S. Space Force public website depicted the seal but because it was limited to internal, official use, the seal's image was covered with a red X ("United States Space Force Symbols," accessed at https://www.spaceforce.mil/About-Us/About-Space-Force/USSF-Symbols/) (5 Oct 22). Note that many, including the president, erroneously referred to the seal as the logo.

76. Memorandum, SecAF Barbara Barrett to "Air and Space Professionals," [USSF official logo and motto], 22 Jul 20, including quotes (copy at AFHRA); Barbara Sprunt, "Trump, Unveiling Space Force Flag, Touts What He Calls New 'Super-Duper Missile,'" National Public Radio (NPR.org), 15 May 20. Note that the USSF public website referred to the "Delta symbol" rather than using the preferred term, "logo." There were various delta symbols around, but there was only one official Space Force logo, hence the preferred use of "logo."

77. Elizabeth Howell, "Watch William Shatner gaze at Earth from space in awe during Blue Origin's launch (video)," Space.com, 14 Oct 21, including quote.

78. Memorandum, SecAF Barrett to HQ USSF, Subj: "Redesignation of Patrick Air Force Base," 16 Mar 20, including quote 1 (copy at AFHRA); E-mail, HAF TMT to USAF Pentagon and Various Offices, Subj: "Renaming of Air Force

NOTES TO PAGES 144–148   219

Installations to Space Force Installations," 5 Feb 20, including quote 2 (copy at AFHRA); Christian Davenport, *The Space Barons: Elon Musk, Jeff Bezos, and the Quest to Colonize the Cosmos* (New York: Public Affairs, 2018), 203, including quote 3; Rachel S. Cohen, "Cape Canaveral, Patrick Named First Space Force Installations," *Air Force Magazine*, 9 Dec 20.

79. OHI, Ziarnick, 14 Oct 21, including quote 1; Brent D. Ziarnick, "An aggressive Space Force begins with a Space Force Reserve," *The Hill* (op-ed), 1 May 20, including quote 2, accessed at https://thehill.com/opinion/national-security/494796-an-aggressive-space-force-begins-with-a-space-force-reserve (5 Oct 22); OHI, Fischer, 3 Jan 20, including quote 3; Peter Garretson, "Demanding more of Space Force," AerospaceAmerica.aiaa.org, vol. 59, no. 5 (Jun 2021), 44–46; Bryan Bender, "'We're in a sprint here': The Space Force struggles to blaze its own path," Politico.com, 6 Oct 21.

80. OHI, Thompson, 13 Feb 20. Benjamin S. Lambeth used the same dog-and-truck analogy when referring to the 2001 Space Commission; see his *Mastering the Ultimate High Ground: Next Steps in the Military Uses of Space* (Santa Monica, CA; Arlington, VA; and Pittsburgh, PA: RAND, 2003), 129–30.

Epilogue. Service Fundamentals, 2021

1. Memorandum, [Acting SecAF] John P. Roth, to ALMAJCOM-FLDC-MD-FOA-DRU, Subj: "Redesignation of Air Force Installations to Space Force Installations," 21 Apr 21, w/Atch 1 ("Installation Re-designation Dates"), including quote (copy at AFHRA); Alexus Wilcox, "Peterson, Schriever, Cheyenne Mountain cultivate a new identity," *Peterson-Schriever Garrison Public Affairs*, 26 Jul 21.

2. Zachary Stieber and Jan Jekielek, "Exclusive: Space Force Officer, Punished After Denouncing Marxism, to Leave Military," *Epoch Times*, 18 Aug 21, including quotes 1–3 (quotes 1–2, Lohmeier quoted by Stieber/Jekielek; quote 3, Whiting quoted by Stieber/Jekielek); Rachel Cohen, "Air Force inspector general takes over review of fired Space Force commander's speech," *Air Force Times*, 21 May 21, including quote 4 (Whiting quoted by Cohen), accessed at https://www.airforcetimes.com/news/your-air-force/2021/05/21/air-force-inspector-general-takes-over-review-of-fired-space-force-commanders-speech/ (5 Oct 22); "Wicker Asks Department of Defense to Explain Firing of Space Force Commander," *Press Releases, U.S. Senator Roger Wicker*, 21 May 21, including quote 5 (from Wicker's letter to Secretary Austin), accessed at https://www.wicker.senate.gov/public/index.cfm/2021/5/wicker-asks-department-of-defense-to-explain-firing-of-space-force-commander (5 Oct 22); Kristen Holmes and Barbara Starr, "Space Force commander fired after comments made on conservative podcast," CNN.com, 17 May 21; Personal discussion, Lt.

220 NOTES TO PAGES 148-150

Col. Peter A. Garretson, USAF (Ret.), with Marion, 29 Oct 21; E-mail, Garretson to Marion, Subj: "Re: Lt Col Matt Lohmeier—aide to Gen Raymond at one time?" 23 Mar 22. As an ACSC student, then–Major Lohmeier studied and later published on the Air Force's "traditional mind" toward space power—supporting the joint fight—and the transition to the "emergent mind of space," which he argued was "directly tied to national security, because unfettered access to and freedom of action in space are vital national interests." Only the latter mind was "capable of advancing space power," he concluded; see Matthew L. Lohmeier, *The Better Mind of Space*, Wright Flyer Papers, No. 79 (Maxwell AFB, AL: Air University Press, September 2020), 11, 21.

3. Hon. Heather Wilson Papers, Ltr, Sen. John McCain to Wilson, 30 Mar 17, including quote, AFHRA, call no. 168.7768–2; Bryan Bender, "Space Force under fire after officer sacked for comments," Politico.com, 17 May 21. One could argue that USAF departmental distraction from its primary purpose of warfighting continued; see Ltr, Department of the Air Force, Hq USAF, to "Airmen and Guardians," [Assessment of Racial Disparity Review], 9 Sep 21 (copy at AFHRA). At about the same time as the letter, an article highlighted a recent interview with the chief of the Space Force, General Raymond, who expressed concern that China was building "everything from reversible jammers of our GPS system . . . to jamming of communications satellites," in addition to "killer satellites" whose robotic arms are capable of disabling an adversary's satellites; see Ryo Nakamura, "US Space Force chief convinced China would use satellite killers," NIKKEI Asia, 9 Sep 21, accessed at https://asia.nikkei.com/Editor-s-Picks/Interview/US-Space-Force-chief-convinced-China-would-use-satellite-killers (5 Oct 22).

4. Oriana Pawlyk, "The Space Force Has its First Marines—and Soldiers and Sailors," Military.com, 2 Jul 21, including quote (Thompson quoted by Pawlyk), accessed at https://www.military.com/daily-news/2021/07/02/space-force-has-its-first-marines-and-soldiers-and-sailors.html (5 Oct 22). Some personnel from other services served an assignment with USSF and then returned to their permanent branch of service.

5. Pawlyk, "The Space Force Has its First Marines," Military.com, 2 Jul 21.

6. Nathan Strout, "The Space Force wants to manage acquisitions by portfolio," c4isrnet.com, 4 Aug 21, including quotes, accessed at https://www.c4isrnet.com/battlefield-tech/space/2021/08/04/the-space-force-wants-to-manage-by-portfolio/ (5 Oct 22).

7. Samantha Masunaga, "Space Force acquisitions and launch division will be based in L.A. area," *Los Angeles Times*, 8 Apr 21, including quotes (Thompson quoted by Masunaga, quotes 1–2), accessed at https://www.latimes.com/business/story/2021-04-08/space-force-el-segundo-space-systems-command

NOTES TO PAGES 150–153

-headquarters-la-air-force-base (5 Oct 22); Sandra Erwin, "End of an era: Space and Missile Systems Center is now Space Systems Command," *Space News*, 13 Aug 21; Neil Sheehan, *A Fiery Peace in a Cold War: Bernard Schriever and the Ultimate Weapon* (New York: Random House, 2009), 231–32; "Space Force activates Space Training and Readiness Command," *Secretary of the Air Force Public Affairs*, 23 Aug 21; Abraham Mahshie, "STAR Command Stands Up," *Air Force Magazine*, 23 Aug 21. Of the two other field commands, the Space Operations Command was established in October 2020, the Space Training and Readiness Command in August 2021.

8. Mahshie, "STAR Command Stands Up," *Air Force Magazine*, 23 Aug 21.

9. Mahshie, "STAR Command Stands Up," *Air Force Magazine*, 23 Aug 21, including quotes (Bratton quoted by Mahshie, quote 2), accessed at https://www.air forcemag.com/article/star-command-stands-up/ (5 Oct 22); "Brigadier General Shawn N. Bratton," *National Guard Bureau*, August 2021; Oral History Interview (OHI), Col. Niki J. Lindhorst, USSF, conducted by Marion, Maxwell AFB, AL, 11 Apr 22 (AFHRA, call number S239.0512–2847, audio only).

10. OHI, Lindhorst, 11 Apr 22, including quotes.

11. OHI, Lindhorst, 11 Apr 22; "Space Force to partner with Johns Hopkins University SAIS for service-specific IDE, SDE," Secretary of the Air Force Public Affairs, Oct. 26, 2022; Rachel S. Cohen, "Space Force picks Johns Hopkins University as war college," Federal Times, Nov. 4, 2022.

12. Davis Winkie and Rachel Cohen, "Do we need a Space National Guard? Colorado says yes, but Congress is not so sure," *Air Force Times*, 13 Apr 21, including quotes 1–3 (Loh, Eifert, Lengyel quoted by Winkie/Cohen), accessed at https://www.airforcetimes.com/news/your-air-force/2021/04/13/do-we -need-a-space-national-guard-colorado-says-yes-but-congress-is-not-so-sure/ (5 Oct 22); Bryan Bender and Connor O'Brien, "Battle brews over creating Space National Guard," *Politico*, 21 Oct 21, including quote 4 (Hokanson quoted by Bender/O'Brien), accessed at https://www.politico.com/news/2021/10/21/ space-national-guard-political-battle-516422 (5 Oct 22).

13. Caitlin Sullivan, "Colorado lawmakers introduce bipartisan legislation to create Space Force reserve," *KOAA News5*, 30 Aug 21, including quote 1, accessed at https://www.koaa.com/news/covering-colorado/colorado-lawmakers-in troduce-bipartisan-legislation-to-create-space-force-reserve (5 Oct 22); Forrest L. Marion and Jon T. Hoffman, *Forging A Total Force: The Evolution of the Guard and Reserve* (Washington, DC: Historical Office, Office of the Secretary of Defense, 2018), 109, 119, 150–51, 173–77, including quote 2. Note, as of 2021 there were between about fifteen hundred and two thousand National Guard members in eight States who performed space missions; see Winkie

222   NOTES TO PAGES 153–155

and Cohen, "Do we need a Space National Guard?" *Air Force Times*, 13 Apr 21; Jacqueline Feldscher, "Proposed Space National Guard Gathers Momentum," *Defense One*, 4 May 21.

14. Sandra Erwin, "House Armed Services Committee approves Space National Guard, challenges DoD on space programs," *Space News*, 1 Sep 21, including quote 1 (amendment quoted or paraphrased by Erwin), accessed at https://spacenews.com/house-armed-services-committee-approves-space-national-guard-challenges-dod-on-space-programs/ (5 Oct 22); Bender and O'Brien, "Battle brews over creating Space National Guard," *Politico*, 21 Oct 21, including quote 2; Brooke Singman, "White House 'strongly opposes' creation of Space National Guard in NDAA," *Fox News*, 22 Sep 21, including quote 3 (Office of Management and Budget quoted by Singman), accessed at https://www.foxnews.com/politics/white-house-opposes-space-national-guard-ndaa (5 Oct 22); Tom Roeder, "Space Force abolished? House bill would do just that," *Gazette* (Colorado Springs), 22 Sep 21.

15. Breck Dumas, "Space Force unveils its Guardians Ideal to fine-tune hiring," *Fox Business*, 22 Sep 21, including quotes 1–2, accessed at https://www.foxbusiness.com/technology/space-force-fine-tunes-hiring (5 Oct 22); Brent D. Ziarnick, "Space Force Reserve too important to be dictated by active duty," *Air Force Times* (op-ed), 20 Apr 21, including quote 3; OHI, Dr. Brent D. Ziarnick (ACSC), conducted by Marion, Maxwell AFB, AL, 14 Oct 21.

16. Ziarnick, "Space Force Reserve too important to be dictated," *Air Force Times* (op-ed), 20 Apr 21, including quotes 1–2; Marion and Hoffman, *Forging A Total Force*, 194–97, including quotes 3–4 (quote 3, Col. David E. Shaver quoted by authors; quote 4, former Assistant Secretary of Defense for Reserve Affairs Dennis M. McCarthy quoted by authors).

17. Konstantin Toropin, "The Space Force Finally Has Its Own Rank Insignia," Military.com, 20 Sep 21, including quotes, accessed at https://www.military.com/daily-news/2021/09/20/space-force-finally-has-its-own-rank-insignia.html (5 Oct 22). The article provided illustrations depicting the new rank insignia, with a detailed description of the elements. The first orbital chevron (E-7) symbolized low-Earth orbit; the second orbital chevron (E-8) signified medium-Earth orbit; and the third (E-9), geosynchronous orbit.

18. Bill Shatner, "William Shatner wants to know: What the heck is wrong with you, Space Force?" *Military Times*, 26 Aug 20, including quotes, accessed at https://www.militarytimes.com/opinion/commentary/2020/08/26/what-the-heck-is-wrong-with-you-space-force/ (5 Oct 22); "Space Force releases service-specific rank names," *Secretary of the Air Force Public Affairs*, [Space Force News], 29 Jan 21, accessed at https://www.spaceforce.mil/News/Article/2487814/space-force-releases-service-specific-rank-names/ (5 Oct 22).

NOTES TO PAGES 156–158   223

The USSF grades E-1 through E-4 were designated as "specialists," the only deviation from traditional USAF rank names.

19. Stephen Losey, "The Space Force Unveils its New, Sci-Fi Worthy Uniform," *Military.com*, 21 Sep 21, including quotes 1–3 (quote 3, Raymond paraphrased by Losey), accessed at https://www.military.com/daily-news/2021/09/21/space-force-unveils-its-new-sci-fi-worthy-uniform.html (5 Oct 22); Rachel S. Cohen, "The Space Force's new service dress and PT uniforms have landed," *Air Force Times*, 21 Sep 21, including quote 2 (Col. Catie Hague quoted by Cohen), accessed at https://www.airforcetimes.com/news/your-air-force/2021/09/21/the-space-forces-new-service-dress-and-pt-uniforms-have-landed/ (5 Oct 22); David Roza, "The Space Force knows their pants look terrible: 'We are still working to get the fit right.'" *Task & Purpose*, 5 Oct 21, including quotes 4–5 (social media quotes quoted by Roza), accessed at https://taskandpurpose.com/news/space-force-uniform-prototype-pants/ (5 Oct 22); Bill Chappell, "The New Space Force Uniforms Are Causing a Stir," National Public Radio, NPR.org 22 Sep 21.

20. "BREAKING ISS astronauts forced to board Crew Dragon and Soyuz to prepare for a possible evacuation," *AIRLIVE*, 15 Nov 21, including quote 1 (Shoigu quoted by *AIRLIVE*), accessed at https://www.airlive.net/breaking-iss-astronauts-forced-to-board-crew-dragon-and-soyuz-to-prepare-for-a-possible-evacuation/ (5 Oct 22); Andrew Follett, "Russia Just Showed How Vulnerable America Is to 'Scorched Earth' Space War," NationalReview.com, 27 Nov 21, including quotes 2–3, accessed at https://www.nationalreview.com/2021/11/russia-just-showed-how-vulnerable-america-is-to-scorched-earth-space-war/ (5 Oct 22); Eric Berger, "Russia threatens criminal charges against a NASA astronaut," ArsTechnica.com, 30 Nov 21.

21. "Statement of General James H. Dickinson, Commander, United States Space Command," [presentation to] Senate Armed Services Committee, [subject] Fiscal Year 2022 Priorities and Posture of USSPACECOM, 21 Apr 21, 4–6, including quotes 1–4, accessed at https://www.armed-services.senate.gov/imo/media/doc/Dickinson04.20.2021.pdf (5 Oct 22); Brian G. Chow and Brandon Kelley, "Hyten's Parting Shot: U.S. Must Step Up Response to Chinese Space Weapons," *National Interest*, 24 Nov 21, including quotes 5–6 (quote 6, Hyten quoted by Chow/Kelley), accessed at https://nationalinterest.org/feature/hyten%E2%80%99s-parting-shot-us-must-step-response-chinese-space-weapons-197098 (28 Dec 21); Ken Moriyasu, "China can 'grapple' US satellites with robotic arm, commander says," *Nikkei Asia*, 21 Apr 21; Frank Fang, "China's Advancing Space Program Leaves US Vulnerable in Event of Space War, Expert Warns," *The Epoch Times*, 20 Jun 21 (updated 6 Jul 21); Dino A. Lorenzini and Charles L. Fox, "2001: A U.S. Space Force," *Naval War College*

224 NOTES TO PAGES 158–159

Review, vol. 34, no. 2 (Mar–Apr 1981): 50–53. In fairness, Lorenzini/Fox emphasized not ground-based, but space-based high-energy lasers. For more on their work, see the Prologue.

22. Frederick J. Shaw, ed., *Locating Air Force Base Sites, History's Legacy* (Washington, DC: Air Force History and Museums Program, 2004), 118–19, including quote; Rachel S. Cohen, "Colorado Pushes Back on Decision to Base U.S. Space Command in Alabama," *Air Force Magazine*, 13 Jan 21; Leada Gore, "Trump on Space Command move: 'I single-handedly said let's go to Alabama,'" AL.com, 20 Aug 21. In 1964, the facts "concerning airlift modernization and Hunter's shortcomings demonstrated that the Pentagon had based its closure decision upon sound technical criteria" (Shaw, *Locating Air Force Base Sites*, 119). In 2020, the five other finalists were Albuquerque, NM; Bellevue, NE; Cape Canaveral, FL; Colorado Springs, CO; and San Antonio, TX (Gore, "Trump on Space Command move"). Air Force documentation showed Alabama had scored higher than Colorado on eleven of twenty-one categories.

23. Cohen, "Colorado Pushes Back on Decision," *Air and Space Forces Magazine*, 13 Jan 21, including quote 1, accessed at https://www.airforcemag.com/air-force -picks-alabama-to-host-space-command-hq/ (5 Oct 22); Gore, "Trump on Space Command move," AL.com, 20 Aug 21, including quote 2 (Trump quoted by Gore), accessed at https://www.al.com/news/2021/08/trump-on-space -command-move-i-single-handedly-said-lets-go-to-alabama.html (5 Oct 22); Jason Lemon, "Trump's Pre-Rally Boast of 'Single-Handedly' Giving Alabama Space Command HQ Angers Colorado," *Newsweek*, 21 Aug 21, including quote 3 (Suthers quoted by Lemon), accessed at https://www.newsweek .com/trumps-pre-rally-boast-single-handedly-giving-alabama-space-com mand-hq-angers-colorado-1621777 (5 Oct 22); Ellen Mitchell, "House committee votes to temporarily postpone Space Command relocation," *The Hill*, 2 Sep 21, accessed at https://thehill.com/policy/defense/570598-house-commit tee-votes-to-temporarily-postpone-space-command-relocation (5 Oct 22). At the end of September 2021, Colorado's representatives in Washington wrote to the Air Force Secretary asking him to halt activities regarding the relocation of U.S. Space Command's headquarters from Colorado Springs to Huntsville, Alabama, until the reviews by the DoD inspector general and the GAO were completed; see Ellen Mitchell, "Lawmakers ask Air Force to 'pause all actions' on Space Command move," *The Hill*, 30 Sep 21.

24. *Evaluation of the Air Force Selection Process for the Permanent Location of the U.S. Space Command Headquarters (DODIG-2022–096)*, 10 May 22, including quotes, accessed at https://www.dodig.mil/reports.html/article/3027137/eval uation-of-the-air-force-selection-process-for-the-permanent-location-of-the/ (9 Dec 22).

NOTES TO PAGES 159–162

25. Sandra Erwin, "For U.S. Space Force, Raymond's retirement marks the end of an era," *Space News*, 30 Oct 22, including quotes 1–4, accessed at https://space news.com/for-u-s-space-force-raymonds-retirement-marks-the-end-of-an -era/ (5 Dec 22); Valerie Insinna, "'Father of the Space Force' Raymond retires, as Saltzman takes command," *Breaking Defense*, 2 Nov 22, including quote 5, accessed at https://breakingdefense.com/2022/11/father-of-the-space-force -raymond-retires-as-saltzman-takes-command/ (5 Dec 22).

26. E-mail, Ambassador Barbara Barrett to Marion, Subj: "FW: ACTION: Review paragraph," 14 Dec 22, including quote (copy at AFHRA).

27. OHI, Mr. Stephen L. Kitay (former Deputy Assistant Secretary of Defense—Space Policy), conducted by Marion (via telephone), 16 May 22, including quotes.

28. History, Air Force Systems Command, Jul 1965–Jun 1966, vol. 3 (Supporting Documents), Document no. 14, address by General B. A. Schriever, "The Spectrum of Deterrence," 19 Oct 65, including quotes (AFHRA call no. K243.01) [published as *Air Force Systems Command News Release*, 19 Oct 65]. In General Dickinson's remarks before the SASC in 2021, he referred to the "changing strategic environment" that resembled the American experience in the Vietnam conflict, in which our troops were found "vulnerable to asymmetric and decentralized attacks"; see "Statement of General James H. Dickinson," SASC, FY 2022 Priorities and Posture of USSPACECOM, 21 Apr 21.

29. History, Air Force Systems Command, Jul 1964–Jun 1965, vol. 3 (Supporting Documents), Tab 10, including quote; Sheehan, *A Fiery Peace in a Cold War*, 433, 470.

226

SELECTED BIBLIOGRAPHY

Primary Materials

GOVERNMENT DOCUMENTS AND REPORTS

Barrett, Barbara M. [Secretary of the Air Force]. Memorandum, Barrett to "Air and Space Professionals," [USSF official logo and motto], 22 Jul 20.

———. Memorandum, Barrett to Department of the Air Force, Subj: "Department of the Air Force Priorities," 27 Feb 20.

———. [Secretary of the Air Force]. Memorandum, Barrett to HQ USSF, Subj: "Redesignation of Patrick Air Force Base," 16 Mar 20.

Cohen, William S. [Secretary of Defense]. *Annual Report to the President and the Congress.* Washington, DC, 1998.

———. Memorandum, Cohen to Secretaries of the Military Departments et al., Subj: "Department of Defense Space Policy," 9 Jul 99.

———. *Space Policy, Department of Defense Directive (DoDD) 3100.10.* Washington, DC, 9 Jul 99.

Crosier, Clinton E. [Maj. Gen.] (USSF PTF [Planning Task Force]). Document, "Read Ahead, U.S. Space Force Planning Task Force Phase 1 Deliverables, Vector Check with SecAF and CSAF, Mon., 6 May 2019, 1400," 2 May 19.

"Fact Sheet, National Space Policy," The White House, 19 Sep 96.

Forsyth, James W. [Dean, ACSC]. Memorandum, Forsyth to Major General Thompson, Subj: "Space Content in ACSC Curriculum," 25 Apr 17.

Gossick, Lee V. "The Implications of Space in Global Power Relationships." Air War College Thesis No. 1595, Maxwell AFB, Ala., 1959.

Hearing on [NDAA] for Fiscal Year 2017 . . . Before the Committee on Armed Services, House of Representatives, One Hundred Fourteenth Congress, Second Session, Subcommittee on Strategic Forces Hearing on Fiscal Year 2017 Budget Request for National Security Space . . . March 15, 2016. Washington, DC: GPO, 2017.

Hearing on [NDAA] for Fiscal Year 2017 . . . Before the Committee on Armed Services, House of Representatives, One Hundred Fourteenth Congress, Second Session, Subcommittee on Strategic Forces Hearing on The Missile Defeat Posture and Strategy of the United States—The Fiscal Year 2017 President's Budget Request... April 14, 2016. Washington, DC: GPO, 2017.

Joint Doctrine Publication 0–40, UK Space Power. Bristol: UK Ministry of Defence, 2022.

Moseley, T. Michael [Chief of Staff, USAF]. *The Nation's Guardians, America's 21st Century Air Force*. [CSAF White Paper], 29 Dec 07.

National Defense Authorization Act for Fiscal Year 2018, Conference Report to Accompany H.R. 2810 [115th Congress, 1st Session, House of Representatives, Report 115–404]. Washington, DC: GPO, 9 Nov 17.

Public Law 113-291 [113th Congress]—Dec. 19, 2014, Carl Levin and Howard P. "Buck" McKeon National Defense Authorization Act [NDAA] for Fiscal Year 2015. Washington, DC: GPO, 2015.

Public Law 115-91, 115th Congress, National Defense Authorization Act for Fiscal Year 2018. Washington, DC: GPO, 12 Dec 17.

Public Papers of the Presidents of the United States, Barack Obama, 2010 (In Two Books), Book 1—January 1 to June 30, 2010. Washington, DC: U.S. GPO, 2013.

Roth, John P. [Acting Secretary of the Air Force]. Memorandum, Roth to ALMA-JCOM-FLDCMD-FOA-DRU, Subj: "Redesignation of Air Force Installations to Space Force Installations," 21 Apr 21, w/Atch 1.

Schriever, [General Bernard] A. "The Spectrum of Deterrence." *Air Force Systems Command News Release*, 19 Oct 65.

Shanahan, Patrick M. [Acting Secretary of Defense]. Memorandum, Shanahan to Chief Management Officer of the Department of Defense, Secretaries of the Military Departments et al., Subj: "U.S. Space Force Planning Team," 21 Feb 19.

[Space Development Agency]. Fact Sheet, "Space Development Agency: What You Need To Know," ca. late 2020.

"Stenographic Transcript Before the . . . United States Senate," [Alderson Court Reporting]. Washington, DC, 17 May 2017.

The Aerospace Force: Defending America in the 21st Century. Washington, DC, 2000 [White Paper].

[Trump, Donald J.]. "Presidential Documents, Space Policy Directive-1 of December 11, 2017, Reinvigorating America's Human Space Exploration Program." *Federal Register*, vol. 82, no. 239, 11 Dec 17.

[Trump, Donald J.]. "Reviving the National Space Council," Executive Order 13803, *Federal Register*, 30 Jun 17.

Wilson, Heather A. [Secretary of the Air Force]. Memorandum, Wilson to Chief Management Officer of the Department of Defense, Secretaries of the Military Departments et al., Subj: "Establishment of the US Space Force Planning Task Force," 22 Feb 19.

BIBLIOGRAPHY

U.S. AIR FORCE HISTORIES AND FILES (HELD AT AIR FORCE HISTORICAL RESEARCH AGENCY, AFHRA)

History, Air Force Space Command, Jan 1994–Dec 2003 (AFHRA call number K496.01). (Information extracted from this document is not of a critical nature.)

History, Air Force Space Command, Jan 2009–Dec 2010 (AFHRA call number K496.01). (Information extracted from this document is not of a critical nature.)

History, Headquarters, United States Air Force, 2 Sep 05–1 Aug 08 (AFHRA call number K168.01). (Information extracted from this document is not of a critical nature.)

History, Lineage and Honors, Space Operations Command (U.S. Space Force), AFHRA, Oct 2021.

"Looking into the Aviation Future." *Plane News*, 25 Jan 1919 (AFHRA call number 167.612–3).

ORAL HISTORY INTERVIEWS (BY THE AUTHOR UNLESS NOTED OTHERWISE, ALL HELD AT AFHRA)

Anonymous, USAF (Ret.), Randolph AFB, TX, Sep. 2022 (audio only).

Ambassador Barbara M. Barrett (Secretary of the Air Force), remote via telephone from Maxwell AFB, AL, 13 Apr 22 (transcript).

Col. Brian Bolio, USA, by Gregory W. Ball, USSF/HO, remote via telephone from Colorado Springs, CO, 23 Apr 20 (audio only).

Lt. Col. Charles J. Cooper, USSF, by Gregory W. Ball, USSF/HO, 4 Jun 20 (audio only).

Maj. Gen. Clinton E. Crosier, deputy chief of staff, Strategy, Integration and Requirements, Hq USAF, Arlington, VA, by Gregory W. Ball and Wade A. Scrogham, USSF/HO, Peterson AFB, CO, 12 Feb 20 (transcript). (Information extracted from this document is not of a critical nature.)

Maj. Jerry Drew, USA, by Gregory W. Ball, USSF/HO, Peterson AFB, CO, 3 May 19 (transcript).

Col. Jack Fischer, USAF, by Gregory W. Ball, USSF/HO, Schriever AFB, CO, 3 Jan 20 (transcript).

Lt. Col. Peter A. Garretson, USAF (Ret), Maxwell AFB, AL, 29 Oct 21 (audio only).

Hon. Speaker Newton L. Gingrich (U.S. House of Representatives), remote via telephone from Maxwell AFB, AL, 21 Mar 22 (transcript).

Gen. C. Robert Kehler, AFSPC/CC, by George W. Bradley III, AFSPC/HO, Peterson AFB, CO, 22 Dec 10 (transcript).

BIBLIOGRAPHY

Stephen L. Kitay, DASD (Space Policy), remote via telephone from Maxwell AFB, Ala., 16 May 22 (audio only).

Stephen L. Kitay, DASD (Space Policy), and Col. Casey M. Beard, OSD/SP, by Gregory W. Ball and Wade A. Scrogham, USSF/HO, Peterson AFB, CO, 13 Feb 20 (transcript). (Information extracted from this document is not of a critical nature.)

Lt. Gen. Steven L. Kwast (AU/CC), by Robert Kane (AU/HO), Maxwell AFB, AL, 18 Sep 17 (transcript).

Col. Niki J. Lindhorst (USSF), Maxwell AFB, AL, 11 Apr 22 (audio only).

Ms. Michelle Linn, Hq USSF/S4, by Gregory W. Ball, USSF/HO, Peterson AFB, CO, 28 Feb 20 (transcript). (Information extracted from this document is not of a critical nature.)

Gen. Lance W. Lord, USAF (Ret.), by George W. Bradley III and Rick Sturdevant, AFSPC/HO, Peterson AFB, CO, 29 Jan 07 (transcript).

Lt. Gen. William T. Lord, USAF (Ret.), by Daniel P. Williams (Hq CCC/HO) and Forrest L. Marion (AFHRA), Peterson SFB, CO, 6 Mar 23 (audio only).

Col. Anthony Lujan, USAF, by Gregory W. Ball, USSF/HO, Peterson AFB, CO, 31 May 19 (transcript).

Col. Stuart Pettis, USAF, by Gregory W. Ball and Wade A. Scrogham, USSF/HO, Pentagon, Arlington, VA, 11 Feb 20 (transcript).

Dr. Michael V. Smith (ACSC), Maxwell AFB, AL, 3 Aug, 12–13 Aug 20 (audio only).

Col. Suzanne M. Streeter, USSF, by Gregory W. Ball, USSF/HO, 26 Feb 20 (transcript).

Lt. Gen. David D. Thompson, USSF/CV, by Gregory W. Ball and Wade A. Scrogham, USSF/HO, Peterson AFB, CO, 13 Feb 20 (transcript). (Information extracted from this document is not of a critical nature.)

Hon. Robert S. Walker (U.S. House of Representatives), remote via telephone from Maxwell AFB, AL, 19 Apr 22 (audio only).

Maj. Gen. Stephen N. Whiting, USSF/CD, by Gregory W. Ball, USSF/HO, Peterson AFB, CO, 18 Mar 20 (transcript). (Information extracted from this document is not of a critical nature.)

Hon. Dr. Heather A. Wilson, secretary of the Air Force, by Dr. James Malachowski and Ms. Aungelic Nelson, AF/HO, Pentagon, 8 May 19 (transcript). (Information extracted from this document is not of a critical nature.)

Hon. Dr. Heather A. Wilson, former secretary of the Air Force, El Paso, TX, 8 Aug 22 (transcript).

Dr. Brent D. Ziarnick (ACSC), Maxwell AFB, AL, 14 Oct 21 (audio only).

BIBLIOGRAPHY 231

WEBINAR

Barrett, Barbara M. (Secretary of the Air Force) and Raymond, John W. (General, USSF), by Thomas Dorame. *Space Foundation*, 6 May 20 (audio only, copy at AFHRA).

SECRETARY OF THE AIR FORCE DR. HEATHER A. WILSON PAPERS
(Accessioning in progress at AFHRA, call no. 168.7768)

Air Force Future Operating Concept, A View of the Air Force in 2035, Sep. 2015, AFHRA, call no. 168.7768–3.

Draft of Suggested Testimony for SASC on 17 May 17, [Wilson's handwritten notes, separate page], n.d., AFHRA, call no. 168.7768–6.

Letter, Sen. John McCain to Wilson, 30 Mar 17, AFHRA call no. 168.7768–2.

Memorandum, Subj: "Air Force Directive Publication Reduction," 3 Aug 17, AFHRA, call no. 168.7768–115.

Remarks by Secretary of Defense James Mattis, Secretary of the Air Force Swearing-In Ceremony, 16 May 2017, AFHRA, call no. 168.7768–76.

USAF Strategic Master Plan [Wilson's handwritten note on title page], May 2015, AFHRA, call no. 168.7768–3.

PERSONAL DISCUSSIONS

Lt. Col. Peter A. Garretson, USAF (Ret.), Maxwell AFB, AL, 29 Oct 21.

Dr. Richard P. Hallion, Shalimar, FL, 4 Dec 20, 20 Aug 21, 15 Dec 21.

Lt. Col. Michael M. Trimble, USAF, Maxwell AFB, AL, 29 Jun 22.

TELEPHONE DISCUSSIONS

Gen. Kevin P. Chilton, USAF (Ret.), 22 Sep 21.

Hon. Matthew P. Donovan (undersecretary/acting secretary of the Air Force), 27 May 21.

PERSONAL PAPERS (PROVIDED TO AUTHOR)

Hon. Matthew P. Donovan (undersecretary/acting secretary of the Air Force)
Document (draft), "Toward an Independent Space Force: Is It Time for a Space Corps?" Jun–Jul 2017.

Lt. Col. Peter A. Garretson, USAF (Ret.)
Document (draft), "Contingency Plan for a US Space Corps," n.d.
Document (draft), "Which Civilian Control of the Military?" n.d.
Document, "Space Force 2019: The Cost of One Year's Delay," 11 May 19.
Memorandum (unsigned), "Environment Contrary to Academic Freedom," n.d.

232 BIBLIOGRAPHY

Col. (Dr.) Michael V. Smith, USAF (Ret.)
Talking Paper, "CSAF Position Regarding US Space Corps," 31 Mar 17.
Talking Paper, "Ten Myths Regarding the US Space Corps," 31 Mar 17.

Secondary Sources

BOOKS

Baiocchi, Dave, and William Welser IV. *Confronting Space Debris: Strategies and Warnings from Comparable Examples Including Deepwater Horizon.* Santa Monica, Calif.: RAND, 2010.

Davenport, Christian. *The Space Barons: Elon Musk, Jeff Bezos, and the Quest to Colonize the Cosmos.* New York: Public Affairs, 2018.

Dolman, Everett C. *Astropolitik: Classical Geopolitics in the Space Age.* London and Portland, Ore.: Frank Cass Publishers, 2002.

Gavin, James M. *War and Peace in the Space Age.* New York: Harper and Brothers, 1958.

Graham, Daniel O. *High Frontier: A New National Strategy.* Washington, DC: High Frontier, 1982.

———. *We Must Defend America: A New Strategy for National Survival.* Chicago: Regnery Gateway, 1983.

Guardians of the High Frontier: The Heritage of Air Force Space Command. Peterson AFB, CO: AFSPC History Office, Apr 2018.

Hallion, Richard P.; Roger Cliff, and Phillip C. Saunders, eds. *The Chinese Air Force: Evolving Concepts, Roles, and Capabilities.* Washington, DC: National Defense University Press, 2012.

Hays, Peter L.; James M. Smith, Alan R. Van Tassel, and Guy M. Walsh, eds. *Spacepower for a New Millennium: Space and U.S. National Security.* New York and St. Louis: McGraw-Hill Companies, 2000.

Johnson-Freese, Joan. *Heavenly Ambitions: America's Quest to Dominate Space.* Philadelphia: University of Pennsylvania Press, 2009.

———. *Space Warfare in the 21st Century: Arming the Heavens.* London and New York: Routledge, 2017.

Lambeth, Benjamin S. *Mastering the Ultimate High Ground: Next Steps in the Military Uses of Space.* Santa Monica, CA, Arlington, VA, and Pittsburgh, PA: RAND, 2003.

Lupton, David E. *On Space Warfare: A Space Power Doctrine.* Maxwell AFB, AL: Air University Press, Jun. 1988.

Lutes, Charles D., and Peter L. Hays, eds., et al. *Toward a Theory of Spacepower, Selected Essays.* Washington, DC: Institute for National Strategic Studies, National Defense University, 2011.

BIBLIOGRAPHY

Mastalir, Anthony J. *The US Response to China's ASAT Test: An International Security Space Alliance for the Future.* Maxwell AFB, AL: Air University Press, Aug 2009, Drew Paper No. 8.

Mowthorpe, Matthew. *The Militarization and Weaponization of Space.* New York and Toronto: Lexington Books, 2004.

Neufeld, Jacob. *Bernard A. Schriever, Challenging the Unknown.* Washington, DC: Office of Air Force History, 2005.

O'Hanlon, Michael E. *Neither Star Wars nor Sanctuary: Constraining the Military Uses of Space.* Washington, DC: Brookings Institution Press, 2004.

PLA Aerospace Power: A Primer on Trends in China's Military Air, Space, and Missile Forces. 2nd ed. Maxwell AFB, AL: China Aerospace Studies Institute, 2017.

Pollpeter, Kevin L.; Michael S. Chase, and Eric Heginbotham. *The Creation of the PLA Strategic Support Force and Its Implications for Chinese Military Space Operations.* Santa Monica, CA: RAND, 2017.

Sheehan, Neil. *A Fiery Peace in a Cold War: Bernard Schriever and the Ultimate Weapon.* New York: Random House, 2009.

Smith, Jeffrey J. *Tomorrow's Air Force: Tracing the Past, Shaping the Future.* Bloomington and Indianapolis: Indiana University Press, 2014.

Spires, David N. *Beyond Horizons: A History of the Air Force in Space, 1947–2007.* 2nd. ed. Peterson AFB, CO: Air Force Space Command, 2007.

Temple, L. Parker III. *Implosion: Lessons from National Security, High Reliability Spacecraft, Electronics, and the Forces Which Changed Them.* Hoboken, NJ: John Wiley and Sons, 2013.

United Nations Treaties and Principles on Outer Space. New York: United Nations, 2002.

REPORTS, ARTICLES, AND PAMPHLETS

"Allard Commission: Executive Summary of Independent Assessment Panel on the Organization and Management of National Security Space." *Army Space Journal* 8, no. 2, Sum. 2009.

"Army Reform Launched with Lebed on Sidelines." *Current Digest of the Post-Soviet Press* 48, no. 40, 30 Oct 96.

Barnet, Todd. "United States National Space Policy, 2006 & 2010." *Florida Journal of International Law* 23, 2011.

Bjorklund, Michael. "A Report on the First National Space Forum." *Space Times,* Jul–Aug 1997.

Bradley, George W. III. "The Navstar Global Positioning System: Origins and Development." *Space Times,* Nov–Dec 1997.

Broad, William J., and Kenneth Chang. "Obama Reverses Bush's Space Policy." *New York Times,* 28 Jun 10.

BIBLIOGRAPHY

Butler, Amy. "Departing from Ryan's Rhetoric, Jumper Notes Unique Space Needs." *Inside the Air Force* 12, no. 42, 19 Oct 01.

Carns, Michael P.C.. *National Security Industrial Association SPACECAST 2020 Symposium, Washington, D.C., 9–10 November 1994.* Maxwell AFB, AL: Air Education and Training Command, ca. 1994.

Chilton, Kevin P. "Cyberspace Leadership: Towards New Culture, Conduct, and Capabilities." *Air & Space Power Journal* 23, no. 3, Fall 2009.

Cohen, Rachel S. "Appropriators: No Space Development Agency Funds Until We Get More Info." *Air Force Magazine*, 14 May 19.

———. "Cape Canaveral, Patrick Named First Space Force Installations." *Air Force Magazine*, 9 Dec 20.

———. "US Space Command Takes Reins on Space Ops." *Air Force Magazine*, Oct 2019.

Colby, Elbridge. "US Needs to Prepare for Space War." *Defense News*, 22 Feb 16.

Day, Dwayne A. "Recon for the Rising Sun." *Spaceflight* 41, Oct 1999.

———. "The Air Force in Space: Past, Present and Future." *Space Times*, Mar–Apr 1996.

Dugan, Michael J. "Forgotten, But Not Gone . . . Thinking About Air & Space Power." Air Force Association National Symposia, 5 Feb 99.

Eberhart, Ralph E. [untitled address]. Air Force Association National Symposium, 17 Nov 2000.

Erwin, Sandra. "House members energized by Trump's sudden attention to space warfare." *Space News*, 14 Mar 18.

Estes, Howell M. III. "The Air Force at a Crossroad." Air Force Association National Symposia, 14 Nov 97.

"First 'Announced' NRO Payload." *Spaceflight* 39, Mar 1997.

Furniss, Tim. "Space News Round-Up," *Spaceflight* 41, Jul 1999.

———. "Space News Round-Up." *Spaceflight* 41, Aug 1999.

———. "Space News Round-Up." *Spaceflight* 41, Sep 1999.

———. "Space News Round-Up." *Spaceflight* 42, Jan 2000.

Glenshaw, Paul. "The First Space Ace." *Air & Space Magazine*, Apr 2018.

Goswami, Namrata. "China in Space: Ambitions and Possible Conflict." *Strategic Studies Quarterly* 12, no. 1, Spr. 2018.

Hansen, Richard E. "Freedom of Passage on the High Seas of Space." *Strategic Review*, Fall 1977.

Hutzler, Charles. "Rocket Launch Advances China's Space Program." *Washington Times*, 11 Jan 01.

"John Glenn, The Come-Back Astronaut." *Spaceflight* 40, Nov 1998.

Jones, Sam. "Barack Obama to drop Nasa moon mission in budget cutbacks." *Guardian*, 1 Feb 10.

BIBLIOGRAPHY

Jordan, Bryant. "Will the Air Force lose its space program?" *Air Force Times*, 8 Feb 99.

Kidger, Neville. "Early orbital operations." *Spaceflight* 42, Nov 2000.

———. "Tito recalls historic 'tourist' flight." *Spaceflight* 43, Sep 2001.

Leavitt, William. "How Much of a Spurt SINCE SPUTNIK." *Air Force Magazine* 42, no. 1, Jan. 1959.

Lorenzini, Dino A., and Charles L. Fox. "2001: A U.S. Space Force." *Naval War College Review* 34, no. 2, Mar–Apr 1981.

Luker, George. "Army Space: Schriever IV." *Army Space Journal* 7, no. 2, Spr. 2008.

Mahshie, Abraham. "STAR Command Stands Up." *Air Force Magazine*, 23 Aug 21.

McKinley, Cynthia A. S. "The Guardians of Space: Organizing America's Space Assets for the Twenty-First Century." *Aerospace Power Journal*, Spr. 2000.

"Military Affairs." *Current Digest of the Post-Soviet Press* 48, no. 43, 20 Nov 96.

Myers, Richard B. "Achieving the Promise of Space—The Next Step." Air Force Association National Symposia, 4 Feb 99.

———. [untitled address]. Air Force Association National Symposium and Annual Air Force Ball, 19 Nov 99.

Naegele, Tobias. "Launching the Space Force." *Air Force Magazine* 103, no. 1 & 2, Jan–Feb 2020.

"Our National Space Effort." *Air Force Magazine* 42, no. 2, Feb. 1959.

Pace, Scott. "American space strategy: Choose to steer, not drift." *Space Policy* 30, no. 1, Feb. 2014.

Peters, F. Whitten. [untitled address]. Air Force Association National Symposium, 17 Nov 2000.

Porterfield, Mannix. "Explosion kills 29 in worst mine tragedy in 40 years." *Register-Herald* [Beckley, W.Va.], 31 Dec 10, updated 30 Sep 15.

"Remarks of Congressman Mike Rogers, Chairman, House Armed Services Strategic Forces Subcommittee, Presented to the 2017 Space Symposium." *Strategic Studies Quarterly (SSQ)*, Sum. 2017.

Rife, Shawn P. "On Space-Power Separatism." *Airpower Journal* 13, no. 1, Spr. 1999.

"Rodionov Proposes Changes in Military Doctrine." *Current Digest of the Post-Soviet Press* 48, no. 50, 8 Jan 97.

"Russian Rocket Engines." *Spaceflight* 38, Feb 1996.

"Russian Space Future Dims," *Spaceflight* 39, Mar 1997.

Ryan, Michael E. "Aerospace Domain." Air Force Association National Symposium and Annual Air Force Ball, 19 Nov 99.

———. "From Above and Beyond." Air Force Association National Symposia, 4 Feb 99.

———. "On Becoming a Space and Air Force." Air Force Association National Symposia, 14 Nov 97.

236 BIBLIOGRAPHY

———. [untitled address]. Air Force Association National Symposia, 17 Nov 2000.

"Ryan says Space Force unwarranted for next 50 years." *Aerospace Daily* 197, no. 26, 9 Feb. 01.

Schuiling, Roelof L. "Discovery delivers second crew to Space Station." *Spaceflight* 43, Jun 2001.

———. "STS-95: 'The John Glenn Flight.'" *Spaceflight* 41, Feb 1999.

Scott, William B. "Innovation Is Currency of USAF Space Battlelab." *Aviation Week & Space Technology* 152, no. 14, 3 Apr 2000.

Seligman, Lara. "Before Resigning, Air Force Secretary Heather Wilson Irked Trump." *Foreign Policy*, 8 Mar 19.

———. "SpaceX Wins US Air Force Contract For GPS III Launch." *Defense News*, 2 May 16.

Smith, Bob. "The Challenge of Space Power." *Airpower Journal* 13, no. 1, Spr. 1999.

"Space and Missile Systems Center becomes part of Air Force Space Command." *News Release United States Air Force*, 2 Oct 01.

"Space tourist Tito touches down." *Spaceflight* 43, Jul 2001.

"SpaceX Head Musk Visits Pentagon." *Defense News*, 13 Jun 16.

Sturdevant, Rick W. "Report on the AAS National Conference 'Space Exploration and Development: Beyond the Space Station.'" *Space Times*, Jan–Feb 1997.

Tirpak, John A. "Future Engagement." *Air Force Magazine* 80, no. 1, Jan 1997.

Ulsamer, Edgar. "Space Shuttle Mired In Bureaucratic Feud." *Air Force Magazine* 63, no. 9, Sep 1980.

"US Air Force Loses Early Warning Satellite." *Spaceflight* 41, Jun 1999.

"US companies gloomy about space work." *Spaceflight* 43, Jun 2001.

Whittington, Mark R. "Was NASA's Charles Bolden right all along about Muslim outreach?" *Foreign Policy Journal*, 23 Sep 16.

Zissis, Carin. "China's Anti-Satellite Test." [Backgrounder by] *Council on Foreign Relations*, 22 Feb 07.

Government Documents and Reports

Defense Space Activities: Status of Reorganization, GAO-02–772R. Washington, DC: U.S. General Accounting Office, Jun 2002.

Department of Defense Directive 5101.2, DoD Executive Agent for Space. Washington, DC, 3 Jun 03.

Report of the Commission to Assess United States National Security Space Management and Organization [Pursuant to Public Law 106-65]. Washington, DC, 11 Jan 01.

Report on A Space Roadmap for the 21st Century Aerospace Force, Volume 3: Appendices F–J [SAB-TR-98–01]. United States Air Force Scientific Advisory Board, December 2000.

BIBLIOGRAPHY   237

USAF Historical Study No. 85, USAF Credits for the Destruction of Enemy Aircraft, World War II. Washington, DC, 1978.

Internet Sources

REPORTS, ARTICLES, AND PAMPHLETS

"Aligning with the Space Enterprise Vision: Overcoming the Threat to Space Systems." *MITRE Corporation* (mitre.org), January 2017. Note the most recent access was at https://apps.dtic.mil/sti/pdfs/AD1107865.pdf (5 Oct 22).

Altvater, B. J., Samantha Clark, and Jeff Bozeman. "Senators Question the Administration's Space Force Proposal." GlobalPolicyWatch.com, 15 Apr 19.

Bahney, B. W., J. J. Pearl, and M. A. Markey. "Grounded: The Logic of Anti-Satellite Threats to Military Space Systems." *Lawrence Livermore National Laboratory (LLNL)-JRNL-689357* [osti.gov], 18 Apr 16.

Bender, Bryan. "Space Force under fire after officer sacked for comments." Politico.com, 17 May 21.

Bender, Bryan, and Connor O'Brien. "Battle brews over creating Space National Guard." Politico.com, 21 Oct 21.

Berger, Eric. "Russia threatens criminal charges against a NASA astronaut." ArsTechnica.com, 30 Nov 21.

Bloemhard, Heather. "National Space Council Reestablished." *American Astronomical Society* (aas.org), 11 Jul 17.

Bodner, Matthew. "Russian Military Merges Air Force and Space Command." TheMoscowTimes.com, 3 Aug 2015.

"Boeing Inertial Upper Stage Mock-up." *The Museum of Flight, The Boeing Company* (MuseumofFlight.org), n.d.

"BREAKING ISS astronauts forced to board Crew Dragon and Soyuz to prepare for a possible evacuation." AirLive.net, 15 Nov 21.

Brissett, Wilson. "The Space Corps Question." AirForceMag.com, 29 Aug 17.

Chappell, Bill. "The New Space Force Uniforms Are Causing a Stir." National Public Radio (NPR.org), 22 Sep 21.

"China eyes more military bases in Africa." TheDailyGuardian.com, 19 May 21.

Chow, Brian G. "Trump's Space Force announcement could propel us to deal with space 'Pearl Harbor.'" SpaceNews.com, 20 Jun 18.

———. "Worker-Bee Satellites Will Weaponize Space—and Help Us Keep the Peace." DefenseOne.com, 5 Jun 18.

Chow, Brian G., and Brandon Kelley. "Hyten's Parting Shot: U.S. Must Step Up Response to Chinese Space Weapons." NationalInterest.org, 24 Nov 21.

Cohen, Rachel S. "Air Force inspector general takes over review of fired Space Force commander's speech." AirForceTimes.com, 21 May 21.

―――. "Colorado Pushes Back on Decision to Base U.S. Space Command in Alabama." AirForceMag.com, 13 Jan 21.

―――. "The Space Force's new service dress and PT uniforms have landed." AirForceTimes.com, 21 Sep 21.

Cohen, Zachary. "Lawmakers scrap 'Space Corps' proposal." CNN.com, 8 Nov 17.

Corrin, Amber. "Air Force unveils $500M satellite museum piece." c4isrnet.com, 22 Dec 17.

Davenport, Christian. "Some in Congress are pushing for a 'Space Corps,' dedicated to fighting wars in the cosmos." WashingtonPost.com, 15 Sep 17.

David, Leonard. "New Bush Space Policy Unveiled, Stresses U.S. Freedom of Action." Space.com, 7 Oct 06.

Dumas, Breck. "Space Force unveils its Guardians Ideal to fine-tune hiring." Fox Business.com, 22 Sep 21.

Donovan, Matthew. "Acting Air Force Secretary Donovan: America needs a Space Force—Here's why." FoxNews.com, 21 Jun 19.

―――. "Unleashing the Power of Space: The Case for a Separate U.S. Space Force." WarontheRocks.com, 1 Aug 19.

Erwin, Sandra. "Air Force secretary raises space awareness inside Pentagon; Startups grab spotlight at satellite industry's annual DC trade show." SpaceNews .com, 13 Mar 18.

―――. "Deputy Defense Secretary Shanahan to take over duties of principal space adviser." SpaceNews.com, 18 Jan 18.

―――. "End of an era: Space and Missile Systems Center is now Space Systems Command." SpaceNews.com, 13 Aug 21.

―――. "GAO completes investigation of the decision to relocate U.S. Space Command." SpaceNews.com, 12 Apr 22.

―――. "House Armed Services Committee approves Space National Guard, challenges DoD on space programs." SpaceNews.com, 1 Sep 21.

―――. "House Armed Services Committee votes to create a U.S. Space Corps." SpaceNews.com, 13 Jun 19.

―――. "Kennedy sees growing congressional support for Space Development Agency." SpaceNews.com, 11 Jun 19.

―――. "On-orbit satellite servicing: The next big thing in space?" SpaceNews.com, 17 Nov 17.

―――. "Senate Armed Services bill shakes up management of Air Force space acquisitions." SpaceNews.com, 12 Jun 19.

―――. "Space Force proponents in Congress warn Air Force: 'We will watch you like a hawk.'" SpaceNews.com, 11 Dec 19.

―――. "Space reforms coming: 2018 NDAA drops legislative bombshells on U.S. Air Force." SpaceNews.com, 9 Nov 17.

BIBLIOGRAPHY

———. "Trump: 'We are going to have the Space Force.'" SpaceNews.com, 18 Jun 18.

———. "U.S. Space Force nameplates introduced for camouflage uniforms." SpaceNews.com, 18 Jan 20.

Fabey, Mike. "Space Corps proposal will 'figure' itself out, Wilson says." SpaceNews.com, 13 Sep 17.

Fecht, Sarah. "Senate Votes to Legalize Space Mining." *Popular Science* (PopSci.com), 12 Nov 15.

Feldscher, Jacqueline. "Proposed Space National Guard Gathers Momentum." DefenseOne.com, 4 May 21.

Follett, Andrew. "Russia Just Showed How Vulnerable America Is to 'Scorched Earth' Space War." NationalReview.com, 27 Nov 21.

Foust, Jeff. "A change in tone in national space policy." TheSpaceReview.com, 6 Jul 10.

Freedberg, Sydney J., Jr. "Rogers 'Pissed' At Air Force Opposition to Space Corps." BreakingDefense.com, 22 Jun 17.

———. "Space Corps, What Is It Good For? Not Much: Air Force Leaders." BreakingDefense.com, 21 Jun 17.

Garamone, Jim. "Space Force Personnel to Be Called Guardians." *DOD News* (Defense.gov), 19 Dec 20.

Garretson, Peter. "Air Force Suppressed Space Force Debate; Lt. Gen. Kwast Spoke Truth to Power." BreakingDefense.com, 8 Aug 19.

Gertz, Bill. "Russia Conducts Fifth Test of New Anti-Satellite Missile." *Washington Free Beacon* (FreeBeacon.com), 21 Dec 16.

Gore, Leada. "Trump on Space Command move: 'I single-handedly said let's go to Alabama.'" AL.com, 20 Aug 21.

Gould, Joe. "Trump, Mattis lose as 'Space Corps' proposal survives in defense policy bill." DefenseNews.com, 13 Jul 17.

Grush, Loren. "SpaceX successfully landed its Falcon 9 rocket after launching it to space." TheVerge.com, 21 Dec 15.

Gruss, Mike. "Delays in U.S. Military Satellite Studies Could Be Limiting," SpaceNews.com, 7 May 15.

———. "Pentagon Says 2013 Chinese Launch May Have Tested Antisatellite Technology." SpaceNews.com, 14 May 15.

———. "Rogers: U.S. Air Force Wasted $518 Million on Weather Satellite." SpaceNews.com, 7 Jan 16.

Hitchens, Theresa. "A Pause Button for Militarizing Space." *Center for International & Security Studies at [University of] Maryland]* (cissm.umd.edu), 1 Apr 16.

———. "Space Force Nears Year Mark, Acquisition Remains a Quagmire." BreakingDefense.com, 2 Oct 20.

Holmes, Kristen, and Starr, Barbara. "Space Force commander fired after comments made on conservative podcast." CNN.com, 17 May 21.

BIBLIOGRAPHY

"How NASA Helped 'The 33' Chilean Miners." NASA.gov, 13 Nov 15.

Howell, Elizabeth. "Watch William Shatner gaze at Earth from space in awe during Blue Origin's launch (video)." Space.com, 14 Oct 21.

Hyten, John E. *A Sea of Peace or a Theater of War: Dealing with the Inevitable Conflict in Space.* University of Illinois at Urbana-Champaign: ACDIS [occasional paper], Apr 2000. https://www.ideals.illinois.edu/bitstream/handle/2142/102028/ASeaofPeaceoraTheaterofWarDealingwiththeInevitableConflictinSpace.pdf?sequence=1&isAllowed=y.

Insinna, Valerie. "Air Force Launches Space Consortium That Puts Startups to Work on Prototypes," DefenseNews.com, 18 Oct 16.

———. "Air Force Secretary Barbara Barrett chats about her top four priorities." DefenseNews.com, 27 Feb 20.

———. "Key lawmaker vows to continue Space Corps fight." DefenseNews.com, 2 Dec 17.

———. "Space Development Agency on track to become part of Space Force in 2022, director says." DefenseNews.com, 21 Jan 20.

Jones, Dustin. "U.S. Space Command Headquarters May Land in Alabama." National Public Radio (NPR.org), 13 Jan 21.

Kania, Elsa B. "China Has a 'Space Force.' What Are Its Lessons for the Pentagon?" DefenseOne.com, 29 Sep 18.

Keck, Zachary. "China Secretly Tested an Anti-Satellite Missile." TheDiplomat.com, 19 Mar 14.

"Kennedy Space Center, NASA Orbiter Fleet, Space Shuttle Overview: Atlantis (OV-104)." NASA.gov, 12 Apr 13.

Kheel, Rebecca. "Trump unveils Space Force logo." TheHill.com, 24 Jan 20.

Koren, Marina. "What Does Trump Mean By 'Space Force'?" TheAtlantic.com, 13 Mar 18.

Kwast, Steve. "Opinion: 'There won't be many prizes for second place.'" Politico.com, 10 Aug 18.

Lemon, Jason. "Trump's Pre-Rally Boast of 'Single-Handedly' Giving Alabama Space Command HQ Angers Colorado." Newsweek.com, 21 Aug 21.

Losey, Stephen. "Laughlin misconduct included vulgar call sign for female student pilot." AirForceTimes.com, 6 Nov 18.

———. "The Space Force Unveils its New, Sci-Fi Worthy Uniform." Military.com, 21 Sep 21.

Mackenzie, Christina. "French Air Force changes name as it looks to the stars." DefenseNews.com, 15 Sep 20.

Masunaga, Samantha. "Space Force acquisitions and launch division will be based in L.A. area." *Los Angeles Times* (LATimes.com), 8 Apr 21.

BIBLIOGRAPHY 241

Mehta, Aaron. "Former US SecDefs: Stronger Military Ties with China Key to Peace." DefenseNews.com, 14 Jan 16.

Mehta, Aaron, and Valerie Insinna. "Pentagon officially stands up Space Development Agency, names first director." DefenseNews.com, 13 Mar 19.

"Military/National Security Space Activities." SpacePolicyOnline.com, updated 25 May 21.

Mitchell, Ellen. "House committee votes to temporarily postpone Space Command relocation." TheHill.com, 2 Sep 21.

Moriyasu, Ken. "China can 'grapple' US satellites with robotic arm, commander says." *Nikkei Asia* (asia.nikkei.com), 21 Apr 21.

Moskowitz, Clara. "NASA chief says agency's goal is Muslim outreach, forgets to mention space." *Christian Science Monitor* (CSMonitor.com), 14 Jul 10.

"NASA Administrator Jim Bridenstine explains Trump's Space Force." Politico .com, 27 Jun 18.

"NASA Administrator Statement on Space Policy Directive-2." NASA Release 18–042 (NASA.gov), 24 May 18.

"NASA Astronauts Launch from America in Historic Test Flight of SpaceX Crew Dragon." NASA Release 20–057 (NASA.gov), 30 May 20.

Pawlyk, Oriana. "Air Force Issues Gag Order on Press Engagements: Memo." Military.com, 13 Mar 18.

———. "The Space Force Has its First Marines—and Soldiers and Sailors." Military.com, 2 Jul 21.

Pope, Charles. "Barrett highlights space, modernization, alliances, people as pressing priorities." Secretary of the Air Force Public Affairs (arnold.af.mil), 27 Feb 20.

———. "Barrett publicly sworn in as secretary of the Air Force." Secretary of the Air Force Public Affairs (af.mil), 2 Nov 19.

———. "Gen Goldfein hosts inaugural space conference for US, partner nations." Secretary of the Air Force Public Affairs (af.mil), 17 Apr 19.

"President Donald Trump impeached." History.com ("This Day in History," December 18, 2019).

"President Obama Signs Bill Recognizing Asteroid Resource Property Rights into Law." Press release, *Planetary Resources* (SpaceRef.com), 25 Nov 15.

Roeder, Tom. "Space Force abolished? House bill would do just that." *Gazette* [Colorado Springs] (Gazette.com), 22 Sep 21.

"Rogers Says Air Force Cannot Fix Space, so Congress Must." AirForceMag.com, 22 Jun 17.

Roza, David. "The Space Force knows their pants look terrible: 'We are still working to get the fit right.'" TaskandPurpose.com, 5 Oct 21.

Shalal, Andrea. "Analysis points to China's work on new anti-satellite weapon." Reuters.com, 18 Mar 14.

Shatner, Bill. "William Shatner wants to know: What the heck is wrong with you, Space Force?" MilitaryTimes.com, 26 Aug 20.

Singman, Brooke. "White House 'strongly opposes' creation of Space National Guard in NDAA." FoxNews.com, 22 Sep 21.

Smith, Marcia. "No Space Corps in Final FY2018 NDAA." spacepolicyonline.com, 8 Nov 17.

———. "Text of President Trump's Space Policy Directive 2, May 24, 2018." SpacePolicyOnline.com, 24 May 18.

———. "Trump Talks Mars, Rockets, Space Force—But Not the Moon." Space PolicyOnline.com, 13 Mar 18.

Smith, M. [Michael] V. "America needs a space corps." TheSpaceReview.com, 13 Mar 17.

"Space Force activates Space Training and Readiness Command." Secretary of the Air Force Public Affairs (SpaceForce.mil), 23 Aug 21.

Spitzer, Michelle. "NASA Chief Bolden's Muslim Remark to Al-Jazeera Causes Stir." Space.com, 7 Jul 10.

Sprunt, Barbara. "Trump, Unveiling Space Force Flag, Touts What He Calls New 'Super-Duper Missile.'" National Public Radio (NPR.org), 15 May 20.

Stockton, Nick. "Congress Says Yes to Space Mining, No to Rocket Regulations." Wired.com, 18 Nov 15.

Strout, Nathan. "The Space Force wants to manage acquisitions by portfolio." c4isrnet.com, 4 Aug 21.

———. "The Space Development Agency's first director is already out." c4isrnet .com, 21 Jun 19.

Sullivan, Caitlin. "Colorado lawmakers introduce bipartisan legislation to create Space Force reserve." (koaa.com), 30 Aug 21.

Swarts, Phillip. "Space Corps proposal becoming flashpoint in DoD budget negotiations." SpaceNews.com, 22 Jun 17.

Tadjdeh, Yasmin. "Future of Space Development Agency Debated." National DefenseMagazine.org, 23 Jul 20.

Tellis, Ashley J. "India's ASAT Test: An Incomplete Success." *Carnegie Endowment for International Peace* (CarnegieEndowment.org), 15 Apr 19.

Thompson, Amy. "SpaceX launches 60 new Starlink internet satellites, nails latest rocket landing at sea." Space.com, 24 Mar 21.

Thompson, Loren. "Heather Wilson Was Uniquely Qualified to Be Air Force Secretary. So Why Is She Leaving?" Forbes.com, 8 Mar 19.

Toropin, Konstantin. "The Space Force Finally Has Its Own Rank Insignia." Military.com, 20 Sep 21.

Tritten, Travis J. "Mattis urges House to abandon Space Corps proposal." Real ClearDefense.com, 13 Jul 17.

BIBLIOGRAPHY

"Trump introduces idea of 'Space Force.'" CNBC.com, 13 Mar 18.

Venable, John. "Backgrounder: Independent Capability Assessment of U.S. Air Force Reveals Readiness Level Below Carter Administration Hollow Force." *Heritage Foundation* (Heritage.org), no. 3208, 17 Apr 17.

Wall, Mike. "China Launches High-Altitude Rocket on Apparent Science Mission: Reports." Space.com, 15 May 13.

———. "'Get a haircut,' real Space Force chief tells Netflix 'Space Force' star Steve Carell." Space.com, 7 May 20.

———. "Trump Says US May Need a 'Space Force.'" Space.com, 13 Mar 18.

Weeden, Brian. "Anti-Satellite Tests in Space—The Case of China." *Secure World Foundation* (SWFound.org), 16 Aug 13.

Weitering, Hanneke. "France Is Launching a 'Space Force' with Weaponized Satellites." Space.com, 2 Aug 19.

Wilcox, Alexus. "Peterson, Schriever, Cheyenne Mountain cultivate a new identity." Peterson-Schriever Garrison Public Affairs (Schriever.SpaceForce.mil), ca. 26 Jul 21.

Wilson, Jim, ed. "Former Administrator Charles F. Bolden." NASA.gov, March 2016 (updated 3 Aug 17).

Winkie, Davis, and Rachel Cohen. "Do we need a Space National Guard? Colorado says yes, but Congress is not so sure." AirForceTimes.com, 13 Apr 21.

Ziarnick, Brent D. "An aggressive Space Force begins with a Space Force Reserve." TheHill.com (op-ed), 1 May 20.

———. "Space Force Reserve too important to be dictated by active duty." Air ForceTimes.com (op-ed), 20 Apr 21.

Executive and Legislative Branch Documents

"Actions—H.R. 2810—115th Congress (2017–2018): National Defense Authorization Act for Fiscal Year 2018." Library of Congress (congress.gov).

[Bush, George W.]. "U.S. National Space Policy." NASA (history.NASA.gov), Aug–Oct 2006.

"Department of the Air Force expands potential basing locations for U.S. Space Command Headquarters." *Space Force News* (SpaceForce.mil), 15 May 20.

"Evaluation of the Air Force Selection Process for the Permanent Location of the U.S. Space Command Headquarters (DODIG-2022–096)." Department of Defense Inspector General (dodig.mil), 10 May 22.

"Fact Sheet, National Space Policy." [The White House, National Science and Technology Council]. ClintonWhiteHouse4.archives.gov, 19 Sep 96.

Kyl, Jon. "China's Anti-Satellite Weapons and American National Security." [Address delivered to U.S. Senate, 29 Jan 07]. Heritage Foundation (heritage .org), 1 Feb 07.

BIBLIOGRAPHY

[Obama, Barack H.]. *National Space Policy of the United States of America, Jun. 28, 2010*. history.NASA.gov, 28 Jun 10.

"President Clinton Issues New National Space Policy." [The White House, Office of the Press Secretary, 19 Sep 96]. ClintonWhiteHouse4.archives.gov, 19 Sep 96.

"Presidential Documents, Space Policy Directive-3 of June 18, 2018, National Space Traffic Management Policy." FederalRegister.gov, vol. 83, no. 120, 21 Jun 18.

"Presidential Documents, Space Policy Directive-4 of February 19, 2019, Establishment of the United States Space Force." FederalRegister.gov, vol. 84, no. 37, 25 Feb 19.

"President Opens Door to Commercial GPS Markets; Move Could Add 100,000 New Jobs to Economy by Year 2000." [The White House, Office of the Press Secretary, 29 Mar 96]. clintonwhitehouse4.archives.gov, 29 Mar 96.

"Remarks by President Trump at a Meeting with the National Space Council and Signing of Space Policy Directive-3." TrumpWhitehouse.archives.gov, 18 Jun 18.

"Remarks by Vice President Pence on the Future of the U.S. Military in Space," Press release from White House. spaceref.com, 9 Aug 18.

"Roll Call Vote 116th Congress—1st Session." United States Senate (senate.gov), n.d.

"SECAF: Accelerating defendable space, multi-domain operations key to future readiness." Secretary of the Air Force Public Affairs (afspc.af.mil), 21 Mar 18.

"Space Force releases service-specific rank names." Secretary of the Air Force Public Affairs, *Space Force News* (SpaceForce.mil), 29 Jan 21.

"Statement of General James H. Dickinson, Commander, United States Space Command." [presentation to] Senate Armed Services Committee, [subject] Fiscal Year 2022 Priorities and Posture of USSPACECOM, 21 Apr 21. armed-services.senate.gov, 21 Apr 21.

Summary of the 2018 National Defense Strategy of the United States of America. DoD. Defense.gov, 2018?

"Text of Space Policy Directive-4: Establishment of the United States Space Force." TrumpWhiteHouse.archives.gov, 19 Feb 19.

"Toward the Creation of a U.S. 'Space Force.'" Congressional Research Service (sgp.fas.org), 16 Aug 18.

[Trump, Donald J.]. "National Security Strategy of the United States of America." TrumpWhiteHouse.archives.gov, Dec. 2017.

"USSF Organization." SpaceForce.mil, n.d.

"Wicker Asks Department of Defense to Explain Firing of Space Force Commander." Press releases, U.S. Senator Roger Wicker, 21 May 21. Wicker.Senate.gov, 21 May 21.

[Wilson, Heather A.]. "Letter to Airmen on Space—19 Jun 18.pdf." MilitaryNews .com, 20 Jun 18.

"With the stroke of a pen, U.S. Space Force becomes a reality." Secretary of the Air Force Public Affairs (SpaceForce.mil), 20 Dec 19.

INDEX

A11 office (deputy chief of staff for space), 91, 94, 95, 203n31, 204–5n38

Adams, John, 140

aerospace: air and space integration, 23–24, 28–29, 42–43, 52, 91, 95, 180n61, 203n29; demarcation between air and space, 22, 180n58; seamless aerospace domain to encompass air and space, 22–25, 95; space race and, xvii

Afghanistan: Afghan Air Force, 195n39; Enduring Freedom operation, 41–42, 186nn40–41; U.S.–Afghan Women's Council, 126–27

air chiefs conference, 123

Air Corps Tactical School, xv, 106

Air Education and Training Command (AETC), 105–6, 208–9n64

Air Force, U.S. (USAF): budget and funding structures of, 9–10, 12, 17–18, 24, 26, 34, 82–83, 91, 94, 99–100, 177n24, 199n5; evolution to Space and Air Force, 8–11, 16, 18, 28–29, 176–77n22; *Global Engagement* vision statement of, 9, 176–77n22; independence of, xii–xiii, xv–xvii, xix, xxxvi; missions and responsibilities of, xviii, xxv–xxvii; NRO relationship with, 33–34; partnership between space industry and, 23; promotion or career advancement for uniformed personnel assigned to USSF installations, 120; readiness of, 91, 203n31; realignment recommendations from space commission, 32, 35, 36–39, 185nn31–32; seamless aerospace domain to encompass air and space under, 22–25, 95; Space Force–Air Force secretary proposal

by Rogers, 92, 203n32; space technology and capabilities of, xvii, xviii–xix, 8–11, 28–29, 32; stewardship of space by, 23–24, 26, 28–29, 95; uniforms of Airmen assigned to Space Force installations, 119

Air Force, U.S. Department of the: officer guideline recommendations from space commission, 31–32, 37–38, 183n17, 185n32; response to space commission report and implementation of recommendations, 35–40, 51–52, 185nn31–33; Space Corps creation in, advocacy for, 90; Space Force relationship to, 101–2, 111, 113; two distinct services under, 131, 145

Air Force Academy, U.S., 136, 149

Air Force Association (AFA) gatherings and symposia, 9–10, 16–21, 22–24, 94, 131

Air Force Cyber Command, 192n16

Air Force Materiel Command (AFMC), 32, 37

Air Force Space Command (AFSPC): attachment points/relationships for, 62–63, 193nn24–25; budget of, 9–10, 177n24; collocation of Army and AFSPC at Peterson AFB, 119, 157; commanders of, xx, 8, 26, 32, 37–39, 62, 169n7, 180–81n62, 183n17, 193n24, 205n42; cyber mission move to, 59–60; disestablishment of, 124, 213n30; establishment of, xviii, xxix, xxxvi, 172n16; Forward Element, 204–5n38; missions and responsibilities of, 59–60, 62–63; NDAA signing and personnel assignment to Space Force, 130, 215n45;

247

248 INDEX

personnel for, background and training of, 14, 178n36; Peterson AFB as home to, xxxvi, 51, 172n16; realignment recommendations from space commission, 32, 35, 36–39, 185n31; redesignation of Space Command as, xxix, 172n16; service acquisition executive, commander as, 204–5n38; Task Force Tango at, 116–18, 144–45, 211–12n15

Air Force Systems Command, 30, 107, 161–62

Air Force Warfighting Integration Capability (AFWIC), 114–15

Air National Guard (ANG), 61–62, 152

air operations groups redesignation to air and space operations centers, 109, 209n73

Air University (AU): Air Command and Staff College (ACSC), xxvi–xxvii, 22, 70, 83–84, 143–44, 170n3 (prologue), 187–88n59; Air Corps Tactical School as predecessor of, xv, 106; declassification of space-related information for presentation at, 84; gag order on space at, 103–6; Gingrich visits to and speeches at Maxwell AFB and, 98–99, 206n50; Kwast leadership of, 104–6; opportunity-driven advocacy for space at, 70; professional education for space at, 151; School of Advanced Airpower Studies, 83, 199n7; Space Force branding and, 143–44; space-related curriculum at, 69–70, 83–84, 143–44, 172n17, 200n8; strategy-related projects at, 104–5

Air War College (AWC), xxxii, xxxvi, 151, 172n17

aircraft, xv, 4, 24

Aldrin, Edwin E. "Buzz," Jr., 53, 54, 57

Allard Commission and Wayne Allard, 36, 49–51, 52, 200–201n15

Anti-Ballistic Missile (ABM) Treaty, xxxiii–xxxiv

anti-satellite (ASAT) weapons and capabilities: Chinese testing and capabilities, xxxii, 6–7, 31, 46–49, 52, 66–67, 68, 71, 78–79, 120–21, 187–88nn59–60, 188n63, 194n37, 196n49; debris from, 47, 68, 77, 120, 121, 156, 188n60; Indian testing and capabilities, 120–22; laser testing for, 20; Russian testing and capabilities, 67, 71–72, 78–79, 156, 196n49; Soviet capabilities, xxxii; U.S. space assets as targets of, 67, 68–69, 72, 100, 195n38; U.S. testing, 188n60

arms race, xxxiv–xxxv

Army, U.S.: airpower and aviation program of, xv, xvi–xvii, xxxvi, 106; collocation of Army and AFSPC at Peterson AFB, 119, 157; evolution of aviation in, 16, 36–37; space professionals in, 84–85; space technology and capabilities of, xvii, xviii, 32

Army Air Corps, U.S., xv, 84

Army Air Forces, U.S. (USAAF), xiii, xiii–xiv, xviii, 36–37

Army Signal Corps, U.S., 16, 36–37

Army Space and Missile Defense Command, U.S., 119, 129–30, 157

artificial intelligence (AI), xvii, xix

asteroids: mining of, 74; sending humans to, 74, 97

Atlas rockets, xvi, xvii, 67–68, 68

Austin, Lloyd, 147–48, 159

badges/space badges, 39, 84–85

Ball, Gregory W., 141

Barrett, Barbara M, 124–25, 126–28, 131, 134, 135, 138, 141–42, 149, 159, 214–15n42, 214n37

base operating support (BOS)/garrison support, 118–20, 145

Beard, Casey, 102

Behnken, Robert, 135, 216–17n55

Bezos, Jeff, 54, 78, 142

Biden, Joseph R., 48, 158

Blue Origin, 54, 56, 75, 142, 155, 190–91n9

blue-water school, 70

Boeing, 53, 56, 58

Bolden, Charles F., 58–59

Bolio, Brian, 128–29

Bratton, Shawn, 150–51

Bridenstine, Jim, 97, 101

Buckley AFB/Buckley Space Force Base, 146–47

Bush, Laura, 126–27

INDEX

249

Bush administration and George W. Bush: Barrett role in, 126–27; election of Bush, 25, 26; focus of after 9/11, 50, 51–52; missile defense policy of, 174n11; NASA exploration of deep space, opinion about, 191n11; space policy of, 45–46, 51–52, 63–65, 66, 160, 187n53, 193n27

Cape Canaveral Space Force Station, 143
Carell, Steve, 136
Carter, Ashton B., 57
Center for Strategic and International Studies, 132–33
Challenger, 53, 174–75n13, 190n1
Cheyenne Mountain Space Force Station, 147
Chilean copper mine crisis and rescue, 55
Chilton, Kevin P., 60–61, 193n24
China: aggressiveness of, 31, 76–78, 156–57; ASAT testing and capabilities of, xxxii, 31, 46–49, 52, 66–67, 68, 71, 78–79, 120–21, 187–88nn59–60, 188n63, 194n37, 196n49; ICBM development and capabilities, 78, 198n67; jamming GPS signals by, 220n3; sovereignty and territorial claims by, 74–75; space technology and capabilities of, xi, xxxv, 6–7, 27, 31, 46–49, 66–67, 68–69, 76–78, 106–7, 110, 156–57, 194n37; technology sharing with, 6–7
Chow, Brian, 106–7
civil aviation, xv
civil space agencies and programs: cooperation between military, civil, and commercial practitioners, 15, 55–58, 65, 78–79, 191n11; innovation in, 144; opposition to separate military and civil programs, xxxii; overlap between civil, commercial, and NSS sectors, 3–4, 173–74n7; space access for, xvi; Space Force creation out of military agencies and, xxxv; space policy and guidelines for, 3–4, 46; tourism/space tourism, 38, 185n33; uncertainty of roles and missions in post-Apollo era, xxix. *See also* National Aeronautics and Space Administration (NASA)

Clapper, James, 67
Clausewitz, Carl von, 195n38
Clinton administration, space policy of, 1–6, 11, 32–33, 45–46, 63, 65–66, 160, 189n71, 194n34
coal mine accident, 55, 190n6
Coast Guard, U.S., 17–18
Cohen, William S., 11, 13–14, 28, 76
Colby, Elbridge, 76–77
Cold War: agreements between superpowers during, 107; Air Force role during, xvi; NRO establishment during, 175n15; post–Cold War culture of Air Force, 19; post–Cold War space policy, 1, 4–5; technological superiority to U.S. competitors during, xxx
Colorado Air National Guard, 61–62
Colorado National Guard, 62, 152
Colorado Springs: National Security Space Institute (NSSI) in, 40; Space Symposium at, 80–86. *See also* Peterson AFB
Columbia, 53, 190n1
combined air operations center (CAOC), xxiv, 41–42, 135
Combined Space Operations Center, 134–35
commerce in space, 12–13
Commercial Space Launch Competitiveness Act, U.S., 73–75, 197n56
commercial space programs and companies: competition for experienced personnel for, 18; cooperation between military, civil, and commercial practitioners, 15, 55–58, 65, 78–79, 191n11; extraction of space-based resources by, 73–75; federal funding for, 65, 194n34; growth of activities and industries, 16–17; imagery for OEF from, 42, 186n43; interest in other countries, 173–74n7; NASA reliance on nontraditional space companies/NewSpace actors, 54, 55–58, 78, 191n11; overlap between civil, commercial, and NSS sectors, 3–4, 173–74n7; partnership between Air Force and space industry, 23; Space Force links to, 159; space policy and guidelines for, 3–4, 46; traffic management policy for, 98

INDEX

communications: 9/11 attacks and importance of satellites for, 41; space and cyber professionals communication with USAF, 15; space-based capabilities for, xix

Congress, U.S.: action to establish Space Force by, 111, 112, 124–26, 127–28, 213–14nn30–31; advocacy for Space Force by, 88–89; hearings on military space organization, policy, and programs, 90–92, 99–100, 110, 203n29; hearings on Space Force by, 123–24; separate space service, discussion about in, 2, 85–86

Constellation program, 53–54, 57

Cooper, Charles, 117

Cooper, Jim, 69, 81, 88, 92, 93, 100, 124, 126, 160

Corbett, Julian, 12–13, 178n33

COVID-19 pandemic, xxiii–xxv, xxvii, 134, 136, 143, 216n53

critical race theory (CRT), 147–48

Crosier, Clinton E.: career of, 109, 114; Initial Space Force Staff (ISFS) planning by, 122–23, 128; NDAA signing ceremony, feelings about, 129; planning task force under, 94, 114–16, 117, 122–23, 125, 144–45; on prohibition against saying warfighting and space together, 109; retirement of, 114, 115, 122

Crow, Jason, 152

culture and cadre-building: air and space integration and, 28–29, 42–43, 52, 91, 95, 203n29; change in Air Force culture to embrace space, 10–11, 18–19, 28–29, 84–85; comments to and slights of space officers by fighter pilots, 28–29; cyberspace culture, development of, 60–61; decline in Air Force culture, 18–19; identity, cultural touchpoints, and values of Space Force, 85, 139–44, 218nn75–76; identity relationship to aircraft type rather than Air Force, 19, 179n49; institutional resistance to exploring potential of space, 14–15; institutional resistance to Space Force, xix–xx; NRO culture comparison to Air Force culture, 33; prohibition against saying warfighting and space together, 109–10; space as separate culture, 42–43, 52, 61; space culture of warfighting, 107–10, 111, 209n71; warfighting culture of Air Force, 87, 116, 148, 220n3

Cyber Mission Force, 59–60

cyber/cyberspace/cybersecurity: budget for cybersecurity, 61; communication of requirements with USAF, 15; networks, sensors, platforms, and weapons linking in, xvii, xix; priority of and culture development, 59–61; technology and capabilities of military services for, xvii, 59–62, 192n16; threats from adversaries in, xvii

Davenport, Christian, 54, 58, 75, 84

debris and effects of debris on space activities, 47, 68, 77, 98, 106–7, 120, 121, 136, 156, 188n60

Defense, U.S. Department of (DoD)/Pentagon: changes under Rumsfeld and tourist attraction status of Pentagon, 27; cybersecurity budget of, 61; DCI relationship and meetings with defense secretary, recommendation for, 31, 34; diversity promotion in, 147–48; 9/11 attack on Pentagon, 40–41; reliance on commercial satellites by, 20; Rumsfeld as secretary of, 25, 26–27, 51–52, 181n2; Space Force as independent service in, 85, 89–90; space knowledge and expertise vacuum in, 107; space policy of, 11

Defense Advanced Research Projects Agency (DARPA), xxx, 34, 132, 133

Defense Space Council, 94, 95

Defense Support Program (DSP) satellites, 44

DeKok, Roger D., 12, 35–36, 37

deputy chief of staff for space (A11 office), 91, 94, 95, 203n31, 204–5n38

Desert Storm, Operation, xix, 4, 8–9, 23, 42, 44, 169n7, 176nn20–21, 186n41

deterrence, 135–36, 161

Dickinson, James H., 130, 156–57, 225n28

Dickman, Robert S., 53, 200–201n15

INDEX

Discovery, 38

dog-catching-car/truck analogy, 144, 219n80

Dolman, Everett C., 4, 30–31, 97, 105

Donovan, Matthew P. "Matt": advocacy for Space Force by, 124–25; Air Force acting secretary service of, xxvii, 170n3 (prologue); Air Force undersecretary service of, xxvii, 90, 94, 95, 170n3 (prologue); on congressional testimony of Wilson and Goldfein, 90; on gag order controversy, 103, 105; professional education of, xxvi–xxvii, 83, 170n3 (prologue); seamless air-space doctrine, impossibility of, 95; on Senate NDAA version, 94, 204n37; space culture views of, 108–9; on transgender policy of Trump, 207n51; working relationship under Wilson, 88

Drew, Jerry, 119–20

Dugan, Michael J. "Mike," 18–19, 176n21

Dunford, Joseph F., Jr., 101, 124

Eberhart, Ralph, 24, 37, 39, 180–81n62, 181n2

Eifert, James, 152

Eisenhower, Dwight D., xvi, 109

Enduring Freedom, Operation (OEF), 41–42, 186nn40–41

Esper, Mark T., 119, 141–42

Estes, Howell M., III, 9–10, 11

Falcon/Falcon 9 rockets, 56–57, 58, 75, 135, 190–91n9

Fast Space study, 105

Fischer, Jack, 116–17, 144

Foreign Intelligence Surveillance Act (FISA), 217n62

Fox, Charles, xxix–xxx, xxxii, xxxiii, xxxiv–xxxv, xxxvi, 157, 171n6, 171n9, 223–24n21

French Air Force, space command, 123

gag order controversy, 103–6

Gagarin, Yuri, 3, 27

Garretson, Peter, 70, 99, 105, 125, 144

garrison support/base operating support (BOS), 118–20, 145

Gates, Robert M., 46–47, 188n63

Gingrich, Newt L., xi–xii, 14–15, 31, 57, 97, 98–99, 102–3, 106

Glenn, John, 3, 27, 56

Goldfein, David, 87–88, 90–92, 103, 110, 114–15, 123, 131, 135–36, 140, 203n29

Gortney, William E., 77–78

Gossick, Lee V., xxxii, 171n8

GPS (Global Positioning System): Air Force use of, 4; ASAT targeting of satellites, 72; civil-commercial-NSS overlap of program, 4; Clinton policy and guidelines for, 4; errors and interference with timing signal, 21, 30; function and components of system, xxxi; funding for operational and control systems, 18, 20–21; jamming signals of, 44, 220n3; Lorenzini role in development of and program for, xxx; 9/11 attacks and reliance on, 41; satellite constellation for, 4, 17, 20–21, 30–31, 60, 182–83n13; satellite system as alternative to, 132; weapon cuing and GPS–guided weaponry, xix, 43–44, 72, 187n48

grade insignia, service ranks, and uniforms, 85, 154–55, 222–23nn17–18

Graham, Daniel O, xxx, 170–71n5

Griffin, Michael D., 132–33

Guardians, 140–41

Guetlein, Michael, 150

Hallion, Richard P. "Dick," xi–xxi, xxv–xxvii, xxxv, 169n1

Harrison, Todd, 132–33

High Frontier, xxx, 14, 170–71n5

Horner, Charles "Chuck," xx, 12, 15, 18, 29

hospital ships, 216n53

Hubble telescope, 55

Hurley, Douglas, 135, 216–17n55

Hyten, John E.: coordination of government space policy, criticism of, 2; on Cyber Mission Force, 59–60, 61; on funding for and delays in replacement of older still-functioning systems, 17, 20; reserve service use for cyber, 61; on Russian engine use and development of a new engine, 68; space war warnings from, 77; studying and over-studying space problems, concern about, xxxiii, 171n10; technology transfer concerns, competition, and U.S. business policies, 7; threat-based military space architecture development, requirements for, 133; weakness of U.S. in space, concern about, 79, 81, 157

India, ASAT testing and capabilities of, 120–22
informatized warfare, 73
Initial Space Force Staff (ISFS), 122–23, 128
Institute for Defense Analyses, Science and Technology Policy Institute (IDA-STPI), xii, 169n1
intelligence, surveillance, and reconnaissance (ISR) capabilities, xix, 10–11, 67, 73
intelligence career field, promotion of, 136–38
intercontinental ballistic missiles (ICBMs): ABM system to protect against, xxxiv; Chinese development and capabilities, 78, 198n67; development of, xvii; modernization of Minuteman, 18; passage through space by, 178n36; road-mobile ICBMs, 77, 78, 198n67; Soviet threat and development of, xvi, 31
International Space Station (ISS), 3, 23, 55, 58, 135, 156, 191n11
Iran, xi, 77, 135
Iraq: Desert Storm operation in, xix, 4, 8–9, 23, 42, 44, 169n7, 176nn20–21, 186n41; Iraqi Freedom operation, 43–44, 187n48; jamming GPS signals by Iraqis, 44

James, Deborah Lee, 54, 69, 93–94
Johnson-Freese, Joan, 45–46, 65, 188n63
joint direct attack munitions (JDAMs), xix, 43–44, 72, 187n48
Jumper, John P., 42–43, 52, 95, 200–201n15

Kehler, Robert, 62–63, 193nn24–25
Kennedy, John F., xx, xxxv
Kennedy Space Center, 53, 54–57

killer-bee/worker-bee satellites, 106–7, 220n3
Kitay, Stephen L. "Steve," 67, 88, 92–93, 100–101, 102, 160–61
Korean War, xvi, 72
Kosovo, 23, 28, 180n61
Kwast, Steven L. "Steve," 70, 99, 104–6, 110, 143, 151, 208–9n64
Kyle, Jon, 48, 49–50, 188–89n66

Lambeth, Benjamin, 14, 22, 42, 180n58, 181n2, 219n80
Lamborn, Doug, 152, 210n4
laser program, space-based, xxx, xxxiii, xxxiv, 20, 67, 171n9
Lewis, Mark J., xii, 132
Limited Test Ban Treaty, xxxiii–xxxiv
Lindhorst, Niki J., 150, 151
Linn, Michelle, 118–19, 212n17
Liquori, William J., 116–17
Lockheed Martin, xx, 38, 53, 56, 58
logo, 141–42, 218nn75–76
Loh, Michael A., 61–62, 152
Lohmeier, Matthew, 147–48, 219–20n2
Lord, Lance W., 26, 39, 183n17
Lorenzini, Dino, xxvi–xxvii, xxix–xxx, xxxii, xxxiii, xxxiv–xxxv, xxxvi, 30, 157, 171n6, 171n9, 223–24n21
Lorenzini, Edward "Ed," xxvi, 170n3 (prologue)
Los Angeles AFB, 149–50, 220–21n7
Loverro, Douglas, 69, 78–79
Lujan, Anthony, 117–18
Lupton, David E., xxxv–xxxvi, 51, 170n2 (prologue), 172n17

Macron, Emmanuel, 123
Mahan, Alfred Thayer, 30–31, 178n33
major force program (MFP) for space, 15, 16, 34, 178n39, 184n24
Marine Corps, U.S.: airpower and aviation program of, xvi–xvii; Department of the Navy relationship to, 16, 101, 102, 113, 119, 203n32; uniforms of Navy corpsmen assigned to units, 119
Marion, Jerry B, xxiii
Mars, 55, 57–58, 97
Marshall, George C., xiii–xiv, 27

INDEX

253

Mattis, James, 86–87, 88, 89, 90, 207n51
Maxwell AFB, xxv, 98–99, 206n50. *See also* Air University (AU)
McCain, John, 87, 95, 116, 148, 220n3
McCartney, Forrest S., 107
McKinley, Cynthia, 17–18, 23
Meyerrose, Dale W., 15
military purposes for space: Air Force doctrine on, xxxiii; defense of U.S. in and from space, xxxiii; high ground, seizing by U.S., xxxiii, xxxiv–xxxv; increase in activity for, xix, xxx; OST and prohibition of, xxxiv; space culture of warfighting, 107–10, 111, 209n71; weaponization of space, xix, 156–57; weapons in space, difficulty in defining, xxxiv
military services: airpower and aviation programs of, xv, xvi–xvii, xviii, xxxvi, 106; consequences of forming, or not forming, new, xiv; cyber technology and capabilities of, xvii, 59–62, 192n16; hollow force status and readiness of, 91; inferiority of U.S. for WWII, xv–xvi; institutional resistance to Space Force, xix; military exchanges with PLA, 76; resources for space-related activities, 2; response to new branches or commands, xi, 94; space technology and capabilities of, xvii, xviii–xix, xxx, xxxii, xxxiv–xxxv, 8–11, 28–29, 32
military space agencies and programs: advocacy and promotion of separate service for space, xxix–xxx, xxxiv–xxxvi, 15–16, 18, 24–25, 85–86, 170n2 (prologue); Air Force dominance in, xviii, xxix; Air Force stewardship of, 23–24, 26, 28–29, 95; ambitious agenda for, xxix; bureaucracy reduction in, 85–86; career development for space leaders, 29, 43, 182n10; communication of requirements with USAF, 15; congressional hearings on, 90–92, 99–100, 110, 203n29; cooperation between military, civil, and commercial practitioners, 15, 55–58, 65, 78–79, 191n11; cooperation between NRO and, 86; opposition to separate civil and military programs, xxxii; overlap between civil, commercial,

and NSS sectors, 3–4, 173–74n7; personnel for, 14, 178n36; rapid research, development, and acquisition of capabilities through operational flexibility, xx; space access for, xix; space as supporting force, 11, 13–14, 108–9; space corps creation, space commission recommendation on, 34–35, 68–69; Space Force creation out of civil agencies and, xxxv; tracking objects in space as standard practice, 136; uncertainty of roles and missions in post-Apollo era, xxix
missiles: Bush policy on missile defense, 174n11; China technology and capabilities, 7; Clinton policy on missile defense, 4–6, 174n9, 174n11; development of, xvii; missile lag in U.S., 171n8; Rumsfeld commission on, 5, 174n11, 181n64; Russia technology and capabilities, 77–78; threat to U.S from, 5, 174n12; U.S. strategy and budget, 77. *See also* intercontinental ballistic missiles (ICBMs)
Mitchell, William "Billy," xiii, xv, xxxvi, 106
moon: OST and uses of, xxxiv; public interest in space after landing on, xxxii–xxxiii; race to land on, xxx, 54; returning to, 57–58, 97
Moorman, Thomas A., 8, 169n7
Moseley, T. Michael, 47, 59, 62–63, 81, 192n16
motto, 142
Muir-Harmony, Teasel, xii
Musk, Elon, 15, 54, 57, 58, 75, 78, 159. *See also* SpaceX
Muslim world, NASA outreach to, 58–59, 191n14
Myers, Richard B., 16–17, 18, 19–21

National Aeronautics and Space Administration (NASA): budget and funding for, 55; Clinton policy and support for, 3; Glenn's return to space on NASA flight, 3; Obama speech at Kennedy Space Center, 53, 54–57; public awareness of work of, xxxii–xxxiii; reliance on nontraditional space companies/NewSpace actors, 54, 55–58, 191n11;

resources for, 2; risk aversion of, 53; seats for NASA astronauts on Russian *Soyuz* rockets, 54, 135, 156

National Defense Authorization Act (NDAA, 2000), 26

National Defense Authorization Act (NDAA, 2001), 181n2

National Defense Authorization Act (NDAA, 2015), 68–69

National Defense Authorization Act (NDAA, 2018): passage and signing of, 92, 93, 96; Senate version of, 94, 204n37; separate space service under, discussion about, 2, 88, 173n4; Space Corps creation under, advocacy for and pushback about, 90–96, 203nn31–32, 204–5n38, 205n42

National Defense Authorization Act (NDAA, 2019/2020): signing of and signing ceremonies, 128–30, 137, 144, 160–61, 215n43, 215n45; Space Force authorization under, xxiii–xxiv, 125–26, 127–28

National Geospatial-Intelligence Agency, 137

National Missile Defense Act, 174n11

National Reconnaissance Office (NRO): Air Force relationship with, 33–34; cooperation between military space and, 86; Desert Storm as first space war, opinion about, 169n7; directors of, 33, 38; establishment of, 32, 175n15; missions and responsibilities of, 32–33; secrecy of satellite work of, xxxii, 6, 32–34, 109, 175n15, 184n22; Space Force relationship with, 149

national security: cybersecurity as national security priority, 59; great power competition and threat to, xxvii; non-state terrorist threats to, xxvii; space as national security priority, 31, 45–46, 48, 50–51, 52, 78–79, 188–89n66; technology transfer concerns, U.S. business policies, and, 7, 175n17; vulnerability of satellites to attacks and malfunctions and, 30–31

National Security Agency (NSA), 137

National Security Council (NSC), 1

national security space (NSS): agenda and strategy for, 50–51, 52; Allard Commission on, 49–51, 52; budget and funding for, 50–51, 94, 99–100; Clinton policy on, 4–6; compartmentalized and classified state of, 109, 169n7; cooperation between military space and NRO, 86; Desert Storm as first space war, opinion about, 169n7; international agreements and initiatives in, xxxiii–xxxiv, 64–65, 73–74, 107; management and organization of, 5, 24, 26, 50–51, 52, 81–82, 96, 174n9, 189n69; Obama policy on, 65, 78–79; overlap between civil, commercial, and NSS sectors, 3–4, 173–74n7; separate military department responsible for, plan for establishment of, 96. *See also* Rumsfeld Space Commission

National Security Space Institute (NSSI), 40

National Space Council: languished state of, 2, 189n71, 202n26; policy development by, 2; reestablishment recommendation of Allard Commission, 50; revival under Trump, xii, 2, 97–98, 160

NATO (North Atlantic Treaty Organization), xvi, 123

Naval Academy, U.S., 70

Navy, U.S.: airpower and aviation program of, xv, xvi–xvii; MUOS satellite program of, 85, 200n12; operations mindset of and protection of a carrying trade, 70; space technology and capabilities of, xvii, xviii; uniforms of Navy corpsmen assigned to Marine Corps units, 119

Navy, U.S. Department of the, 16, 101, 102, 113, 119, 203n32

net-centric warfare, 28, 49, 189n67

9/11 attacks, xxv–xxvi, 40–41, 51

North American Aerospace Defense Command (NORAD), 32, 37–38, 39, 147, 180–81n62

North Atlantic Treaty Organization (NATO), xvi, 123

North Korea, xi, 5, 77, 174n12, 198n67

nuclear program and weapons, xv, xvi, xxxiii–xxxiv, 189–90n74

INDEX

Obama administration and Barack H. Obama: cyberspace policy of, 59; Kennedy Space Center speech of, 53, 54–57; priority of space under, 55, 78–79; space policy of, 1, 58–59, 63–69, 78–79, 96–97, 160, 193n30, 205–6n45

officers: comments to and slights of space officers by fighter pilots, 28–29; commissioning into Space Force, 136; guideline recommendations from space commission, 37–38, 185n32; space officer development and senior, career space professionals, 14–15, 29, 43, 52, 81–82, 83–85, 86, 182n10, 200–201n15

O'Hanlon, Michael, 4–5, 20, 43–44, 186n41

Outer Space Treaty (OST), xxxiii–xxxiv, 64–65, 73–74

Pace, Scott, 57–58, 97–98, 102

Patrick AFB/Patrick Space Force Base, 119, 120, 142–43

peaceful purposes for space: Air Force doctrine on, xxxiii; China policy on, 47, 49; increase in activity for, xxx; OST to support, xxxiv; U.S. policy on, xxxii, 64, 109, 123, 159–60, 193n30

Pearl Harbor/Space Pearl Harbor, 31, 110, 183n15

Pence, Mike, 96, 98–99, 101–2, 103, 124, 129, 141, 209n71, 213–14n31

People's Liberation Army (PLA) and People's Liberation Army Air Force (PLAAF): leadership decision about ASAT test, 188n63; military exchanges with, 76; priority of space for, 48–49; Rocket Force (PLARF), 72; Strategic Support Forces (PLASSF), 72–73; technology sharing with, 6–7

Peters, F. Whitten, 24–25, 181n2

Peterson AFB: AFSPC establishment at, xxxvi, 51, 172n16; collocation of AFSPC and Army at, 119, 129–30, 157; redesignation as Space Force base, 146–47; remote NDAA signing ceremony at, 129–30, 137, 215n43; Schriever wargame series at, 51, 150, 189–90n74; U.S. Space Command

location in, 138–39, 157–59, 210n4, 224nn22–23

Pettis, Stuart, 125

policy/space policy: Bush administration, 45–46, 51–52, 63–65, 66, 160, 187n53, 193n27; Clinton administration, 1–6, 11, 32–33, 45–46, 63, 65–66, 160, 189n71, 194n34; DoD policy, 11; Obama administration, 1, 58–59, 63–69, 78–79, 96–97, 160, 193n30, 205–6n45; Trump administration, 88–89, 96–103, 112–13, 160, 163–68, 205–6n45, 207n51

Powers, Francis Gary, 109

Principal Department of Defense Space Advisor (PDSA), 94–95

Putin, Vladimir, 77–78, 156

ranks, grade insignia, and uniforms, 85, 154–55, 222–23nn17–18

Raymond, John W. "Jay": air chiefs conference attendance by, 123; Bolio relationship with, 128; Chief of Space Operations service of, 113, 128–30, 139–40; Chinese satellite technology, concern about by, 220n3; combat and combat support functions in USSF, opinion about, 212n17; culture and identity of Space Force, role in, 139–40, 141–42, 155, 159; on current state of space, 135–36; international partnerships in space, promotion by, 134–35; leadership and legacy of, 159; retirement of, 159; return to Peterson AFB after NDAA signing, 130, 137; threat-based military space architecture development, requirements for, 133; vision for Space Force of, 159

Raymond, Molly, 130

RD-180 rocket engines, 67–68

Ream, Peggy, 209n73, 213n30

Redstone Arsenal, Huntsville, 139, 157–58, 224n23

reserves/reserve components: Air Force reserves, 192n22; military services reserves, 61–62, 192n22; partisanship and the Space Guard, 153; Space Force reserves, 136, 152–54, 221–22n13

256 INDEX

rockets and rocketry: booster rocket failures, 5–6, 174–75n13; RD-180 rocket engines, 67–68; reuse of first stage boosters, 56–57, 75, 190–91n9; Soviet threat and development of, xvi, xxxv, 8. *See also specific rockets*

Rodney Dangerfield command, 62, 193nn24–25

Rogers, Mike: advocacy for independent space service by, 69, 85–86, 88, 90, 91–92, 93, 96, 98–99, 100, 110; advocacy for Space Force by, 124–25; budget and funding structures, concerns about, 82–83, 199n5; coordination of government space policy, criticism of, 2, 51; Hyten remarks to subcommittee of on cybersecurity, 61; ICBM development and capabilities, concern about, 77–78; Maxwell AFB visits of, 98–99; on Russian engine use and development of a new engine, 68; Space Force–Air Force secretary proposal by, 92, 203n32; space organization and management and development of space professionals as priority of, 80–86, 160

Roth, John, 146–47

Royal Air Force (RAF), xii–xv, xvii, xix

Royal Flying Corps (RFC), xiii, xiv, xviii

Royal Naval Air Services (RNAS), xiii, xviii

Rumsfeld, Donald H.: career of, 27, 182n3; defense secretary role of, 25, 26–27, 51–52, 181n2; missile defense commission led by, 5, 174n11, 181n64; transformation of military as goal of, 35

Rumsfeld Space Commission: chairman and members of, 26, 27–28, 181n2; establishment and purpose of, 24, 26, 27, 50, 189n69; option for new space service, 16, 25; recommendation for MFP for space, 15, 34, 178n39, 184n24; report and recommendations from, xxx, 25, 26–27, 30–35, 51–52, 84, 110, 181n2, 200–201n15; response to report and implementation of recommendations of, 35–40, 51–52, 185nn31–33; space corps creation, recommendation on, 34–35, 68

Russia: Aerospace Forces of, 70–71; ASAT testing and capabilities of, 67, 71–72, 78–79, 156, 196n49; Crimea annexation by, 67, 195n39; military capabilities of, 7–8, 175–76n19; missile development and capabilities, 77–78; rocket engines from, 67–68; seats for NASA astronauts on *Soyuz* rockets of, 54, 135, 156; space technology and capabilities of, xi, 7–8, 67–69, 77–78, 106–7, 110, 135, 156–57, 175–76n19

Ryan, John D., 23, 30

Ryan, Michael E. "Mike," 8–9, 11, 18, 22, 23–24, 28, 36–37, 180n61

Saltzman, B. Chance, 159

satellites: budget and management of military satellites, 82–83; China capabilities, 6–7; DoD reliance on commercial satellites, 20; Enduring Freedom operations bandwith requirements, 41–42, 186n41; GPS satellite constellation, 4, 17, 20–21, 30–31, 60, 182–83n13; imagery for OEF from commercial satellites, 42, 186n43; Iraqi Freedom operation use of and bandwidth requirements, 43–44; jam-resistant technology for, 100; licensing of, 7, 175n17; military satellite responsibilities of Air Force, 33–34; MUOS satellite program, 85, 200n12; national security vulnerability to attacks and malfunctions of, 30–31; 9/11 attacks and importance of satellites, 41; NRO satellites, xxxii, 6, 32–33, 109, 175n15; operations mindset of and protection of information carried by, 70; resiliency of and development of next-generation, 69, 196n44; space access for, xvi; SpaceX launch of, 15, 75; Starlink internet satellites, 56, 190–91n9; system as alternative to GPS, 132; threat-based military space architecture development, requirements for, 133–34; worker-bee-killer bee satellites, 106–7, 220n3. *See also* anti-satellite (ASAT) weapons and capabilities

INDEX

257

Schriever, Bernard A., xx, 5, 33, 39, 107, 110, 150, 161–62, 169–70n8, 184n22
Schriever AFB: redesignation as Space Force base, 146–47; renaming Falcon AFB as, 5; Schriever Space Force Base redesignation of, 108; training for warfighting at, 108
Schriever Space Scholars program and symposium, 99, 105, 147
Schriever wargame series, 51, 150, 189–90n74
Science and Technology Policy Institute (STPI), xii, 169n1
sea comparison to space, 12–13
seal, 141–42, 218nn75–76
September 11 attacks, xxv–xxvi, 40–41, 51
Serbia, 23, 28, 71, 180n61
Shanahan, Patrick, 95, 102, 113–14, 116, 132
Shatner, William, 142, 155
Shaw, John E., 116
Shepperd, Donald W., 126
Smith, Bob: advocacy for independent space service by, 11–16, 18, 34; coordination of government space policy, criticism of, 2, 51, 52; House committee role of, 11, 177n30; options for U.S. dominance in space, 15–16, 178n39, 184n24; priorities of, 14–16, 83, 86, 160
Smith, Jeffrey J., 10–11, 19
Smith, Michael V., 12, 22, 70, 80, 99, 177n31, 180n58, 187–88n59
Smithsonian Institution, National Air and Space Museum (SI-NASM), xii
Soviet Strategic Rocket Forces, xxxv, 8
Soviet Union (USSR): air capabilities of, xiv; ASAT capabilities of, xxxii; breakup of, 7–8; military capabilities of, xxx; nuclear threat from, xvi; space technology and capabilities of, xxx, xxxii, xxxiii, xxxiv–xxxv, 3, 27, 31, 171n9
space: air chiefs conference on, 123; commercialization of, 73–75, 105, 110; declassification of space-related information, 84; dominance in, importance of, 16, 70; as geographic theater of national power, 70; international partnerships in, 134–35; options for U.S.

dominance in, 15–16, 178n39, 184n24; planetary motion, understanding of, xxiii; sea comparison to, 12–13, 93, 104–5; seamless aerospace domain to encompass air and space, 22–25, 95; sovereignty claims in and extraction of space-based resources, 73–75; strategic development for space power, 104–6, 161–62, 225n28; weakness of U.S., perception of adversaries of, 79
Space and Missile Systems Center (SMC), 32, 36, 37–39, 83, 133, 149–50, 185nn31–32
Space Command, xxix, xxxvi, 172n16. *See also* Air Force Space Command (AFSPC)
Space Command, U.S. (USSPACECOM): commanders of, 9, 16, 17, 24, 32, 37–38, 39, 180–81n62; competition for experienced personnel for, 18; disestablishment of, 192n18, 210n2; establishment of, xxix, 119–20; location of and permanent basing for, 138–39, 157–59, 210n4, 224nn22–23; missions and responsibilities of, 210n4; reestablishment of, 113, 137, 210n4; unified combatant command role of, xxix, 119–20, 210n4
space community: budget and funding structures for projects, 24, 34, 82, 94, 99–100, 199n5; disarray and disinterest in, xxix; rapid research, development, and acquisition of capabilities through operational flexibility, xx; recognition of need for purpose-focused force, xvii–xix, xxxii–xxxvi; threat to losing superiority and capabilities, xvii, 19–22
Space Corps, 90–96, 125–26, 203nn31–32, 204–5n38, 205n42
Space Development Agency (SDA), 108, 131–34, 149, 209n71
Space Force, 136
Space Force, U.S. (USSF): acquisitions reform under, 149–50; advocacy and support for, xi–xii, xvii–xxi, xxix–xxx, xxxiv–xxxvi, 85–86, 88–89, 98–103, 105–6, 107, 110, 124–25, 170n2 (prologue), 207n51, 213–14n31; bureaucracy reduction in, 118, 149–50, 159,

212n17; challenges faced by, xix–xx; Chief of Space Operations position in, 113, 128–30, 139–40; combat and combat support functions in, 212n17; congressional action for establishment of, 111, 112, 124–26, 127–28, 213–14nn30–31; criticism and skepticism about and resistance to, xi–xii, 88–89, 90, 91, 93, 103, 106–7, 204n36; Department of the Air Force relationship to, 101–2, 111, 113; establishment of, xi–xii, xxiii–xxiv, 128–30, 160–61, 215n43, 215n45; field command structure, roles, and responsibilities, planning for, 117–18, 211–12n15; headquarters of, 138; importance of and need for purpose-focused force, xvii–xix, xxxii–xxxvi; as independent service under DoD, 85, 89–90; leadership of, xx; missions and responsibilities of, 113, 131; name of as not open to discussion, 102–3; Naval Academy graduates as asset to, 70; NDAA 2018 for creation of, advocacy for and pushback about, 90–96, 203nn31–32, 204–5n38, 205n42; NDAA signing ceremonies and establishment of, 128–30, 144, 160–61, 215n43, 215n45; operations mindset of and protection of a carrying trade, 70; partisan and polarized society and views about, xi–xii, xx, 147–48, 159, 219–20n2; personnel and billets for, 122–23, 128, 130, 130–31, 137–38, 140–41, 215n45; personnel transferring into, 140, 148–49, 220n4; planning for, 94, 101, 110–11, 112, 113–20, 122–23, 144–45, 211–12n15; priorities for, 131; promotion of, 134–36; rapid research, development, and acquisition of capabilities for, xx; Space Force–Air Force secretary proposal by Rogers, 92, 203n32; space policy directives to develop proposal to establish, 88–89, 96–103, 112–13, 163–68, 205–6n45, 207n51; symposium discussions about creation of, xii–xiii, 169n1; uniforms of Airmen assigned to, 119

Space Force, U.S. (USSF) installations: promotion or career advancement for Air Force uniformed personnel assigned to, 120; redesignation of Air Force bases as, 142–43, 146–47; uniforms of Airmen assigned to, 119

Space Force, U.S. Department of the, 102, 113

Space Guard, U.S., 17–18, 152–53

Space National Guard, 61–62, 152–53, 221–22n13

Space Operations Command, 147, 151, 214–15n42, 220–21n7

space programs: civilian projects, xxxii; military projects, xxxii; NewSpace actors for conducting business of space, 54, 55–58, 78, 191n11; studying and over-studying space problems, xxxiii, 171n10. *See also* National Aeronautics and Space Administration (NASA)

space race, xvii, xxx

Space Rapid Capabilities Office, 149

Space Shuttle program, xvii, xxix, xxx, xxxii, 3, 53, 171n6, 190n1

Space Symposium, 80–86, 90

space systems: C3ISR and C4ISR systems, 67, 73; networks, sensors, platforms, and weapons, xvii, xix, 67, 68–69, 73, 195n38; operations mindset of and protection of information grid, 70; threat-based military space architecture development, requirements for, 133–34; U.S. assets as targets of adversaries, 67, 68–69, 72, 73, 76–78, 79, 100, 106–7, 124, 156–57, 195n38; U.S. dependence on, 70

Space Systems Command (SSC), 133, 149–50

Space Training and Readiness Command (STARCOM), 150–51, 220–21n7

space war: consequences of losing, xx–xxi; Desert Storm operation as first, xix, 8–9, 44, 169n7, 176nn20–21; informatized warfare, 73; Iraqi Freedom operation as first space applications war, 44; limited level, maintaining a space war at, 189–90n74; preparations for, 69, 76–77, 161–62, 225n28; prohibition against saying warfighting and space together, 109–10; Schriever wargame series for, 51, 189–90n74; space culture of warfighting, 107–10, 111, 209n71; space supporting air warfare not space warfare, 11, 13–14, 108–9; training for warfighting, 108, 209n71

Space-Based Infrared System (SBIRS), 17

Spacecast 2020 study, 3

spaceman, xxxvi

SpaceX: government reliance on strategies and technologies of, 54, 56; photo-op with Obama and rocket of, 58, 75; reuse of first stage boosters by, 56–57, 75, 190–91n9; satellite launches by, 15, 75; spacecraft for NASA crews and space-flights, 135, 216–17n55

Special Operations Command, U.S., 15, 34, 184n24

Spires, David N., xxix, 6, 17, 22, 23, 33, 41, 110, 186n41

Spurring Private Aerospace Competitive-ness and Entrepreneurship (SPACE) Act, 73–75, 197n56

Squadron Officer School, 19, 179n49, 183n17

Starlink internet satellites, 56, 190–91n9

Strategic Air Command (SAC), xvi, 171n9

Strategic Arms Reduction Treaty (START), 174n9

Strategic Command, U.S. (USSTRAT-COM), 12, 17, 51, 60–61, 81, 192n18, 210n2

Strategic Defense Initiative (SDI), xxx, 170–71n5

Streeter, Suzanne, 129–30, 136–38

Sun Tzu, 121

synergistic-operations perspective, 10–11

Task Force Tango, 116–18, 144–45, 211–12n15

technology and capabilities for space: air and space integration, 23–24, 28–29, 42–43, 52, 91, 95, 180n61, 203n29; of China, xi, xxxv, 6–7, 27, 31, 46–49, 66–67, 68–69, 76–78, 106–7, 110, 156–57, 194n37; of military services, xvii, xviii, xviii–xix, xxx, xxxii, xxxiv–xxxv,

8–11, 28–29, 32; military services cyber capabilities, xvii; of Russia, xi, 7–8, 67–69, 76, 77–78, 106–7, 110, 135, 156–57, 175–76n19; of Soviets, xxx, xxxii, xxxiii, xxxiv–xxxv, 3, 27, 31, 171n9; Space Pearl Harbor warning, 31, 110, 183n15; strategic development for space power, 104–6, 161–62, 225n28

Tellis, Ashley, 121–22

Terino, John, xxvi, 83–84

Thompson, David D.: A11 confirmation and firing of, 95; AFSPC vice commander service of, 95, 106–7; applications to Space Force, comment about, 148; chances of getting Space Force, changing views on, 125; changing view on Space Force by, 106–7; on Congress actions and laws, 112; long-anticipated Space Force as a thing, 130; NDAA signing ceremony, feelings about, 129; space curriculum clarification to, 83; on Space Force planning task forces, 118, 211–12n15; Space Force vice commander service of, 95, 106, 144; space professionals, support for, 200–201n15; vice chief of space operations, USSF, service of, 112, 148

Thor rockets, xvi, xvii

Thornberry, Mac, 92

Thule Air Base/Thule Space Base, 143

Titan rockets, xvi, 5–6, 33, 174–75n13, 175n15

Tito, Dennis A., 38

tourism/space tourism, 38, 185n33

Tournear, Derek M., 133–34

Towberman, Roger A., 140, 154, 218n71

traffic management policy for space, 98

transatmospheric vehicles, xvii

transgender policy, 87, 116, 207n51

Trump, Ivanka, 127, 129

Trump administration and Donald J. Trump: advocacy for Space Force by, 88–89, 92–93, 98–103, 110, 124–25, 207n51; culture and identity of Space Force, role in, 141–42; impeachment of, 129; NDAA signing ceremony, 128–29, 144, 215n45; resistance to Space Force by, 88, 90; space advocacy by Trump, xi–xii; Space Force creation under, xi–xii, xxiii–xxiv; space policy and space policy directives of, 88–89, 96–103, 112–13, 160, 163–68, 205–6n45

uniforms, grade insignia, and service ranks, 85, 154–55, 222–23nn17–18
United Kingdom, RAF establishment and WWII outcome for, xii–xv
unmanned aerial vehicles (UAVs), 42, 43–44, 44

Vandenberg AFB, 6, 33, 134–35, 150, 214–15n42

Walker, Robert S. "Bob," 2, 3, 97, 98, 160
Wallop, Malcolm, 171n9
Warakomski, Shay, 147
wargaming and exercises, 51, 83–84, 100, 150, 189–90n74, 206n50
Warner, John, 37, 185n32
war/warfare: linkage of space-based capabilities for, xix; space as supporting force, 11, 13–14, 108–9; victory through massing force against center of gravity of enemy, 67, 195n38; warfighting culture of Air Force, 87, 116, 148, 220n3. *See also* space war
weaponization of space, xix. *See also* military purposes for space
weapons, GPS–guided and weapon cuing, xix, 43–44, 72, 187n48
weather: JDAMs and, 43; space-based capabilities for information on, xix
weather satellites: Chinese weather satellite, destruction of, 46–48, 68, 120, 187–88nn59; Defense Meteorological Satellite Program (SMSP), 82–83; U.S. weather satellite, destruction of, 188n60
West Virginia coal mine accident, 55, 190n6
White, Thomas D., 23, 43
Whiting, Stephen N.: base renaming ceremony role of, 147; bureaucracy

reduction, opinion about, 107; chances of getting Space Force, changing views on, 125; culture and identity of Space Force, role in, 139–40, 141; deputy commander role of, 102, 140; Lohmeier investigation by, 147–48; remote NDAA signing ceremony role of, 129–30, 215n43; on Space Force as separate service, 102; on uniforms of Airmen assigned to Space Force installations, 119
Wicker, Roger, 147–48
Wilson, Charles, 110
Wilson, Heather A.: background and education of, 86; budget and funding focus of Air Force under, 82–83, 99–100; changing view on Space Force by, 123–24; congressional testimony on military space organization, policy, and programs, 90–92, 99–100, 110, 203n29; Crosier appointment for planning task force by, 115; departure as secretary, 89, 126, 127; gag order controversy under, 103–6; planning task force activity approval by, 116, 122; qualifications of, 86–87, 89; resistance to Space Force by, 88–89, 90, 91, 93, 103, 204n36; SDA mission concerns of, 133; secretary of Air Force appointment, 86–90; space culture views of, 108, 109; Space Force announcement, prior knowledge of, 99, 101; Space Force memorandum from, 101
Worden, Simon P., 21–22
worker-bee/killer-bee satellites, 106–7, 220n3
World War I, xii
World War II (WWII), xii–xvi, xxxvi

Xi Jinping, 72

Ziarnick, Brent, 143–44, 153–54

ABOUT THE AUTHOR

Forrest L. Marion graduated from the Virginia Military Institute with a degree in civil engineering and earned a master's degree in military history from the University of Alabama and a doctorate in U.S. history from the University of Tennessee. He is a retired U.S. Air Force Reserve officer and served as staff/oral historian (federal civil service) at the Air Force Historical Research Agency from 1998 to 2023, including three overseas deployments (two in military status) and two stateside deployments. He is the author of three military history works. From 2011 to 2015, he worked primarily for the Office of the Secretary of Defense Historical Office on a coauthored his-tory of the reserve components.

The Naval Institute Press is the book-publishing arm of the U.S. Naval Institute, a private, nonprofit, membership society for sea service professionals and others who share an interest in naval and maritime affairs. Established in 1873 at the U.S. Naval Academy in Annapolis, Maryland, where its offices remain today, the Naval Institute has members worldwide.

Members of the Naval Institute support the education programs of the society and receive the influential monthly magazine *Proceedings* or the colorful bimonthly magazine *Naval History* and discounts on fine nautical prints and on ship and aircraft photos. They also have access to the transcripts of the Institute's Oral History Program and get discounted admission to any of the Institute-sponsored seminars offered around the country.

The Naval Institute's book-publishing program, begun in 1898 with basic guides to naval practices, has broadened its scope to include books of more general interest. Now the Naval Institute Press publishes about seventy titles each year, ranging from how-to books on boating and navigation to battle histories, biographies, ship and aircraft guides, and novels. Institute members receive significant discounts on the Press' more than eight hundred books in print.

Full-time students are eligible for special half-price membership rates. Life memberships are also available.

For more information about Naval Institute Press books that are currently available, visit www.usni.org/press/books. To learn about joining the U.S. Naval Institute, please write to:

Member Services
U.S. Naval Institute
291 Wood Road
Annapolis, MD 21402-5034
Telephone: (800) 233-8764
Fax: (410) 571-1703
Web address: www.usni.org